M A S T E R I N G

KOREAN

HEAR IT · SPEAK IT · WRITE IT · READ IT

Developed for the
FOREIGN SERVICE INSTITUTE,
DEPARTMENT OF STATE

by B. Nam Park

BARRON'S

Cover design by Milton Glaser, Inc.

This course was developed for the Foreign Service Institute, Department of State, by B. Nam Park.

The title of the original course is Korean Basic Course

This edition published in 1988 by Barron's Educational Series, Inc.

All inquiries should be addressed to:
Barron's Educational Series, Inc.
250 Wireless Boulevard
Hauppauge, New York 11788

Paper Edition

International Standard Book No. 0-8120-3375-2

A large part of the text of this book is recorded on the accompanying tapes as follows:

Introductory Unit	Tape 1A, 1B	Unit 10	Tape 8A, 8B
Unit 1	Tape 1B	Unit 11	Tape 8B, 9A
Unit 2	Tape 2A	Unit 12	Tape 9B
Unit 3	Tape 2B	Unit 13	Tape 10A
Unit 4	Tape 3A, 3B	Unit 14	Tape 10B
Unit 5	Tape 4A, 4B	Unit 15	Tape 11A
Unit 6	Tape 5A, 5B	Unit 16	Tape 11B
Unit 7	Tape 6A, 6B	Unit 17	Tape 12A
Unit 8	Tape 7A	Unit 18	Tape 12B
Unit 9	Tape 7B		

PRINTED IN THE UNITED STATES OF AMERICA

234 800 9876543

Preface

This course in Mastering Korean is part of a series being offered by Barron's Educational Series, Inc. If you are a serious language student, this course will provide you with the opportunity to become truly fluent in modern Korean.

This is one of the famous language courses developed by the Foreign Service Institute of the United States. These courses were designed to train United States Government representatives who need to be able to communicate clearly and accurately in a foreign language.

Mastering Korean provides an excellent opportunity for you to learn Korean on your own, studying at your own pace. In addition, these tapes are ideal for students who are studying modern Korean in a school and would like to supplement their classroom work with additional practice in the spoken language.

TABLE OF CONTENTS

Tape 1A

INTRODUCTORY UNIT

Introduction

This volume is designed to teach spoken Korean to English speakers. The Korean presented in this book is representative of the "standard" speech of educated Koreans in Seoul, which has been the capital city and cultural, educational and political center of the country for over five hundred years. In Korea, as in every other nations, there is considerable local variation in pronunciation and vocabulary as well as in styles of speech. However, in schools all over Korea the language presented here is used and taught as the national standard and, if you learn it well, you will be speaking a form of Korean which has prestige throughout the country and which will be understood everywhere.

This course is written primarily for use in an intensive language program of twenty or more hours per week; but it can also be used for other situations, such as a language program in which one or more part-time students attend class for three to six hours per week, or for individual study with the aid of recorded tapes.

Acquiring proficiency in the use of language is like acquiring proficiency in any other skill, for example, driving an automobile -- you must practice until the mechanics of driving -- or speaking -- are reflex. It is the aim of this course, therefore, to bring students to "automacity" in speaking and understanding everyday Korean.

The following points are emphasized:

1. ALWAYS SPEAK AT A NORMAL CONVERSATIONAL SPEED. Do not speak slower than a "normal rate of speed."
2. CORRECT MISTAKES IMMEDIATELY.
3. REVIEW CONSTANTLY. As the student proceeds through the course, he should master everything thoroughly. Each new unit presupposes thorough mastery of what has been covered before. Otherwise, do not go ahead.

Organization and Use of This Course

Each unit in Korean Basic Course (Units 1-18) consists of four major parts: Basic Dialogue or other "basic sentences," Notes on Dialogues, Grammar Notes, Drills and Exercises.

Basic Dialogues

Each unit begins with a connected dialogue of about ten sentences between two or (occasionally) more speakers. Each dialogue is to be practiced, memorized and acted out until it has been so "overlearned" that the utterances and their sequence are understood and can be produced automatically without conscious thought or hesitation. In some units, there is a group of two or (rarely) more short dialogues which are related to one another. In such a unit, the dialogues may be treated as one connected dialogue.

In the Basic Dialogues, new words and phrases ("build-ups") are introduced immediately before each sentence. They are not part of the Dialogue itself.

Notes on Dialogues and Grammar Notes

Notes on Dialogues and Grammar Notes follow the Basic Dialogue section. The Notes are intended to be self-explanatory and to be read after the Basic Dialogue has been introduced. The Notes on Dialogues are numbered according to the sentences in the dialogue, and are intended to give additional information on the use of the words, phrases, or sentences. The Grammar Notes are systematic presentations of new patterns or major grammatical constructions that occur for the first time in the Basic Dialogues or other "basic sentences" in the unit.

The Grammar Notes are written to give some basic understanding of Korean to the beginning student, and are intended to be immediately and practically relevant.

Drills

The Drills in this Course are of a considerable variety. However, each unit basically has five kinds of drills:

Substitution Drills

Transformation (or Grammar) Drills

Response Drills

Combination Drills

Expansion Drills

It is to be noted that each drill has its own specific purpose, but the final goal of all the drills is to lead the student to develop his proficiency in free conversation. Without sufficient drill practice, he cannot achieve such proficiency.

a. Substitution Drills

In this course, there are several kinds of substitution drills: Simple Substitution, Multiple Substitution, Alternate Substitution, Correlation Substitution, etc. In substitution drills - of whatever kind - the student will be required to produce the given pattern sentence, and then he will be required to make substitutions in one or more "slots." Sometimes, he may be asked to form a properly arranged sentence by inserting a correlated cue. The basic aims of a substitution drill are twofold: the first is to make the student's control of the pattern sentences automatic and reflex, in order to develop fluency in actual free conversation; the second is to practice useful lexical items in the given sentence patterns. The lexical items are either those which have occurred previously or new related ones. New words and phrases added in the substitution drills are marked with an asterisk to the left of the sentence on their first occurrence. New words and phrases are used only in substitution drills. Substitution drills are printed in two columns, with English equivalents on the right and drill sentences with cues underlined on the left. English equivalents are not provided except for the model sentences at the beginning of each drill; but only in Substitution Drills are English equivalents provided for subsequent sentences.

b. Response Drills

These are mostly question-and-answer drills designed to help the student develop ability to respond to questions normally. A model is provided at the beginning of the drill. The student is required to produce a response for each question or remark.

c. Transformation Drills

The student is required to produce sentences parallel in an easily generalizable way to the pattern sentence. For example, the student may be asked to transform a negative to an affirmative pattern; or a statement to a question. Transformation Drills are sometimes designated as Grammar Drills in this course.

d. Combination Drills

These are drills in which the student is asked to produce one long pattern by combining two short patterns.

e. Expansion Drills

Starting from a short sentence, the student expands the sentence each time in specific ways.

Exercises

The exercises are of two sorts: (1) they ask the student to complete unfinished utterances or to give appropriate responses to the questions based on reality relevant to each situation; (2) they offer suggestions about additional practice and review for what has been covered in the unit.

The student should be able to do all these exercises fluently and accurately before going on to the next unit.

Romanization

The symbols used to represent Korean sounds are based on a phonemic analysis (see Pronunciation), but each word is transcribed morphophonemically - that is, each word is always written with the same sequence of symbols, even though its pronunciation may be changed by what precedes or follows it. However, if a word has two shapes, our selection is made on the basis of the final sound of the preceding word. The stems of inflected words (i.e., verbs) are written the same way always, even if phonetic changes take place when certain endings or suffixes are added to them.

Words are separated by spaces. A Korean word is a form which may be either (1) inflected or uninflected, (2) bound or free. Free forms can occur alone, while bound forms can occur only with other forms. If a bound form occurs with another form, the combination is a single word unless at least one of the bound forms also occurs with free forms in other constructions.

The first letter of a sentence (except ɪ or ə) is capitalized. So is the first letter of a proper noun wherever it occurs.

Korean Orthography (Hankɪl)

In this volume, the dialogue portions of each unit are accompanied by Korean orthography (Hankɪl) throughout the text. And in the glossary at the end of the text, Hankɪl is provided for all entries, in addition to English equivalents.

We follow the standard Korean spelling rules in this text regardless of the transcription. Spaces within a phrase or sentence are based on Hankɪl writing rules; for example, particles are not separated from the words preceding them.

Since Hankıl is relatively easy to learn, it may be introduced gradually during the middle part of the text, replacing the Romanized transcription completely by the time this volume is completed. A student should thus be able to read in Hankıl at normal speed.

It is not the intention of this text to teach spoken Korean through Hankıl from the very beginning, since it requires some time before the student can read it fluently. Hankıl can be easily mastered by reading (in Hankıl) dialogues which have already been memorized by the student.

It is suggested that students interested in written Korean (which requires the knowledge of Chinese characters in addition to Hankıl) use an appropriate basic reading text.

Special Symbols

Symbol	In a KOREAN sequence	In an ENGLISH sequence
( )	Optional addition, no change of meaning. a(b) = a or ab; b is optional. Muəs (ıl) hasimnikka? "What do [you] do?"	Explanatory information, not required in English. Korean (language)

(' ')	---	Literal translation. [I]'m fine. ('[I] exist well.')
[ ]	---	English items not represented in Korean. [I]'m fine. ('[I] exist well.')
a/b	Alternate forms (like English a/an). i/ka, ıl/lıl	---
/ /	'Sentence' pronunciation of preceding words (like English can't you /kancha/) əttəhsımnikka?/əttəssımnikka/ haksæng/hakssæng/ Hankuk mal/hangkungmal/	---
;	---	(In 'Build-ups') or child; baby
*	(In substitution drills) new lexical item.	---
?	End of question-sentence.	---
.	End of other kinds of sentences.	---
,	After (1) sentence adverbs and adverb phrases, (2) subordinate clauses.	---
-	(1) Connects parts of compound words (like English sister-in-law), (2--in Grammar Notes) indicates end of verb stem or beginning of some verb endings.	---

Pronunciation

Standard Korean, spoken by educated natives of Seoul, has an inventorv of 8 vowels, 2 semi-vowels and 19 consonants:

(a) Vowels

i		i	u
e		ə	o
	æ	a	

(b) Semi-vowels

w	y

(c) Consonants

p	t	c	k	
pp	tt	cc	kk	
ph	th	ch	kh	h
	s			
	ss			
m	n	ng		
	l			

Note: The symbols pp, tt, cc, kk, ph, th, ch, kh, ss, ng in the above chart are unit sounds, not combination sounds.

The Korean phonological system can be described in terms of possible syllable formation:

(a) 8 single vowels
(b) 144 consonant + vowel
(c) 11 semi-vowel + vowel
(d) 108 consonant + y (semi-vowel) + vowel
(e) 90 consonant + w (semi-vowel) + vowel
(f) 1 i + y
(g) 1 w + ə + y
(h) 8 consonant + w + ə + y
(i) 56 vowel + consonant
(j) 1008 consonant + vowel + consonant
(k) 42 y + vowel + consonant
(l) 35 w + vowel + consonant
(m) 756 consonant + y + vowel + consonant
(n) 630 consonant + w + vowel + consonant

The most common syllable types, however, are the first five kinds: (a) 8 single vowels, (b) 144 consonant + vowel, (c) 11 semi-vowel + vowel, (d) 108 consonant + y + vowel, (e) 90 consonant + w + vowel.

The following chart shows the formation of the basic Korean syllables. It is essential that the student should ultimately be able to pronounce and distinguish each syllable type correctly.

Basic Syllable Chart

Practice 1

1	2	3	4	5	6	7	8	9	10	11	12	13	14	15	16	17	18	19	20
a	ka	kka	kha	na	ta	tta	tha	la	ma	pa	ppa	pha	sa	ssa	ca	cca	cha	ha	ang
ə	kə	kkə	khə	nə	tə	ttə	thə	lə	mə	pə	ppə	phə	sə	ssə	cə	ccə	chə	hə	əng
o	ko	kko	kho	no	to	tto	tho	lo	mo	po	ppo	pho	so	sso	co	cco	cho	ho	ong
u	ku	kku	khu	nu	tu	ttu	thu	lu	mu	pu	ppu	phu	su	ssu	cu	ccu	chu	hu	ung
ı	kı	kkı	khı	nı	tı	ttı	thı	lı	mı	pı	ppı	phı	sı	ssı	cı	ccı	chı	hı	ıng
i	ki	kki	khi	ni	ti	tti	thi	li	mi	pi	ppi	phi	si	ssi	ci	cci	chi	hi	ing
e	ke	kke	khe	ne	te	tte	the	le	me	pe	ppe	phe	se	sse	ce	cce	che	he	eng
æ	kæ	kkæ	khæ	næ	tæ	ttæ	thæ	læ	mæ	pæ	ppæ	phæ	sæ	ssæ	cæ	ccæ	chæ	hæ	æng
ya	kya	kkya	khya	nya	tya	ttya	thya	lya	mya	pya	ppya	phya	sya	ssya	cya	ccya	chya	hya	yang
yə	kyə	kkyə	khyə	nyə	tyə	ttyə	thyə	lyə	myə	pyə	ppyə	phyə	syə	ssyə	cyə	ccyə	chyə	hyə	yəng
yo	kyo	kkyo	khyo	nyo	tyo	ttyo	thyo	lyo	myo	pyo	ppyo	phyo	syo	ssyo	cyo	ccyo	chyo	hyo	yong
yu	kyu	kkyu	khyu	nyu	tyu	ttyu	thyu	lyu	myu	pyu	ppyu	phyu	syu	ssyu	cyu	ccyu	chyu	hyu	yung
ye	kye	kkye	khye	nye	tye	ttye	thye	lye	mye	pye	ppye	phye	sye	ssye	cye	ccye	chye	hye	yeng
yæ	kyæ	kkyæ	khyæ	nyæ	tyæ	ttyæ	thyæ	lyæ	myæ	pyæ	ppyæ	phyæ	syæ	ssyæ	cyæ	ccyæ	chyæ	hyæ	yæng
wa	kwa	kkwa	khwa	nwa	twa	ttwa	thwa	lwa	mwa	pwa	ppwa	phwa	swa	sswa	cwa	ccwa	chwa	hwa	wang
wə	kwə	kkwə	khwə	nwə	twə	ttwə	thwə	lwə	mwə	pwə	ppwə	phwə	swə	sswə	cwə	ccwə	chwə	hwə	wəng
wi	kwi	kkwi	khwi	nwi	twi	ttwi	thwi	lwi	mwi	pwi	ppwi	phwi	swi	sswi	cwi	ccwi	chwi	hwi	wing
we	kwe	kkwe	khwe	nwe	twe	ttwe	thwe	lwe	mwe	pwe	ppwe	phwe	swe	sswe	cwe	ccwe	chwe	hwe	weng
wæ	kwæ	kkwæ	khwæ	nwæ	twæ	ttwæ	thwæ	lwæ	mwæ	pwæ	ppwæ	phwæ	swæ	sswæ	cwæ	ccwæ	chwæ	hwæ	wæng

End of Tape 1A

Tape 1B

1	2	3	4	5	6	7	8	9	10	11	12	13	14	15	16	17	18	19	20
아	가	까	카	나	다	따	타	라	마	바	빠	파	사	싸	자	짜	차	하	앙
어	거	꺼	커	너	더	떠	터	러	머	버	뻐	퍼	서	써	저	쩌	처	허	엉
오	고	꼬	코	노	도	또	토	로	모	보	뽀	포	소	쏘	조	쪼	초	호	옹
우	구	꾸	쿠	누	두	뚜	투	루	무	부	뿌	푸	수	쑤	주	쭈	추	후	웅
으	그	끄	크	느	드	뜨	트	르	므	브	쁘	프	스	쓰	즈	쯔	츠	흐	응
이	기	끼	키	니	디	띠	티	리	미	비	삐	피	시	씨	지	찌	치	히	잉
에	게	께	케	네	데	떼	테	레	메	베	뻬	페	세	쎄	제	쩨	체	헤	엥
애	개	깨	캐	내	대	때	태	래	매	배	빼	패	새	쌔	재	째	채	해	앵
야	갸	꺄	캬	냐	댜	땨	탸	랴	먀	뱌	뺘	퍄	샤	쌰	쟈	쨔	챠	햐	양
여	겨	껴	켜	녀	뎌	뗘	텨	려	며	벼	뼈	펴	셔	쎠	져	쪄	쳐	혀	영
요	교	꾜	쿄	뇨	됴	뚀	툐	료	묘	뵤	뾰	표	쇼	쑈	죠	쬬	쵸	효	용
유	규	뀨	큐	뉴	듀	뜌	튜	류	뮤	뷰	쀼	퓨	슈	쓔	쥬	쮸	츄	휴	융
예	계	꼐	켸	녜	뎨	뗴	톄	례	몌	볘	뼤	폐	셰	쎼	졔	쪠	쳬	혜	옝
얘	걔	꺠	컈	냬	댸	떄	턔	럐	먜	뱨	뺴	퍠	섀	썌	쟤	쨰	챼	햬	얭
와	과	꽈	콰	놔	돠	똬	톼	롸	뫄	봐	뽜	퐈	솨	쏴	좌	쫘	촤	화	왕
워	궈	꿔	쿼	눠	둬	뚸	퉈	뤄	뭐	붜	뿨	풔	숴	쒀	줘	쭤	춰	훠	웡
위	귀	뀌	퀴	뉘	뒤	뛰	튀	뤼	뮈	뷔	쀠	퓌	쉬	쒸	쥐	쮜	취	휘	윙
외	괴	꾀	쾨	뇌	되	뙤	퇴	뢰	뫼	뵈	뾔	푀	쇠	쐬	죄	쬐	최	회	욍
왜	괘	꽤	쾌	놰	돼	뙈	퇘	뢔	뫠	봬	뽸	퐤	쇄	쐐	좨	쫴	쵀	홰	왱

Syllable Final Consonant Chart

Possible syllable final consonants within or at the end of words.	Actual syllable-final sounds
(1) -k, -kk, -kh	/ -k/
(2) -t, -tt, -th, -s, -ss, -c, -cc, -ch	/ -t/
(3) -p, -pp, -ph	/ -p/
(4) -h	/ --/
(5) -l	/ -l/
(6) -m	/ -m/
(7) -n	/ -n/
(8) -ng	/ -ng/

Practice 2

(1)	kak, kakk, kakh	/kak/
(2)	tat, tatt, tath, tas, tass	/tat/

	tac tacc tach	/tat/
(3)	pap papp paph	/pap/
(4)	ah	/a/
(5)	lal	/lal/
(6)	mam	/mam/
(7)	nan	/nan/
(8)	ang	/ang/

Every syllable-final consonant within or at the end of a word becomes the initial consonant of the following syllable when a vowel occurs immediately after it. If two consonants occur in a cluster, the first of the cluster belongs to the preceding syllable and the second goes to the following syllable. Morphophonemic boundry within a word is not indicated. Thus, the consonant combinations -p p-, -t t-, -c c-, -k k-, -s s-, -p h-, -t h-, -c h-, -k h-, which may be divided morphemically so that the first consonant of the cluster belongs to the preceding syllable and the second to the following syllable, are not distinguished syllabically from the unit consonants pp, tt, cc, kk, ss, ph, th, ch, kh, even though the Korean orthography does distinguish them. In Korean, every syllable contains a vowel; therefore, there are as many syllables as there are vowels.

Practice 3

(1) kaka
kakka
kakha

(2) tata
tatta
tatha
tasa
tassa
taca
tacca
tacha

(3) papa
pappa
papha

(4) aha

(5) lala

(6) mama

(7) nana

(8) anga

1	Symbol:	Closest English Sound:	Short Description:
	a	'a' in 'father'	short
	ə	'u' in 'but'	open; phonetically [ɔ] or [ʌ]
	o	'o' in 'for'	rounded; with lips protruded
	u	'u' in 'food'	short with lip-rounding
	ɪ	'u' in 'put'	long and unrounded
	i	'ee' in 'meet'	short
	e	'e' in 'pen'	lower than English 'e'
	æ	'a' in 'bat'	short

Practice 4

1. /a/

a	'oh'
ai	'child'
ca	'well'

2. /ə/

əsə	'quickly'
əce	'yesterday'
cə	'I' (polite form)

3. /o/

O	'a family name''
oi	'cucamber'
Co	'a family name'

4. /u/

un	'luck'
au	'younger brother'
kutu	'shoe'

5. /ɪ/

ɪn	'silver'
ɪysa	'doctor'
kɪm	'gold'

6. /i/

i	'lice'
Kim	'a family name'
pi	'rain'

7. /e/

ne	'yes'
eku	'gee'
ke	'crab'

8. /æ/

æki	'child'
pæu	'actor'
kæ	'dog'

2	Symbol:	Closest English Sound:	Short Description: initially	medially	finally
	k	'c' in 'can'	slightly aspirated	sometimes voiced intervocalically	unreleased
	kk	'c' in 'scan'	unaspirated; tense	unaspirated; tense	unreleased
	kh	'k' in 'keen'	heavily aspirated	heavily aspirated	unreleased

Practice 5

1. /k/		2. /kk/		3. /kh/	
Kim	'a family name'	kkum	'dream'	khi	'height'
koki	'meat'	kkachi	'magpie'	kho	'nose'
aka	'baby'	akka	'a little while ago'	cokha	'nephew'
kuk	'soup'	cakku	'repeatedly'		

3	Symbol:	Closest English Sound:	Short Description: initially	medially	finally
	t	't' in 'top'	slightly aspirated	sometimes voiced intervo-callically	unreleased
	tt	't' in 'stop'	unaspirated; tense	unaspirated; tense	unreleased
	th	't' in 'teen'	neavily aspirated	heavily aspirated	unreleased

Practice 6

1. /t/		2. /tt/		3. /th/	
tal	'moom'	ttal	'daughter'	thal	'mask' or 'trouble'
eti	'where'	itta	'later'	ithil	'two days'
pata	'sea'	patta	'receive'	pithal	'slope'
tot	'sail'	tto	'again'	tho	'particle (in grammar)'

4	Symbol:	Closest English Sound:	Short Description: initially	medially	finally
	p	'p' in 'pin'	slightly aspirated	sometimes voiced intervo-callically	unreleased
	pp	'p' in 'spin'	unaspirated; tense	unaspirated; tense	unreleased
	ph	'p' in 'peen'	heavily aspirated	heavily aspirated	unreleased

Practice 7

1. /p/		2. /pp/		3. /ph/	
pal	'foot'	ppalkan	'red'	phal	'arm'
pul	'fire'	ppul	'horn'	phul	'grass'
ipal	'hair-cut'	ippal	'tooth'	naphal	'trumpet'
nap	'lead'	nappin	'bad'	nophi	'height'

5 Symbol:	Closest English Sound:	Short Description: initially	medially	finally
c	'ch' in 'chick'	slightly aspirated	sometimes voiced intervocallically	unreleased
cc	'j' in 'Jack'	unaspirated; tense	unaspirated; tense	unreleased
ch	'ch' in 'cheek'	heavily aspirated	heavily aspirated	unreleased

Practice 8

1. /c/		2. /cc/		3. /ch/	
cam	'sleep'	ccam	'spare time'	cham	'truth'
ceul	'scale'	ccok	'side'	chima	'skirt'
ice	'now'	ecci	'how'	kicha	'train'
ece	'yesterday'	eccase	'why'	achim	'morning'

6 Symbol:	Closest English Sound:	Short Description:
s	's' in 'Smith'	regularly voiceless; unreleased in final position
ss	'ts' in 'puts'	voiceless; tense; unreleased in final position

Practice 9

1. /s/		2. /ss/	
sal	'flesh'	ssal	'rice'
si	'poetry'	ssi	'seed'

Pusan	'name of a city'	pissan	'expensive'
susul	'operation'	malssɯm	'speech'

7	Symbol:	Closest English Sound:	Short Description: initially	medially	finally
	m	'm' in 'mother'	consonantal	consonantal	syllabic
	n	'n' in 'name'	consonantal	consonantal	syllabic
	ng	'ng' in 'sing'	--	consonantal	syllabic

Practice 10

1. /m/		2. /n/		3. /ng/	
mal	'horse'	nal	'day'	kang	'river'
Mikuk	'America'	nui	'sister'	congi	'paper'
imi	'already'	əni	'which'	pang	'room'
mom	'body'	mən	'far'	səng	'castle'

8	Symbol:	Closest English Sound:	Short Description: initially	medially	finally
	l	'l' in 'light' or 'ball'	front l	flap	back l

Practice 11

1. /l/

lætio	'radio'
palam	'wind'
salang	'love'
kəlsang	'chair'
pal	'foot'

9	Symbol:	Closest English Sound:	Short Description: initially	medially	finally
	h	'h' in 'hire'	strong friction	weak friction	--

Practice 12

1. /h/

hana	'one'	ohu	'afternoon'
hilin	'cloudy'	inhi	'girl's name'
hakkyo	'school'	ahin	'90'
huson	'descendent'		

10	Symbol:	Closest English Sound:	Short Description:
	w before a, ə, i, e, æ	'wh' in 'why'	lip rounding
	y before a, ə, o, u, e, æ	'y' in 'yet'	palatalizing

Practice 13

1. /w/

wi	'stomach'
wənki	'energy'
wæ	'why'
cəngwən	'garden'
I-wəl	'February'

2. /y/

yək	'station'
yuli	'glass'
yaku	'baseball'
uyu	'milk'
wəlya	'moon-night'

제 1 과 인사

(대화 A)

안녕

1. 김 : 안녕하십니까?

2. 제임스 : 예, 안녕하십니까?

처음

뵙습니다

3. 김 : 처음 뵙습니다.

김

기수

4. 김 기수 입니다.

이름

저

저의, 제

저의 이름, 제 이름

저의 이름은

제임스입니다

5. 제임스 : 제 이름은 제임스입니다.

선생

선생은

미국

사람

미국 사람

UNIT 1. Greetings

BASIC DIALOGUES FOR MEMORIZATION

Dialogue A

Kim

annyəng	peace; tranquility
1. Annyəng-hasımnikka?	How are you? ('Are you at peace?')

James

2. Ne, annyəng-hasımnikka?	Fine. How are you? ('Yes, how are you?')

Kim

chəım	first time
pwepsımnita/pwepssımnita/	(I see you)
3. Chəım pwepsımnita.	('I'm glad to meet you.') ('I see you for the first time.')
Kim	(family name)
Kisu	(given name)
4. Kim Kisu imnita.	[I] am Kisu Kim.

James

ilım	name
cə	I
cə e } ce }	my
cə e ilım } ce ilım }	my name
ce ilım ın	as for my name
Ceimsı imnita	[it] is James
5. Ce ilım ın Ceimsı imnita.	My name is James. ('As for my name, it is James.')

Kim

sənsæng	teacher; you (polite)
sənsæng ın	as for the teacher; as for you
Mikuk	America; the United States
salam	person
Mikuk salam	an American
6. Sənsæng ın Mikuk salam imnikka?	Are you an American?

6. 김 : 선생은 미국 사람입니까?

예

그렇습니다

7. 제임스 : 예, 그렇습니다.

무엇

무엇을

하십니까

8. 김 : 선생은 무엇을 하십니까?

저는

학생

학생입니다

9. 제임스 : 저는 학생입니다.

공부

공부합니까

10. 김 : 무엇을 공부합니까?

한국

말

한국 말

공부합니다

11. 제임스 : 한국 말을 공부합니다.

(대화 B)

제임스 선생

12. 김 : 제임스 선생, 안녕하십니까?

James

	ne	yes
	kıləhsımnita/kıləssımnita/	[it]is so; [that]'s right
7.	Ne, kıləhsımnita. Kurlahsimnita	Yes, I am. ('Yes, that's right.')

Kim

	muəs	what(thing)?
	muəs ıl	what (as direct object)
	hasimnikka	do [you] do?
8.	Sənsæng ın muəs (ıl) hasimnikka?	What do you do? ('As for you, what do [you] do?')

James

	cə nın	I (as a topic); as for me
	haksæng/hakssæng/	student
	haksæng imnita	[I] am a student
9.	Cə nın haksæng imnita.	I am a student.

Kim

	kongpu	studying
	kongpu-hamnikka	do [you] study?
10.	Muəs ıl kongpu-hamnikka?	What do [you] study?

James

	Hankuk/Hangkuk/	Korea
	mal	language; utterance; speech
	Hankuk mal/Hangkungmal/	Korean (language)
	kongpu-hamnita	[I] study
11.	Hankuk mal ıl kongpu-hamnita.	[I] study Korean.

Dialogue B

Kim

	Ceimsı Sənsæng	Mr. James
12.	Ceimsı Sənsæng, annyəng-hasimnikka?	Good morning, Mr. James.

아

13. 제임스 : 아, 안녕하십니까, 김 선생?

잘

있읍니다

14. 김 : 예, 잘 있읍니다.

요즘

어떻게

지나십니까

15. 제임스 : 요즘 어떻게 지나십니까?

덕분에

16. 김 : 덕분에 잘 지납니다.

재미

어떻습니까

17. 선생은 재미 어떻습니까?

그저

18. 제임스 : 그저 그렇습니다.

부인

부인도, 부인께서도

19. 김 : 부인께서도 안녕하십니까?

20. 제임스 : 예, 잘 있읍니다.

James

a	oh
13. A, annyəng-hasimnikka, Kim Sənsæng?	Oh, how are you, Mr. Kim?

Kim

cal	well
issimnita	[there] is; [there] exists
14. Ne, cal issimnita.	(Yes) I'm fine. ('I exist well.')

James

yocım	these days; lately
əttəhke/əttəhke/	how; in what way
cinasimnikka	are [you] getting along?
15. Yocım əttəhke cinasimnikka?	How are you getting along these days?

Kim

təkpun e/təkppune/	(at favor)
16. Təkpun e cal cinamnita.	I'm doing fine, thank you. ('I'm getting along well at your favor.')
cæmi	fun; interest
əttəhsımnikka/əttəssımnikka/	how is [it]?
17. Sənsæng ın cæmi əttəhsımnikka?	And how are you? ('As for you, how is fun?')

James

kıcə	just
18. Kıcə kıləhsımnita.	Just so-so. ('It is just so.')

Kim

pu	your wife; lady
puin to / puin kkesə to	your wife also
19. Puin (kkesə) to annyəng-hasimnikka?	How is your wife? ('Is your wife also at peace?')

James

20. Ne, cal issımnita.	She is fine. ('Yes, [she] exists well.')

21. 미안합니다.

22. 고맙습니다.

23. 천만에 말씀입니다.

24. 실례합니다.

25. 실례했읍니다.

26. 실례하겠읍니다.

27. 안 됐읍니다.

28. (아니요) 괜찮습니다.

29. 안녕히 가십시요.

30. 안녕히 계십시요.

31. 또 뵙겠읍니다.

ADDITIONAL GREETING EXPRESSIONS

21.	Mianhamnita.	I'm sorry Thank you for your trouble.
22.	Komapsɨmnita.	Thank you.
23.	Chənman e malssɨm imnita.	You're welcome. Not at all. Don't mention it.
24.	Sillye-hamnita./silyehamnita/	Excuse me (on leaving, on interrupting).
25.	Sillye-hæssɨmnita.	Excuse me (for what was done).
26.	Sillye-hakessɨmnita.	Excuse me (for what I'm going to do).
27.	An twessɨmnita.	That's too bad.
28.	(Aniyo) kwænchanhsɨmnita. /kwænchanssɨmnita/	Not at all. ('No, that's all right,')
29.	Annyənghi kasipsiyo.	Goodbye (to someone leaving). ('Go peacefully.')
30.	Annyənghi kyesipsiyo.	Goodbye (to someone staying). ('Stay peacefully.')
31.	Tto pwepkessɨmnita.	See you again. So long. I'll see you again.

NOTES ON DIALOGUES

(Numbers correspond to the sentence numbers in the dialogues.)

1.2. The expression Annyəng-hasimnikka? ('Are you at peace?') is a general greeting similar to such English expressions as 'How are you?', 'How do you do?', 'Good morning.', 'Good evening.', etc. It is used for first meetings at any time of the day. The usual response to Annyəng-hasimnikka? are Annyəng-hasimnikka?; Ne, annyəng-hasimnikka?

3. Chəɨm pwepsɨmnita. ('I meet you for the first time.') is regularly said by someone who has just been introduced. The response is usually Chəɨm pwepsɨmnita.; Annyəng-hasimnikka?.

4. Kim Kisu is a full name: the family name Kim plus the given name Kisu. Most Korean names consist of three syllables: the first is a family name, the last two are a given name. Cə 'I' is the politest equivalent of na.

6. Sənsæng means either 'teacher' or polite 'you'. After a family name or a family name plus a given name it is used as a title or term of address like English Mr., Mrs., or Miss. This form of address (i.e. Name + Sənsæng) is most commonly used among or to the teachers of all levels, regardless of age and/or sex, but is also commonly used among and to educated male adults. Mr./Mistta/, Mrs./Missessɯ/, and Miss /Missɯ/, followed by the family name are commonly used by Koreans as forms of address when speaking to equals and young people. These forms of address are not applied to individuals older than or superior to the speaker. A full or last name + Ssi 'Mr._____' occurs for other than the addressee to refer to a male adult of any age, rank or status. A family name + Ssi is also used as a term of address directly to the addressee who is a blue-collar worker.

7. Ne, kɯləhsɯmnita. ('What you just said is right, that's so.') is used as a response when you agree to the Yes-No question regardless of whether it is negative or affirmative. Aniyo, the opposite of Ne, means 'What you just said is wrong.' It is used in a parallel way as opposed to Ne. Often Ne and Aniyo are used similarly as 'yes' and 'no' in affirmative Yes-No questions but are the other way around in negative Yes-No questions.

10.11. When a situation is obvious, the subject or topic in a Korean sentence is usually omitted. For example, (Sənsæng ɯn) muəs ɯl kongpu-hamnikka? 'What do you study?'; (Na nɯn) Hankuk mal ɯl kongpu-hamnita. 'I study Korean.' Note that the subjects or topics in brackets may be omitted in speech. Kongpu-hamnita 'studies' is one of many Korean verbs which are formed from nouns. The noun kongpu 'studying' makes a verb (stem) by simply adding another verb (stem) ha- 'to do', that is, kongpu + ha→ kongpu-ha- 'to study'. (See Grammar Notes, the Verbals.) Examples:

Kongpu-hamnita.	'[I] study.'
Kongpu-hamnikka?	'Do [you] study?'

12. Ceimsɯ Sənsæng, annyəng-hasimnikka? ('Mr. James, how are you?') and Annyəng-hasimnikka, Ceimsɯ Sənsæng? ('How are you, Mr. James?') can be freely interchangeable.

15. Yocɯm əttəhke cinasimnikka? ('How do you pass by these days?') is a polite greeting to someone you know well, to ask him how things are going. The usual responses are Təkpun e cal cinamnita. ('I pass by well at your favor.') or Kɯce kɯləhsɯmnita. 'Just so-so.'

19. Puin without being preceded by a name means either 'lady' or 'your wife'. A family name (with or without being followed by a given name) + Sənsæng (or a title) + puin means 'Mrs. _____' or 'Mr. so-and-so's wife'.
Example:

Kim Sənsæng puin 'Mrs. Kim' or 'Mr. Kim's wife'

21. Mianhamnita. is commonly used to apologize, or to express thanks immediately upon receiving something.

23. Chənman e malssım imnita. ('A million words.') is a formal response to 'Thank you.', complimentary statements, and apologies. The English equivalent is 'You're welcome.' or 'Not at all.'

24.25.
26. Sillye-hamnita. ('I commit rudeness.'), Sillye-hæssımnita. ('I committed rudeness.'), Sillye-hakessımnita. ('I'll commit rudeness.') are different only in time: present, past, and future, respectively. The proper one depends on the situation. Sillye-hamnita. and Sillye-hakessımnita. are used interchangeably for what is not done. Sillye-hæssımnita. is used for something already done. 'Excuse me.' in English is used generally for all three expressions.

27. An twessımnita. 'That's too bad.' ('[It] has not become.') is used to express the speaker's sympathy or regret.

28. (Aniyo), kwænchanhsımnita. 'Not at all.' ('(No), that's not bad.') is an informal response to Mianhamnita., Komapsımnita., Sillye-hamnita. (or Sillye-hakessımnita. or Sillye-hæssımnita.), or to An twessımnita.

29.30. When two people part, the one who goes away says Annyənghi kyesipsiyo. ('Stay peacefully.'), and the one who remains says Annyənghi kasipsiyo. ('Go peacefully.'). If both are departing, they both say Annyənghi kasipsiyo.

GRAMMAR NOTES

1. The Verbals and the Copula

In Korean, inflected words, which may be used by themselves as complete sentences, are called Verbals. Korean verbals are made up of two main parts: Verb Stems + Endings.

Neither of the two main components in a verbal occurs alone. The verbals occur in a variety of forms depending on what endings are added to the verb stems, but the verb stems maintain their shapes, in most instances. Hereafter, we will call verb stems as well as all members of the inflected class of words Verbs.

In Korean dictionaries, verbs always are listed with the ending -ta. For instance, ka-ta 'to go', o-ta 'to come', mek-ta 'to eat', ca-ta 'to sheep', ilk-ta 'to read'. This is called the dictionary form of a verb. When -ta is dropped from the dictionary form the Verb Stem remains. It is very important to recognize every verb stem because all the inflected forms are based on them. Examples of Verbals:

(Cə nɪn) Kongpu-hamnita.	'(I)'m studying.'
(Cə nɪn) Hankuk mal ɪl kalɪchimnita.	'(I) teach Korean.'
Cal cinamnita.	'[I]'m fine.' ('I pass by well.')
Komapsɪmnita.	'(I) thank (you).'

Imnita is a verb: i- is its stem and -mnita is its ending. Imnita and the other inflected forms of i- (for example, its dictionary form i-ta) are used in sentences like 'Noun A is Noun B.' Often Noun A is not stated, but is understood. Thus, the verb stem i- is equivalent to one meaning of the English verb 'to be'. Notice, however, that the English verb 'to be' is used not only to connect two nouns ('A is B') as in 'I am a teacher', but is also used in sentences like 'A is in such and such a state', as in 'She is beautiful'. The Korean verb imnita is used only for 'A is B', never in sentences like 'A is beautiful'. Imnita is called the Copula; i- is the stem of the Copula.

The Copula never occurs alone. It is always preceded immediately by a noun and there is no pause between the noun and the Copula.

The Copula is distinguished from other verbals only in that the Copula never occurs as a complete sentence, whereas other verbals may occur as complete sentences. Observe the following Copula expressions:

(Cə nɪn) Kim imnita.	'(I) am Kim.'
(Kɪ kəs;) Muəs imnikka?	'What is (it)?'
(Cə nɪn) Mikuk salam imnita.	'(I) am an American.'
(Ceimsɪ nɪn) Haksæng imnita.	'(James) is a student.'

2. Particles ɪn/nɪn, ɪl/lɪl, e

There is a class of uninflected words in Korean which occurs within a sentence or at the end of a sentence, but never at the beginning of one. These words are never preceded by a pause; they are regularly pronounced as though they were part of the preceding word. All such words are called Particles.

Some particles have only one shape; others occur in either of two shapes determined by the final sound of the preceding word.

(a) ɪn/nɪn 'as for', 'in reference to' is a two-shape particle: ɪn occurs after a word ending in a consonant and nɪn occurs after a word ending in a vowel.

(1) It follows the general topic (often one already under discussion) about which something new or significant is about to be stated or asked: Examples:

Cə nɪn haksæng imnita.	'I am a student.'
Ce ilɪm ɪn Ceimsɪ imnita.	'My name is James.'
Sənsæng ɪn Mikuk salam imnikka?	'Are you an American?'

(2) ɪn/nɪn also occurs as the particle of comparison following a topic which is being compared: A ɪn/nɪn 'A in comparison with (others)' or 'insofar as we're talking about A.' Examples:

Sənsæng ɪn muəs ɪl hasimnikka?	'What are YOU doing?'
Cə nɪn Yəngə nɪn kongpu-hamnita.	'ENGLISH I am studying.'

(ɪn/nɪn never follows an interrogative word (i.e. a word that asks a question: 'What?', 'Who?', 'Where?', etc.)

(b) ɪl/lɪl is a two-shape particle: ɪl occurs after a noun ending in a consonant and lɪl after a noun ending in a vowel. The particle ɪl/lɪl singles out the preceding noun as the direct object of the following inflected expression. Examples:

Muəs ɪl kongpu-hamnikka?	'What do [you] study?'
Hankuk mal ɪl kongpu-hamnita.	'[I] am studying Korean.'
Ilpon mal ɪl kalɪchimnita.	'[He] teaches Japanese.'
Cungkuk mal ɪl mal-hamnita.	'[He] speaks Chinese.'

(c) e

When the particle e occurs between two nouns, it is called the Possessive Particle. Noun 1 + e + Noun 2 means 'Noun 1's Noun 2' or 'Noun 2 of Noun 1. Examples:

cə e ilɪm	'my name'
hakkyo e ilɪm	'the name of the school'
Kim e chæk	'Kim's book'

3. Nouns and Noun phrases.

Korean nouns are uninflected words, that is, they have only one form. (They do not, for example, reflect the singular-plural distinction as English nouns do.) In Korean two or more nouns often make up noun phrases and are used as though they were one word. Compare:

(a) Single nouns:

Mikuk	'America', 'the U.S.'
salam	'person', 'man'
mal	'language', 'utterance'

(b) Noun Phrases:

(1) Country name + salam = Nationality

Mikuk salam	'(an) American' ('America person')
Yəngkuk salam	'(an) Englishman' ('Britian person')
Ilpon salam	'(a) Japanese' ('Japan person')
Cungkuk salam	'(a) Chinese' ('China person')

(2) Country name + mal = language of the country named

Hankuk mal	'Korean (language)' ('Korea language')
Cungkuk mal	'Chinese (language)' ('China language')
Pullansə mal	'French' ('France language')
Yəngə*	'English'

Note 1: Place name + mal = dialect

Səul mal	'Seoul dialect'
Pusan mal	'Pusan dialect'

Note 2: Place name + salam = Person of the place named

Nam-Han salam	'South Korean
Pusan salam	'Pusanian'
Səul salam	'Seoulite'
Nyuyok salam	'New Yorker'

A noun which may occur as a free form is called a Free Noun. Hereafter, any noun or noun phrase which occurs in a position where a free noun can be substituted shall be called a Nominal Expression or simply a Nominal.

---

* Yəngə is a single-word expression for 'English'.
Yəngkuk mal ('British language') is rarely used for English.

DRILLS

A. Substitution Drill

1. Ce ilɪm ɪn Ceimsɪ imnita.	My name is James.
2. Ce ilɪm ɪn <u>Kim</u> imnita.	My name is Kim.
3. Ce ilɪm ɪn <u>Kisu</u> imnita.	My name is Kisu.
4. Ce ilɪm ɪn <u>Kim Kisu</u> imnita.	My name is Kisu Kim.
*5. Ce ilɪm ɪn <u>Pak</u> imnita.	My name is Park (family name).
*6. Ce ilɪm ɪn <u>I Kisu</u> imnita.	My name is Kisu Lee (family name + given name).
*7. Ce ilɪm ɪn <u>Chwe</u> imnita.	My name is Choe (family name).
*8. Ce ilɪm ɪn <u>Cəng</u> imnita.	My name is Chung (family name).

B. Substitution Drill

1. Cə nɪn <u>haksæng</u> imnita.	I am a student.
2. Cə nɪn <u>sənsæng</u> imnita.	I am a teacher.
3. Cə nɪn <u>Hankuk salam</u> imnita.	I am a Korean.
4. Cə nɪn <u>Mikuk salam</u> imnita.	I am an American.
5. Cə nɪn <u>Mikuk haksæng</u> imnita.	I am an American student.
6. Cə nɪn <u>Hankuk haksæng</u> imnita.	I am a Korean student.
7. Cə nɪn <u>Hankuk mal haksæng</u> imnita.	I am a Korean (language) student.
8. Cə nɪn <u>Hankuk mal sənsæng</u> imnita.	I am a Korean (language) teacher.
*9. Cə nɪn <u>Mikuk mal sənsæng</u> imnita.	I am an American (language) teacher.
*10. Cə nɪn <u>Yəngə sənsæng</u> imnita.	I am an English teacher.
*11. Cə nɪn <u>Mikuk salam</u> imnita.	I am an American.

C. Substitution Drill

1. Cə nɪn Hankuk salam imnita.	I am a Korean.
*2. Cə nɪn <u>Yəngkuk salam</u> imnita.	I am an Englishman.
*3. Cə nɪn <u>Ilpon salam</u> imnita.	I am a Japanese.
*4. Cə nɪn <u>Cungkuk salam</u> imnita.	I am a Chinese.
*5. Cə nɪn <u>Tokil salam</u> imnita.	I am a German.
*6. Cə nɪn <u>Pullansə salam</u> imnita.	I am a Frenchman.
*7. Cə nɪn <u>Səul salam</u> imnita.	I am from Seoul.

D. Substitution Drill

1.	Sənsæng ɨn Mikuk salam imnikka?	Are you an American? / Is the teacher an American?
2.	Sənsæng ɨn Hankuk salam imnikka?	Are you a Korean? / Is the teacher a Korean?
3.	Sənsæng ɨn Yəngkuk salam imnikka?	Are you an Englishman? / Is the teacher an Englishman?
4.	Sənsæng ɨn Ilpon salam imnikka?	Are you a Japanese? / Is the teacher a Japanese?
5.	Sənsæng ɨn Cungkuk salam imnikka	Are you a Chinese? / Is the teacher a Chinese?
6.	Sənsæng ɨn Tokil salam imnikka?	Are you a German? / Is the teacher a German?
7.	Sənsæng ɨn Pullansə salam imnikka?	Are you a Frenchman? / Is the teacher a Frenchman?
8.	Sənsæng ɨn Səul salam imnikka?	Are you from Seoul? / Is the teacher from Seoul?
9.	Sənsæng ɨn Kim sənsæng imnikka?	Are you Mr. Kim / Is the teacher Mr. Kim?
*10.	Sənsæng ɨn Hankuk yəca imnikka?	Is the teacher a Korean woman?
*11.	Sənsæng ɨn Mikuk yəca imnikka?	Is the teacher an American woman?
*12.	Sənsæng ɨn Yəngkuk yəca imnikka?	Is the teacher an English woman?

E. Substitution Drill

1.	Sənsæng ɨn Mikuk salam imnikka?	Is the teacher an American?
2.	Kim Sənsæng ɨn Mikuk salam imnikka?	Is Mr. Kim an American?
3.	Ceimsɨ Sənsæng ɨn Mikuk salam imnikka?	Is Mr. James an American?
4.	Pak Sənsæng ɨn Mikuk salam imnikka?	Is Mr. Park an American?
5.	Haksæng ɨn Mikuk salam imnikka?	Is the student an American?
6.	Hankuk mal haksæng ɨn Mikuk salam imnikka?	Is the Korean (language) student an American?
7.	Hankuk mal sənsæng ɨn Mikuk salam imnikka?	Is the Korean (language) teacher an American

F. Substitution Drill

1.	Sənsæng ın muəs (ıl) hasimnikka?	What do you do? / What does the teacher do?
2.	Haksæng ın muəs (ıl) hasimnikka?	What does the student do?
*3.	Tangsin ın muəs (ıl) hasimnikka?	What do you do (to husband or wife, or to the same male adult friend)?
4.	Ceimsı Sənsæng ın muəs (ıl) hasimnikka?	What does Mr. James do?
5.	I Sənsæng ın muəs (ıl) hasimnikka?	What does Mr. Lee do?
6.	Chwe Sənsæng ın muəs (ıl) hasimnikka?	What does Mr. Choe do?
7.	Kim Sənsæng ın muəs (ıl) hasimnikka?	What does Mr. Kim do?
8.	Kim Sənsæng ın muəs (ıl) kongpu-hamnikka?	What does Mr. Kim study?
*9.	Kim Sənsæng ın muəs (ıl) pæumnikka?	What does Mr. Kim learn?
*10.	Kim Sənsæng ın muəs (ıl) kalıchimnikka?	What does Mr. Kim teach?
*11.	Kim Sənsæng ın muəs (ıl) i(l)ksımnikka?	What does Mr. Kim read?

G. Substitution Drill

1.	Kim Sənsæng ın muəs ıl i(l)ksımnikka?	What does Mr. Kim read?
2.	Pak Sənsæng ın muəs ıl i(l)ksımnikka?	What does Mr. Park read?
3.	Pak Sənsæng ın muəs ıl pæumnikka?	What is Mr. Park learning?
4.	Chwe Sənsæng ın muəs ıl pæumnikka?	What is Mr. Choe learning?
5.	Chwe Sənsæng ın muəs ıl kalıchimnikka?	What does Mr. Choe teach?
6.	Mikuk haksæng ın muəs kalıchimnikka?	What is the American student teaching?
*7.	Mikuk haskæng ın muəs ıl mal-hamnikka?	What does the American student say? / What does the American student speak?
8.	Hankuk mal sənsæng ın muəs ıl mal-hamnikka?	What does the Korean teacher say?
9.	Hankuk mal sənsæng ın muəs ıl kongpu-hamnikka?	What is the Korean teacher studying?
10.	Ilpon haksæng ın mues ıl kongpu-hamnikka?	What is the Japanese student studying?

H. Substitution Drill

1.	(Cə nɪn) Hankuk mal ɪl kongpu-hamnita.	I('m) study(ing) Korean.
2.	(Cə nɪn) Mikuk mal ɪl kongpu-hamnita.	I('m) study(ing) the American language.
3.	(Cə nɪn) Ilpon mal ɪl kongpu-hamnita.	I('m) study(ing) Japanese.
4.	(Cə nɪn) Cungkuk mal ɪl kongpu-hamnita.	I('m) study(ing) Chinese.
5.	(Cə nɪn) Yəngə lɪl kongpu-hamnita.	I('m) study(ing) English.
6.	(Cə nɪn) Hankuk mal ɪl kongpu-hamnita.	I('m) study(ing) Korean.
7.	(Cə nɪn) Hankuk mal ɪl kalɪchimnita.	I('m) teach(ing) Korean
8.	(Cə nɪn) Hankuk mal ɪl mal-hamnita.	I speak Korean.
9.	(Cə nɪn) Hankuk mal ɪl pæumnita.	I('m) learn(ing) Korean
10.	(Cə nɪn) Hankuk mal ɪl i(l)ksɪmnita	I('m) read(ing) Korean

I. Substitution Drill

1.	(Sənsæng ɪn) muəs ɪl kongpu-hamnikka?	What do you study?
2.	(Sənsæng ɪn) Hankuk mal ɪl kongpu-hamnikka? hamnikka?	Do you study Korean?
3.	(Sənsæng ɪn) Mikuk mal ɪl kongpu-hamnikka?	Do you study the American language?
4.	(Sənsæng ɪn) Cungkuk mal ɪl kongpu-hamnikka?	Do you study Chinese?
5.	(Sənsæng ɪn) Ilpon mal ɪl kongpu-hamnikka?	Do you study Japanese?
6.	(Sənsæng ɪn) Yəngə lɪl kongpu-hamnikka?	Do you study English?
7.	(Sənsæng ɪn) Tokil mal ɪl kongpu-hamnikka?	Do you study German?
8.	(Sənsæng ɪn) Pullansə mal ɪl kongpu-hamnikka?	Do you study French?

J. Substitution Drill

1. Cə nɪn Yəngə lɪl mal-hamnita.	I speak English.
2. Kim Sənsæng ɪn Yəngə lɪl mal-hamnita	Mr. Kim speaks English.
3. Kim Sənsæng ɪn Pullansə mal ɪl mal-hamnita.	Mr. Kim speaks French.
Kim Sənsæng ɪn Pullansə mal ɪ pæumnita.	Mr. Kim is learning French.
5. Hankuk haksæng ɪn Pullansə mal ɪl pæumnita.	Korean students are learning French.
6. Hankuk haksæng ɪn Tokil mal ɪl pæumnita.	Korean students are learning German.
7. Hankuk haksæng ɪn Tokil mal ɪl ilksɪmnita.	Korean students read German.
8. Yəngkuk haksæng ɪn Tokil mal ɪl ilksɪmnita.	British students read German.
9. Yəngkuk haksæng ɪn Cungkuk mal ɪl ilksɪmnita.	British students read Chinese.
10. Yəngkuk haksæng ɪn Cungkuk mal ɪl kalɪchimnita.	A British student is teaching Chinese.
11. Mikuk haksæng ɪn Cungkuk mal ɪl kalɪchimnita.	An American student is teaching Chinese.

K. Response Drill (based on the dialogues)

Teacher:	Student:
1. Annyəng-hasimnikka?	Ne, annyəng-hasimnikka?
2. Chəɪm pwepsɪmnita.	Annyəng-hasimnikka? Chəɪm pwepsɪmnita.
3. Ce ilɪm ɪn Kim Kisu imnita.	Ce ilɪm ɪn Ceimsɪ imnita.
4. Sənsæng ɪn Mikuk salam imnikka?	Ne, kɪləhsɪmnita.
5. (Sənsæng ɪn) muəs (ɪl) hasimnikka?	Cə nɪn haksæng imnita.; Hankuk mal ɪɪ kongpu-hamnita.
6. Muəs ɪl kongpu-hamnikka?	Hankuk mal ɪl kongpu-hamnita.
7. Ceimsɪ Sənsæng, annyəng-hasimnikka?	Ne, cal issɪmnita.
8. Yocɪm əttəhke cinasimnikka?	(Təkpun e) cal cinamnita.
9. (Sənsæng ɪn) cæmi (ka) əttəhsɪmnikka?	Kɪce kɪləhsɪmnita.

L. Response Drill

Teacher:	Student:
1. Mianhamnita.	Chənman e malssım imnita.
2. Sillye-hamnita.	(Aniyo) kwænchanhsımnita.
3. Sillye-hakessımnita.	(Aniyo) kwænchanhsımnita.
4. Sillyehæssımnita.	(Aniyo) kwænchanhsımnita.
5. Annyənghi kasipsiyo.	Annyənghi kyesipsiyo.
6. Annyənghi kyesipsiyo.	Annyənghi kasipsiyo.
7. Komapsımnita.	Chənman e malssım imnita.
8. Mianhamnita.	(Aniyo) kwænchanhsımnita.
9. An twessımnita.	(Aniyo) kwænchanhsımnita.
10. Tto pwepkessımnita.	Ne, tto pwepkessımnita.

EXERCISES

A. Tell Kim Sənsæng:

1. your name.
2. that you are an American.
3. that you are a student.
4. that you are studying Korean.
5. that you are fine.
6. that Mr. Park teaches Korean.
7. that you are glad to meet him.
8. that you speak Japanese.
9. that you read French.
10. that Mr. Park is learning English.
11. that the Korean (language) teacher is a woman from Seoul.
12. that the American is an English teacher.
13. that the English teacher speaks Chinese.
14. that the Chinese woman teaches German.
15. that the German (language) student speaks Japanese.

B. Conduct the following conversations:

Ask Mr. Kim:	Mr. Kim answers:
1. if he is a Korean.	that he is.
2. what he does.	that he is a teacher.
3. what he teaches.	that he teaches Korean.
4. how he's getting along these days.	that he's doing fine.
5. if the teacher is an American.	that he is.
6. if the student is a Korean.	that he is an Englishman.
7. if he speaks Korean.	that he does.
8. if Mr. James is a Korean (language) student.	that he is.

C. You've met a stranger at a party; tell him:

1. that you are glad to meet him.
2. that your name is so-and-so.
3. that you're studying Korean.
4. that Mr. Park is your Korean teacher.
5. that you'll see him again.

End of Tape 1B

Tape 2A

제 2 과 길 찾기

(대화 A)

잠간
실례
실례합니다

1. A: 잠간 실례합니다.

말 말씀
좀
물어 봅시다

2. 말씀 좀 물어 봅시다.

3. B. 예, 무엇입니까?

대사관
미국 대사관이
어디
어디에
있읍니까

4. A: 미국 대사관이 어디에 있읍니까?

저기
저기에
쪽
왼쪽
왼쪽으로
가십시요

5. B: 저기에 있읍니다 왼쪽으로 가십시요.

UNIT 2. Finding One's Way Around

BASIC DIALOGUES FOR MEMORIZATION

Dialogue A

A

camkan/camkkan/	for a moment
sillye	rudeness
sillye-hamnita	[I] commit rudeness
1. Camkan sillye-hamnita.	Excuse me for a moment.
mal malssım }	word; speech; language
com	a little
mulə popsita/muləpopssita/	let's inquire; let's ask
2. Malssım com mulə popsita.	May I ask you a question? ('Let's inquire a word.')

B

3. Ne, muəs imnikka?	Yes, what is [it]?

A

tæsakwan	embassy
Mikuk Tæsakwan i	the U.S. Embassy (as subject)
əti	what place?
əti e	at what place?; where?
issımnikka	does [it] exist?; is [there]?
4. Mikuk Tæsakwan i əti e issımnikka?	Where is the U.S. Embassy? ('At what place does the U.S. Embassy exist?')

B

cəki	that place; there
cəki e	at that place; over there
ccok	side; direction
wen ccok	the left (side)
wen ccok ılo	to the left
kasipsiyo/kasipssiyo/	(please) go
5. Cəki e issımnita. Wen ccok ılo kasipsiyo.	[It]'s over there. Go to the left.

건물
저 건물
학교

6. A: 저 건물이 학교입니까?

7. B: 예, 그렇습니다.

대단히
고맙습니다

8. A: 대단히 고맙습니다.

아니요
천만에 말씀

9. B: 아니요, 천만에 말씀입니다

(대화 B)

어데
시청

10. A: 시청이 어데 있읍니까'

이 건물

11. B: 이 건물이 시청입니다.

저것
저것은

12. A: 저것은 무엇입니까?

A

kənmul	building
cə kənmul	that building
hakkyo	school
6. Cə kənmul i hakkyo imnikka?	Is that building a school?

B

7. Ne, kɪləhsɪmnita.	Yes, it is.

A

tætanhi	very; very much
komapsɪmnita	[I]'m grateful
8. Tætanhi komapsɪmnita.	Thank you very much.

B

chənman e malssɪm	('a million words')
9. Aniyo, chənman e malssɪm imnita.	(No,) Not at all. ('You're welcome.')

Dialogue B

A

əte	where
sichəng	City Hall
10. Sichəng i əte issɪmnikka?	Where is the City Hall?

B

i kənmul	this building
11. I kənmul i sichəng imnita.	This building is the City Hall.

A

cə kəs	that (thing); the thing over there
cə kəs ɪn	as for that
12. Cə kəs ɪn muəs imnikka?	What is THAT?

그것
여관

13. B: 그것은 여관입니다.

어느 것
백화점

14. A: 어느 것이 백화점입니까?

옆
옆에
시청 옆에

15. B: 백화점은 시청 옆에 있습니다.

공보
공보원
미국 공보원

16. A: 미국 공보원은 어디에 있읍니까?

바로
앞
앞에
바로 앞에

17. B: 바로 앞에 있읍니다.

감사
감사합니다

18. A: 대단히 감사합니다.

19. B: 아니요, 천만에요.

B

kɪ kəs	that; it
yəkwan	inn; hotel
13. Kɪ kəs ɪn yəkwan imnita.	It's a hotel. ('It's an inn.')

A

ənɪ kəs	which one
pækhwacəm	department store
14. ənɪ kəs i pækhwacəm imnikka?	Which one is the department store?

B

yəph	the side
yəph e	beside; by
sichəng yəph e	beside the City Hall; next to the City Hall
15. Pækhwacəm ɪn sichəng yəph e issɪmnita.	The department store is beside the City Hall. ('As for a department store it exists besides the City Hall.')

A

kongpo	public information
kongpowən	information office
Mikuk Kongpowən	USIS
16. Mikuk Kongpowən ɪn ət e issɪmnikka?	Where is USIS? ('As for USIS, where is [it]?')

B

palo	just; right
aph	the front
aph e	at the front
palo aph e	right ahead
17. Palo aph e issɪmnita.	[It]'s right up ahead.

A

kamsa	gratitute
kamsa-hamnita	[I] thank you
18. Tætanhi kamsa-hamnita.	Thanks a lot.

B

19. Aniyo, chənman e yo.	No, not at all

NOTES ON DIALOGUES

(Numbers correspond to the sentence numbers in the dialogues)

1. Camkan sillye-hamnita. 'Excuse me for a moment.' is usually said when you stop a stranger to get some information.

2. Malssɪm com mulə popsita. ('Let us ask [you] a word') is often preceded by Camkan sillye-hamnita. and is regularly used to a stranger from whom you want to inquire about something, such as directions.

3. Muəs 'what (thing)' is always a free noun. It is never used to modify a following noun.

5. Ccok 'direction' occurs after determinatives (See Grammar Note 3) or place names. It never stands along. Examples:

i ccok	'this way'
cə ccok	'that way'
kɪ ccok	'that way'
hakkyo ccok	'the direction of the school'
tæsakwan ccok	'the direction of the embassy'
wen ccok	'the left'
clɪn ccok	'the right'

8.18 Komapsɪmnita. and Kamsa-hamnita. 'Thank you.' are freely interchangeable on any occasion.

10. əte 'where' is the contracted form of əti + e.

13. Yəkwan generally refers to 'inns' or 'hotels' of all sizes. However, modern western-style hotels are often called hothel.

14. ənɪ 'which', 'what' always occurs before a nominal (free or bound) as a determinative. It never occurs as a free form.

19. Chənman e yo. 'Not at all.' is the informal equivalent of Chənman e malssɪm imnita.

GRAMMAR NOTES

1. Formal Polite Speech Sentences

The nucleus of a Korean sentence comes at the end of the sentence. When the nucleus of a normal sentence is a verb, we talk about verb-stems and verb-endings. There are several levels and/or styles of speech which show the relationship between the speaker and the person spoken to and/or about. The distinctions of speech level are shown mostly by the inflected forms of verbs.

In all societies, everywhere, when people talk to one another, they give each other signals (gestures, tones of voice, word-choice, etc.) to show that they understand their personal relationship (equality, dominance, subordination) and the situation (polite-casual, formal-informal, etc.). Sometimes, in our democratic society, we like to pretend these things don't exist, but they do. Very few of us can talk to our boss the way we talk to our best friend. In Korean, the personal relationship signals are built into the language.

Formal Polite Speech is the polite style of speech commonly used between adults who do not have a casual relationship. The four forms of Formal Polite Speech verb-endings are listed below.

(a) Formal Polite Statement Form: -mnita ~ -(s)ımnita

In Formal Polite Statements, -mnita is added to a verb stem ending in a vowel; -(s)ımnita to a verb stem ending in a consonant. Examples:

Stem		Verbal	
ka-	'to go'	Kamnita.	'[I] go.'
o-	'to come'	Omnita.	'[I] come.'
pæu-	'to learn'	Pæumnita.	'[I] learn.'
kongpu-ha-	'to study'	Kongpu-hamnita.	'[I] study.'
ilk-	'to read'	Ilk(s)ımnita.	'[I] read.'
mək-	'to eat'	Mək(s)ımnita.	'[I] eat.'
a(l)-	'to know'	Amnita.	'[I] know.'

(b) Formal Polite Question Form: -mnikka? ~ -(s)ımnikka?

In Formal Polite Questions, -mnikka? is added to a verb stem ending in a vowel, -(s)ımninka? to a verb stem ending in a consonant. Compare:

Kamnita.	'[I] go.'	Kamnikka?	'Do [you] go?'
Omnita.	'[I] come.'	Omnikka?	'Do [you] come?'
Paəumnita.	'[I] learn.'	Paəumnikka?	'Do [you] learn?'
Kongpu-hamnita.	'[I] study.'	Kongpu-hamnikka?	'Do [you] study?'
Ilk(s)ımnita.	'[I] read.'	Ilk(s)ımnikka?	'Do [you] read?'
Mək(s)ımnita.	'[I] eat.'	Mək(s)ımnikka?	'Do [you] eat?'

(c) Formal Polite Imperative Form: -sipsiyo ~ -ısipsiyo

In Formal Polite Requests, -sipsiyo is added to a verb stem ending in a vowel and -ısipsiyo to a verb stem ending in a consonant. Examples:

Stem		Verbal	
ha-	'to do'	Hasipsiyo.	'Please do [it].'
ka-	'to go'	Kasipsiyo.	'Please go.'
o-	'to come'	Osipsiyo.	'Please come.'
mulə po-	'to inquire'	Mulə posipsiyo.	'Please ask.'
iss-	'to exist'	Issısipsiyo.	'Please stay.'
ilk-	'to read'	Ilkısipsiyo.	'Please read.'

(d) Formal Polite Propositative Form: -psita ~ -ıpsita

In Formal Polite Proposals ('Let's ___.'), -psita is added to a verb stem ending in a vowel, and -ıpsita is added to a verb stem ending in a consonant. Examples:

Stem		Verbal	
ka-	'to go'	Kapsita.	'Let's go.'
kalıchi-	'to teach'	Kalıchipsita.	'Let's teach.'
mal-ha-	'to speak'	Mal-hapsita.	'Let's speak.'
mulə po-	'to inquire'	Mulə popsita.	'Let's ask.'
ilk-	'to read'	Ilkıpsita.	'Let's read.'

2. Particles i/ka, lo/ɪlo, e

(a) i/ka

The particle i/ka singles out the preceding word as the emphasized subject of a sentence; i occurs after a word ending in a consonant and ka after a word ending in a vowel. When the particle i/ka is added, the subject is emphatic. Observe the location of the emphasis in the English equivalents. Examples:

Hakkyo ka issɪmnita.	'There is a school.' ('A school exists.')
Cə kənmul i tæsakwan imnita.	'That building is the embassy.'
Ce ka Hankuk mal ɪl pæumnita.	'I am studying Korean.'

(b) lo/ɪlo 'to, toward'

A place nominal + lo/ɪlo followed by such verbs as ka- 'to go', o- 'to come' indicates the direction of the following inflected expression. Lo occurs after a place noun which ends in a vowel and ɪlo after a noun ending in a consonant. Examples:

Hakkyo lo kamnita.	{'[I] go to school.' {'[I]'m going toward the school.'
Cip ɪlo osipsiyo.	'Please come to the house.'
Wen ccok ɪlo kasipsiyo.	'Please go to the left (side).'

(c) e 'at', 'on', 'in', 'to'

A place (or location) noun + e indicates that the action of the following inflected expression takes place at the noun. Examples:

Səul i Hankuk e issɪmnita.	'Seoul is in Korea. ('Seoul is in Korea.')
Tæsakwan i əti e issɪmnikka?	'Where is the Embassy? ('At what place does the Embassy exist?')
Yəkwan ɪn palo aph e issɪmnita.	'A hotel is right ahead.'
Chæk ɪl chæksang e tuəssɪmnita.	'[I] have placed ('put') the book on the desk.

3. Determinatives

There is a small class of uninflected words in Korean which never occur by themselves but are followed by nominals. Words of this class are called Determinatives. A determinitive + a nominal = a noun phrase. In Unit 2, we have the following determinatives: i 'this___', cə 'that___', kɪ 'the (or that)___', ənɪ 'which___', olɪn 'right___', wen 'left___'. Observe the following examples:

i chæk	'this book'
i kəs	'this (thing)'
cə salam	'that man'
cə kəs	'that (thing over there)'
kɪ kənmul	'that ('the') building'
kɪ salam	'that man (mentioned previously)'
ənɪ pækwacəm	'which department store'
ənɪ kəs	'which one'
olɪn ccok	'the right (direction)'
wen ccok	'the left (direction)'

Note that <u>i</u> 'this__ and <u>cə</u> 'that__' before nominals indicate nominals within the sight of the speaker, while <u>kɪ</u> 'that (<u>or</u> the)__' before a nominal refers to a previously mentioned one; <u>olɪn</u> 'the right__' and <u>wen</u> 'the left__' occur only before the word <u>ccok</u>.

4. Post-Nouns: <u>kəs</u>, <u>pun</u>, <u>ccok</u>

<u>Kəs</u> ('thing'), <u>pun</u> ('person'), <u>ccok</u> ('side') belong to a small class of Korean nouns which never occur alone but only after such words as determinatives, free nouns, or other modifier classes of words and make up nominal phrases. Words of this class are called <u>Post-Nouns</u>. Examples:

i kəs	'this (thing)'
cə pun	'that man (honored)'
khɪn kəs	'(a) big one'
wen ccok	'the left (side)'

5. <u>Imnita</u> and <u>Issɪmnita</u>

In Korean there is a distinction between the experssion (a) 'A is B' and (b) 'There is an A.' or 'A exists.' In Unit 1, we learned that the copula <u>i-</u> (of which <u>imnita</u> is one inflected form) is used to denote 'Noun A is Noun B.' In contrast to the copula, the verb <u>iss-</u> (of which <u>issɪmnita</u> is one inflected form) means '(something) exists.' (See Grammar Note 1, Unit 1.) Compare:

(a)

(Kɪ kəs ɪn) chæk imnita.	'[It] is a book.'
I kənmul i hakkyo imnita.	'This building is a school.'
Na nɪn sənsæng imnita.	'I am a teacher.'

(b)

Chæk i issımnita.	'There is a book.' ('A book exists.')
Səul e tæsakwan i issımnita.	'There is an Embassy at Seoul.' ('An exbassy exists at Seoul.')

Note that a nominal i/ka + issımnita preceded by a personal noun as a topic occurs to express that the personal noun has or possesses the nominal. Examples:

Na nın chæk i issımnita.	'I have a book.' ('As for me a book exists.')
Sənsæng ın Hankuk mal sacən i issımnikka?	'Do you have a Korean dictionary?'
Ne, (na nın) sikye ka issımnita.	'Yes, I have a watch.'

DRILLS

A. Substitution Drill

1.	Tæsakwan i əti e issımnikka?	Where is the Embassy?
2.	Mikuk Tæsakwan i əti e issımnikka?	Where is the U.S. Embassy?
3.	Hakkyo ka əti e issımnikka?	Where is the school?
4.	Sichəng i əti e issımnikka?	Where is the City Hall?
5.	Pækhwacəm i əti e issımnikka?	Where is the department store?
6.	Yəkwan i əti e issımnikka?	Where is the inn?
7.	Kongpowən i əti e issımnikka?	Where is the information center?
8.	Mikuk Kongpowən i əti e issımnikka?	Where is the USIS?
9.	Hankuk Tæsakwan i əti e issımnikka?	Where is the Korean Embassy?
10.	Haksæng i əti e issımnikka?	Where is the student?
11.	Hankuk mal sənsæng i əti e issımnikka?	Where is the Korean (language) teacher?
12.	Kı kəs i əti e issımnikka?	Where is it?
*13.	Ai ka əti e issımnikka?	Where is the child?
14.	Puin i əti e issımnikka?	Where is your wife? ('Where is the lady?')

B. Substitution Drill

1.	Cəki e issımnita.	[It]'s over there.
*2.	Yəki e issımnita.	[It]'s over here.
3.	Wen ccok e issımnita.	[It]'s on the left.
*4.	Olın ccok e issımnita.	[It]'s on the right.
5.	Aph e issımnita.	[It]'s in front [of you].
*6.	Twi e issımnita.	[It]'s in the back.
7.	Yəph e issımnita.	[It]'s beside [you].
8.	Hakkyo e issımnita.	[It]'s at school.
9.	Mikuk e issımnita.	[It]'s in America.
10.	Hankuk e issımnita.	[It]'s in Korea.

C. Substitution Drill (Supply i/ka Particle.)

1.	Sicheng i issımnita.	[There] is the City Hall.
2.	Hakkyo (ka) issımnita.	[There] is a school.
3.	Kənmul (i) issımnita.	[There] is a building.
4.	Yəkwan (i) issımnita.	[There] is an inn.
5.	Sənsæng (i) issımnita.	[There] is a teacher.
*6.	Kyosil (i) issımnita.	[There] is a classroom.
*7.	Sikye (ka) issımnita.	[There] is a watch.
*8.	Chæk (i) issımnita.	[There] is a book.
*9.	Chæksang (i) issımnita.	[There] is a {table. desk.}
*10.	ıyca (ka) issımnita.	[There] is a chair.
*11.	Yənphil (i) issımnita.	[There] is a pencil.
*12.	Cito (ka) issımnita.	[There] is a map.
13.	Ai (ka) issımnita.	[There] is a child.

D. Substitution Drill

1.	Tæsakwan i yəki e issımnita.	The Embassy is here ('at this place').
2.	Tæsakwan i cəki e issımnita.	The Embassy is over there ('at that place').
3.	Hakkyo ka cəki e issımnita.	The school is over there.
4.	Hakkyo ka wen ccok e issımnita.	The school is on the left.
5.	Mikuk Kongpowən i wen ccok e issımnita.	USIS is on the left.
6.	Mikuk Kongpowən i i kənmul e issımnita.	USIS is in this building.
7.	Pækhwacəm i i kənmul e issımnita.	The department store is in this building.
8.	Pækhwacəm i aph e issımnita.	The dpeartment store is ahead.
9.	Yəkwan i aph e issımnita.	The inn is ahead.
10.	Yəkwan i yəph e issımnita.	The inn is nearby.

E. Substitution Drill (Supply lo/ılo Particle.)

1.	Wen ccok ılo kasipsiyo.	(Please) go to the left.
*2.	Olın ccok (ılo) kasipsiyo.	(Please) go to the right.
*3.	I ccok (ılo) kasipsiyo.	(Please) go this way.
*4.	Cə ccok (ılo) kasipsiyo.	(Please) go that way.
5.	Hakkyo (lo) kasipsiyo.	(Please) go to school.
6.	Cə kənmul (lo) kasipsiyo.	(Please) go to that building.
7.	Pækhwacəm (ılo) kasipsiyo.	(Please) go to the department store.
8.	Sichəng (ılo) kasipsiyo.	(Please) go to the city hall.
9.	Yəkwan (ılo) kasipsiyo.	(Please) go to the inn.
10.	Tæsakwan (ılo) kasipsiyo.	(Please) go to the Embassy.

F. Substitution Drill

1.	Cə kənmul i hakkyo imnikka?	Is that building a school?
2.	Cə kənmul i tæsakwan imnikka?	Is that building the embassy?
3.	Cə kənmul i Mikuk Tæsakwan imnikka?	Is that building the U.S. Embassy?
4.	Cə kənmul i sichəng imnikka?	Is that building the City Hall?
5.	Cə kənmul i kongpowən imnikka?	Is that building the information center?
6.	Cə kənmul i pækhwacəm imnikka?	Is that building a department store?
7.	Cə kəs i pækhwacəm imnikka?	Is that a department store?
8.	I kəs i pækhwacəm imnikka?	Is this a department store?
9.	Kı kəs i pækhwacəm imnikka?	Is it a department store?
10.	I kənmul i pækhwacəm imnikka?	Is this building a department store?
11.	ənı kəs i pækhwacəm imnikka?	Which is the department store?
12.	ənı kənmul i pækhwacəm imnikka?	Which building is the department store?

G. Substitution Drill (Supply i/ka Particle)

1. Cə kənmul i hakkyo imnikka?	Is that building a school?
2. Cə salam i haksæng imnikka?	Is he ('that person') a student?
3. Cə kəs i yəkwan imnikka?	Is that an inn?
4. Cə kənmul i Mikuk Tæsakwan imnikka?	Is that building the U.S. Embassy?
5. Cə haksæng i Mikuk salam imnikka?	Is that student an American?
6. Cə yəca ka Yəngə sənsæng imnikka?	Is she ('that woman') an English teacher?
7. Cə ccok i Mikuk Kongpowən imnikka?	Is USIS that way?
8. Cə hakkyo ka Hankuk mal hakkyo imnikka?	Is that school a Korean language school?
9. Cə kənmul i pækhwacəm imnikka?	Is that building a department store?
10. Cə puin i Hankuk yəca imnikka?	Is that lady a Korean woman?

H. Substitution Drill

1. Sənsæng e ilɪm ɪn muəs imnikka?	What is your name?
2. Haksæng e ilɪm ɪn muəs imnikka?	What is the student's name?
3. Cə sənsæng e ilɪm ɪn muəs imnikka?	What's that teacher's name?
4. I kənmul e ilɪm ɪn muəs imnikka?	What's the name of this building?
5. Cə hakkyo e ilɪm ɪn muəs imnikka?	What's the name of that school?
6. Cə Mikuk salam e ilɪm ɪn muəs imnikka?	What's the name of that American?
7. Cə Hankuk salam e ilɪm ɪn muəs imnikka?	What's the name of that Korean?
8. Kɪ salam e ilɪm ɪn muəs imnikka?	What's the name of that man?
9. Cə yəkwan e ilɪm ɪn muəs imnikka?	What's the name of that inn?
10. Cə ai e ilɪm ɪn muəs imnikka?	What's the name of that child?
11. Cə puin e ilɪm in muəs imnikka?	What's the name of that lady?

I. Substitution Drill

1.	Pækhwacəm ın hakkyo yəph e issımnita.	The department store is next to the school.
2.	Tæsakwan ın hakkyo yəph e issımnita.	The Embassy is next to the school.
3.	Mikuk Tæsakwan ın hakkyo yəph e issımnita.	The U.S. Embassy is next to the school.
4.	Mikuk Kongpowən ın hakkyo yəph e issımnita.	USIS is next to the school.
5.	Hankuk yəkwan ın hakkyo yəph e issımnita.	The Korean inn is next to the school.
*6.	ınhæng ın hakkyo yəph e issımnita.	The bank is next to the school.
*7.	Sangcəm ın hakkyo yəph e issımnita.	The store is next to the school.
8.	Hothel ın hakkyo yəph e issımnita.	The hotel is next to the school.
*9.	Cip ın hakkyo yəph e issımnita.	The house is next to the school.
*10.	Kongwən ın hakkyo yəph e issımnita.	The park is next to the school.

J. Substitution Drill

1.	Pækhwacəm ın sichəng yəph e issımnita.	The department store is next to the City Hall.
2.	Pækhwacəm ın sichəng aph e issımnita.	The department store is in front of the City Hall.
3.	Pækhwacəm ın sichəng twi e issımnita.	The department store is behind the City Hall.
4.	Pækhwacəm ın sichəng wen ccok e issımnita.	The department store is on the left side of the City Hall.
5.	Pækhwacəm ın sichəng olın ccok e issımnita.	The department store is on the right side of the City Hall.
*6.	Pækhwacəm ın sichəng aph ccok e issımnita.	The department store is on the front side of the City Hall.
*7.	Pækhwacəm ın sichəng twi ccok e issımnita.	The department store is on the back side of the City Hall.
*8.	Pækhwacəm ın sichəng kakkai issımnita.	The department store is near the City Hall.

K. Substitution Drill (Supply ɪn/nɪn Particle.)

1.	Pækhwacəm ɪn sichəng yəph e issɪmnita.	The department store is next to the City Hall.
2.	Sichəng ɪn tæsakwan yəph e issɪmnita.	The City Hall is next to the Embassy.
3.	Hakkyo nɪn yəkwan yəph e issɪmnita.	The school is next to an inn.
*4.	Yəkwan ɪn ɪnhæng yəph e issɪmnita.	The inn is next to a bank.
*5.	ɪnhæng ɪn sangcəm yəph e issɪmnita.	The bank is next to a store.
*6.	Sangcəm ɪn hothel yəph e issɪmnita.	The store is next to a hotel.
*7.	Hothel ɪn cip yəph e issɪmnita.	The hotel is next to a house.
*8.	Cip ɪn kongwən yəph e issɪmnita.	The house is next to a park.
*9.	Kongwən ɪn kil yəph e issɪmnita.	The park is right near the street.

L. Substitution Drill

1.	Pækhwacəm ɪn sichəng yəph e issɪmnita.	The department store is next to the City Hall.
2.	Hakkyo nɪn sichəng aph e issɪmnita.	The school is in front of the City Hall.
3.	Hankuk Tæsakwan ɪn sichəng twi e issɪmnita.	The Korean Embassy is behind the City Hall.
4.	ɪnhæng ɪn sichəng wen ccok e issɪmnita.	The bank is on the left side of the City Hall.
5.	Sangcəm ɪn sichəng olɪn ccok e issɪmnita.	The store is on the right side of the City Hall.
6.	Hothel ɪn sichəng kakkai issɪmnita.	The hotel is near the City Hall.
7.	Kongwən ɪn sichəng aph ccok e issɪmnita.	The park is on the front side of the City Hall.
8.	Cip ɪn sichəng twi ccok e issɪmnita.	The house is on the back side of the City Hall.
9.	Mikuk Kongpowən ɪn sichəng yəph e issɪmnita.	USIS is next to the City Hall.

M. Response Drill

Tutor: Mikuk Tæsakwan i issımnikka?	'Is there a U.S. Embassy?'
Student: Ne, Mikuk Tæsakwan i issımnita.	'Yes, [there] is a U.S. Embassy.'
1. Cəki e issımnikka?	Ne, cəki e issımnita.
2. Cə kəs i hakkyo imnikka?	Ne, cə kəs i hakkyo imnita.
3. Kıləhsımnikka?	Ne, kıləhsımnita.
4. I kənmul i sicheng imnikka?	Ne, i kənmul i sicheng imnita.
5. (Sənsæng ın) Mikuk salam imnikka?	Ne, Mikuk salam imnita.
6. (Sənsæng ın) Hankuk mal ıl kongpu-hamnikka?	Ne, Hankuk mal ıl kongpu-hamnita.
7. Cal issımnikka?	Ne, cal issımnita.
8. Mianhamnikka?	Ne, mianhamnita.
9. Kwænchanhsımnikka?	Ne, kwænchanhsımnita.
10. Hankuk mal ıl pæumnikka?	Ne, Hankuk mal ıl pæumnita.
11. Yəngə lıl mal-hamnikka?	Ne, Yəngə lıl mal-hamnita.
12. Ilpon mal ıl kalıchimnikka?	Ne, Ilpon mal ıl kalıchimnita.

N. Response Drill (Answer the question based on the dialogue.)

1. Sillye-hamnita.	Aniyo, kwænchanhsımnita.
2. Malssım com mulə popsita.	Ne, muəs imnikka.
3. Tætanhi komapsımnita.	Aniyo, chənman e malssım imnita.
4. Yocım əttəhke cinasimnikka?	(Təkpun e) cal cinamnita.
5. Sənsæng ın Mikuk salam imnikka?	Ne, kıləhsımnita.
6. Sənsæng ın muəs hasimnikka?	Hankuk mal ıl kongpu-hamnita.
7. Kim Sənsæng ın muəs ıl kalıchimnikka?	Hankuk mal ıl kalıchimnita.
8. Chæk i əte issımnikka?	Chæksang e issımnita.
9. Səul i əte issımnikka?	Hankuk e issımnita.
10. ıyca ka əti e issımnikka?	Chæksang aph e issımnita.

O. Grammar Drill (Based on Grammar Note 2 supply <u>i/ka</u> in a proper place.)

Tutor: Tæsakwan əte ıssımnikka?
Student: Tæsakwan i əte issımnikka?

1. Sichəng (i) cəki e issımnita.
2. Hakkyo (ka) wen ccok e issımnita.
3. Ceimsı Sənsæng (i) Mikuk salam imnita.
4. Haksæng (i) kongpu-hamnita.
5. Yəki (ka) tæsakwan imnita.
6. ıyca (ka) əti e issımnikka?
7. Kim Kisu (ka) haksæng imnikka?
8. Səul (i) Hankuk e issımnikka?
9. ənı kəs (i) pækhwacəm imnikka?
10. I kənmul (i) sichəng imnikka?

P. Transformation Drill (Transform the sentence as in the example supplying the particle <u>i/ka</u>.)

Tutor:	I kəs i chæk imnita.	'This is a book.'
Student:	Chæk i issımnita.	'There is a book.'

1.	I kəs i hakkyo imnita.	Hakkyo (ka) issımnita.
2.	I kəs i tæsakwan imnita.	Tæsakwan (i) issımnita.
3.	I kəs i sichəng imnita.	Sichəng (i) issımnita.
4.	I kəs i sikye imnita.	Sikye (ka) issımnita.
5.	I kəs i ıyca imnita.	ıyca (ka) issımnita.
6.	I kəs i kyosil imnita.	Kyosil (i) issımnita.
7.	I kəs i Cungkuk Tæsakwan imnita.	Cungkuk Tæsakwan (i) issımnita.
8.	I kəs i chæksang imnita.	Chæksang (i) issımnita.
9.	I kəs i pækhwacəm imnita.	Pækhwacəm (i) issımnita.
10.	I kəs i yəkwan imnita.	Yəkwan (i) issımnita.

Q. Response Drill (Use the particle ɪn/nɪn in place of i/ka and answer the questions as in the example.)

Tutor: Hakkyo ka issɪmnikka?	'Is there a school?'
Student: Ne, hakkyo nɪn issɪmnita.	'Yes, there is a school...(but)...'
1. Cə kəs i pækhwacəm imnikka?	Ne, cə kəs ɪn pækhwacəm imnita.
2. Sichəng i wen ccok e issɪmnikka?	Ne, sichəng ɪn wen ccok e issɪmnita.
3. Ceimsɪ ka Hankuk mal ɪl kongpu-hamnikka?	Ne, Ceimsɪ nɪn Hankuk mal ɪl kongpu-hamnita.
4. ɪyca ka yəki e issɪmnikka.	Ne ɪyca nɪn yəki e issɪmnita.
5. Kim Kisu ka Hankuk salam imnikka?	Ne, Kim Kisu nɪn Hankuk salam imnita.
6. Səul i Hankuk e issɪmnikka?	Ne, Səul ɪn Hankuk e issɪmnita.
7. Pak Sənsæng i Yəngə lɪl kalɪchimnikka?	Ne, Pak Sənsæng ɪn Yəngə lɪl kalɪchimnita.
8. Mikuk salam i Cungkuk mal ɪl pæumnikka?	Ne, Mikuk salam ɪn Cungkuk mal ɪl pæumnita.

R. Grammar Drill (Supply che right particle wherever appropriate: ɪn/nɪn, ɪl/lɪl, e, ɪlo/lo.)

Tutor: Ce ilɪm Ceimsɪ imnita.

Student: Ce ilɪm ɪn Ceimsɪ imnita.

1. Cə (nɪn) haksæng imnita.
2. Muəs (ɪl) kongpu-hamnikka?
3. Hankuk mal (ɪl) pæumnita.
4. Pak Sənsæng ɪn Yəngə (lɪl) kalɪchimnita.
5. Tæsakwan ɪn cəki (e) issɪmnita.
6. Wen ccok (ɪlo) kasipsiyo.
7. Cə kəs (ɪn) muəs imnikka?
8. Palo aph (e) issɪmnita.
9. Hakkyo (lo) kasipsiyo.
10. Olɪn ccok (ɪlo) kasipsiyo.
11. Cə nɪn Yəngə (lɪl) mal-hamnita.
12. Ceimsɪ Sənsæng ɪn Ilpon mal (ɪl) kalɪchimnita.

EXERCISES

A asks B for the following information and B responds.

A asks:	B answers:
1. where the U.S. Embassy is.	that it is next to the City Hall.
2. what that building is.	that it is the USIS building.
3. which building the department store is.	that the department store is in front of USIS.
4. where USIS is.	that it is in front of the department store.
5. where the City Hall is.	that it is in front of USIS.
6. what he does.	that he teaches Korean.
7. how he's doing these days.	that he's doing O.K.
8. whether that building is a department store.	that it is.
9. whether the school is next to the City Hall.	that it is behind the City Hall.
10. whether the school is behind the City Hall.	that it is in front of the City Hall.
11. whether the department store is in front of the U.S. Embassy.	that it is next to the Embassy.
12. whether USIS is beside the Embassy.	that it is in the Embassy building.
13. whether that is the school building.	that it is a department store.
14. where a bank is.	that it is near the park.
15. whether the park is near the street.	that it is beside the street.
16. whether the store is beside the street.	that it is so.

End of Tape 2A

Tape 2B

제 3 과 길 찾기(계속)

(대화 A)

여보세요
길
좀
물어 보겠읍니다
1. A: 여보세요, 길 좀 물어 보겠읍니다.

어디를
찾습니까
2. B: 예, 어디를 찾습니까?

역
서울역
가는 길
아십니까, 압니까
3. A: 서울역에 가는 길을 아십니까?

똑바로
가십시요
4. B: 예, 똑바로 가십시요.

여기에서
멉니까, 멀읍니까
5. A: 여기에서 멉니까?

UNIT 3. Finding One's Way Around (Continued)

BASIC DIALOGUES FOR MEMORIZATION

Dialogue A

A

yəpose yo	hello there!; say!
kil	street; road; way
com	a little
mulə pokessımnita	I will inquire
1. Yəpose yo! Kil com mulə pokessımnita.	Excuse me. May I ask you for directions? ('I'll inquire about the street a little.')

B

əti lıl	where (as direct object)
chacsımnikka/chassımnikka/	do [you] look for?
2. Ne, əti lıl chacsımnikka?	Certainly, where do you want to go? ('What (place) are you looking for?')

A

yək	station
Səul Yək e	to Seoul Station
kanın kil	the way to ('going way')
asimnikka / amnikka	do [you] know?
3. Səul Yək e kanın kil ıl asimnikka?	Can you tell me how to get to Seoul Station? ('Do you know the way to Seoul Station?')

B

ttokpalo	straight ahead, straight
kasipsiyo	(please) go
4. Ne, ttokpalo kasipsiyo.	Go straight ahead.

A

yəki esə	from here
mə(lı)mnikka	is [it] far?
5. Yəki esə məmnikka?	Is [it] far from here?

안 멉니다

가깝습니다

6. B: 아니요, 안 멉니다. 가깝습니다.

7. A: 대단히 고맙습니다.

괜찮습니다

8. B: 아니요, 괜찮습니다.

(대화 B)

어디에

가십니까, 갑니까

9. 박 어디에 가십니까?

정거장

10. 김 : 정거장에 갑니다.

정거장에서

하겠읍니까

무엇을 하겠읍니까

11. 박 : 정거장에서 무엇을 하겠읍니까?

거기

거기에서

만나겠읍니다

친구

B

an məmnita	[it] is not far
kakkapsımnita/kakkapssımnita/	[it]'s near
6. Aniyo, an məmnita. Kakkapsımnita.	No, it's not far. It's near(by).

A

tæetanhi	very; very much
komapsımnita	I'm grateful
7. Tæetanhi komapsımnita.	Thank you very much.

B

kwænchanhsımnita	[that]'s O.K.
8. Aniyo, kwænchanhsımnita.	(No,) Not at all.

Dialogue B

A

əti e	in what place; to what place
kasimnikka } kamnikka }	do [you] go?
9. əti e kasimnikka?	Where are you going? ('Where do you go?')

B

cəngkəcang	railroad station
10. Cəngkəcang e kamnita.	I'[m] go[ing] to the station.

A

cəngkəcang esə	at the station; from the station
hakessımnikka	will you do?
muəs (ıl) hakessımnikka	what will you do?
11. Cəngkəcang esə muəs (ıl) hakessımnikka?	What are you going there for? ('What are you going to do at the station?')

12. 김 : 거기에서 친구를 만나겠읍니다.

누구

13. 박 : 그 친구는 누구 입니까?

그분

그분을

14. 김 : 제임스 선생입니다. 그분을 압니까?

모릅니다

학교 선생

15. 박 : 아니요, 모릅니다. 학교 선생입니까?

아닙니다

외교관

16. 김 : 아니요, 학교 선생이 아닙니다. 외교관입니다.

Additional Expressions for Classroom Use

17. 알겠읍니까?

18. 예, 알겠읍니다.

19. 아니요, 모르겠읍니다.

20. 다시 한번 말씀 하십시요.

21. 잊어 버렸읍니다., 잊었읍니다.

B

kəki	that place
kəki esə	at that place; there
mannakessımnita	[I] will meet
chinku	friend
12. Kəki esə chinku lıl mannakessımnita.	I'm going to meet a friend there.

A

nuku	who; what person
13. Kı chinku nın nuku imnikka?	Who is he ('that friend')?

B

kı pun	he (honored); ('that person')
kı pun ıl	him (as direct object)
14. Ceimsı Sənsæng imnita. Kı pun ıl amnikka?	(He is) Mr. James. Do you know him?

A

molımnita	[I] do not know
hakkyo sənsæng	(school) teacher
15. Aniyo, molımnita. Hakkyo sənsæng imnikka?	No, I don't know [him]. Is he a teacher?

B

an imnita	[he] is not
wekyokwan	diplomat; foreign service personnel
16. Aniyo, hakkyo sənsæng i an imnita. Wekyokwan imnita.	No, [he] is not a (school) teacher. [He] is in the foreign service.

Additional Expressions for Classroom Use

17. Alkessımnikka?	Do you understand? ('Will you know?')
18. Ne, alkessımnita.	Yes, I understand. ('Yes, I'll know.')
19. Aniyo, molıkessımnita.	No, I don't understand. ('No, I'll not know.')
20. Tasi (hanpən) malssım-hasipsiyo.	Please say [it] once more.
21. Icə pəlyessımnita. } Icəssımnita. }	I forgot [it].

NOTES ON DIALOGUES

(Numbers correspond to the sentence numbers in the dialogues.)

1. Yəpose yo. 'Hello there!' ('Please look here.') is the informal polite equivalent of the less frequently used form Yəposipsiyo. Yəpose yo. is said only when you try to get the attention of a passerby and is not said as the equivalent of the English greeting expression 'Hi!' or 'Hello.' Yəpose yo! also occurs regularly when you make and/or receive a phone call.

   Kil com mulə pokessımnita. ('I'll inquire [you] about the street a little.') is used when you ask someone for street directions.

2. The verb stem chac- means 'to look for (something, someone)', 'to find', 'to get (money at the bank)', 'to claim (something)', etc.

3. Səul Yək e kanın kil ıl asimnikka? means literally 'Do you know the street which goes to Seoul Station?' The phrase 'place noun + e kanın kil' is the equivalent of English 'the way to + place noun.'

5. The verb stem in Məmnikka? 'Is [it] far?' is mə(l)-. l in mə(l)- is dropped when either -(ı)mnita or -(ı)mnikka ending is added to the stem.

13. Nuku 'who' or 'what person' is a noun. When nuku is used as the subject of a sentence, with the particle i/ka, it has the irregular form nuka. When other particles follow, the full form nuku occurs. For example, nuku lıl 'whom', nuku wa 'with whom', nuku eke 'to whom', nuku e 'whose', etc.

14. Kı pun 'he (honored)' is the politer equivalent of kı salam ('that person'). Salam is a free noun, whereas pun occurs only as a post-noun.

15. The verb stem molı- 'do not know' is the negative of the verb stem a(l)- 'know'. When one of -(ı)mnita, -(ı)mnikka, -(ı)psita and -(ı)sipsiyo endings is added to the stem a(l)-, l is dropped and is not pronounced.

GRAMMAR NOTES

1. Verbs: Action vs. Description and Intransitive vs. Transitive

Korean verbs fall into two main classes: Action Verbs and Description Verbs.

An action verb is used in sentences like 'X does something' or 'X takes a certain action', whereas a description verb is used in sentences like 'X is in such and such a state'. A Korean action verb corresponds generally to an English verb; a Korean description verb, to English 'be + adjective'.

The only difference between action and description verbs is that most description verbs do not occur in either propositative or imperative sentences. Otherwise, the forms of description verbs are similar to those of action verbs.

Korean verbs are further classified into another two main classes: Transitive and Intransitive. A transitive verb is one which may be preceded by an object, that is, noun + ıl/lıl may procede the verb. There is no change in the verb itself. An intransitive verb is one which is never preceded by an object. Both transitive and intransitive verbs may be preceded by an emphasized subject, that is, noun + i/ka.

All description verbs are intransitive verbs; most action verbs are transitive, but some are intransitive and others are both transitive and intransitive. Examples:

Group 1 (intransitive verbs)

Hakkyo ka kakkapsımnita.	'The school is near.'
Chæk i cohsımnita.	'The book is good.'
Yəki esə tæsakwan i mə(lı)mnikka?	'Is the embassy far from here?'
Haksæng i kongpu-hamnita.	'The student is studying.'
Hakkyo ka sicak-hamnita.	'School begins.'

Group 2 (transitive verbs)

Yəngə lıl pæumnita.	'[I]'m learing English.'
Hankuk mal ıl kalıchimnita.	'[I]'m teaching Korean.'
Yəngə chæk ıl i(l)kımnita.	'[I] read an English book.'
Hakkyo lıl sicak-hamnita.	'[I] begin school.'

Note that inflected forms (e.g. 'verbals') may occur as complete sentences. In Korean when the context or situation is clear as to the subject and/or topic of a sentence, the speaker often omits the subject or the topic, and the sentence consists of the verbal alone, or the verbal plus its modifiers and/or objects. The topic/subject in the following examples may be omitted.

Examples:

(Sənsæng ın) əti e kamnikka? 'Where are (you) going?'
(Cə nın) hakkyo e kamnita. '(I) am going to school.'
Ne, (hakkyo ka) məmnita. 'Yes, [it] ('the school') is far.'

2. Future Tense in Korean

Tenses in a Korean sentence are indicated in verbals. The form -kess- is infixed between the verb stem and the verb ending to mark the future tense. There is a small class of forms which occur after verb stems but always before verb endings. We shall call them Verb Suffixes. The form -kess- is called the Future Tense Suffix. When a verbal is a statement sentence and includes -kess-, it indicates the speaker's intention for the future. If the verbal which includes -kess- is a question sentence, the speaker asks the addressee about his future intention or opinion. If the subject or the topic of the sentence is other than the speaker or the addressee, the sentence which includes -kess- denotes an opinion or presumption about the subject or the topic in the sentence. Examples;

(Cə nın) hakkyo e kakessımnita. 'I will go to school.'
(Ce ka) Yəngə lıl pæukessımnita. 'I will study English.'
(Sənsæng ın) muəs ıl hakessımnikka? 'What are you going to do?' / 'What will you do?'
Chinku lıl mannakessımnikka? 'Are you going to meet a friend?'
Hakkyo ka kakkapkessımnikka? 'Will the school be near (do you think)?'
Kim Sənsæng i cip e isskessımnita. 'Mr. Kim must be home (I suppose).'

3. Honorifics

Whenever the subject and/or the topic in the sentence is honored, a verb suffix -(ı)si- is added immediately after the verb stem. We shall call the suffix -(ı)si- the Honorific Suffix. When -(ı)si- and other suffixes such as the future tense suffix -kess- occur in the same verb, the honorific suffix -(ı)si- always precedes other suffixes. In an inflected form the honorific suffix is not used if the subject in the sentence is inferior to the speaker. Note that the speaker never honors himself, that is, the suffix -(ı)si- in a verbal does not occur when the subject and/or the topic is the speaker. -Si- occurs after a stem ending in a vowel; -ısi- after a stem ending in a consonant. Compare:

a. əti e kamnikka? 'Where are [you] going.'
əti e kasimnikka? 'Where are [you] going?' (H)
əti e kasikessımnikka? 'Where will [you] go?' (H)

b.	Muəs ıl hamnikka?	'What do [you] do?'
	Muəs ıl hasimnikka?	'What do [you] do?' (H)
	Muəs ıl hasikessımnikka?	'What will [you] do?' (H)
c.	Kim Sənsæng i kalıchimnita.	'Mr. Kim's teaching.'
	Kim Sənsæng i kalıchisimnita.	'Mr. Kim's teaching.' (H)
	Kim Sənsæng i kalıchisikessımnita.	'Mr. Kim will teach (I think).' (H)
d.	Cə salam ın Yəngə lıl pæumnita.	'He's learning English.'
	Cə salam ın Yəngə lıl Pæusimnita.	'He's learning English.' (H)
	Cə salam ın Yəngə lıl pæusikessımnita.	'He will learn English.' (H)

4. Negative *an*

There are two ways of expressing negation in Korean statement and question sentences. One simple way is the use of the word *an* immediately before an inflected expression. However, with some verbs, *an* does not normally occur; another form of negation is used. (See Unit 4.) Compare:

a.	Hakkyo e kamnita.	'[I] go to school.'
	Hakkyo e an kamnita.	'[I] don't go to school.'
b.	Kim Sənsæng i omnita.	'Mr. Kim's coming.'
	Kim sənsæng i an omnita.	'Mr. Kim is not coming.'
c.	Ne, kalıchimnita.	'Yes, [I] teach.'
	Aniyo, an kalıchimnita.	'No, [I] don't teach.'

5. Particle *esə* 'from', 'at', 'in', 'on'

A *place nominal + esə* denotes either *dynamic location* or *point of departure* for the following inflected expression depending on what verb follows after it. Examples:

Cə nın *Səul esə* omnita.	'I'm coming *from Seoul*.'
Hakkyo ka *cip esə* məmnita.	'The school is far *from the house*.'
Uli nın *kyosil esə* kongpu-hamnita.	'We study *in the classroom*.'
Cəngkəcang esə chinku lıl mannakessımnita.	'I'll meet a friend *at the station*.'
Kim Sənsæng i *Səul esə* il-hamnita.	'Mr. Kim works *in Seoul*.'

Compare the above construction with *place nominal + e* in Unit 2. Before *issımnita* 'exists', *a place nominal + e* may occur but not *a place nominal + esə*.

6. Particle e 'to'

A place nominal + e followed by either ka- 'to go' or o- 'to come' indicates the direction of the action of the inflected expression. Compare e with lo/ɪlo in Unit 2, Grammar Note 2. Observe the examples:

Cə nɪn hakkyo e kamnita.	'I'm going to school.'
Cə e cip e ośipsiyo.	'Please come to my house.'
Cəngkəcang e kakessɪmnikka?	'Will you go to the station?'
Kim Sənsæng ɪn Mikuk e an omnita.	'Mr. Kim is not coming to America.'

DRILLS

A. Substitution Drills

1.	əti lɪl chacsɪmnikka?	What (place) are [you] looking for?
2.	Muəs (ɪl) chacsɪmnikka?	What are you looking for?
3.	ənɪ hakkyo (lɪl) chacsɪmnikka?	What school are you looking for?
4.	ənɪ haksæng (ɪl) chacsɪmnikka?	Which student are you looking for?
5.	ənɪ kil (ɪl) chacsɪmnikka?	Which street are you looking for?
6.	ənɪ pækhwacəm (ɪl) chacsɪmnikka?	Which department store are you looking for?
7.	Nuku (lɪl) chacsɪmnikka?	Whom are you looking for?
8.	ənɪ kyosil (ɪl) chacsɪmnikka?	Which classroom are you looking for?
9.	ənɪ sənsæng (ɪl) chacsɪmnikka?	Which teacher are you looking for?
10.	ənɪ ai (lɪl) chacsɪmnikka?	Which child are you looking for?
11.	ənɪ pun (ɪl) chacsɪmnikka	Whom (H) are you looking for?

B. Substitution Drill

1.	Səul Yək e kanɪn kil ɪl asimnikka?	Do you know the way to Seoul Station?
2.	Səul Sichəng e kanɪn kil ɪl asimnikka?	Do you know the way to Seoul City Hall?
3.	Cəngkəcang e kanɪn kil ɪl asimnikka?	Do you know the way to the station?
4.	Pækhwacəm e kanɪn kil ɪl asimnikka?	Do you know the way to the department store?
5.	Sicang e kanɪn kil ɪl asimnikka?	Do you know the way to the market place?
6.	Kongwən e kanɪn kil ɪl asimnikka?	Do you know the way to the park?
*7.	Tapang e kanɪn ɪl asimnikka?	Do you know the way to the tearoom?
*8.	Siktang e kanɪn kil ɪl asimnikka?	Do you know the way to the restaurant?
*9.	Kim Sənsæng cip e kanɪn kil ɪl asimnikka?	Do you know the way to Mr. Kim's house?

C. Substitution Drill

1.	Ttokpalo kasipsiyo.	Go straight ahead.
2.	Wen ccok ılo kasipsiyo.	Go to the left.
3.	Olın ccok ılo kasipsiyo.	Go to the right.
*4.	I ccok ılo kasipsiyo.	Go this way (direction).
*5.	Cə ccok ılo kasipsiyo.	Go that way (direction).
6.	Səul Yək ılo kasipsiyo.	Go to Seoul Station.
7.	Cəngkəcang ılo kasipsiyo.	Go to the railroad station.
8.	Sichəng ccok ılo kasipsiyo.	Go toward the City Hall.
9.	Mikuk Tæsakwan ılo kasipsiyo.	Go to the U.S. Embassy.

D. Substitution Drill

1.	Yəki esə məmnikka?	Is it far from here?
2.	Hakkyo esə məmnikka?	Is it far from school?
3.	Cəngkəcang esə məmnikka?	Is it far from the station?
4.	Mikuk Tæsakwan esə məmnikka?	Is it far from the U.S. Embassy?
5.	Səul Yək esə məmnikka?	Is it far from Seoul Station?
6.	Sichəng esə məmnikka?	Is it far from the City Hall?
*7.	Sangcəm esə məmnikka?	Is it far from the store?
8.	Pækhwacəm esə məmnikka?	Is it far from the department store?
*9.	Tapang esə məmnikka?	Is it far from the tearoom?
*10.	Kongwən esə məmnikka?	Is it far from the park?
*11.	Sicang esə məmnikka?	Is it far from the market place?
12.	Mikuk esə məmnikka?	Is it far from America?
*13.	Uphyənkuk esə məmnikka?	Is it far from the post office?
*14.	Samusil esə məmnikka?	Is it far from the office?
*15.	Kıkcang esə məmnikka?	Is if far from the theatre?

E. Substitution Drill

1.	Na nɪn cəngkəcang e kamnita.	I['m] go[ing] to the railroad station.
2.	Na nɪn kongwən e kamnita.	I['m] go[ing] to the park.
3.	Na nɪn kɪkcang e kamnita.	I['m] go[ing] to the theatre.
4.	Na nɪn ɪnhæng e kamnita.	I['m] go[ing] to the bank.
5.	Na nɪn sangcəm e kamnita.	I['m] go[ing] to the store.
6.	Na nɪn Cungkuk siktang e kamnita.	I['m] go[ing] to a Chinese restaurant.
7.	Na nɪn Səul Uphənkuk e kamnita.	I['m] go[ing] to the Seoul Post Office.
8.	Na nɪn Hankuk ɪnhæng e kamnita.	I['m] go[ing] to the Bank of Korea.
9.	Na nɪn Səul Pækhwacəm e kamnita.	I['m] go[ing] to the Seoul Department Store.
*10.	Na nɪn tæsakwan siktang e kamnita.	I['m] go[ing] to the Embassy dinning hall.
*11.	Na nɪn na e samusil e kamnita.	I['m] go[ing] to my office.
*12.	Na nɪn Ceimsi Sənsæng cip e kamnita.	I['m] go[ing] to Mr. James' house.

F. Substitution Drill

1.	Kəki esə muəs (ɪl) hakessɪmnikka?	What are you going to do there? ('What will you do there?')
2.	Cəngkəcang esə muəs (ɪl) hakessɪmnikka?	What are you going to do at the station?
3.	Tapang esə muəs (ɪl) hakessɪmnikka?	What are you going to do at the tea-room?
4.	Kongwən esə muəs (ɪl) hakessɪmnikka?	What are you going to do in the park?
5.	Hakkyo esə muəs (ɪl) hakessɪmnikka?	What are you going to do at school?
6.	Hakkyo esə muəs (ɪl) chackessɪmnikka?	What are you going to look for at school?
7.	Hakkyo esə muəs (ɪl) pæukessɪmnikka?	What are you going to study at school?
8.	Hakkyo esə muəs (ɪl) kalɪchikessɪmnikka?	What are you going to teach at school?
9.	Hakkyo esə muəs (ɪl) mal-hakessɪmnikka?	What are you going to say at school?
10.	Hakkyo esə muəs (ɪl) mulə pokessɪmnikka?	What are you going to inquire about at school?
11.	Hakkyo esə muəs (ɪl) kongpu-hakessɪmnikka?	What are you going to study at school?
12.	Hakkyo esə muəs (ɪl) ilkkessɪmnikka?	What are you going to read at school?

G. Substitution Drill

1.	Kɪ chinku nɪn nuku imnikka?	Who is that friend [of yours]?
2.	Kɪ salam ɪn nuku imnikka?	Who is that man?
3.	Cə haksæng ɪn nuku imnikka?	Who is that student over there?
4.	Cə Mikuk salam ɪn nuku imnikka?	Who is that American over there?
5.	Cə Ilpon salam ɪn nuku imnikka?	Who is that Japanese over there?
6.	Cə pun ɪn nuku imnikka?	Who is that man (honored)?
7.	Cə Mikuk wekyokwan ɪn nuku imnikka?	Who is that American diplomat?
8.	Kɪ Hankuk haksæng ɪn nuku imnikka?	Who is the Korean student?
9.	Hankuk mal sənsæng ɪn nuku imnikka?	Who is the Korean (language) teacher?
10.	Cə puin ɪn nuku imnikka?	Who is that lady?
11.	Cə ai nɪn nuku imnikka?	Who is that child?

H. Response Drill

Tutor:	əti lɪl chacsɪmnikka? /Səul Yək/	'What (place) are you looking for?' /Seoul Station/
Student:	Səul Yək ɪl chacsɪmnita.	'I'm looking for Seoul Station.'
1.	Muəs ɪl chacsɪmnikka? /Hankuk mal chæk/	Hankuk mal chæk ɪl chacsɪmnita.
2.	əti e kasimnikka? /uphyənkuk/	Uphyənkuk e kamnita.
3.	Kɪ Mikuk salam ɪn nuku imnikka? /Ceimsɪ/	Ceimsɪ imnita.
4.	Sənsæng ɪn muəs hakessimnikka? /Hankuk mal kongpu/	(Na nɪn) Hankuk mal kongpu (lɪl) hakessɪmnita.
5.	Cəngkəcang esə nuku lɪl manakessɪmnikka? /chinku/	Chinku lɪl manakessɪmnita.
6.	Pækhwacəm i əti e issɪmnikka? /uphyənkuk twi e/	Uphyənkuk twi e issɪmnita.
7.	Kim Sənsæng ɪn hakkyo esə muəs ɪl kalɪchimnikka? /Yəngə/	Yəngə lɪl kalɪchimnita.
8.	ənɪ kənmul i ɪnhæng imnikka? /wen ccok kənmul/	Wen ccok kənmul i ɪnhæng imnita.
9.	əti esə chinku lɪl mannakessɪmnikka? /tapang/	Tapang esə mannakessɪmnita.
10.	Səul Yək ɪn əti lo kamnikka? /olɪn ccok/	Olɪn ccok ɪlo kamnita.

11. Nuka Hankuk mal ıl pæumnikka? /Mikuk salam/	Mikuk salam i pæumnita.
12. Sənsæng samusil i əti e issımnikka? /tæsakwan kənmul/	Tæsakwan kənmul e issımnita.

I. Response Drill

Tutor: Hakkyo sənsæng imnikka?	'Is [he] a school teacher?'
Student: Aniyo, (hakkyo sənsæng i) an imnita.	'No, [he] is not.'
1. I kəs i chæksang imnikka?	Aniyo, (chæksang i) an imnita.
2. (Hakkyo ka) məmnikka?	Aniyo, an məmnita.
3. Cəngkəcang e kamnikka?	Aniyo, an kamnita.
4. Kı pun ıl amnikka?	Aniyo, molımnita.
5. Hankuk mal ıl pæumnikka?	Aniyo, an pæumnita.
6. Chinku lıl mannakessımnikka?	Aniyo, an mannakessımnita.
7. Yəngə lıl kalıchimnikka?	Aniyo, an kalıchimnita.
8. Hakkyo ka kakkapsımnikka?	Aniyo, an kakkapsımnita.
9. Hakkyo e kakessımnikka?	Aniyo, an kakessımnita.
10. Kil ıl mulə pokessımnikka?	Aniyo, an mulə pokessımnita.
11. Yənphil ıl chackessımnikka?	Aniyo, an chackessımnita.

J. Grammar Drill (based on Grammar Note 2)

Tutor: Yəngə lıl pæumnikka?	'[Are] you learn[ing] English?'
Student: Yəngə lıl pæukessımnikka?	'Will you learn English?'
1. Hakkyo e kamnikka?	Hakkyo e kakessımnikka?
2. Muəs ıl hamnikka?	Muəs ıl hakessımnikka?
3. Nuku lıl mannamnikka?	Nuku lıl mannakessımnikka?
4. Ilpon mal ıl pæumnikka?	Ilpon mal ıl pæukessımnikka?
5. Pækhwacəm ıl chacsımnikka?	Pækhwacəm ıl chackessımnikka?
6. (Sənsæng ın) cip e issımnikka?	(Sənsæng ın) cip e isskessımnikka?
7. Nuku lıl pwepsımnikka?	Nuku lıl pwepkessımnikka?
8. Nuka Yəngə lıl kalıchimnikka?	Nuka Yəngə lıl kalıchikessımnikka?

K. Response Drill

Tutor: Kongpu-hakessımnikka?	'Will you study?'
Student: Ne, (na nın) kongpu-hakessımnita.	'Yes, I'll study.'
1. Hankuk mal ıl pæukessımnikka?	Ne, (na nın) Hankuk mal ıl pæukessımnita.
2. Cip e isskessımnikka?	Ne (na nın) cip e isskessımnita.
3. Chinku lıl mannakessımnikka?	Ne, (na nın) chinku lıl mannakessımnita.
4. Yəngə lıl kalıchikessımnikka?	Ne, (na nın) Yəngə lıl kalıchikessımnita.
5. ınhæng e kakessımnikka?	Ne, (na nın) ınhæng e kakessımnita.
6. Hakkyo e an kakessımnikka?	Ne, (na nın) hakkyo e an kakessımnita.
7. Kı chæk ıl chackessımnikka?	Ne, (na nın) kı chæk ıl chackessımnita.
8. Kil ıl mulə pokessımnikka?	Ne, (na nın) kil ıl mulə pokessımnita.
9. Kı kəs ıl hakessımnikka?	Ne, (na nın) kı kəs ıl hakessımnita.
10. Hankuk mal ıl mal-hakessımnikka?	Ne, (na nın) Hankuk mal ıl mal-hakessımnita.

L. Response Drill

Tutor: Muəs ıl kongpu-hakessımnikka? /Cungkuk mal/	'What will you study?' /Chinese/
Student: Cungkuk mal ıl kongpu-hakessımnita.	'I will study Chinese.'
1. əti e kasikessımnikka? /cəngkəcang/	Cəngkəcang e kakessımnita.
2. əti esə chinku lıl mannakessımnikka? /tapang/	Tapange esə mannakessımnita.
3. ənı mal ıl pæukessımnikka? /Hankuk mal/	Hankuk mal ıl pæukessımnita.
4. Nuku e samusil ıl chackessımnikka? /Kim Sənsæng/	Kim Sənsæng e samusil ıl chackessımnita.
5. Sənsæng ın cip esə muəs ıl hakessımnikka? /chæk/	(Cip esə) chæk ıl ilkkessımnita.
6. Tapang esə nuku lıl mannakessımnikka? /chinku/	Chinku lıl mannakessımnita.
7. Nuka Yəngə lıl kalıchikessımnikka? /Mikuk salam/	Mikuk salam i kalıchikessımnita.

M. Grammar Drill (as a level drill based on Grammar Note 3)

Tutor: Muəs ıl kongpu-hamnikka?	'What are you studying?'
Student: Muəs ıl kongpu-hasimnikka?	'What are you studying?'
1. əti e kamnikka?	əti e kasimnikka?
2. Muəs ıl hamnikka?	Muəs ıl hasimnikka?
3. ənı mal ıl pæumnikka?	ənı mal ıl pæusimnikka?
4. Nuku lıl chacsımnikka?	Nuku lıl chacısimnikka?
5. Nuka Yəngə lıl kalıchimnikka?	Nuka Yəngə lıl kalıchisimnikka?
6. Səul Yək e kanın kil ıl amnikka?	Səul Yək e kanın kil ıl asimnikka?
7. Kı chinku nın nuku imnikka?	Kı chinku nın nuku isimnikka?
8. Cə pun ın hakkyo sənsəng imnikka?	Cə pun ın hakkyo sənsəng isimnikka?
9. (Sənsəng ın) wekyokwan imnikka?	Sənsəng ın wekyokwan isimnikka?
10. I salam ıl molımnikka?	I salam ıl molısimnikka?
11. Hankuk mal ıl mal-hamnikka?	Hankuk mal ıl mal-hasimnikka?

N. Response Drill (as a level drill)

Tutor: Ceimsı Sənsæng ın əti e kamnikka? /hakkyo/	'Where does Mr. James go?' /school/
Student: Hakkyo e kasimnita.	'He goes to school.'
1. Ceimsı Sənsæng ın muəs ıl kongpu-hamnikka? /Hankuk mal/	Hankuk mal ıl kongpu-hasimnita.
2. Ceimsı Sənsæng ın nuku lıl chacsımnikka? /Pak Sənsæng/	Pak Sənsæng ıl chacısimnita.
3. Ceimsı Sənsæng ın nuku lıl mannamnikka? /chinku/	Chinku lıl mannasimnita.
4. Ceimsı Sənsæng ın Səul Yək e kanın kil ıl amnikka? /aniyo/	Aniyo, molısimnita.
5. Ceimsı Sənsæng ın Yəngə lıl kalıchimnikka? /aniyo/	Aniyo, an kalıchisimnita.
6. Ceimsı Sənsæng ın wekyokwan imnikka? /ne/	Ne, wekyokwan isimnita.
7. Ceimsı Sənsæng ın Yəngə lıl pæumnikka? /aniyo/	Aniyo, an pæusimnita.
8. Ceimsı Sənsæng ın Yəngə lıl ilksımnikka? /aniyo/	Aniyo, an ilkısimnita.

EXERCISES

1. Ask a passerby:

    a. if he knows the way to USIA.
    b. if it is near.
    c. if the building (over there) is the railroad station.
    d. if he is going in the direction of the City Hall.
    e. if the park is far.
    f. if the station is to the left of the market place.

2. Mr. Kim asks: / You answer that:

Mr. Kim asks:	You answer that:
a. where you're going.	you're going to the station.
b. what you'll do there.	you'll meet a friend.
c. who your friend is.	he is an American.
d. what your friend does.	he is in the foreign service.
e. how you know him.	he is with the U.S. Embassy.
f. if your friend speaks Korean.	he speaks a little.
g. if you know Mr. Park.	you know him well.
h. if you are a Korean teacher.	you are not.
i. if you're going to learn Japanese.	you're not.

3. Tell Pak Sənsəng the following:

    1. The department store is near the street.
    2. The classroom is in this building.
    3. The park is behind my house.
    4. The store is next to the theatre.
    5. The bank is on the left side of the City Hall.
    6. The market (place) is in front of the Chinese restaurant.
    7. The USIS is this way.
    8. The Ambassador's office is on your right.
    9. The school building is next to the inn.
    10. This is the map of that lady's child.

4. Find out the following information from Pak Sənsəng:

    1. Which building is the department store.
    2. Where he is going.
    3. What Mr. James does.

4. Whom he's going to meet.
5. Who teaches Korean.
6. Which classroom he is looking for.
7. Who his friend is.
8. How he knows him.
9. If he knows the way to the City Hall.
10. If he is going to be home.

5. Tell Pak Sənsæng that:

1. you're looking for Kim's house.
2. you're in the foreign service.
3. you're going to meet James at the restaurant.
4. your office is not far from here.
5. you will be home.
6. you don't know that Korean's name.
7. this Korean lady is not {in the foreign service. / a diplomat.}
8. the Bank of Korea is straight ahead.
9. you're not going to come to school.
10. the post office is not near.

End of Tape 2B

Tape 3A

제 4 과　　물건 사기

(대화 A)

어제
갔읍니까

1. 이 : 김 선생, 어제 어디에 갔읍니까?

시내
상점
갔었읍니다

2. 김 : 시내 상점에 갔었읍니다.

샀어요

3. 이 : 무엇을 샀어요?

용품
일상 용품

4. 김 : 일상 용품을 좀 샀읍니다.

오늘
또
가겠어요
안 가겠어요

5. 이 : 오늘은 시내에 또 안 가겠어요?

글쎄
글쎄요
책방

UNIT 4. Shopping

BASIC DIALOGUES FOR MEMORIZATION

Dialogue A

Lee

əce	yesterday
kassımnikka	did [you] go?
1. Kim Sənsæng, əce əti e kassımnikka?	Where did you go yesterday, Mr. Kim?

Kim

sinæ	downtown
sangcəm	store
kassəssımnita	[I] went; [I] had gone
2. Sinæ sangcəm e kassəssımnita.	[I] went to a store downtown.

Lee

sassə yo	did [you] buy?
3. Muəs ıl sassə yo?	What did [you] buy?

Kim

yongphum	necessary goods
ilsang yongphum	daily necessities
4. Ilsang yongphum ıl com sassımnita.	[I] bought some daily necessities.

Lee

onıl	today
tto	again
kakessə yo	will you go?
an kakessə yo	('will you not go?')
5. Onıl ın sinæ e tto an kakessə yo?	Are you going downtown again today? ('Will you not go downtown again?')

Kim

kılsse } kılsse yo }	well; maybe
chækpang	bookstore
tıllıkessımnita	[I]'ll stop by
com	a little; a little while
6. Kılsse yo. Nan nın chækpang e com tıllıkessımnita.	Maybe. I'll stop by a bookstore (for a while).

들르겠읍니다
좀

6. 김 : 글쎄요. 나는 책방에 좀 들르겠읍니다.

그럼
같이
나와
나와 같이
갑시다

7. 이 : 그럼, 나와 같이 갑시다.

그럽시다
그러합시다
사겠어요

8. 김 : 예, 그럽시다. 선생은 무엇을 사겠어요?

나도
보겠읍니다
값
비쌉니까?

9. 이 : 나도 책을 좀 보겠읍니다. 책 값이 비쌉니까?

그리
비싸지 않습니다
쌉니다

10. 김 : 아니요, 그리 비싸지 않습니다. 쌉니다.

Lee

kıləm	if so; then
kathi	together
na wa	with me
na wa kathi	(together) with me
kapsita	let us go
7. Kıləm, na wa kathi kapsita.	Then, let's go together.

Kim

kıləhapsita / kıləpsita	let's do so
sakessə yo	will you buy?
8. Ne, kıləpsita. Sənsæng ın muəs ıl sakessə yo?	Let's (do so). What are you going to buy?

Lee

na to	I also; me too
pokessımnita	I'll see [it]; I'll look at [it]
kaps	price
pissamnikka	is [it] expensive?
9. Na to chæk ıl com pokessımnita. Chæk kaps i pissamnikka?	I would like to see some books too. ('I'll also see books a little.') Are books expensive?

Kim

kıli	so; like that
pissaci anhsımnita/anssımnita/	[it] is not expensive
ssamnita	[it] is cheap
10. Aniyo, kıli pissaci anhsımnita. Ssamnita.	No, [they]'re not so expensive. [They] are [fairly] cheap.

Dialogue B
(--at the store--)

Cəmwən

əsə	quickly; (please)
osipsiyo	come!
əsə osipsiyo	(welcome!); come in
11. əsə osipsiyo. Muəs ıl sasikessımnikka?	Please come in. May I help you? ('What would you like to buy?')

(대화 B)

어서
오십시요
어서 오십시요

11. 점원 : 어서 오십시요. 무엇을 사시겠읍니까?

여기에서
수건
팝니까, 팔읍니까

12. 이 : 여기에서 수건을 팝니까?

색
무슨 색
원하세요

13. 점원 : 예, 팝니다. 무슨 색을 원하세요.

노란 색
좋아합니다

14. 이 : 노란 색을 좋아합니다. 노란 것이 있어요?

여러 가지
어떻습니까

15. 점원 : 여러 가지가 있읍니다. 이것이 어떻습니까?

얼마
좋습니다

16. 이 : 예, 좋습니다. 그것 얼마입니까?

Lee

	yəki esə	here; at this place
	sukən	towel
	phalımnikka / phamnikka	do [you] sell?
12.	Yəki esə sukən ıl phamnikka?	Do you carry towels here? ('Do you sell towels here?')

Cəmwən

	musın	what sort of
	sæk	color
	wənhase yo	do [you] want?
13.	Ne, phamnita. Musın sæk ıl wənhase yo?	Yes, we do. What color would you like? ('What sort of color do you want?')

Lee

	nolan sæk	yellow color
	cohahamnita	[I] like; [I] prefer
14.	Nolan sæk ıl cohahamnita. Nolan kəs i issə yo?	('[I] like yellow color.') Yellow, please. ('Do you have yellow ones?')

Cəmwən

	yələ kaci	several kinds; many kinds
	əttəhsımnikka	how is [it]?
15.	Yələ kaci ka issımnita. I kəs i əttəhsımnikka?	We have several kinds. How do you like this one? ('How is this one?')

Lee

	əlma	how much
	cohsımnita	[that]'s good
16.	Ne, cohsımnita. Kı kəs, əlma imnikka?	On, that's nice. How much is it?

Cəmwən

	osip	50
	osip Wən	fifty Won W50
17.	Osip Wən e phamnita.	W50. ('We sell it for W50')

오십

오십 원

17. 점원 : 오십 원에 팝니다.

하나

주십시요

18. 이 : 그것 하나 주십시요.

19. 점원 : 예, 여기(에) 있읍니다.

Lee

hana	one
cusipsiyo	give [me]
18. Kɪ kəs, hana cusipsiyo.	Please give [me] one [of them].

Cəmwən

19. Ne, yəki (e) issɪmnita.	Here you are.

NUMERALS (1)

1	il	11	sip-il	21	isip-il	31	samsip-il
2	i	12	sip-i	22	isip-i	40	sasip
3	sam	13	sip-sam	23	isip-sam	50	osip
4	sa	14	sip-sa	24	isip-sa	60	yuksip ~ nyuksip
5	o	15	sip-o	25	isip-o	70	chilsip
6	yuk	16	sip-yuk /simnyuk/	26	isip-yuk /isimnyuk/	80	phalsip
7	chil	17	sip-chil	27	isip-chil	90	kusip
8	phal	18	sip-phal	28	isip-phal	91	kusip-il
9	ku	19	sip-ku	29	isip-ku	99	kusip-ku
10	sip	20	i-sip	30	samsip	100	(il)pæk

101	pæk-il	200	ipæk	1,001	chən-il
102	pæk-i	300	sampæk	1,011	chən-sip-il
103	pæk-sam	400	sapæk	1,111	chən-pæk-sip-il
104	pæk-sa	500	opæk	2,000	ichən
105	pæk-o	600	yukpæk /nyukpæk/	3,000	samchən
106	pæk-yuk	700	chilpæk	4,000	sachən
107	pæk-chil	800	phalpæk	5,000	ochən
108	pæk-phal	900	kupæk	6,000	yukchən ~ nyukchən
109	pæk-ku	999	kupæk-kusip-ku	7,000	chilchən
110	pæk-sip	1,000	(il)chən	10,000	(il)man
		100,000	sipman /simman/	1,000,000	pækman /pæŋgman/

수자 (1)

1	일	11	십 일	21	이십 일	31	삼십 일
2	이	12	십 이	22	이십 이	40	사십
3	삼	13	십 삼	23	이십 삼	50	오십
4	사	14	십 사	24	이십 사	60	육십
5	오	15	십 오	25	이십 오	70	칠십
6	육	16	십 육	26	이십 육	80	팔십
7	칠	17	십 칠	27	이십 칠	90	구십
8	팔	18	십 팔	28	이십 팔	91	구십 일
9	구	19	십 구	29	이십 구	99	구십 구
10	십	20	이십	30	삼십	100	(일)백

101	백 일	200	이백	1,001	천 일
102	백 이	300	삼백	1,011	천 십 일
103	백 삼	400	사백	1,111	천 백 십 일
104	백 사	500	오백	2,000	이천
105	백 오	600	육백	3,000	삼천
106	백 육	700	칠백	4,000	사천
107	백 칠	800	팔백	5,000	오천
108	백 팔	900	구백	6,000	육천
109	백 구	999	구백 구십 구	7,000	칠천
110	백 십	1,000	(일)천	10,000	(일)만
				100,000	십만
				1,000,000	백만

NOTES ON DIALOGUES

(Numbers correspond to the sentence numbers.)

2. Sinæ ('the inside of city') originally meant any part of a city which had walls around it. Today, it refers to the downtown area in general.

3. Sassə yo? 'Did [you] buy?' is the informal polite equivalent of the formal polite form Sassımnikka?

5. Tto 'again', 'also', 'too', is an adverb which occurs before a sentence, a verbal, or other words of a modifier class.

6. Kılsse yo. 'Well..' is a kind of hesitating response to or comment upon someone's question, statement, suggestion or command.

9. Chæk kaps 'the price of the book' is a noun phrase which literally means 'book price'. Kaps 'price' occurs after certain nouns. For example, cip kaps 'the rent' or 'the price of a house', ppəsı kaps 'bus fare', ımsik kaps 'food price'.

10. Kıli before verbs or words of a modifier class in a negative statement means '(not) so','(not) very' or '(not)that'. In propositative, imperative and question sentences, it means 'like that', 'such a' or 'in such a way'.

11. əsə osipsiyo.('Come quickly.') is a general greeting expression for welcoming; it is commonly used by business people to customers.

12. Yəki esə X ıl/lıl pha(lı)mnikka? ('Do you sell X here?') is one common way of asking store clerks a certain item you want to buy. Yəki e X i/ka issımnikka? ('Do you have X here?' or 'Is there X here?') is another common question in such a situation. The stem of pha(lı)mnikka? 'Do [you] sell?' is pha(l)-.

13. Musın 'what sort of', 'what', occurs before a noun, and asks about the type or the characteristics of the noun: musın chæk 'what kind of book', musın mal 'what language', musın salam 'what kind of person', musın cip 'what type of house', musın cha 'what kind of car'.

14. Nolan 'yellow', hayan 'white', phalan 'blue', kkaman 'black', ppalkan 'red', are all modifier class words formed from the verb stems nola- 'to be yellow', haya- 'to be white', phala- 'to be blue', kkama(h)- 'to be black', ppalka- 'to be red', by the addition of the modifier ending -n/ın/nın (See Unit 5). The verb stem cohaha- 'to like' has an unpredictable negative form: silhəha- 'to dislike'.

15. Yələ 'several', 'many' ('more than a few but not too many in number') is a numeral which may occur before free or post nouns only as a determinative: yələ kaci 'many kinds', yələ salam 'several people', yələ pun 'many people (H)'. Kaci 'kind' occurs only as a post-noun preceded by numerals of Korean origin, and never occurs after other modifiers. Examples:

yələ kaci	'several kinds'
han kaci	'one kind'
tu kaci	'two kinds'
se kaci	'three kinds'

In the verbal əttəhsımnikka? ' 'How is [it]?', əttəh- 'how is' is its verb stem, of which inflected forms are used only as question words. Most Korean question words are either nouns or adverbs.

16. The verb stem coh- 'to be good', 'to be nice', 'to be O.K.', has as its antonymous verb stem nappı- 'to be bad'. əlma ımnikka? 'How much is [it]?' is a fixed expression when you ask about the price of something. əlma 'how much' occurs always as a noun and is never used as a modifier.

GRAMMAR NOTES

1. Informal Polite Speech

We noticed in the Grammar Notes of Unit 2 that Formal Polite Speech is a level and/or style of speech. In standard Korean, there is another style and/or level of speech which is no less polite than the Formal Polite but is considered more casual and friendly. This style of speech is called Informal Polite Speech. Usually both styles are mixed in one's speech, but in general women tend to use more informal polite speech than men. Informal Polite Speech is often called Yo speech style, because any sentence which ends in the particle yo is Informal Polite Speech. Regardless of the sentence type (i.e. statement, question, imperative, propositative), yo at the end of an utterance is the sign that is an Informal Polite sentence.

When the particle yo occurs immediately after a verb which does not have a verb-ending but is inflected from the stem in a certain form ending in a vowel, the inflected form which precedes yo is called an Infinitive. Note that an infinitive is a word, whereas a verb stem is not a word. An infinitive is formed from a verb stem by a certain phonetic change at the end of the stem.

Infinitives are formed not only from verb stems but also from verb stem plus suffix(es), that is, verb stem + (ı)si + (tense suffixes) can be made into infinitives by adding ə at the end of the suffixes. For example, the verb stem ha- 'to do' + (suffixes) can have the following kinds of infinitive:

hæ (or haye), hasie (or hase), hakessə, hæssə (or hayəssə), hasikessə, hasiəssə, etc.

For the time being, however, our term Infinitive refers to the inflected form without any suffix. Yo may be added to the infinitive to make an informal polite speech present form. The verbs we have had so far are listed below. Compare:

	Stem	Formal Polite Present statement	Informal Polite Present
'to do'	ha-	hamnita	hæ yo
'to study'	kongpu-ha-	kongpu-hamnita	kongpu-hæ yo
'to pass by'	cina-	cinamnita	cina yo
'to exist'	iss-	issɪmnita	issə yo
'to learn'	pæu-	pæumnita	pæwə yo
'to teach'	kalɪchi-	kalɪchimnita	kalɪchiə yo
'to read'	ilk-	ilk(s)ɪmnita	ilkə yo
'to ask'	mulə po-	mulə pomnita	mulə pwa yo
'to go'	ka-	kamnita	ka yo
'to be so'	kɪləh-	kɪləhsɪmnita	kɪləhæ yo or kɪlæ yo
'to know'	a(l)-	amnita	alə yo
'to look for'	chac-	chac(s)ɪmnita	chacə yo
'to be far'	mə(l)-	məmnita	mələ yo
'to meet'	manna-	mannamnita	manna yo
'to come'	o-	omnita	wa yo
'to buy'	sa-	samnita	sa yo
'to stop by'	tɪllɪ-	tɪllɪmnita	tɪllə yo
'to look at'	po-	pomnita	pwa yo or poa yo
'to be expensive'	pissa-	pissamnita	pissa yo
'to be cheap'	ssa-	ssamnita	ssa yo
'to sell'	pha(l)-	pha(lɪ)mnita	phalə yo
'to like'	cohaha-	cohahamnita	cohahæ yo
'to want'	wənha-	wənhamnita	wənhæ yo
'to ge good'	coh-	cohsɪmnita	coha yo
'to give'	cu-	cumnita	cuə yo

Note that the verbs which occur hereafter will be treated individually for the formation of Infinitives. Refer to the following rules and the glossary at the end of the book for the infinitive form of each verb.

Observe the following regularities in forming infinitives from verb stems. Do not try to memorize the rules at this point; rather it is simpler to memorize each inflected form as a separate word. It is not necessary to memorize the verbs listed below. Add yo to the infinitive to make informal polite speech:

a. Stems ending in a or ə do not change:

ka-	ka yo	'goes'
sa-	sa yo	'buys'
sə-	sə yo	'stands'

Exception:

ha-	hæ yo or hayə yo	'does'

b. Stems ending in e, æ or we have alternative forms:

mæ-	mæ yo or mæə yo	'ties'
twe-	twe yo or tweə yo	'becomes'

c. Stems ending in o change o to wa:

o-	wa yo	'comes'
po-	pwa yo	'sees'

d. Stems ending in ɪ change ɪ to ə:

khɪ-	khə yo	'is big'
ssɪ-	ssə yo	'writes'

e. Stems ending in u add ə:

cu-	cuə yo	'gives'
tu-	tuə yo	'places'

f. The copula stem i- changes to iye or iyə.

g. Stems ending in i have three alternatives:

swi-	swiə yo or swiyə yo or swyə yo	'rests'
masi-	masiə yo or masiyə yo or masyə yo	'drinks'
kitali-	kitaliə yo or kitaliyə yo or kitalyə yo	'waits (for)'
kalɪchi-	kalɪchiə yo or kalɪchiyə yo or kalɪchyə yo	'teaches'

h. Stems ending in consonants: these are divided into several groups on the basis of the morphophonemic changes of the final sounds.

Most consonant stems belong to Group 1, and are called <u>ə</u>-adding stems; Group 2 stems are called <u>a</u>-adding stems; Group 3, <u>wə</u>-replacing stems; Group 4, <u>l</u>-dropping stems; Group 5, <u>l</u>-doubling stems. Note that there is a small number of verbs which are not classed into one of the 5 groups. They will be treated separately as irregular verbs.

<u>Group 1</u>

mək-	məkə yo	'eats'
cuk-	cukə yo	'dies'
cap-	capə yo	'holds'
ip-	ipə yo	'wears'
nəlp-	nəlpə yo	'is wide'
pis-	pisə yo	'combs'
iss-	issə yo <u>or</u> isse yo	'exists'
əps-	əpsə yo <u>or</u> əpse yo	'does not exist'
pəs-	pəsə yo	'takes off (clothes, hats, shoes)'
alh-	alhə yo	'aches', 'gets sick'

<u>Group 2</u>

cop-	copa yo	'is narrow'
noph-	nopha yo	'is high'
pokk-	pokka yo	'roasts (beans)'
noh-	noha yo	'places', 'puts'

<u>Group 3</u>

swip-	swiwə yo	'is easy'
əlyəp-	əlyəwə yo	'is difficult'
kakkap-	kakkawə yo	'is near'
alımtap-	alimtawə yo	'is beautiful'

<u>Group 4</u>

mə(l)-	mələ yo	'is far'
ki(l)-	kilə yo	'is long(in length)'
a(l)-	alə yo	'knows'
sa(l)-	salə yo	'lives'
mantı(l)-	mantilə yo	'makes'

<u>Group 5</u>

molı-	molla yo	'does not know'

talı-	talla yo	'is different'
pulı-	pullə yo	'calls'
hılı-	hıllə yo	'flows'

2. Past Tenses

A past tense form of a Korean verb denotes either 'something was in such state' or 'something which has been done', or 'someone took such and such action'.

There are two past tenses in Korean: Simple Past and Remote Past. The simple past designates any action or description which has been finished before the speech takes place. The remote past denotes an action which was done or happened a relatively long time ago, or a description of a condition which ended a relatively long time ago. The remote past also is used to indicate the more remote of two or more past actions or descriptions occuring in the same context.

Past tenses in Korean are formed by infixing the suffixes -(a, ə, yə)ss- for the Simple Past and -(a, ə, yə)ssəss- for the Remote Past between verb stems and endings. We shall call the suffixes the Past Tense Suffixes. Depending on the final sound of a verb stem, a certain vowel change takes place between verb stem and the past tense suffix. The verb element preceding -ss(əss)- is identical with the infinitive form, so it may be simpler to consider that the past tense is formed by infixing -ss(əss)- between infinitive and ending.
Compare:

	Stem	F. P. Present	Inf. P. Present	F.P. Past	Inf.P. Past
'to do'	ha-	hamnita	hæ yo	hæssımnita	hæssə yo
'to go'	ka-	kamnita	ka yo	kassımnita	kassə yo
'to come'	o-	omnita	wa yo	wassımnita	wassə yo
'to see'	po-	pomnita	pwa yo	pwassımnita	pwassə yo
'to buy'	sa-	samnita	sa yo	sassımnita	sassə yo
'to be cheap'	ssa-	ssamnita	ssa yo	ssassımnita	ssassə yo
'to be expensive'	pissa-	pissamnita	pissa yo	pissassımnita	pissa yo
'to pass by'	cina-	cinamnita	cina yo	cinassımnita	cinassə yo
'to want'	wənha-	wənhamnita	wənhæ yo	wənhæssımnita	wənhæssə yo
'to give'	cu-	cumnita	cuə yo	cuəssımnita	cuəssə yo
'to meet'	manna-	mannamnita	manna yo	mannassımnita	mannassə yo
'to exist'	iss-	issımnita	issə yo	issəssımnita	issəssə yo
'to read'	ilk-	ilksımnita	ilkə yo	ilkəssımnita	ilkəssə yo
'to be far'	mə(l)-	məmnita	mələ yo	mələssımnita	mələssə yo

'to know'	a(l)-	amnita	alə yo	aləssımnita	aləssə yo
'to be near'	kakkap-	kakkapsımnita	kakkawə yo	kakkawəssımnita	kakkawəssə yo
'to be different'	talı-	talımnita	talla yo	tallassımnita	tallassə yo
'not to know'	molı-	molımnita	molla yo	mollassımnita	mollassə yo

3. Particle to

To is a one-shape particle, which following a noun or another particle means 'also' or 'too' in an affirmative sentence; '(not) either' in a negative sentence. When to occurs after the object, topic, or emphasis subject of a sentence, the particles ın/nın, ıl/lıl, i/ka respectively are dropped.

Examples:

Na to amnita.	'I know [it], too.'
I kəs to chæk imnikka?	'Is this also a book?'
Ilpon mal to pæwəssımnita.	'[I] have studied Japanese also.'
Kim Sənsæng to molımnita.	'Mr. Kim doesn't know [it], either.'

4. Particle wa/kwa 'with', 'and'

Wa occurs after a word ending in a vowel; kwa after a word ending in a consonant. It occurs in the following two constructions:

a. Personal noun + wa/kwa means 'with the P. N.'

Examples:

Na wa (kathi) kapsita.	'Let us go with me.'
Chinku wa mannassımnita.	'[I] met with a friend.'
Kim Sənsæng kwa okessə yo.	'I'll come with Mr. Kim.'

b. Noun 1 + wa/kwa + Noun 2 means 'N 1 and N 2'

Examples:

chæk kwa yənphil	'a book and a pencil'
hakkyo wa cip	'a school and a house'

5. -ci + anhsımnita

-Ci is a verb ending which is added to a verb stem, or to a verb stem plus other suffix(es). Hereafter, we shall call such a verb form the ci form.

The ci form is an inflected word which occurs before a small class of words. The verb anh- 'not' occurs only after the ci form and is used to mean the verb in the ci form is in negative. The distinction of tenses, levels of speech may be made in the verb anh-.

Compare:

Kaci anh(s)ımnita.	'[I] don't go.'
Kaci anh(s)ımnikka?	'Don't [you] go?'
Kaci anhkessımnita.	'I will not go.'
Kaci anhəssımnita.	'I did not go.'
Kaci anhə yo.	'[I] don't go.'
Kaci anhkessə yo.	'[I]'ll not go.'
Kaci anhəssə yo.	'[I] didn't go.'

6. Numerals

In Korean, there are two series of numbers, both of which occur either as free nouns or before a special class of nouns called Counters. One of the two series of the Korean numbers was borrowed from Chinese characters; the other is of Korean origin. The counters are a class of words which occur only as post-nouns preceded by numbers. Some counters occur after the character numbers; some occur after the numbers of Korean origin; others occur after both sets of numbers. Therefore, it is important to know which series of numbers a certain counter goes with. For example, the counter Wən 'Korean monetary unit' occurs only after the character numbers as do all other monetary units, whereas the counter sal 'year(s) old (age counter)' occurs only with the numbers of Korean origin. Some counters like kwən 'book counter' occur after both series. In Unit 4 we have the numbers of the Chinese character origin, and in Unit 5 the numbers of Korean origin are listed. When the numbers of Korean origin are used as modifiers, the final sounds of the first four are dropped, thus making hana 'one' han, tul 'two' tu, ses 'three' se, nes 'four' ne. Others do not change (See Unit 5).

DRILLS

A. Substitution Drill

1.	əce əti e kassımnikka?	Where did [you] go yesterday?
2.	Onıl əti e kassımnikka?	Where did [you] go today?
*3.	Achim e əti e kassımnikka?	Where did [you] go in the morning?
*4.	Ohu e əti e kassımnikka?	Where did [you] go in the afternoon?
*5.	Cənyək e əti e kassımnikka?	Where did [you] go in the evening?
*6.	Pam e əti e kassımnikka?	Where did [you] go at night?
*7.	Kıcəkke əti e kassımnikka?	Where did [you] go the day before yesterday?
*8.	Onıl achim e əti e kassımnikka?	Where did [you] go this morning?
*9.	əce pam e əti e kassımnikka?	Where did [you] go last night?
*10.	Kıcəkke ohu e əti e kassımnikka?	Where did [you] go in the afternoon, the day before yesterday?
11.	Onıl ohu e əti e kassımnikka?	Where did [you] go this afternoon?
12.	Onıl ohu e əti e kakessımnikka?	Where will [you] go this afternoon?
*13.	Næil əti e kakessımnikka?	Where will [you] go tomorrow?
*14.	Mole əti e kakessımnikka?	Where will [you] go the day after tomorrow?
*15.	Næil pam e əti e kakessımnikka?	Where will [you] go tomorrow night?

B. Substitution Drill

1.	Ilsang yongphum ıl sassımnita.	[I] bought some daily necessities.
2.	Chæk ıl sassımnita.	[I] bought a book.
3.	Sukən ıl sassımnita.	[I] bought a towel.
4.	I kəs ıl sassımnita.	[I] bought this.
*5.	Nolan sukən ıl sassımnita.	[I] bought a yellow towel.
*6.	Nolan sæk yənphil ıl sassımnita.	[I] bought a yellow pencil.
7.	Yələ kaci lıl sassımnita.	[I] bought several kinds.
8.	Nolan kəs ıl sassımnita.	[I] bought a yellow one.
*9.	Ppalkan kəs ıl sassımnita.	[I] bought a red one.
*10.	Hayan kəs ıl sassımnita.	[I] bought a white one.
*11.	Phalan kəs ıl sassımnita.	[I] bought a blue one.
*12.	Kkaman kəs ıl sassımnita.	[I] bought a black one.
13.	Hana lıl sassımnita.	[I] bought one.
14.	Hankuk mal chæk ıl sassımnita.	[I] bought a Korean book.

C. Substitution Drill

1.	Chæk kaps i pissamnikka?	Are the books expensive?
2.	Chæk kaps i ssamnikka?	Are the books cheap?
3.	Chæk kaps i əttəhsımnikka?	How expensive are books?
4.	Chæk kaps i kwænchanhsımnikka?	Is the price of books reasonable ('not bad')?
5.	Chæk kaps i əlma imnikka?	How much is the book? ('What is the price of the book?')
6.	Chæk kaps i kıcə kıləhsımnikka?	Is the (price of) book just so?
7.	Chæk kaps i pissamnikka?	Are the books expensive?
8.	Cip kaps i pissamnikka?	Are the houses expensive?
9.	Ilsang younphum kaps i pissamnikka?	Are the daily necessities expensive?
*10.	Kutu kaps i pissamnikka?	Are the shoes expensive?
*11.	Yangpok kaps i pissamnikka?	Are the suits expensive?

D. Substitution Drill

1.	I sukən sæk ın nolahsımnita.	The color of this towel is yellow.
*2.	I sukən sæk ın ppalkahsımnita.	The color of this towel is red.
*3.	I sukən sæk ın hayahsımnita.	The color of this towel is white.
*4.	I sukən sæk ın kkamahsımnita.	The color of this towel is black.
*5.	I sukən sæk ın phalahsımnita.	The color of this towel is blue.
*6.	I sukən sæk ın nuləhsımnita.	The color of this towel is yellowish.
*7.	I sukən sæk ın pulkımnita.	The color of this towel is reddish.
*8.	I sukən sæk ın himnita.	The color of this towel is whitish.
*9.	I sukən sæk ın kəmsımnita.	The color of this towel is dark.
*10.	I sukən sæk ın phulımnita.	The color of this towel is bluish.

E. Substitution Drill

1.	Musın sæk ıl wənhase yo?	What color would you like? ('What color do you want?')
2.	Musın sukən ıl wənhase yo?	What kind of towels would you like?
3.	Musın chæk ıl wənhase yo?	What books would you like?
4.	Musın yənphil ıl wənhase yo?	What kind of pencils would you like?
5.	Musın sikye lıl wənhase yo?	What kind of watches would you like?
6.	Musın moca lıl wənhase yo?	What kind of hats would you like?
7.	Musın phen ıl wənhase yo?	What kind of pens would you like?
8.	Musın phen ıl phamnikka?	What kind of pens do you carry ('sell')?
9.	Musın phen ıl sakessə yo?	What kind of pens will you buy?

10. Musın phen ıl cohahamnikka?	What kind of pens do you prefer?
11. Musın phen ıl pokessımnikka?	What kind of pens would you like to see?

F. Substitution Drill

1. Yəki esə sukən ıl phamnikka?	Do you carry towels here? ('Do you sell towels here?')
*2. Yəki esə yangpok ıl phamnikka?	Do you carry suits here?
*3. Yəki esə son-sukən ıl phamnikka?	Do you carry handkerchiefs here?
*4. Yəki esə yangmal ıl phamnikka?	Do you carry socks here?
*5. Yəki esə kutu lıl phamnikka?	Do you carry shoes here?
*6. Yəki esə nekthai lıl phamnikka?	Do you carry neckties here?
*7. Yəki esə waisyassı lıl phamnikka?	Do you carry dress shirts here?
*8. Yəki esə kongchæk ıl phamnikka?	Do you carry notebooks here?
*9. Yəki esə sinmun ıl phamnikka?	Do you carry newspaper here?
*10. Yəki esə capci lıl phamnikka?	Do you carry magazines here?
*11. Yəki esə tampæ lıl phamnikka?	Do you carry cigarettes here?
*12. Yəki esə cito lıl phamnikka?	Do you carry maps here?

G. Substitution Drill

1. I kəs i əttəhsımnikka?	How do you like this? ('How is this?')
*2. I son-sukən (i) əttəhsımnikka?	How do you like this handkerchief ('hand towel')?
3. I kutu (ka) əttəhsımnikka?	How do you like these shoes?
4. I sikye (ka) əttəhsımnikka?	How do you like this watch?
5. I waisyassı (ka) əttəhsımnikka?	How do you like this dress shirt?
6. I kongchæk (i) əttəhsımnikka?	How do you like this notebook?
7. I sinmun (i) əttəhsımnikka?	How do you like this newspaper?
8. I capci (ka) əttəhsımnikka?	How do you like this magazine?
9. I yangpok (i) əttəhsımnikka?	How do you like this suit?
*10. I yangmal (i) əttəhsımnikka?	How do you like these socks?
11. I sæk (i) əttəhsımnikka?	How do you like this color?
12. I sangcəm (i) əttəhsımnikka?	How do you like this store?
13. I pækhwacəm (i) əttəhsımnikka?	How do you like this department store?
*14. I os (i) əttəhsımnikka?	How do you like this { this dress? / these clothes? }
*15. I pang (i) əttəhsımnikka?	How do you like this room?

H. Substitution Drill

1.	Kı kəs, əlma imnikka?	How much is that?
*2.	Cə moca, əlma imnikka?	How much is that hat?
*3.	Cə kkaman yangpok, əlma imnikka?	How much is that black suit?
*4.	Cə hayan kutu, əlma imnikka?	How much are these white shoes?
*5.	I nolan son-sukən, əlma imnikka?	How much is this yellow handkerchief?
*6.	I phalan yangmal, əlma imnikka?	How much are these blue socks?
*7.	Kı hayan waisyassı, əlma imnikka?	How much is the dress shirt?
*8.	Kı ppalkan sukən, əlma imnikka?	How much is the red towel?
*9.	Kı kkaman yangmal, əlma imnikka?	How much are the black socks?

I. Substitution Drill

1.	I chæk, əlma e phamnikka?	How much do you sell this book for? ('At what price do you sell this book?')
*2.	Kı moca, əlma e phamnikka?	How much do you sell that hat for?
*3.	Cə kkaman yangpok, əlma e phamnikka?	How much do you sell that black suit for?
*4.	Cə hayan kutu, əlma e phamnikka?	How much do you sell these white shoes for?
*5.	I nolan son-sukən, əlma e phamnikka?	How much do you sell this yellow handkerchief for?
*6.	I phalan yangmal, əlma e phamnikka?	How much do you sell these blue socks for?
*7.	I hayan waisyassı, əlma e phamnikka?	How much do you sell this dress shirts for?
*8.	I ppalkan sukən, əlma e phamnikka?	How much do you sell this red towel for?
*9.	Kı kkaman yangmal, əlma e phamnikka?	How much do you sell those black socks for?

End of Tape 3A

Tape 3B

J. Substitution Drill

1.	I moca nın o-sip Wən imnita.	This hat is W 50.
2.	Cə sikye (nın) i Wən imnita.	That watch is W 2.
3.	Kı kutu (nın) sa Wən imnita.	Those shoes are W 4.
*4.	I mannyənphil (ın) yuk Wən imnita.	This fountain pen is W 6.
*5.	Cə kılim (ın) phal Wən imnita.	That picture is W 8.
*6.	Kı os (ın) sip Wən imnita.	That dress is W 10.
7.	I sinmun (ın) sip-il Wən imnita.	This newspaper is W 11.
8.	Cə capci (nın) sip-sam Wən imnita.	That magazine is W 13.
9.	Kı syassı (nın) sip-o Wən imnita.	That shirt is W 15.

10.	I son-sukən (ın) sip-chil Wən imnita.	This handkerchief is W 17.
11.	Cə ıyca (nın) sip-ku Wən imnita.	That chair is W 19.

K. Grammar Drill (as a response drill based on Grammar Note 2)

Tutor:	əce hakkyo e kassımnikka?	'Did you go to school yesterday?'
Student:	Ne, kassımnita.	'Yes, I did.'
1.	Moca lıl sassımnikka?	Ne, sassımnita.
2.	Chækpang e tılləssımnikka?	Ne, tılləssımnita.
3.	Kim Sənsæng ıl mannassımnikka?	Ne, mannassımnita.
4.	Kı chæk ıl ilkəssımnikka?	Ne, ilkəssımnita.
5.	Pak Sənsæng i cip e issəssımnikka?	Ne, cip e issəssımnita.
6.	Haksæng ıl chacəssımnikka?	Ne, (haksæng ıl) chacəssımnita.
7.	Pak Sənsæng i Hankuk mal ıl kalıchyəssımnikka?	Ne, (Pak Sənsæng i) kalıchyəssımnita.
8.	Ceimsı Sənsæng ıl pwassımnikka?	Ne, pwassımnita.
9.	Cungkuk mal ıl pæwəssımnikka?	Ne, (Cungkuk mal ıl) pæwəssımnita.
10.	I yənphil ıl wənhæssımnikka?	Ne, (kı yənphil ıl) wənhæssımnita.
11.	Kil ıl mulə pwassımnikka?	Ne, (kil ıl) mulə pwassımnita.
12.	Kı chæk ıl phalassımnikka?	Ne, phalassımnita.
13.	Kı sæk ıl cohahæssımnikka?	Ne, (kı sæk ıl) cohahæssımnita.

L. Response Drill

Tutor:	əce əti e kassımnikka? /sinæ/	'Where did you go yesterday?' /downtown/
Student:	Sinæ e kassımnita.	'[I] went downtown.'
1.	Muəs ıl sassımnikka? /ilsang yongphum/	Ilsang yongphum ıl sassımnita.
2.	əce əti e tılləssımnikka? /chækpang/	Chækpang e tıllassımnita.
3.	Musın sæk ıl wənhæssımnikka? /nolan sæk/	Nolan sæk ıl wənhæssımnita.
4.	Muəs i issəssımnikka? /yələ kaci/	Yələ kaci ka issəssımnita.
5.	Nuku lıl cohahæssımnikka? /Ceimsi/	Ceimsı lıl cohahæssımnita.
6.	Kı kəs, əlma e phaləssımnikka? /o-sip Wən/	O-sip Wən e phaləssımnita.
7.	Nuka cip e wassımnikka? /Mikuk salam/	Mikuk salam i wassımnita.
8.	Muəs ıl chacəssımnikka? /haksæng/	Haksæng ıl chacəssımnita.
9.	Muəs ıl kongpu-hæssımnikka? /Hankuk mal/	Hankuk mal ıl kongpu-hæssımnita.

10.	Muəs ɪl pæwəssɪmnikka? /Ilpon mal/	Ilpon mal ɪl pæwəssɪmnita.
11.	Nuka Hankuk mal ɪl kalɪchyəssɪmnikka? /Pak Sənsæng/	Pak Sənsæng i kalɪchyəssimnita.
12.	əti esə kɪ chæk ɪl pwassɪmnikka? /sinæ chækpang/	Sinæ chækpang esə pwassimnita.

M. Response Drill (based on Grammar Note 5)

Tutor:	Hakkyo e kamnikka?	'Do you go to school?'
Student:	Aniyo, kaci anhsɪmnita.	'No, I don't (go).'

1.	Hankuk mal ɪl pæumnikka?	Aniyo, pæuci anhsɪmnita.
2.	Chæk kaps i pissamnikka?	Aniyo, pissaci anhsɪmnita.
3.	Cip kaps i ssamnikka?	Aniyo, ssaci anhsɪmnita.
4.	Onɪl chækpang e tɪllɪmnikka?	Aniyo, tɪllɪci anhsɪmnita.
5.	Kim Sənsæng ɪl mannamnikka?	Aniyo, mannaci anhsɪmnita.
6.	Kɪ chæk ɪl ilksɪmnikka?	Aniyo, ilkci anhsɪmnita.
7.	Hankuk mal ɪl mal-hamnikka?	Aniyo, mal-haci anhsɪmnita.
8.	Pak Sənsæng i cip e issɪmnikka?	Aniyo, (cip e) issci/icci/ anhsɪmnita.
9.	I sæk ɪl cohahamnikka?	Aniyo, cohahaci anhsɪmnita.
10.	Yəki esə chæk ɪl phamnikka?	Aniyo, pha(l)ci anhsɪmnita.
11.	I kəs ɪl wənhamnikka?	Aniyo, wənhaci anhsɪmnita.
12.	Hakkyo ka məmnikka?	Aniyo, mə(l)ci anhsɪmnita.
13.	Tæsakwan i kakkapsɪmnikka?	Aniyo, kakkapci anhsɪmnita.

N. Response Drill

Tutor:	Hakkyo e kakessɪmnikka?	'Are [you] going to school?' ('Will you go to school?')
Student:	Aniyo, kaci anhkessɪmnita.	'No, [I]'m not (going).' ('No, I'll not go.')

1.	Hankuk mal ɪl pæukessɪmnikka?	Aniyo, pæuci anhkessɪmnita.
2.	Onɪl chækpang e tɪllɪkessɪmnikka?	Aniyo, tɪllɪci anhkessɪmnita.
3.	Kim Sənsæng ɪl mannakessɪmnikka?	Aniyo, mannaci anhkessɪmnita.
4.	Kɪ chæk ɪl ilkkessɪmnikka?	Aniyo, ilkci anhkessɪmnita.
5.	Hankuk mal ɪl mal-hakessɪmnikka?	Aniyo, mal-haci anhkessɪmnita.
6.	Kutu lɪl sakessɪmnikka?	Aniyo, saci anhkessɪmnita.
7.	Moca lɪl phalkessɪmnikka?	Aniyo, pha(l)ci anhkessɪmnita.
8.	Nolan syassɪ lɪl pokessɪmnikka?	Aniyo, poci anhkessɪmnita.
9.	Kil ɪl mulə pokessɪmnikka?	Aniyo, mulə poci anhkessɪmnita.
10.	Kim Sənsæng ɪl chackessɪmnikka?	Aniyo, chacci anhkessɪmnita.

O. Response Drill (based on Grammar Note 5 with Past Tense)

Tutor:	əce sinæ e kassımnikka?	'Did you go downtown yesterday?'
Student:	Aniyo, kaci anhəssımnita.	'No, I didn't (go).'

1.	Hankuk mal ıl pæwəssımnikka?	Aniyo, pæuci anhəssımnita.
2.	Kı chæk ıl ilkəssımnikka?	Aniyo, ilkci anhəssımnita.
3.	Kim Sənsæng ıl mannassımnikka?	Aniyo, mannaci anhəssımnita.
4.	Kutu lıl sassımnikka?	Aniyo, saci anhəssımnita.
5.	Kil ıl mulə pwassımnikka?	Aniyo, mulə poci anhəssımnita.
6.	Kim Sənsæng ıl chacəssımnikka?	Aniyo, (Kim Sənsæng ıl) chacci anhəssımnita.
7.	Chæksang ıl phaləssımnikka?	Aniyo, phalci anhəssımnita.
8.	Samusil e tılləssımnikka?	Aniyo, tıllıci anhəssımnita.
9.	Sənsæng ın Yəngə lıl kalıchyəssımnikka?	Aniyo, kalıchici anhəssımnita.
10.	Hakkyo ka mələssımnikka?	Aniyo, mə(l)ci anhəssımnita.
11.	Chæk kaps i pissassımnikka?	Aniyo, pissaci anhəssımnita.
12.	Phalan sæk ıl wənhæssımnikka?	Aniyo, (phalan sæk ıl) wənhaci anhəssımnita.
13.	Ceimsı Sənsæng ıl aləssımnikka?	Aniyo, alci anhəssımnita.

P. Response Drill (as a level drill based on Grammar Note 1)

Tutor:	Hakkyo e ka yo?	'Do you go to school?'
Student:	Ne, (hakkyo e) ka yo.	'Yes, I do (go to school).'

1.	Hankuk mal ıl kongpu-hæ yo?	Ne, (Hankuk mal ıl) kongpu-hæ yo.
2.	Chæk kaps i ssa yo?	Ne, (chæk kaps i) ssa yo.
3.	Yangpok i pissa yo?	Ne, (yangpok i) pissa yo.
4.	Hakkyo ka mələ yo?	Ne, (hakkyo ka) mələ yo.
5.	Cəngkəcang i kakkawə yo?	Ne, (cəngkəcang i) kakkawə yo.
6.	Sənsæng ın Mikuk salam iye yo?	Ne, Mikuk salam iye yo.
7.	Sənsæng ın cal issə yo?	Ne, cal issə yo.
8.	Ceimsı Sənsæng ın Yəngə lıl mal-hæ yo?	Ne, Yəngə lıl mal-hæ yo.
9.	Sənsæng ın cə salam ıl alə yo?	Ne, (cə salam ıl) alə yo.
10.	Pækhwacəm i sichəng yəph e issə yo?	Ne, sichəng yəph e issə yo.
11.	Yəki esə sukən ıl phalə yo?	Ne, (sukən ıl) phalə yo.
12.	Nolan sæk ıl wənhæ yo?	Ne, (nolan sæk ıl) wənhæ yo.
13.	Hankuk mal ıl cohahæ yo?	Ne, (Hankuk mal ıl) cohahæ yo.

14.	Onɪl chækpang e tɪllə yo?	Ne, (chækpang e) tɪllə yo.
15.	Kɪ chæk i coha yo?	Ne, (kɪ chæk i) coha yo.
16.	Sangcəm ɪl chacə yo?	Ne, sangcəm ɪl chacə yo.
17.	Səngsæng ɪn Hankuk mal ɪl pæwə yo?	Ne, cə nɪn Hankuk mal ɪl pæwə yo
18.	Kim Sənsæng i kalɪchiə yo?	Ne, Kim Sənsæng i kalɪchiə yo.

Q. Response Drill (as a level drill based on Grammar Note 1)

Tutor: Hakkyo e kamnikka? 'Do you go to school?'
Student: Ne, (hakkyo e) ka yo. 'Yes, I do ('go to school').

1.	Hankuk mal ɪl kongpu-hamnikka?	Ne, kongpu-hæ yo.
2.	Chæk kaps i ssamnikka?	Ne, ssa yo.
3.	Yangpok i pissamnikka?	Ne, pissa yo.
4.	Hakkyo ka məmnikka?	Ne, mələ yo.
5.	Cəngkəcang i kakkapsɪmnikka?	Ne, kakkawə yo.
6.	Sənsæng ɪn Mikuk salam imnikka?	Ne, Mikuk salam iye yo.
7.	Kim Sənsæng ɪn cip e issɪmnikka?	Ne, (cip e) issə yo.
8.	Cə salam ɪl amnikka?	Ne, alə yo.
9.	Yəki esə sukən ɪl phamnikka?	Ne, phalə yo.
10.	Kkaman sæk ɪl wənhamnikka?	Ne, kkaman sæk ɪl wənhæ yo.
11.	I kyosil ɪl cohahamnikka?	Ne, cohahæ yo.
12.	Haksæng ɪl chacsɪmnikka?	Ne, haksæng ɪl chacə yo.
13.	Cə salam ɪl molɪmnikka?	Ne, molla yo.

R. Level Drill (based on Grammar Note 1)

Tutor: Hakkyo e kasimnikka?
Student: Hakkyo e kase yo?
{ 'Do you go to school?' / 'Are you going to school?' }

1.	Hankuk mal ɪl kongpu-hasimnikka?	Hankuk mal ɪl kongpu-hase yo?
2.	Cungkuk mal ɪl pæusimnikka?	Cungkuk mal ɪl pæuse yo?
3.	Hankuk mal chæk ɪl ilkɪsimnikka?	Hankuk mal chæk ɪl ilkɪse yo?
4.	Kim Sənsæng ɪn kutu lɪl sasimnikka?	Kim Sənsæng ɪn kutu lɪl sase yo?
5.	Sənsæng i haksæng ɪl chacɪsimnikka?	Sənsæng i haksæng ɪl chacɪse yo?
6.	Annyəng-hasimnikka?	Annyəng-hase yo?
7.	Yocɪm əttəhke cinasimnikka?	Yocɪm əttəhke cinase yo?
8.	Ceimsɪ Sənsæng ɪl asimnikka?	Ceimsɪ Sənsæng ɪl ase yo?
9.	Onɪl Mikuk salam i Hankuk e osimnikka?	Onɪl Mikuk salam i Hankuk e ose yo?

10. Yəngə sənsæng i Hankuk mal chæk ıl ilkısimnikka?	Yəngə sənsæng i Hankuk mal chæk ıl ilkıse yo?
11. Ceimı Sənsæng i na e samusil e tıllısimnikka?	Ceimsı Sənsæng i na e samusil e tıllıse yo?
12. Pak Sənsæng ın wekyokwan isimnikka?	Pak Sənsæng ın wekyokwan ise yo?

S. Response Drill (as a grammar drill based on Grammar Notes 2 and 5)
(Answer in Informal Polite Speech for the Formal Polite using the stimulus /ne/ or /aniyo/.)

Tutor: Hakkyo e kakessımnikka? /aniyo/	'Are you going to school?' /no/
Student: Aniyo, kaci anhkessə yo.	'No, I'm not (going to go).'
1. Hankuk mal ıl kongpu-hakessımnikka? /ne/	Ne, kongpu-hakessə yo.
2. I chæk ıl ilkkessımnikka? /aniyo/	Aniyo, ilkci anhkessə yo.
3. Mikuk salam chinku lil mannakessımnikka? /ne/	Ne, mannakessə yo.
4. Kil ıl mulə pokessımnikka? /aniyo/	Aniyo, mulə poci anhkessə yo.
5. I chæksang ıl phalkessımnikka? /ne/	Ne, phalkessə yo.
6. Cə e samusil e tıllıkessımnikka? /aniyo/	Aniyo, tillici anhkessə yo.
7. Yəngə lil kalıchikessımnikka? /ne/	Ne, kalıchikessə yo.
8. Cip e isskessımnikka/ikkessımnikka/? /aniyo/	Aniyo, (cip e) issci anhkessə yo.

T. Response Drill (as a level drill based on Grammar Note 1)
(Answer in Informal Polite Speech using the stimulus.)

Tutor: Kim Sənsæng ın əti e kasiəssımnikka? /sicang/	'Where did Mr. Kim go?' /market place/
Student: Sicang e kassə yo.	'[He] went to the market place.'
1. Kim Sənsæng ın əti e kasiəssımnikka? /chækpang/	Chækpang e kasiəssə yo.
2. Muəs ıl sassımnikka? /Hankuk kılim/	Hankuk kılim ıl sassə yo.
3. Ceimsı Sənsæng i muəs ıl mulə pwassımnikka? /kil/	Kil ıl mulə pwassə yo.

4. Nuka sənsæng cip e tılləssımnikka? /chinku/ — Chinku ka tılləssə yo.
5. Sənsæng e yangpok əlma e sassımnikka? /o-sip Wən/ — O-sip Wən e sassə yo.
6. Kı Mikuk salam ın nuku iyəssımnikka? /Ceimsı Sənsæng/ — Ceimsı Sənsæng iyəssə yo.
7. Sənsæng ın əce musın chæk ıl ilkəssımnikka? /Ilpon mal chæk/ — Ilpon mal chæk ıl ilkəssə yo.
8. I chæk, əlma e phaləssımnikka? /o-sip Wən/ — O-sip Wən e phaləssə yo.
9. Hankuk mal ın nuka kalıchyəssımnikka? /Pak Sənsæng/ — Pak Sənsæng i kalıchyəssə yo.
10. Nuka Yəngə sənsæng iəssımnikka? /Mikuk yəca/ — Mikuk yəca ka Yəngə sənsæng iəssə yo.

U. Response Exercise (Answer the questions on the basis of the dialogues at the beginning of this Unit: Formal Polite question in Informal Polite and vice versa.)

Tutor:	əce əti e kassımnikka?	'Where did you go yesterday?'
Student:	Sinæ sangcəm e kassə yo.	'I went to a store downtown.'

1. Pækhwacəm esə muəs ıl sassə yo?
2. Onıl ın sinæ e an kakessımnikka?
3. Chæk kaps i pissa yo?
4. Chækpang esə sukən ıl phamnikka?
5. Musın sæk ıl wənhase yo?
6. Sənsæng ın nolan waisyassı lıl cohahæssımnikka?
7. Sənsæng e moca, əlma ye yo?
8. Sənsæng e kutu, əlma e sassımnikka?
9, Səul e os kaps i ssamnikka?
10. Sənsæng ın onıl achim e muəs hakessə yo?
11. əce cənyək e muəs hæssımnikka?
12. Onıl pam e cip e isskessə yo?
13. əce ohu e əti e kassə yo?
14. Næil nac e ce samusil e tıllıkessımnikka?
15. Sənsæng ın yosæ musın chæk ıl ilkıse yo?

EXERCISES

Conduct the following conversations, once in Formal Polite Speech and once in Informal Polite Speech:

A. You ask Mr. Kim:	Mr. Kim answers:
a. where he's going to go this afternoon.	that he's going to the market place.
b. what he'll buy.	that he's going to buy some pictures.
c. what kind of pictures he likes.	that he likes Korean pictures.
d. what he's going to do at school.	that he's going to study.
e. what books he's going to read.	that he's going to read English books.
f. where he'll stop by.	that he's going to stop by his friend's office.
g. who is going to teach English.	that he (i.e. Mr. Kim) will teach it.
h. whom he's going to meet.	that he's going to meet a friend.
i. where he's going to teach Korean.	that he will teach [it] at a school.
j. How much he is going to pay for shoes.	that he's going to pay W 95.
k. where he'll be tonight.	that he'll be in class.

B. Ask Mr. Kim:	Mr. Kim answers:
a. if the books are expensive.	that they are not (expensive).
b. if he's going downtown.	that he is (going downtown).
c. if downtown is near.	that it is far.
d. if he has black shoes.	that he doesn't.
e. if they sell many kinds.	that they don't.
f. if they sell towels here.	that they do.
g. where Mr. Lee's office is.	that he doesn't (know).
h. if he wants a pencil.	that he wants paper.
i. if he wants several kinds.	that he does.
j. if he'll drop in the school.	that he won't.
k. if he's looking for USIS.	that he's looking for the Embassy.
l. if he knows the way to Seoul Station.	that he doesn't know.
m. where he went yesterday.	that he went to a store.
n. what he bought.	that he bought some daily necessities.
o. how much he paid for the pen.	that he paid W 35.
p. how much the book was.	that it was W 55.
q. what color he liked.	that he liked blue color.

r.	what book he read yesterday.	that he read a Korean book.
s.	where he stopped by this morning.	that he stopped by his friend's office.
t.	who taught Korean.	that Mr. Park taught it.
u.	whom he met at school.	that he met an American teacher.
v.	what the man's name was.	that (it) was James.
w.	what the American asked [him].	that he asked him for directions.
x.	how much the <u>cəmwən</u> sold this book for.	that he sold it for W 65.
y.	how much he paid for his shoes	that he paid W 73.
z.	whom he looked for.	that he looked for his teacher.

C. Say the following in Korean:

a. W 12
b. W 23
c. W 34
d. W 45
e. W 56
f. W 67
g. W 78
h. W 89
i. W 103
j. W 214
k. W 358
l. W 893
m. W 2,539
n. W 7,927
o. W10,111
p. W11,123

D. Mr. James asks the price of the following objects and you answer with the given price.

	Mr. James	You
a.	this yellow towel	W 28
b.	that Seoul map	W 52
c.	those red shoes	W 250
d.	those black suits	W 3,210
e.	these blue socks	W 8
f.	that hat	W 79
g.	that American watch	W 1,700
h.	this dress shirt	W 95
i.	your fountain pen	W 55
j.	that chair	W 527
k.	this woman's dress	W 250

E. Pak Sənsæng will respond with /Ne, kıləpsita./ 'Yes, let's do so.' when you propose to:

a. go downtown with him.
b. see the picture.
c. buy some daily necessities.
d. stop by a bookstore.
e. sell the house.
f. ask the street directions.
g. find Mr. Kim.
h. meet friends.
i. read that book.
j. come again tomorrow.
k. learn Chinese.
l. stay at home.
m. find out that Korean's name.

End of Tape 3B

Tape 4A

제 5 과 물건 사기 (계속)

(대화 A)

(-책방에서-)

사전

좋은 사전

1. 김 : 실례합니다. 여기 좋은 사전이 있읍니까?

영한 사전

사전 말입니까

2. 점원 : 영한 사전 말입니까?

3. 김 : 예.

4. 점원 : 예, 있읍니다.

보여 주십시오

5. 김 : 좀 보여 주십시오.

자

6. 점원 : 자, 여기 있읍니다.

어떤

어떤 사전

7. 김 : 이것은 어떤 사전입니까?

UNIT 5. Shopping (Continued)

BASIC DIALOGUES FOR MEMORIZATION

Dialogue A

(--Kim stopped by a bookstore--)

Kim

	sacən	dictionary
	cohın sacən	a good dictionary
1	Sillye-hamnita. Yəki cohın sacən i issımnikka?	Excuse me. Do you have a good dictionary here?

Cəmwən

	Yəng-Han sacən	English-Korean dictionary
	sacən mal imnikka	do you mean [a] dictionary?
2.	Yəng-Han sacən mal imnikka?	Do you mean an English-Korean dictionary?

Kim

3.	Ne.	Yes.

Cəmwən

4.	Ne, issımnita.	Yes, we do.

Kim

	poyə cusipsiyo	please show [me]
5.	Com poyə cusipsiyo.	May I see it? ('Please show [it to me].')

Cəmwən

	ca	well; here
6.	Ca, yəki issımnita.	Here you are! ('Here! [it] is.')

Kim

	əttən	what kind of
	əttən sacən	what kind of dictionary
7.	I kəs ın əttən sacən imnikka?	Is this a good dictionary? ('What kind of dictionary is this?')

대단히 좋습니다
그러나
다른 것

8. 점원 : 대단히 좋습니다. 그러나 다른 것도 있습니다.

어떻습니까

9. 김 : 다른 것은 어떻습니까?

비싼 사전
그리고
큰 책

10. 점원 : 다른 것은 좀 비싼 사전입니다. 그리고 큰 책입니다.

작은 것

11. 김 : 나는 작은 것이 좋습니다. 이 작은 것을 사겠읍니다.

또
필요합니까

12. 점원 : 또 다른 것이 필요합니까?

종이
펜과 종이

13. 김 : 아, 펜과 종이는 어디에서 팝니까?

Cəmwən

tæetanhi cohsımnita	[it]'s very good
kılәna	but; however
talın kəs	different one; other one
8. Tæetanhi cohsımnita. Kılәna, talın kəs to issımnita.	[It] is very good. But we also have another one.

Kim

əttəhsımnikka	how is [it]?
9. Talın kəs ın əttəhsımnikka?	Is the other one good? ('How is the other one?')

Cəmwən

pissan sacən	[an] expensive dictionary
kıliko	and
khın chæk	a big book
10. Talın kəs ın com pissan sacən imnita. Kıliko, khın chæk imnita.	The other one is [a] fairly expensive (dictionary). And, [it]'s a big book.

Kim

cakın kəs	a small one
11. Na nın cakın kəs i cohsımnita. I cakın kəs ıl sakessımnita.	A small one is fine for me. I'll take this small one.

Cəmwən

tto	again; besides; also
philyo	necessity; need
philyo-hamnikka	do [you] need?; is [something] needed?
12. Tto takın kəs i philyo-hamnikka?	Do you need anything else? ('Is other thing also needed?')

Kim

congi	paper
phen kwa congi	pen and paper
13. A, phen kwa congi nın əti esə pha(lı)mnikka?	Oh, where can I buy a pen and paper? ('As for pens and paper, where do [they] sell?')

다음
다음 집
문방구점

14. 점원 : 다음 집이 문방구점입니다.

(대화 B)

(-문방구점에서-)

드릴까요

15. 점원 : 어서 오십시요. 무엇을 드릴까요?

16. 김 : 종이와 펜이 있읍니까?

원하십니까

17. 점원 : 예, 있읍니다. 종이는 무슨 종이를 원하세요?

타이프 종이

18. 김 : 타이프 종이를 원합니다.

두 가지
두 가지 종이

19. 점원 : 아, 그러세요? 두 가지 종이가 있읍니다.

20. 김 : 얼마예요?

Cəmwən

taım	next; next time
taım cip	the next door ('next house')
munpangkucəm	stationary shop
14. Taım cip i munpangkucəm imnita.	There's a stationary shop next door. ('Next door is a stationary shop.')

Dialogue B

(--Kim enters next door--)

Cəmwən

tılil kka yo	shall [I] give [you]?
15. əsə osipsiyo. Muəs ıl tılil kka yo?	Come in. What would you like? ('What shall I give you?')

Kim

16. Congi wa phen i issımnikka?	Do you have paper and pens?

Cəmwən

wənhasimnikka	do [you] want?
17. Ne, issımnita. Congi nın musın congi lıl wənhase yo?	Yes, we have. What kind of paper do you want?

Kim

thaiphı congi	typewriter paper
18. Thaiphı congi lıl wənhamnita.	I want typewriter paper.

Cəmwən

tu kaci	two kinds
tu kaci congi	two kinds of paper
19. A, kıləse yo? Tu kaci congi ka issımnita.	Fine. ('Oh, is that so?') We have two kinds of typewriter paper.

Kim

20. əlma (i)ye yo?	How much are [they]?

한 가지
쉰
쉰 장
오십 원

21. 점원 : 한 가지는 쉰 장에 칠십 원입니다. 그리고, 다른 것은 오십 원에 팝니다.

더
더 쌉니다
더 싼 것
좀 더 싼 것
없어요

22. 김 : 좀 더 싼 것은 없어요?

지금

23. 점원 : 예, 좀 더 싼 것은 지금 없습니다.

그러면
오십 원 짜리

24. 김 : 그러면, 오십 원 짜리를 주십시오.

Cəmwən

	han kaci	one kind
	swin	fifty
	swin cang	fifty sheets; fifty pieces
	o-sip Wən	W50
21.	Han kaci nın swin cang e chil-sip Wən imnita. Kıliko, talın kəs ın o-sip Wən e phamnita.	One (kind) is W70 for 50 sheets, and the other is W50. ('We sell it for W50.')

Kim

	tə	more
	tə ssamnita	[it]'s cheaper
	tə ssan kəs	cheaper one; cheaper kind
	com tə ssan kəs	a little cheaper one
	əpsə yo	don't [you] have?; isn't [there]?
22	Com tə ssan kəs ın əpsə yo?	Don't you have anything cheaper?

Cəmwən

	cikım	now
23.	Ne, tə ssan kəs ın cikım əpsımnita.	No, not right now. ('We don't have a cheaper kind now.')

Kim

	kıləmyən	then; if so
	o-sip Wən ccali	W50 worth; in the value of W50
24.	Kıləmyən, o-sip Wən ccali lıl cusipsiyo.	Then I'll take the 50 Won kind. ('Then give me the W50's.')

수자 (2)

1	하나	11	열 하나	21	스물 하나
2	둘	12	열 둘	29	스물 아홉
3	셋	13	열 셋	30	서른
4	넷	14	열 넷	40	마흔
5	다섯	15	열 다섯	50	쉰
6	여섯	16	열 여섯	60	예순
7	일곱	17	열 일곱	70	일흔(이른)
8	여덟	18	열 여덟	80	여든
9	아홉	19	열 아홉	90	아흔
10	열	20	스물(스무)	99	아흔 아홉

100	(일)백	200	이백	300	삼백
101	백 하나	210	이백 열	401	사백 하나
102	백 둘	220	이백 스물	502	오백 둘
103	백 셋	230	이백 서른	603	육백 셋
104	백 넷	240	이백 마흔	704	칠백 넷
105	백 다섯	250	이백 쉰	805	팔백 다섯
106	백 여섯	260	이백 예순	906	구백 여섯
107	백 일곱	270	이백 일흔	911	구백 열 하나
108	백 여덟	280	이백 여든	922	구백 스물 둘
109	백 아홉	290	이백 아흔	1,000	(일)천
119	백 열 아홉	300	삼백	10,000	(일)만

NUMERALS (2)

1	han(a)	11	yəl-han(a)	21	sımul-han(a)
2	tu(l)	12	yəl-tu(l)	29	sımul-ahop
3	se(s)	13	yəl-se(s)	30	səlhın səlın
4	ne(s)	14	yəl-ne(s)	40	mahın
5	tasəs	15	yəl-tasəs	50	swin
6	yəsəs	16	yəl-yəsəs	60	yesun
7	ilkop	17	yəl-ilkop	70	il(h)ın
8	yətəl yətə(l)p	18	yəl-yətəl	80	yətın
9	ahop	19	yəl-ahop	90	ahın
10	yəl	20	sımu(l)	99	ahın-ahop

100	(il)-pæk	200	ipæk	300	sampæk
101	pæk-han(a)	210	ipæk-yəl	401	sapæk-han(a)
102	pæk-tu(l)	220	ipæk-sımul	502	opæk-tu(l)
103	pæk-se(s)	230	ipæk-səlhın	603	yukpæk-se(s)
104	pæk-ne(s)	240	ipæk-mahın	704	chilpæk-ne(s)
105	pæk-tasəs	250	ipæk-swin	805	phalpæk-tasəs
106	pæk-yəsəs	260	ipæk-yesun	906	kupæk-yəsəs
107	pæk-ilkop	270	ipæk-il(h)ın	911	kupæk-yəl-han(a)
108	pæk-yətəl(yətəp)	280	ipæk-yətın	922	kupæk-sımul-tu(l)
109	pæk-ahop	290	ipæk-ahın	1,000	(il)chən
119	pæk-yəl-ahop	300	sampæk	10,000	(il)man

NOTES ON DIALOGUES

(Numbers correspond to the sentence numbers.)

1. Yəki (e) X i/ka issımnikka? ('Is there X here?') is another expression commonly used in the situations similar to Yəki esə X ıl/lıl phamnikka? ('Do [you] sell X at this place?'). It means something like 'Do you carry X here (where X is a certain thing you want to buy)?'. Cohın 'good, nice' is a noun-modifier word which is formed from the verb stem coh- 'to be good' (See Grammar Note 1).

2. Mal imnikka? 'Do you mean...?' is always immediately preceded by something. The affirmative response to X mal imnikka? 'Do you mean X?' is Ne, X mal imnita. 'Yes, I mean X.' Yəng-Han 'English-Korean' is the contracted form of either Yəngə Hankuk mal 'English-Korean language' or Yəngkuk Hankuk 'Britian-Korea'. This kind of contraction in one word made out of two or more words appears often in Korean. In each case, the first syllables of the words are brought together to make the contraction. Examples: Han-Yəng 'Korea(n)-English (Britian), Han-Il 'Korea(n)-Japan(ese)', Cung-Tok 'Sino-German', Han-Mi 'Korea-U.S.'.

6. Ca 'well', 'here!' occurs always at the beginning of the sentence followed by a pause to signify that the speaker is going to suggest or produce something.

7. əttən 'what sort of' is a question noun-modifier word which denotes the quality or characteristics of the following noun. Compare with musın 'what kind of' which denotes the type, essense or denomination of the following noun.

8. Talın 'different', 'other' is a noun-modifier word which is formed from the verb stem talı- 'to be different'.

10. Kılıko 'And' occurs at the beginning of the sentence and is followed by a pause.

11. The verb stem of the noun-modifier word cakın 'small' is cak- 'to be small in size'; cək- means 'to be little in quantity'.

12. The verb stem philyo-ha- 'to be needed','to be necessary', is an intransitive verb which may be preceded by the emphasized subject but never by an object. Examples:

Talın kəs i philyo-hamnita.	'[I] need another one' ('A different thing is needed'.)

Chæk i philyo-hamnikka?	'Do you need a book?' ('Is a book needed?')

14. Taɪm 'the next time', 'next' occurs either as a free noun or as a determinative.

15. The verb stem tɪli- 'to give' is the politest equivalent of cu-. A sentence which ends in -(ɪ)l kka yo? is always a question sentence (See Grammar Note 2).

22. Tə 'more', '-er' occurs immediately before description verbs or other adverbs (See Grammar Note 3). The antonym of tə is the adverb təl 'less..'.

24. Ccali 'worth', 'value' is a post-noun which occurs only after s stated amount of money. If followed by another noun, the phrase ending in ccali describes the value of the noun. If not followed by another noun, the phrase ending in ccali indicates the denomination of money in the stated amount. Examples:

pæk Wən ccali sikye	a watch which is W100 worth
o-sip Wən ccali moca	a hat which is W50 worth
sip Wən ccali	W10 bill
o-sip Pul ccali	$50 bill

GRAMMAR NOTES

1. -n/ɪn/nɪn

The verb ending -n/ɪn/nɪn is added to a verb stem, or to a verb stem plus other suffix(es): -n is added to a description verb stem which ends in a vowel; -ɪn to a description verb stem which ends in a consonant; -nɪn, to an action verb stem. The inflected form which ends in -n/ɪn/nɪn occurs only before a noun as a modifier of the noun, and never alone nor before other classes of words. It shows only the present action or state of the modified noun. We shall call the words of this class Present Noun-Modifier Words and the -n/ɪn/nɪn ending the Present Noun-Modifier Ending. Examples:

up

pissan sikye	'(an) expensive watch'
mən hakkyo	'a school which is far'
nolan yənphil	'(a) yellow pencil'
kkamhan moca	'(a) black hat'

Group 2

cohın chæk	'(a) good book'
copın kil	'(a) narrow street'
nəlpın kyosil	'(a) large classroom'

Group 3

kanın salam	'a man who is going'
canın ai	'a sleeping child'
kalıchinın yəca	'a woman who is teaching'
chæk ıl ilknın haksæng	'a student who is reading a book'
næ ka pæunın mal	'the language that I'm learning'

2. -l/ıl kka yo? 'Shall I...?', 'Shall we...?', 'Will [it]... (do you think)?'

The construction -l/ıl kka yo? occurs only as a final form of a question sentence. If the subject or the topic in the sentence is the speaker, he asks the addressee's consent or permission for the action he is going to take. If the subject or the topic of the sentence includes both the speaker and addressee, the speaker asks the addressee whether he is interested in doing something. If the subject or the topic in the sentence is other than the speaker or the speaker plus addressee, the speaker asks the addressee for his opinion about the possibility of the action or description occurring in the future. Note: -l is added to a stem ending in a vowel; -ıl to a stem ending in a consonant (See Grammar Note 3, Unit 9). Examples:

Tapang e kal kka yo?	{'Shall I go to the tearoom?' 'Shall we go to the tearoom?'
Sənsæng cip e tıllıl kka yo?	{'Shall I stop by your house?' 'Shall we stop by the teacher's house?'
Kim Sənsæng i ol kka yo?	'Will Mr. Kim come?'
Hakkyo ka məl kka yo?	'(Do you think) the school will be far?'

3. Adverbs

Adverbs are a class of words which may or may not be inflected. They occur before and modify other inflected expressions (i.e. verbals, noun-modifiers, sentences, other adverbs). This class of words is distinguished from noun-modifiers (See Grammar Note 1) which occur only before nouns. There are some nouns which occur sometimes as adverbs also. For examples: are two kinds of adverbs: (1) one kind may be separated by a pause from the subsequent inflected expressions, and (2) the other kind occur without pause as an integral prat of an inflected expressions. The adverbs of group (1) are called Sentence Adverbs; those of the group (2), simply Adverbs. We have had so far the following kinds of adverbs.

kɪliko 'and'; kɪləna 'but'; kɪləmyən 'then'; ne 'yes'; aniyo 'no'; əttəhke 'how'; tto 'again', 'also'; kɪli '(not) so', 'in such a way'; com 'a little'; əsə 'please', 'quickly'; ttokpalo 'straight ahead'; cal 'well', etc.

Some of these adverbs occur at the beginning of sentences which succeed always other sentences: others occur before inflected expressions which do not need to be preceded by other sentences.

(a). tə 'more', '-er' and təl 'less'

Tə and təl occur without pause before noun-modifier words, verbals or other adverbs. They denote the comparative degree of the following descriptive expression. Compare:

1.	Kɪ kəs i cohsɪmnita.	'[It] is good.'
	Kɪ kəs i tə cohsɪmnita.	'[It] is better.'
	Kɪ kəs i təl cohsɪmnita.	'[It] is poorer.'
2.	I chæk i pissamnita.	'This book is expensive.'
	I chæk i tə pissamnita.	'This book is more expensive.'
	I chæk i təl pissamnita.	'This book is less expensive.'
3.	əlyəun mal	'[a] difficult language'
	tə əlyəun mal	'[a] more difficult language'
	təl əlyəun mal	'[a] less difficult language'
4.	Kim Sənsæng i Yəngə lɪl cal hamnita.	'Mr. Kim speaks English well.'
	Kim Sənsæng i Yəngə lɪl tə cal hamnita.	'Mr. Kim speaks English better.'
	Kim Sənsæng i (Ceimsɪ pota) Yəngə lɪl təl cal hamnita.	'Mr. Kim speaks English less well (than James).'

(b). tætanhi 'very'

Tætanhi 'very' occurs without pause before noun-modifiers, verbals or other adverbs. Compare:

1.	Chæk i pissamnita.	'The book is expensive.'
	Chæk i tætanhi pissamnita.	'The book is very expensive.'
2.	Ssan kutu lɪl sassə yo.	'[I] bought cheap shoes.'
	Tætanhi ssan kutu lɪl sassə yo.	'[I] bought very cheap shoes.'

3. Kim Sənsæng i Yəngə lıl cal mal-hæ yo — 'Mr. Kim speaks English well.'

Kim Sənsæng i Yəngə lıl tætanhi cal mal-hæ yo. — 'Mr. Kim speaks English very well.'

4. Counters: cang, can, kwən, kæ, pun, mali, pəl, tæ

In Unit 4, we noticed that certain counters such as Wən 'Korean monetary unit' occur only after numerals of character origin. The counters cang, can, kwən, kæ, pun, etc. are some of the commonly used counters which occur only after Korean numerals.

(a). Cang is used in counting such things as paper, letters, towels, sheets, flat glasses, etc.

thaipı congi tasəs cang	'5 sheets of typing paper'
phyənci tu cang	'two letters'
tamyo se cang	'three blankets'

(b). Can is used in counting cups or glasses of liquid.

khəphi han can	'a cup of coffee'
sul tu can	'two glasses of wine'

(c). Kwən is used in counting books.

yəksa chæk yələ kwən	'several volumes of history books'
Yəngə chæk tu kwən ıl sassə yo.	'I bought two English books.'

(d). Kæ is used in counting common object nouns such as pencils, desks, chairs, etc.

Yənphil han kæ cuse yo.	'Give me a pencil.'
Chæksang i tasəs kæ issə yo.	'There are five desks.'
Iyca ka myəch* kæ issımnikka?	'How many chairs are there?'

*myəch 'how many' is a determinative which occurs before counters as a question word.

(e). Pun or salam is used in counting persons. Pun is the honorific equivalent of salam.

sənsæng se pun	'three teachers'
haksæng tu salam	'two students'
Mikuk salam yələ pun	'several Americans'

(f). Mali is used in counting animals.

mal han mali	'one horse'
so tu mali	'two cattle'
kæ se mali	'three dogs'
koyangi ne mali	'four cats'

(g). Pəl is used in counting suits

yangpok tu pəl	'two suits'

(h). Tæ is used in counting vehicles, airplanes, machines, etc.

catongcha yələ tæ	'several automobiles'
pihængki se tæ	'three airplanes'

Note that all the counters occur typically after the determinative myəch 'how many?'. Also note that in Korean things are counted in the following manner: Nominal + Numeral + Counter.

DRILLS

A. Substitution Drills

1. Yəki Hankuk mal sacən i issımnikka?	Do you have a Korean dictionary here?
2. Yəki Yəng-Han sacən (i) issımnikka?	Do you have an English-Korean dictionary here?
3. Yəki thaiphı congi (ka) issımnikka?	Do you have typewriter paper here?
4. Yəki munpangkucəm (i) issımnikka?	Is there a stationary shop here?
5. Yəki yələ kaci congi (ka) issımnikka?	Do you have several kinds of paper here?
6. Yəki cohın sacən (i) issımnikka?	Do you have a good dictionary here?
7. Yəki əttən sacən (i) issımnikka?	What kind of dictionary do you have here?
8. Yəki talın kəs (i) issımnikka?	Do you have a different one here?
9. Yəki khın chæk (i) issımnikka?	Do you have a big book here?
10. Yəki cakın sacən (i) issımnikka?	Do you have a small dictionary here?
11. Yəki pissan sacən (i) issımnikka?	Do you have any expensive dictionaries here?
12. Yəki ssan congi (ka) issımnikka?	Do you have cheap paper here?

B. Subsitution Drill

1. Yəng-Han sacen mal imnikka?	Do you mean an English-Korean dictionary?
2. I cip mal imnikka?	Do you mean this house?
3. Pissan congi mal imnikka?	Do you mean expensive paper?
4. Yələ kaci mal imnikka?	Do you mean several kinds?
5. Khın sukən mal imnikka?	Do you mean a big towel?
6. Mikuk salam mal imnikka?	Do you mean the Americans?
7. ənı kəs mal imnikka?	Which do you mean?
8. Musın sacən mal imnikka?	What dictionary do you mean?
*9. ənce mal imnikka?	When do you mean?
10. Nuku mal imnikka?	Whom do you mean?
11. Muəs mal imnikka?	What do you mean?
12. əti mal imnikka?	Where do you mean?
13. əttəhke mal imnikka?	How do you mean?
14. Myəch salam mal imnikka?	How many people do you mean?

C. Substitution Drill

1.	Kı kəs, com poyə cusipsiyo.	Please show [me] that.
*2.	Cə kılim, com poyə cusipsiyo.	Please show [me] that picture.
3.	Kı capci, com poyə cusipsiyo.	Please show me that magazine.
4.	Cə sinmun, com poyə cusipsiyo.	Please show me that newspaper.
5.	Nolan yangmal, com poyə cusipsiyo.	Please show me some yellow socks.
6.	Phalan kəs, com poyə cusipsiyo.	Please show me a blue one.
7.	Kkamhan kutu, com poyə cusipsiyo.	Please show me some black shoes.
8.	Hayan waisyassı, com poyə cusipsiyo.	Please show me some white shirts.
9.	Ppalkan os, com poyə cusipsiyo.	Please show me a red dress.

D. Substitution Drill

1.	Talın kəs to issımnita.	[We] also have a different one(s).
2.	Cohın kəs to issımnita.	[We] also have a good one.
3.	Pissan kəs to issımnita.	[We] also have an expensive one.
4.	Ssan kəs to issımnita.	[We] also have a cheap one.
5.	Khın kəs to issımnita.	[We] also have a big one.
6.	Cakın kəs to issımnita.	[We] also have a small one.
7.	Nolan kəs to issımnita.	[We] also have a yellow one.
8.	Ppalkan kəs to issımnita.	[We] also have a red one.
9.	Phalan kəs to issımnita.	[We] also have a blue one.
*10.	Kathın kəs to issımnita.	[We] also have the same thing.
*11.	Alimtaun kəs to issımnita.	[We] also have a beautiful one.
*12.	Yeppın kəs to issımnita.	[We] also have a pretty one.
*13.	Nəlpın kəs to issımnita.	[We] also have a wide one.
*14.	Copın kəs to issımnita.	[We] also have a narrow one.

E. Substitution Drill

1.	Talın kəs ın əttəhsımnikka?	How is the other one?
2.	Talın kəs ın əlma imnikka?	How much is the other one?
3.	Talın kəs ın cohsımnikka?	Is the other one good?
4.	Talın kəs ın nappımnikka?	Is the other one bad?
5.	Talın kəs ın khımnikka?	Is the other one big?
6.	Talın kəs ın caksımnikka?	Is the other one small?
7.	Talın kəs ın əpsımnikka?	Don't you have a different one?
8.	Talın kəs ın issımnikka?	Do you have another one?
9.	Talın kəs ın talımnikka?	Is the other one different?
*10.	Talın kəs ın alımtapsımnikka?	Is the other one beautiful?
*11.	Talın kəs ın yeppımnikka?	Is the other one pretty?
*12.	Talın kəs ın nə(l)psımnikka?	Is the other one wide?
*13.	Talın kəs ın ċopsımnikka?	Is the other one narrow?
*14.	Talın kəs ın kathsımnikka?	Is the other one the same?
*15.	Talın kəs ın swipsımnikka?	Is the other one easy?
*16.	Talın kəs ın əlyəpsımnikka?	Is the other one difficult?

F. Substitution Drill

1.	Talın kəs i philyo-hamnikka?	Do [you] need anything else?
2.	Yəng-Han sacən (i) philyo-hamnikka?	Do you need an E-K dictionary?
3.	Han-Yəng sacən (i) philyo-hammikka?	Do you need a K-E dictionary?
4.	Phen kwa congi (ka) philyo-hamnikka?	Do you need a pen and paper?
5.	Chæksang kwa ıyca (ka) philyo-hamnikka?	Do you need a desk and a chair?
6.	Moca wa kutu (ka) philyo-hamnikka?	Do you need a hat and shoes?
7.	Yəphil kwa kongchæk (i) philyo-hamnikka?	Do you need a pencil and a note-book?
8.	Sacən kwa congi (ka) philyo-hamnikka?	Do you need a dictionary and paper?

G. Substitution Drill

1.	Phen kwa congi nın əti esə phamnikka?	Where can I buy pens and paper? ('Where do [they] sell pens and paper?')
2.	Yangmal (kwa) yangpok ın əti esə phamnikka?	Where can I buy socks and suits?
3.	Sinmum (kwa) capci nın əti esə phamnikka?	Where can I buy newspapers and magazines?
4.	Sikye (wa) son-sukən ın əti esə phamnikka?	Where can I buy watches and handkerchiefs?
5.	Congi (wa) phen ın əti esə phamnikka?	Where can I buy paper and pens?
6.	Yangmal (kwa) kutu nın əti esə phamnikka?	Where can I buy socks and shoes?
7.	Chæksang (kwa) ıyca nın əti esə phamnikka?	Where can I buy tables and chairs?
8.	Moca (wa) kutu nın əti esə phamnikka?	Where can I buy hats and shoes?
9.	Yənphil (kwa) kongchæk ın əti esə phamnikka?	Where can I buy pencils and notebooks?

H. Substitution Drill

1.	Muəs ıl tılil kka yo?	What would you like? ('What shall I give you?')
2.	ənı chæk (ıl) tılil kka yo?	Which book would you like?
3.	Musın sæk (ıl) tılil kka yo?	What color would you like?
4.	Talın kəs (ıl) tılil kka yo?	Would you like a different one?
5.	Tə ssan congi (lıl) tılil kka yo?	Would you like cheaper paper?
6.	Tə pissan sikyo (lıl) tılil kka yo?	Would you like a more expensive watch?
7.	Tə cohın kəs (ıl) tılil kka yo?	Would you like a better one?
8.	Tə cakın kəs (ıl) tılil kka yo?	Would you like a smaller one?
9.	Tə khın kəs (ıl) tılil kka yo?	Would you like a bigger one?
10.	Tə hayan kəs (ıl) tılil kka yo?	Would you like a whiter one?

I. Transformation Drill (based on Grammar Note 1)

Tutor: Chæk i pissamnita.	'The book is expensive.'
Student: Pissan chæk i issımnita.	'There's an expensive book.'
1. Sacən i cohsımnita.	Cohın sacən i issımnita.
2. Cip i khımnita.	Khın cip i issımnita.
3. Mannyənphil i caksımnita.	Cakın mannyəphil i issımnita.
4. Yangpok i kkamhamnita.	Kkamhan yangpok i issımnita.
5. Waisyassı ka hayamnita.	Hayan waisyassı ka issımnita.
6. Yənphil i nolahsımnita.	Nolan yənphil i issımnita.
7. Os i ppalkahsımnita.	Ppalkan os i issımnita.
8. Sicang i kakkapsımnita.	Kakkaun sicang i issımnita.
9. Kılim i alımtapsımnita.	Alımtaun kılim i issımnita.
10. Kyosil i nəlpsımnita.	Nəlpın kyosil i issımnita.
11. Samusil i copsımnita.	Copın samusil i issımnita.
12. Sæk i talımnita.	Talın sæk i issımnita.
13. Sacən i pissamnita.	Pissan sacən i issımnita.
14. Kılim i kathsımnita.	Kathın kılim i issımnita.
15. Chæk i swipsımnita.	Swiun chæk i issımnita.
16. Mal i əlyəpsımnita.	əlyəun mal i issımnita.

J. Transformation Drill (based on Grammar Note 1)

Tutor: Haksæng i kongpu-hamnita.	'A student (is) study(ing).'
Student: Kongpu-hanın haksæng i issımnita.	'There is a student who is studying.'
1. Salam i omnita.	Onın salam i issımnita.
2. Mikuk salam i Hankuk mal ıl (mal-) hamnita.	Hankuk mal ıl (mal-)hanın Mikuk salam i issımnita.
3. Hankuk haksæng i Mikuk e kamnita.	Mikuk e kanın Hankuk haksæng i issımnita.
4. Sənsæng i Yəngə lıl kalıchimnita.	Yəngə lıl kalıchinın sənsæng i issımnita.
5. Puin i kutu lıl samnita.	Kutu lıl sanın puin i issımnita.
6. Ai ka chæk ıl ilksımnita.	Chæk ıl ilknın ai ka issımnita.
7. Mikuk yəca ka kil ıl mulə pomnita.	Kil ıl mulə ponın Mikuk yəca ka issımnita.

8. Hańkuk yəca ka Cungkuk mal ɪl kalɪchimnita. — Cungkuk mal ɪl kalɪchinɪn Hankuk yəca ka issɪmnita.

9. Haksæng i kɪ pun ɪl amnita. — Kɪ pun ɪl anɪn haksæng i issɪmnita.

10. Yəca ka kɪlim ɪl pomnita. — Kɪlim ɪl ponɪn yəca ka issɪmnita.

End of Tape 4A

Tape 4B

K. Response Drill (based on Grammar Note 4)

Tutor: Congi ka myəch cang issɪmnikka? /tu(l)/ — 'How many sheets of paper are there? /two/

Student: Tu cang issɪmnita. — 'There are two sheets [of paper]'.

1. Sənsæng i myəch pun issɪmnikka? /se(s)/ — Se pun issɪmnita.
2. Yənphil ɪl myəch kæ sassɪmnikka? /tasəs/ — Tasəs kæ sassɪmnita.
3. Haksæng i myəch salam issɪmnikka? /ne(s)/ — Ne salam issɪmnita.
4. Mikuk haksæng i myəch salam kongpu-hamnikka? /ilkop/ — Ilkop salam (i) kongpu-hamnita.
5. Kyosil e ɪyca ka myəch kæ issɪmnikka? /ahop/ — Ahop kæ issɪmnita.
6. Yəki e chæk i myəch kwən issɪmnikka? /yəl-se(s)/ — Yəl-se kwən issimnita.
7. Khophi lɪl myəch can masimnikka? /yələ/ — Yələ can masimnita.
8. Hakkyo e kyosil i myəch kæ issɪmnikka? /sɪmu(l)/ — Sɪmu kæ issɪmnita.
9. Kæ lɪl myəch mali pwassɪmnikka? /tasəs/ — Tasəs mali pwassɪmnita.
10. Yangpok ɪl myəch pəl sassɪmnikka? /tu(l)/ — Tu pəl sassɪmnita.

L. Expansion Drill (Supply the proper counter /pun, salam, kæ, cang, kwən/ and expand the sentence as in the example.)

Tutor: Sənsæng i issımnita. /hana/	'There is (a) teacher.' /one/
Student: Sənsæng i han pun issımnita.	'There is one teacher.'
1. Yənphil i issımnita. /tul/	Yənphil i tu kæ issımnita.
2. Haksæng i issımnita. /nes/	Haksæng i ne salam issımnita.
3. Congi ka issımnita. /yəsəs/	Congi ka yəsəs cang issımnita.
4. Chæksang ıl sassımnita. /tasəs/	Chæksang ıl tasəs kæ sassımnita.
5. Sinmun ıl sassımnita. /hana/	Sinmun ıl han cang sassımnita.
6. Kyosil e ıyca ka issımnita. /ilkop/	Kyosil e ıyca ka ilkop kæ issımnita.
7. Yəngə chæk ıl sakessımnita. /yətəl/	Yəngə chæk ıl yətəl kwən sakessımnita.
8. Na nın achim e khəphi lıl masimnita. /se(s)/	Na nın achim e khəphi lıl se can masimnita.
9. Congi lıl cusipsiyo. /tul/	Congi lıl tu cang cusipsiyo.
10. Mikuk salam ıl pwassımnita. /ses/	Mikuk salam ıl se salam pwassımnita.

M. Response Drill (Use <u>tætanhi</u> in the proper place.)

Tutor: Kı sacən i cohsımnikka?	'Is that dictionary good?'
Student: Ne, tætanhi cohsımnita.	'Yes, [it] is very good.'
1. Kı chæk i pissamnikka?	Ne, tætanhi pissamnita.
2. Cəngkəcang i kakkapsımnikka?	Ne, tætanhi kakkapsımnita.
3. Hankuk yəca ka yeppımnikka?	Ne, tætanhi yeppımnita.
4. Samusil i copsımnikka?	Ne, tætanhi copsımnita.
5. I chæk i talımnikka?	Ne, tætanhi talımnita.
6. Cə kutu ka kkamahsımnikka?	Ne, tætanhi kkamahsımnita.
7. Ian-Yəng sacən i philyo-hamnikka?	Ne, tætanhi philyo-hamnita.
8. Pak Sənsæng i cal kalıchimnikka?	Ne, tætanhi cal kalıchimnita.
9. Ceimsi Sənsæng i Yəngə lıl cal (mal-)hamnikka?	Ne, tætanhi cal (mal-)hamnita.
10. Os i ppalkahsımnikka?	Ne, tætanhi ppalkahsımnita.

N. Response Drill

Tutor: Muəs ıl tılil kka yo? /khal/	'What would you like? ('What shall I give you?') /knife/
Student: Khal ıl cusipsiyo.	'Please give [me] a knife.'
1. ənı chæk ıl tılil kka yo? /Hankuk mal sacən/	Hankuk mal sacən ıl cusipsiyo.
2. Musın sæk il tılil kka yo? /phalan sæk/	Phalan sæk ıl cusipsiyo.
3. Talın kəs ıl tılil kka yo? /kı kəs/	Kı kəs ıl cusipsiyo.
4. Pissan yənphil ıl tılil kka yo? /com ssan kəs/	Com ssan kəs ıl cusipsiyo.
5. Yəng-Han sacən ıl tılil kka yo? /Han-Yəng sacən/	Han-Yəng sacən ıl cusipsiyo.
6. Cakın sukən ıl tılil kka yo? /khın son-sukən/	Khın son-sukən ıl cusipsiyo.
7. Nolan sæk yangmal ıl tılil kka yo? /kkaman yangmal/	Kkaman yangmal ıl cusipsiyo.
8. Mikuk moca lıl tılil kka yo? /Ilpon moca/	Ilpon moca lıl cusipsiyo.

O. Response Drill

Tutor: Cip e kal kka yo?	{'Should I go home?' / 'Do you want me to go home?'}
Student: Ne, kasipsiyo.	'Yes, you should ('please go').'
1. I chæk ıl sal kka yo?	Ne, sasipsiyo.
2. Kim Sənsæng il mannal kka yo?	Ne, mannasipsiyo.
3. Kil ıl mulə pol kka yo?	Ne, mulə posipsiyo.
4. Yəki e issıl kka yo?	Ne, {issısipsiyo. / kyesipsiyo.}
5. I chæk ıl phal(ıl) kka yo?	Ne, phalısipsiyo.
6. Yəng-Han sacən ıl tılil kka yo?	Ne, cusipsiyo.
7. Kılim ıl kılil kka yo?	Ne, kılisipsiyo.
8. Sənsæng cip e tıllıl kka yo?	Ne, tıllısipsiyo.
9. Kı ai lıl chacıl kka yo?	Ne, chacısipsiyo.
10. I chæk ıl ilkıl kka yo?	Ne, ilkısipsiyo.

P. Response Drill.

Tutor: Hakkyo lo kal kka yo? /cip/	'Shall we go to school?' /house/
Student: Cip ılo kapsita.	'Let's go to the house, [instead].'
1. Hankuk mal ıl pæul kka yo? /Yəngə/	Yəngə lıl pæupsita.
2. Pækhwacəm esə sal kka yo? /sangcəm/	Sangcəm esə sapsita.
3. Kim Sənsæng ıl mannal kka yo? /Ceimsı Sənsæng/	Cemisı Sənsæng ıl mannapsita.
4. Onıl pækhwacəm e tıllıl kka yo? /næil/	Næil tıllıpsita.
5. Onıl ın Cungkuk mal ıl (mal-)hal kka yo? /Yəngə/	Yəngə lıl (mal-)hapsita.
6. Sinumn ıl ilkıl kka yo? /capci/	Capci lıl ilkıpsita.
7. Kyosil esə kongpu-hal kka yo? /samusil/	Samusil esə kongpu-hapsita.
8. Cənyək e samusil e issıl kka yo? /cip/	Cip e issıpsita.

Q. Response Drill (Answer the question in Informal Polite Speech beginning with Aniyo.)

Tutor: Hakkyo e kassımnikka?	'Did you go to school?'
Student: Aniyo, kaci anhəssə yo.	'No, I didn't (go).'
1. Kı sacən i cohsımnikka?	Aniyo, cohci anhə yo.
2. Cakın kəs ıl sakessımnikka?	Aniyo, saci anhkessə yo.
3. Tto talın kəs i philyo-hamnikka?	Aniyo, philyo-haci anhə yo.
4. Phen kwa congi lıl phaləssımnikka?	Aniyo, phalcı anhəssə yo.
5. Congi lıl wənhasimnikka?	Aniyo, wənhaci anhə yo.
6. Sinæ e munpangkucəm i issəssımnikka?	Aniyo, əpəssə yo.
7. Kil ıl mulə pwassımnikka?	Aniyo, mulə poci anhəssə yo.
8. Tə ssan kəs ın əpsımnikka?	Aniyo, issə yo.
9. Yəki esə phen ıl pha(lı)mnikka?	Aniyo, phalci anhə yo.
10. Chæk kaps i ssamnikka?	Aniyo, ssaci anhə yo.
11. Yəng-Han sacən i issımnikka?	Aniyo, əpsə yo.
12. Nolan sæk ıl cohahamnikka?	Aniyo, cohahaci anhə yo.

R. Grammar Drill

Tutor: I kəs i issımnita. /talın kəs/	'[We] have this.' /a different one/
Student: Talın kəs to issımnikka?	{'Do you have any others?' 'Do you have a different one, too?'
1. Cakın chæk i cohsımnita. /khın chæk/	Khın chæk to cohsımnikka?
2. Congi ka philyo-hamnita. /yənphil/	Yənphil to philyo-hamnikka?
3. I kəs ın pissamnita. /cə kəs/	Cə kəs pissamnikka?
4. Na nın Hankuk mal ıl pæumnita. /Ceimsı/	Ceimsi to Hankuk mal ıl pæumnikka?
5. Sukən ıl sassımnita. /yangpok/	Yangpok to sassımnikka?
6. Sacən ıl wənhamnita. /capci/	Capci to wənhamnikka?
7. Yəki esə kutu lıl phamnita. /moca/	Yəki esə moca to phamnikka?
8. Pak Sənsæng i kalıchimnita. /I Sənsæng/	I Sənsæng to kalıchimnikka?
9. Ceimsı Sənsæng ıl mannamnita. /chinku/	Chinku to mannamnikka?
10. Hankuk mal i swipci anhsımnita. /Ilpon mal/	Ilpon mal to swipci anhsımnikka?
11. Hankuk mal ıl mal-haci anhsımnita. /Cungkuk mal/	Cungkuk mal to mal-haci anhsımnikka?

S. Grammar Drill

Tutor: Hakkyo ka məmnita. /sinæ/	'The shcool is far.' /downtown/
Student: Sinæ to məmnita.	'Downtown is far, too.'
1. Chæk i philyo-hamnita. /yənphil/	Yənphil to philyo-hamnita.
2. I kəs i issımnita. /talın kəs/	Talın kəs to issımnita.
3. Na nın Yəngə lıl mal-hamnita. /Ceimsı/	Ceimsı to Yəngə lıl mal-hamnita.
4. Na nın Hankuk mal ıl kalıchimnita. /Yəngə/	Na nın Yəngə to kalıchimnita.
5. Khın sacən i cohsımnita. /cakın sacən/	Cakın sacən to cohsımnita.
6. Moca lıl sal kka hamnita. /kutu/	Kutu to sal kka hamnita.
7. Yəkı esə capci lıl pha(lı)mnita. /sinmun/	Yəki esə sinmun to pha(lı)mnita.
8. Kyosil i nəlphsımnita. /samusil/	Samusil to nəlphsımnita.

9. Mikuk yəca nın alımtapsimnita. /Hankuk yəca/	Hankuk yəca to alımtapsımnita.
10. Kim Sənsæng ıl chacsımnita. /I Sənsæng/	I Sənsæng to chacsımnita.

T. Grammar Drill

Tutor: Mikuk pæsakwan i kakkapsımnita. /Mikuk Kongpowən/	'The U.S. Embassy is near.' /USIA/
Student: Mikuk Kongpowən i tə kakkapsımnita.	'USIA is nearer.'
1. Yənphil i pissamnita. /mannyənphil/	Mannyənphil i tə pissamnita.
2. I kılim i alımtapsımnita. /cə kılim/	Cə kılim i tə alımtapsımnita.
3. Hankuk mal kyosil i nəlpsımnita. /Cungkuk mal kyosil/	Congkuk mal kyosil i tə nəlpsımnita.
4. Næ moca ka cohsımnita. /Kim Sənsæng moca/	Kim Sənsæng moca ka tə cohsımnita.
5. Ilpon mal i swipsımnita. /Cungkuk mal/	Cungkuk mal i tə swipsımnita.
6. Cungkuk mal i əlyəpsımnita. /Hankuk mal/	Hankuk mal i tə əlyəpsımnita.
7. Khın sacən i ssamnita. /cakın sacən/	Cakın sacən i tə ssamnita.
8. Ilpon ın caksımnita. /Hankuk/	Hankuk ın tə caksımnita.
9. Na nın sinmun ıl cohahamnita. /capci/	Na nın capci lıl tə cohahamnita.
10. Pak Sənsæng ın Yəngə lıl cal hamnita. /Kim Sənsæng/	Kim Sənsæng ın (Yəngə lıl) tə cal hamnita.

U. Response Exercise (Answer the question based on reality.)

Tutor: Yənphil kwa chæk ɪn ənɪ kəs i tə pissamnikka? — 'Which one is more expensive, a pencil or a book?'

Student: Chæk i tə pissamnita. — 'A book is more expensive.'

1. Yəngə wa Hankuk mal ɪn ənɪ mal i tə swipsɪmnikka? — Yəngə ka tə swipsɪmnita.
2. Hankuk mal kyosil kwa Cungkuk mal kyosil ɪn ənɪ kəs i tə nəlpsɪmnikka? — Cungkuk mal kyosil i tə nəlpsɪmnita.
3. Yəngə wa Hankuk mal ɪn ənɪ mal i tə əlyəpsɪmnikka? — Hankuk mal i tə əlyəpsɪmnita.
4. Hankuk kwa Ilpon ɪn əti ka tə caksɪmnikka? — Hankuk i tə caksɪmnita.
5. Kim Sənsæng kwa Pak Sənsæng ɪn nuka Yəngə lɪl tə cal hamnikka? — Kim Sənsæng i tə cal hamnita.
6. Sənsæng e yangpok kwa moca nɪn ənɪ kəs i tə ssamnikka? — Moca ka tə ssamnita.
7. Nyuyok kwa Wəsingthon ɪn əti lɪl tə cohahamnikka? — Wəsingthon ɪl tə cohahamnita.

V. Transformation Drill

Tutor: I chæk i ssamnita. — 'This book is cheap.'

Student: Tə ssan chæk i issɪmnita. — 'There's a cheaper one (book).'

1. I kɪlim i alɪmtapsɪmnita. — Tə alɪmtawn kɪlim i issɪmnita.
2. I kyosil i nəlphsɪmnita. — Tə nəlpɪn kyosil i issɪmnita.
3. I samusil i copsɪmnita. — Tə copɪn samusil i issɪmnita.
4. I sacən i cohsɪmnita. — Tə cohɪn sacən i issɪmnita.
5. I mal i swipsɪmnita. — Tə swiwn mal i issɪmnita.
6. I kyosil i caksɪmnita. — Tə cakɪn kyosil i issɪmnita.
7. I chæk i əlyəpsɪmnita. — Tə əlyəun chæk i issɪmnita.
8. I mannyənphil i ssamnita. — Tə ssan manyənphil i issɪmnita.
9. I kəs ɪl cohahamnita. — Tə cohahanɪn kəs i issɪmnita.
10. I pun i (Yəngə lɪl) cal hamnita. — (Yəngə lɪl) tə cal hanɪn pun i issɪmnita.

EXERCISES

1. Mr. Kim asks you: — You respond:

Mr. Kim asks you:	You respond:
a. to show him the dictionary.	'Which one do you mean?'
b. to give him that.	'What do you mean?'
c. to go downtown together.	'When do you mean?'
d. to study Korean together.	'Where do you mean?'
e. if you know him.	'Who(m) to you mean?'
f. if Korean is difficult.	'Yes, it is.'
g. if you have read a book.	'What kind of book do you mean?'
h. if she teaches Korean.	'Who do you mean?'
i. to buy this suit.	'How much do you want?'

2. You ask the store-clerk: — He replies:

You ask the store-clerk:	He replies:
a. if he carries any good K-E dictionary.	'Yes, we do.'
b. to show you one.	'Here you are.'
c. how it is.	'It's very good, but we have another kind.'
d. how the other one is.	'It's a little larger one.'
e. which one is better.	'They are the same.'
f. if the bigger one is more expensive.	'The price is also the same.'
g. where they sell fountain-pens and notebooks.	'(They sell) at the stationary-store.'
h. how much they charge for a cup of coffee.	'W20.'
i. if the department stores also carry magazines and newspapers.	'Yes, they do.'

3. Ask Mr. Kim:

a. How many cups of coffee he drinks in the morning.

b. How many students there are.

c. How many books he has read.

d. How many chairs there are in the room.

e. How many sheets of paper he needs.

f. How many colors he wants.

g. How many hats he'll buy.

h. How many teachers he has.

i. How many suits he has.

j. How many horses there are on the street.

4. Tell Pak Sənsæng that:

a. You like a bigger one.

b. You want a little more expensive watch.

c. You need a pencil and paper.

d. A beautiful woman came to your house.

e. There is no English-Korean dictionary here.

f. French is easy, but Korean is very difficult

g. The sotre on the left is a stationary shop, and the building on the right is a department store.

h. The dictionary is small, but it is a very good one.

i. The small one is fine for you, but you need the other one, too.

j. You are studying Korean, and your friend is teaching German.

k. You met a pretty Korean girl.

l. There is a child who is reading a newspaper.

m. You know an American who speaks Korean.

n. You don't know the lady who is buying shoes.

o. You have learned Korean, but you don't speak well.

p. Korean is not easy, but you like it.

q. Mr. Park doesn't speaks Chinese, but he reads it well.

End of Tape 4B

Tape 5A

제 6 과 시간

(대화 A)

지금
몇, 몇
몇 시
1. A: 지금 몇 시이에요?

여덟 시
오 분
오 분 전
2. B: 여덟 시 오 분 전입니다.

일
시작
시작합니까
3. A: 몇 시에 일이 시작합니까?

아침
여덟 시 삼십 분
4. B: (아침) 여덟 시 삼십 분에 시작합니다.

하루
시간
몇 시간
5. A: 그럼, 하루에 몇 시간 일을 하세요?

UNIT 6. Time

BASIC DIALOGUES FOR MEMORIZATION

Dialogue A

A

cikɪm	now
myəch mech/met/ }	how many?; what?
myəch-si/myəssi/	what time
1. Cikɪm myəch-si (i)ye yo?	What time is it (now)?

B

yətəl(p)-si/yətəlssi/	8 o'clock
o pun	5 minute(s)
o pun cən	5 minutes of; 5 minutes before
2. Yətəl(p)-si o pun cən imnita.	It's five minutes before 8.

A

il	work; job
sicak	beginning
sicak-hamnikka	do [you] begin?; does [it] begin?
3. Myəch-si e il i sicak-hamnikka?	What time do you start work? ('What times does work begin?')

B

achim	morning
yətəl(p)-si samsip pun	8:30
4. (Achim) yətəl(p)-si samsip pun e sicak-hamnita.	I start at 8:30. ('It begins at 8:30 a.m.')

A

halu	one day
sikan	time; hour
myəch sikan/myəssikan/	how many hours?
5. Kɪləm, halu e myəch sikan il ɪl hase yo?	How many hours do you work a day (then)?

여덟 시간(동안)
일합니다
6. B: 여덟 시간(동안) 일합니다.

대개
집에
7. A: 대개 몇 시에 집에 가세요?

다섯 시 쯤
사무실
떠납니다
사무실을 떠납니다
8. B: 대개 다섯 시 쯤 사무실을 떠납니다.

(대화 B)

며칠
9. A: 오늘이 며칠이지요?

삼월
일일
10. B: 삼월 일일입니다.

달
이 달
벌써
11. A: 이 달이 벌써 삼월입니까?

B

yətəl(p) sikan (tongan)	for eight hours
il-hamnita	[I] work
6. Yətəl(p) sikan (tongan) il-hamnita.	I work (for) eight hours.

A

tækæ	usually
cip e	to the house; home
7. Tækæ myəch-si e cip e kase yo?	What time to you usually go home?

B

tasəs-si ccɪm	around 5 o'clock
samusil	office
ttənamnita	[I] leave
samusil ɪl ttənamnita	[I] leave office
8. Tækæ tasəs-si ccɪm samusil ɪl ttənamnita.	I usually leave my office around 5 o'clock.

Dialogue B

A

myəchil	what day?; what date?; some days
9. Onɪl i myəchil ici yo?	What's today's date?

B

Sam-wəl	March
il il	the 1st(day of the month)
10. Sam-wəl il il imnita.	(It's) March 1st.

A

tal	month; moon
i tal	this month
pəlssə	already
11 I tal i pəlssə Sam-wəl imnikka?	Is it March already? ('Is this month already March?')

이월
이십 팔일
12. B: 예, 그렇습니다. 어제가 이월 이십 팔일이었읍니다.

무슨 요일
13. A: 그러면, 오늘이 무슨 요일이에요?

목요일
14. B: 목요일입니다.

일하러
일하러 갑니다
15. A: 어제 일하러 갔읍니까?

16. B: 아니요, 일하러 가지 않었읍니다.

주일
이 주일
사흘
지난 사흘
지난 사흘 동안
쉬었읍니다
17. 이 주일에는 지난 사흘 동안 쉬었읍니다.

왜요
몸
아픕니까
(몸이) 아펐읍니까
18. A: 왜요? 몸이 아펐읍니까?

B

I-wəl	February
isip-phal il	28th (of the month)
12. Ne, kɪləhsɪmnita. əce ka I-wəl isip-phal il iəssɪmnita.	Yes, it is. Yesterday was February 28th.

A

musɪn yoil	what day of the week?
13. Kɪləmyən, onɪl i musɪn yoil iye yo?	What day of the week is it (today), then?

B

Mokyoil	Thursday
14. Mokyoil imnita.	[It's] Thursday.

A

il-halə	in order to work; to work
il-halə kamnita	[I] go to work
15. əce il-halə kassɪmnikka?	Did [you] go to work yesterday?

B

16. Aniyo, il-halə kaci anhəssɪmnita.	No, I didn't (go to work).
cuil	week
i cuil	this week
sahɪl	three days
cinan sahɪl	last three days
cinan sahɪl tongan	for the last three days
swiəssɪmnita	[I] rested; [I] took a rest
17. I cuil e nɪn cinan sahɪl tongan swiəssɪmnita.	This week I took three days off. ('As for in this week I took a rest for the last three days.')

A

wæ yo	how come?; why?
mom	body
aphɪmnikka	are [you] sick?; are [you] hurt?
(mom i) aphəssɪmnikka	were [you] sick?
18. Wæ yo? Mom i aphəssɪmnikka?	Why? Were you sick?

휴가

받었었읍니다

19. B: 아니요, 휴가를 받었었읍니다.

B

	hyuka		vacation
	patəssəssımnita		[I] received, [I] had received
19.	Aniyo. Hyuka lıl patəssəssımnita.	No.	I took a vacation.

NOTES ON DIALOGUES

(Numbers correspond to the sentence numbers.)

1. Myəch and its variant mech 'how many', 'what', 'some', occurs either as a free noun or as a determinative. Before counters or certain nouns in question sentences, it means 'how many' or 'what'; in a statement sentence it means 'some'. As a free noun myəch means 'how many' in a question sentence, and 'some' or 'several' in a statement sentence. Myəch plus certain counters make up (question) noun phrases. For example, myəch-si 'what time' is a noun phrase which is used only in asking time. Each phrase of this type should be memorized as a phrase. Myəch is pronounced as /myəs/ before s; /myən/ before n; /myət/ before t, etc. When a vowel follows, the final sound ch is released and forms a syllable with the following vowel: myəch-si/myəssi/ 'what time', myəch salam/myəssalam/ 'how many poeple', myəch nal/myənnal/ 'how many days', myəch tal/myəttal/ 'how many months', myəch i/myəchi/ 'how many (as a subject)' in Myəch i issə yo? 'How many are there?'.

2. Pun 'minute' is a time counter which occurs only after numerals of Chinese character origin. Numeral + pun designates either a point in time or a duration of time. Example:

han-si o pun	'5 minutes after 1 o'clock'
o pun	'five minutes'

3. The verb stem sicak-ha- 'to begin' is formed from the noun sicak 'the beginning' by adding ha-. Sicak-ha- is used either as a transitive verb or as an intransitive verb. Compare:

Il i sicak-hamnita.	'The work begins.'
Il ıl sicak-hamnita.	'[I] begin the work.'

The antonym of sicak-ha- is either kkıth-na- 'to end', 'to be over' (intransitive verb), or kkıth-næ- 'to finish' (transitive verb).

5. Kıləm 'then' is the contracted form of kıləmyən 'if so' which is a sentence adverbial. Both forms occur at the beginning of a sentence and are followed by a pause. Sikan 'hour', 'time', occurs either as a time counter or as a free noun. As a counter after Korean numerals sikan means 'hour': han sikan 'one hour', tu sikan 'two hours', se sikan 'three hours', myəch sikan 'how

many hours', yələ sikan 'many hours', etc. As a free noun, it means 'time': Sikan i issımnikka? 'Do you have time?'.

Il-ha- 'to work' is a verb stem formed from the noun il 'work', 'job'. The antonym of il-ha- is no(l)- 'not to work', 'to play', 'to loaf'.

6. Tongan 'for', 'during' is a post-noun. The nominal that precedes usually is a time expression, and 'time expression + tongan' is an adverbial expression. Example: han sikan tongan 'for an hour', halu tongan 'for one day', il pun tongan 'for one minute', Il-wəl tongan 'during January', kı tongan 'in the meantime'.

8. Ccım 'about', 'around' is a post-noun which occurs after other nominal expressions (e.g. time, place names, quality or quantity expressions) and denotes approximation of the preceeding expressions. Examples:

han tal ccım	'about one month'
han tal tongan ccım	'for about one month'
Il-wəl ccım	'around January'
han sikan ccım	'about an hour'

The antonym of the verb stem ttəna- 'to leave' is tah- 'to arrive'.

9. Myəchil 'what date', 'some days' is one word; not a two-word compound of myəch + il.

11. The opposite word for pəlssə 'already' is acik '(not) yet' which also means 'still'. Compare:

Hakkyo ka acik sicak-haci anhəssımnita.	'School has not begun yet.'
Cə nın acik Hankuk mal ıl paəumnita.	'I'm still studying Korean.'

13. Yoil 'day of the week' occurs as a post-noun after certain nouns or determinatives. Examples: ənı yoil 'which day of the week', musın yoil 'what day of the week'.

14. Mokyoil 'Thursday' is one word. So is Ilyoil 'Sunday', Wəlyoil 'Monday', Hwayoil 'Tuesday', Suyoil 'Wednesday', Kɪmyoil 'Friday', Thoyoil 'Saturday'.

17. Halu 'one day', sahɪl 'three days' belong to a small class of one-word time expressions which enumerate days: halu 'one day', ithɪl 'two days', sahɪl 'three days', nahɪl 'four days', tassæ 'five days', yəssæ 'six days', ile 'seven days', yətɪle 'eight days', ahɪle 'nine days', yəlhɪl 'ten days'. This class of time expressions also is used infrequently to designate days of the month.

19. Hyuka 'vacation', 'leave' is distinguished from panghak 'school vacation'.

GRAMMAR NOTES

1. Time counters: nyən 'year', hæ 'year', -wəl 'month', tal 'month', cuil 'week', il 'day', nal 'day', -si 'o'clock', sikan 'hour', pun 'minute'. Korean time counters are classed in two groups: (a) those which occur after the numerals of Korean origin, and (b) those which occur after numerals of Chinese character origin. It is imperative to know the series of numerals with which each time counter is used.

The counters hæ 'year', tal 'month', cuil 'week', nal 'day', -si 'o'clock', sikan 'hour' occur after numerals of Korean origin.

The counters nyən 'year', -wəl 'month', cuil 'week', il 'day', pun 'minute' occur after numerals of Chinese character origin.

The above time counters are divided into three sub-classes without regard to the series of numerals with which they occur:

(a) Those which name:
1. the calendar months.............................. -wəl
2. hours.. -si

(b) Those which count:
1. the number of months............................. tal
2. the number of weeks.............................. cuil
3. the number of hours.............................. sikan
4. the number of days (for only 20 days, 30 days, 40 days, 50 days, 60 days)...................... nal

(c) Those which either:

1. name calendar years or enumerate years.............. nyən
2. name dates or enumerate days........................ il
3. specify the minutes or enumerate the minutes........ pun

Note that expressions of time in Korean are listed from the largest unit to the smallest unit: that is, in the order of year, month, day, hours, minute and second.

Note 1: Cuil 'week' is preceded by either set of numerals.

Note 2: For the words expressing the number of days from 1 day to 10 days, see number 17 of Notes on Dialogues in this Unit.

Note 3: The two time counters -wəl and -si are added to the numbers with a hyphen to signify that they occur only as parts of words which are expressions of time, i.e., -wəl for the names of months and -si for the hours of a day, respectively.

2. -ci yo?

We noticed in Unit 4 that the ci form occurs before the verb anh- 'not'. The ci form immediately followed by yo? (i.e. -ci yo?) occurs as an informal polite question sentence final form. If -ci yo? occurs without a preceding question word, the speaker expects the addresee to answer yes; if -ci yo? follows after a question word in the same sentence it simply substitutes for -(ı)mnikka? or (infinitive) + yo?. Compare: Give attention to the final intonations.

Group 1

Kim Sənsæng i Yəngə lıl mal-haci yo?	'Mr. Kim speaks English, doesn't he?'
Hakkyo ka məlci yo?	'The school is far, isn't it?'
Hankuk mal i əlyəpci yo?	'Korean is difficult, isn't it?'
Sənsæng ın Mikuk salam ici yo?	'You are an American, aren't you?'

Group 2

I kəs i muəs ici yo?	'What's this?'
Hakkyo ka əti e issci yo?	'Where is the school?'
Nuku lıl mannassci yo?	'Whom did [you] meet?'
Myəch-si e il ıl sicak-haci yo?	'(At) What time do [you] begin the work?'

Note that -ci yo may also occur as an informal polite final form of a statement, propositative or imperative sentence. We will learn more about it later.

3. -(ɪ)lə 'in order to-'

The verb ending -(ɪ)lə is added to an action verb stem, or to an action verb stem plus honorific suffix -(ɪ)si: -lə is added to a stem ending in a vowel and -ɪlə to a stem ending in a consonant. Tense suffixes do not occur in the inflected form ending in -(ɪ)lə. The (ɪ)lə form denotes that the following inflected expression in the same sentence occurs for the purpose of the action inflected by the -(ɪ)lə form. The verbs which follow the -(ɪ)lə form are usually ka- 'to go', o- 'to come', or tani- 'to attend'. Examples:

Na nɪn chæk (ɪl) ilkɪlə hakkyo e tɪllɪkessə yo.	'I will stop by school to read books.'
Chinku lɪl mannalə wassɪmnita.	'I came to meet a friend.'
Hankuk mal ɪl pæulə hakkyo e tanimnita.	'I am attending school to learn Korean.'
Chæk (ɪl) salə sinæ e an kakessə yo?	'Wouldn't you go downtown to buy books?'

4. Adverb phrases

In Unit 1 we learned that two or more nouns make up Noun Phrases, and that they occur as though they were one noun. Note that a noun phrase is used as a nominal. In Unit 5, we defined Adverbs. (See Grammar Notes 3, Unit 5.) If two or more words occur together and are used as if they were one adverb we shall call them Adverb Phrases. Hereafter, we shall use the term Adverbial for any word or phrase which occurs in a position where an adverb may be substituted. Note that some adverbials also occur as nominals but most adverbials are used only as adverbials. Nouns + particles are often used as adverb phrases. Examples:

(a) Question Adverb Phrases:

əti esə	'from where ('from what place') or where ('at what place')'
əti e əti lo	'to (or toward) where ('to what place')'
əti kkaci	'(as far as) where'
nuku wa	'with whom'
nuku eke	'(to) whom'
əlma e	'(for) how much ('at what price')'
əlma tongan	'(for) how long'
əlma na	'how (much)'
ənce kkaci	'until when'
ənce puthə	'from (or since) when'
myəch-si e	'(at) what time'

myəchil e	'(on) what date'
musın } tal e ənı }	'(in) what month'
musın } hæ e ənı }	'(in) what year'
musın yoil e	'(on) what day of the week'
myəch sikan tongan	'(for) how many hours'
myəch pun tongan	'(for) how many minutes'
myəchil tongan	'(for) how many days'
myəch tal tongan	'(for) how many months'
myəch nyən } tongan myəch hæ }	'(for) how many years'

(b) Time Adverb Phrases

achim e	'in the morning'
nac e	'at noon'
ohu e	'in the afternoon'
cənyək e	'in the evening'
pam e	'at night'
onıl achim e	'this morning'
næil nac e	'tomorrow noon'
molæ ohu e	'in the afternoon of the day after tomorrow'
kılphi cənyək e	'in the evening of two days after tomorrow'
əce pam e	'last night'
i tal e	'this month'
i cuil e	'this week'
cinan cuil e	'last week'
cinan tal e	'last month'
taım hæ e	'next year'
taım tal e	'next month'
taım cuil e	'next week'

DRILLS

A. Substitution Drill

1.	Myəch-si imnikka?	What time is [it]?
2.	Myəchil imnikka?	What date is [it]?
*3.	Musın hæ imnikka?	What year is [this]?
4.	Musın yoil imnikka?	What day (of the week) is [it]?
5.	Musın tal imnikka?	What month is [it]?
6.	əni cuil imnikka?	Which week (of the month) is [it]?
*7.	Musın nal imnikka?	What date / What day } is [it]?
8.	ənce imnikka?	When will it be?

B. Substitution Drill

1.	Onıl i myəchil ici yo?	What's the date today?
2.	Næil (i) myəchil ici yo?	What's the date tomorrow?
3.	Mole (ka) myəchil ici yo?	What's the date the day after tomorrow?
4.	Kılphi (ka) myəchil ici yo?	What's the date two days after tomorrow?
5.	əce (ka) myəchil ici yo?	What was the date yesterday?
6.	Kıcəkke (ka) myəchil ici yo?	What was the date the day before yesterday?
7.	Kı cən nal (i) myəchil ici yo?	What was the date the day before that?
8.	Næil (i) myəchil ici yo?	What is the date tomorrow?
9.	Næil (i) musın yoil ici yo?	What day (of the week) is it tomorrow?
10.	Næil (i) musın nal ici yo?	What day is it tomorrow?

C. Substitution Drill

1.	Onıl ın Suyoil imnita.	Today is Wednesday.
*2.	Onıl ın Wəlyoil imnita.	Today is Monday.
*3.	Onıl ın Hwayoil imnita.	Today is Tuesday.
*4.	Onıl ın Mokyoil imnita.	Today is Thursday.
*5.	Onıl ın Kımyoil imnita.	Today is Friday.
*6.	Onıl ın Thoyoil imnita.	Today is Saturday.
*7.	Onıl ın Ilyoil imnita.	Today is Sunday.
8.	Onıl ın Suyoil imnita.	Today is Wednesday.

D. Substitution Drill

1.	Cikım i myəch-si imnikka?	What time is it now?
2.	Onıl (i) myəchil imnikka?	What date is it today?
*3.	Kımnyən (i) musın hæ imnikka?	What year is it this year?
*4.	I hæ (ka) musın hæ imnikka?	What year is it this year?
5.	əce (ka) musın yoil imnikka?	What day of the week was yesterday?
6.	I tal (i) musın tal imnikka?	What month is this month?
*7.	Cinan tal (i) musın tal imnikka?	What month was last month?
8.	Næil (i) musın nal imnikka?	What day is tomorrow?
9.	ənce (ka) Suyoil imnikka?	When is Wednesday?
*10.	Cangnyən (i) musın hæ imnikka?	What year was last year?
11.	I cuil (i) ənı cuil imnikka?	Which week (of the month) is this week?
*12.	Næyən (i) musın hæ imnikka?	What year is next year?
*13.	Taım hæ (ka) musın hæ imnikka?	What year is next year?
*14.	Taım tal (i) ənı tal imnikka?	What month is next month?
*15.	Taım cuil (i) ənı cuil imnikka?	Which week of the month is next week?

E. Substitution Drill

1. Onıl ın Il-wəl il il imnita.	Today is January first.
2. Onıl ın I-wəl i il imnita.	Today is February second.
3. Onıl ın Sam-wəl sam il imnita.	Today is March third.
4. Onıl ın Sa-wəl sa il imnita.	Today is April fourth.
5. Onıl ın O-wəl o il imnita.	Today is May fifth.
6. Onıl ın Yu-wəl yuk il imnita.	Today is June sixth.
7. Onıl ın Chil-wəl chil il imnita.	Today is July seventh.
8. Onıl ın Phal-wəl phal il imnita.	Today is August eight.
9. Onıl ın Ku-wəl ku il imnita.	Today is September nineth.
10. Onıl ın Si-wəl sip il imnita.	Today is October tenth.
11. Onıl ın Sipil-wəl sip-il il imnita.	Today is November eleventh.
12. Onıl ın Sipi-wəl sip-i il imnita.	Today is December twelveth.

F. Substitution Drill

1. Cikım in yətəlp-si imnita.	It is 8 o'clock now.
2. Onıl (ın) Wəlyoil imnita.	Today is Monday.
3. Næil (ın) Hwayoil imnita.	Tomorrow is Tuesday.
4. Mole (nın) Suyoil imnita.	The day after tomorrow is Wednesday.
5. Cikım (ın) Sam-wəl imnita.	Now it's March.
6. əce (nın) Ilyoil imnita.	Yesterday was Sunday.
7. Kicəkke (nın) isip il imnita.	The day before yesterday was the 20th.
8. Kılphi (nın) I-wəl il il imnita.	Two days after tomorrow is February first.

G. Substitution Drill

1. Myəch-si e il i sicak-hamnikka?	What time do you start work? ('What time does your work begin?')
2. Myəchil e il i sicak-hamnikka?	What date will you start work?
3. Musın yoil e il i sicak-hamnikka?	What day (of the week) will you start work?
4. ənı cuil e il i sicak-hamnikka?	Which week (of the month) will you start work?
5. Musın tal e il i sicak-hamnikka?	What month will you start work?
6. Musın nal e il i sicak-hamnikka?	What day will you start work?

7.	ənce il i sicak-hamnikka?	When will you start work?
8.	ənce hakkyo (ka) sicak-hamnikka?	When does school start?
9.	ənce kongpu (ka) sicak-hamnikka?	When will your studies begin?
10.	ənce hyuka (ka) sicak-hamnikka?	When does your vacation begin?
*11.	ənce samu (ka) sicak-hamnikka?	When is your office going to open?
*12.	ənce panghak (i) sicak-hamnikka?	When does (school) vacation begin?
*13.	ənce suəp (i) sicak-hamnikka?	When does the class begin?
*14.	ənce suəp (i) kkıth-namnikka?	When does the class end?
*15.	ənce suəp (i) kkıth-nassımnikka?	When was the class over?

H. Substitution Drill

1.	Yətəl-si e sicak-hamnita.	[It] begins at 8 o'clock.
2.	Phal pun e sicak-hamnita.	[It] begins in 8 minutes.
3.	Phal il e sicak-hamnita.	[It] begins on the 8th.
4.	Phal-wəl e sicak-hamnita.	[It] begins in August.
5.	Yətəl(p)-si pan e sicak-hamnita.	[It] begins at 8:30.
6.	Achim ilkop-si e sicak-hamnita.	[It] begins at 7 in the morning.
7.	Cənyək yəsəs-si e sicak-hamnita.	[It] begins at 6 in the evening.
8.	Ohu tasəs-si pan e sicak-hamnita.	[It] begins at 5:30 in the afternoon.
9.	Suyoil pam ahop-si e sicak-hamnita.	[It] begins at 9 o'clock in Wednesday night.
10.	Tasəs-si sip pun cən e sicak-hamnita.	[It] begins at 10 minutes to 5 o'clock.

I. Substitution Drill

1.	Kı salam ın il-halə kassımnita.	He went to work.
2.	Kı salam ın Kongpu-halə kassımnita.	He went to study.
3.	Kı salam ın chæk (ıl) salə kassımnita.	He went to buy a book.
4.	Kı salam ın Hankuk mal (ıl) pæulə kassımnita.	He went to learn Korean.
5.	Kı salam ın chinku (lıl) mannalə kassımnita.	He went to meet a friend.
6.	Kı salam ın il (ıl) chacılə kassımnita.	He went to find a job.

7	Kı salam ın kil (ıl) mulə polə kassımnita.	He went to ask directions.
8	Kı salam ın chæk (ıl) ilkılə kassımnita.	He went to read books.
9.	Kı salam ın hyuka (lıl) patılə kassımnita.	He's gone to ask for a vacation.
10.	Kı salam ın Yəngə (lıl) kalıchilə kassımnita.	He went to teach English.
11.	Kı salam ın Yəngə (lıl) kalıchilə wassımnita.	He came to teach English.
12.	Kı salam ın Yəngə (lıl) kalıchilə omnita.	He comes to teach English.

J. Substitution Drill

1.	I cuil e il-hæssımnita.	[We] worked this week.
2.	I tal e il-hæssımnita.	[We] worked this month.
3.	Cinan tal e il-hæssımnita.	We] worked last month.
4.	Cinan cuil e il-hæssımnita.	[We] worked last week.
5.	Cinan hæ e il-hæssımnita.	[We] worked last year.
6.	Cinan Suyoil e il-hæssımnita.	[We] worked last Wednesday.
7.	Onıl achim e il-hæssımnita.	[We] worked this morning.
8.	Onıl cənyək e il-hæssımnita.	[We] worked this evening.
9.	Onıl pam e il-hæssımnita.	[We] worked tonight.
10.	Onıl ohu e il-hæssımnita.	[We] worked this afternoon.
11.	əce pam e il-hæssımnita.	[We] worked last night.
12.	əce nac e il-hæssimnita.	[We] worked yesterday at noontime.

K. Substitution Drill

1.	ənce Hankuk mal ıl pæwəssımnikka?	When did [you] study Korean?
*2.	Nuka Hankuk mal ıl pæwəssımnikka?	Who studied Korean?
3.	əti esə Hankuk mal il pæwəssımnikka?	Where did [you] study Korean?
*4.	Wæ Hankuk mal ıl pæwəssımnikka?	Why did [you] study Korean?
5.	Myəch salam i Hankuk mal ıl pæwəssımnikka?	How many people studied Korean?

6. ə̲l̲m̲a̲ ̲e̲ Hankuk mal ɪl pæwəssɪmnikka? — How much did you pay for studying Korean?

7. ə̲t̲t̲ə̲h̲k̲h̲e̲ Hankuk mal ɪl pæwəssɪmnikka? — How did you study Korean?

*8. N̲u̲k̲u̲ ̲w̲a̲ Hankuk mal ɪl pæwəssɪmnikka? — With whom did you study Korean?

*9. ə̲l̲m̲a̲ ̲t̲o̲n̲g̲a̲n̲ Hankuk mal ɪl pæwəssɪmnikka? — How long did you study Korean?

*10. M̲y̲ə̲c̲h̲i̲l̲ ̲t̲o̲n̲g̲a̲n̲ Hankuk mal ɪl pæwəssɪmnikka? — How many days have you studied Korean?

*11. M̲y̲ə̲c̲h̲ ̲s̲i̲k̲a̲n̲ ̲t̲o̲n̲g̲a̲n̲ Hankuk mal ɪl pæwəssɪmnikka? — How many hours have you studied Korean?

*12. M̲y̲ə̲c̲h̲ ̲c̲u̲i̲l̲ ̲t̲o̲n̲g̲a̲n̲ Hankuk mal ɪl pæwəssɪmnikka? — How many weeks have you studied Korean?

*13. M̲y̲ə̲c̲h̲ ̲t̲a̲l̲ ̲t̲o̲n̲g̲a̲n̲ Hankuk mal ɪl pæwəssɪmnikka? — How many months have you studied Korean?

L. Substitution Drill

1. Sahɪl tongan cip esə swiəssɪmnita. — I stayed ('rested') at home for three days.

2. S̲e̲ ̲s̲i̲k̲a̲n̲ tongan cip esə swiəssɪmnita. — I stayed at home for three hours.

3. S̲a̲m̲ ̲p̲u̲n̲ tongan cip esə swiəssɪmnita. — I stayed at home for three minutes.

4. S̲e̲ ̲c̲u̲i̲l̲ tongan cip esə swiəssɪmnita. — I stayed at home for three weeks.

5. S̲a̲m̲ ̲c̲u̲i̲l̲ tongan cip esə swiəssɪmnita. — I stayed at home for three weeks.

*6. S̲ə̲k̲ ̲c̲u̲i̲l̲ tongan cip esə swiəssɪmnita. — I stayed at home for three weeks.

*7. S̲ə̲k̲ ̲t̲a̲l̲ tongan cip esə swiəssɪmnita. — I stayed at home for three months.

8. S̲a̲m̲ ̲n̲y̲ə̲n̲ tongan cip esə swiəssɪmnita. — I stayed at home for three years.

9. Y̲ə̲l̲ə̲ ̲n̲a̲l̲ tongan cip esə swiəssɪmnita. — I stayed at home for several days.

10. S̲e̲ ̲s̲i̲k̲a̲n̲ ̲p̲a̲n̲ tongan cip esə swiəssɪmnita. — I stayed at home for three hours and a half.

11. S̲e̲ ̲c̲u̲i̲l̲ ̲p̲a̲n̲ tongan cip esə swiəssɪmnita. — I stayed at home for three weeks and a half.

12. S̲ə̲k̲ ̲t̲a̲l̲ ̲p̲a̲n̲ tongan cip esə swiəssɪmnita. — I stayed at home for three months and a half.

13. Ne cuil pan tongan cip esə swiəssımnita.	I stayed at home for four weeks and a half.
14. Sa cuil pan tongan cip esə swiəssımnita.	I stayed at home for four weeks and a half.
*15. Nək cuil pan tongan cip esə swiəssımnita.	I stayed at home for four weeks and a half.

M. Substitution Drill

*1. (Cə nın) Səul e halu tongan issəssımnita.	I was (or stayed) in Seoul for one day.
*2. (Cə nın) Səul e ithıl tongan issəssımnita.	I was in Seoul for two days.
3. (Cə nın) Səul e sahıl tongan issəssımnita.	I was in Seoul for three days.
*4. (Cə nın) Səul e nahıl tongan issəssımnita.	I was in Seoul for four days.
*5. (Cə nın) Səul e tassæ tongan issəssımnita.	I was in Seoul for five days.
*6. (Cə nın) Səul e yəssæ tongan issəssımnita.	I was in Seoul for six days.
*7. (Cə nın) Səul e ile tongan issəssımnita.	I was in Seoul for seven days.
*8. (Cə nın) Səul e yətıle tongan issəssımnita.	I was in Seoul for eight days.
*9. (Cə nın) Səul e ahıle tongan issəssımnita.	I was in Seoul for nine days.
*10. (Cə nın) Səul e yəlhıl tongan issəssımnita.	I was in Seoul for ten days.
*11. (Cə nın) Səul e yəl-halu tongan issəssımnita.	I was in Seoul for eleven days.
*12. (Cə nın) Səul e yəl-halu tongan məmuləssımnita.	I stayed in Seoul for eleven days.

End of Tape 5A

Tape 5B

N. Substitution Drill

1.	Səul e halu tongan issımnita.	[I] stayed in Seoul for one day.
2.	Wəshingthon e ithıl tongan issəssımnita.	[I] stayed in Washington for two days.
3.	Ilpon e sahıl tongan issəssımnita.	[I] stayed in Japan for three days.
4.	Pusan e nahıl tongan issəssımnita.	[I] stayed in Pusan for four days.
5.	Inchən e tassæ tongan issəssımnita.	[I] stayed in Inchon for five days.
6.	Mikuk e yəssæ tongan issəssımnita.	[I] stayed in America for six days.
7.	Cungkuk e ile tongan issəssımnita.	[I] stayed in China for seven days.
8.	Yəngkuk e yətıle tongan issəssımnita.	[I] stayed in England for eight days.
9.	Nam-Han e ahıle tongan issəssımnita.	[I] stayed in South-Korea for nine days.
10.	Puk-Han e yəlhıl tongan issəssımnita.	[I] stayed in North-Korean for ten days.
11.	Nyuyok e yəl-halu tongan issəssımnita.	[I] stayed in New York for eleven days.
12.	Tokil e yəl-sahıl tongan issəssımnita.	[I] stayed in Germany for thirteen days.
13.	Pullansə e yəl-tassæ tongan issəssımnita.	[I] stayed in France for fifteen days.
14.	Ssolyən e yəl-ile tongan issəssımnita.	[I] stayed in the Soviet Union for seventeen days.
*15.	Kulapha e yəl-ahıle tongan issəssımnita.	[I] stayed in Europe for nineteen days.
*16.	Nammi e sımu nal tongan issəssımnita.	[I] stayed in South America for twenty days.
*17.	Ithæli e sımu-halu tongan issəssımnita.	[I] stayed in Italy for twenty-one days.
*18.	Wəllam e sımu-ithıl tongan issəssımnita.	[I] stayed in Vietnam for twenty-two days.
*19.	Thækuk e sımu-sahıl tongan issəssımnita.	[I] stayed in Thailand for twenty-three days.
*20.	Hwalan e sımu-nahıl tongan issəssımnita.	[I] stayed in Holland for twenty-four days.
*21.	Hocu e sımu-tassæ tongan issəssımnita.	[I] stayed in Australia for twenty-five days.
*22.	Into e sımu-yəssæ tongan issəssımnita.	[I] stayed in India for twenty-six days.
*23.	Tæman e sımu-ile tongan issəssımnita.	[I] stayed in Taiwan for twenty-seven days.

0. Response Drill

Tutor: Cikım myəch-si imnikka? /yəl-si pan/	'What time is it now?' /10:30/
Student: Yəl-si pan imnita.	'[It]'s 10:30.'
1. Onıl i myəchil imnikka? /O il/	O il imnita.
2. Myəch-si e il i sicak-hamnikka? /ahop-si/	Ahop si e sicak-hamnita.
3. əce ka musın yoil iəssımnikka? /Mokyoil/	Mokyoil iəssımnita.
4. ənce hakkyo ka kkıth-namnikka? /ohu tasəs-si/	Ohu tasəs-si e kkıth-namnita.
5. Myəch sikan tongan il (ıl) hamnikka? /yətəl(p) sikan/	Yətəl(p) sikan tongan il hamnita.
6. Sənsæng ın musın yoil e sicang e kamnikka? /Thoyoil/	Thoyoil e sicang e kamnita.
7. əlma tongan Hankuk mal ıl pæwəssımnikka? /tu tal/	Tu tal tongan (Hankuk mal ıl) pæwəssımnita.
8. Myəch salam i Hankuk mal ıl mal-hamnikka? /yələ salam/	Yələ salam i mal-hamnita.
9. Onıl ın myəch-si e cip e kamnikka? /ohu ne-si/	Ohu ne-si e (cip e) kamnita.
10. ənı tal e Hankuk mal kongpu ka sicak-hæssımnikka? /Chil-wəl/	Chil-wəl e sicak-hæssımnita.
11. ənce hyuka lıl patkessımnikka? /taım tal/	Taım tal e (hyuka lıl) patkessımnita.
12. Onıl cənyək e nuku lıl mannakessımnikka? /chinku/	Chinku lıl mannakessımnita.

P. Response Exercise (Answer the question in Informal Polite Speech based on reality.)

Tutor: Yocɪm muəs hase yo? 'What are you doing these days?'

Student: Tæsakwan esə il-hæ yo. 'I'm working at the Embassy.'

1. Onɪl i myəchil iye yo?
2. əce ka musɪn yoil iyəssə yo?
3. ənce Hankuk mal kongpu sicak-hæssə yo?
4. Halu e myəch sikan Hankuk mal ɪl pæuse yo?
5. Sənsæng ɪn əlma toŋan tæsakwan esə il-hæssə yo?
6. Musɪn yoil e tækæ sicang e kase yo?
7. Nuka Hankuk mal ɪl kalɪchyə yo?
8. Haksæng i myəch salam issə yo?
9. Sənsæng e yangpok əlma e sassə yo?
10. əlma tongan Hankuk e issəssə yo?
11. Myəch-si e samusil e tɪllɪkessə yo?

Q. Grammar Drill (Change the sentence ending <u>-(ɪ)mnikka</u>? to <u>-ci yo</u>?)

Tutor: Onɪl i myəchil imnikka? 'What's the date today?'

Student: Onɪl i myəchil ici yo? 'What's the date today?'

1.	Muəs il cohahamnikka?	Muəs ɪl cohahaci yo?
2.	Nuka Hankuk mal ɪl kalɪchimnikka?	Nuka Hankuk mal ɪl kalɪchici yo?
3.	ənce hakkyo ka sicak-hamnikka?	ənce hakkyo ka sicak-haci yo?
4.	Myəch-si e il i kkɪth-namnikka?	Myəch-si e il i kkɪth-naci yo?
5.	ənɪ sangcəm esə sikye lɪl phamnikka?	ənɪ sangcəm esə sikye lɪl phalci yo?
6.	Kɪ kutu, əlma e sassɪmnikka?	Kɪ kutu, əlma e sassci yo?
7.	əlma tongan Hankuk mal ɪl pæwəssɪmnikka?	əlma tongan Hankuk mal ɪl pæwəssci yo?
8.	əce ka musɪn yoil iəssɪmnikka?	əce ka musɪn yoil iəssci yo?
9.	Sənsæng ɪn ənɪ nala esə wassɪmnikka?	Sənsæng ɪn ənɪ nala esə wassci yo?
10.	Tangsin ɪn musɪn nala e kamnikka?	Tangsin ɪn musɪn nala e kaci yo?

R. Transformation Drill (based on Grammar Note 2)

Tutor:	Yətəl(p)-si e il i sicak-hamnita.	'[I] start work at 8 o'clock.' ('The work begins at eight o'clock.')
Student:	Yətəl(p)-si e il i sicak-haci yo?	'You start work at 8 o'clock, don't you?'('The work begins at 8, doesn't it?')
1.	Tasəs-si e cip e kamnita.	Tasəs-si e cip kaci yo?
2.	Tæsakwan i məmnita.	Tæsakwan i məlci yo?
3.	Mom i aphımnita.	Mom i aphıci yo?
4.	Yətəl(p) sikan il ıl hamnita.	Yətəl(p) sikan il ıl haci yo?
5.	Onıl i Sam-wəl il il imnita.	Onıl i Sam-wəl il il ici yo?
6.	Kıləhsımnita.	Kıləhci yo?
7.	Ceimsı Sənsæng ıl asimnita.	Ceimsı Sənsæng ıl asici yo?
8.	Pak Sənsæŋ ıl molısimnita.	Pak Sənsæŋ ıl molısici yo?
9.	Taım tal e hyuka lıl patsımnita.	Taım tal e hyuka lıl patci yo?
10.	Yəki esə son-sukən ıl phamnita.	Yəki esə son-sukən ıl phalci yo?
11.	Chæk kaps i pissamnita.	Chæk kaps i pissaci yo?
12.	Kı ıca ka kwænchanhsımnita.	Kı ıca ka kwænchanhci yo?
13.	Kim Sənsæng e samusil e tıllımnita.	Kim Sənsæng e samusil e tıllıci yo?
14.	Kkaman sæk ıl cohahamnita.	Kkaman sæk ıl cohahaci yo?

S. Combination Drill (based on Grammar Note 3)

Tutor.	Na nın hakkyo e kamnita. Kongpu-hamnita.	'I['m] go[ing] to school.' 'I['m] study[ing].'
Student.	Na nın hakkyo e kongpu-halə kamnita.	'I['m] go[ing] (to school) to study.'
1.	Na nın samusil e kamnita. Il-hamnita.	Na nın (samusil e) il-halə kamnita.
2.	Na nın pækhwacəm e kamnita. Chæk ıl samnita.	Na nın (pækhwacəm e) chæk ıl salə kamnita.
3.	Na nın kyosil e kamnita. Chæk ıl ilksımnita.	Na nın (kyosil e) chæk ıl ilkılə kamnita.
4.	Na nın cəngkəcang e kamnita. Chinku Chinku lıl mannamnita.	Na nın (cəngkəcang e) chinku lıl mannalə kamnita.
5.	Na nın hakkyo e kamnita. Hankuk mal ıl pæumnita.	Na nın (hakkyo e) Hankuk mal ıl pæulə kamnita.

6. Na nın cikım cip e kamnita. Swimnita.	Na nın cikım cip e swilə kamnita.
7. Na nın sinæ e kamnita. Chinku e samusil e tıllımnita.	Na nın (sinæ e) chinku e samusil e tıllılə kamnita.
8. Na nın tapang e kamnita. Cha lıl masimnita.	Na nın (tapang e) cha lıl masilə kamnita.

T. Response Exercise (Answer the questions based on reality.)

1. Cikım myəch-si imnikka?	'What time is it?
2. Onıl i myəchil imnikka?	'What's the day today?'
3. Cikım ın musın tal imnikka?	'What month is it (now)?'
4. Onıl i musın yoil imnikka?	'What day of the week is it today?'
5. Myəch-si e il i sicak-hamnikka?	'What time do you start working?'
6. Myəch-si e hakkyo ka kkıth-namnikka?	'What tome does the school end?'
7. ənce Hankuk e kasimnikka?	'When are you going to Korea?'
8. əlma tongan Hankuk mal ıl pæwəssımnikka?	'How long have you studied Korean?'
9. Musın yoil e sicang e kamnikka?	'What (week)day do you go to the market?
10. Halu e myəch sikan tongan il-hamnikka?	'How many hours a day do you work?'
11. əlma tongan Hankuk e kyesyəssımnikka?	'How long have you been in Korea?'
12. Myəch tal tongan Səul e isskessımnikka?	'How many months will you stay in Korea?'
13. Myəch nyən tongan Səul e isskessımnikka?	'How many years will you stay in Seoul?'

U. Response Drill (Use ccɪm in the proper place in your answer.)

Tutor: ənce il ɪl sicak-hamnikka? /o il/ — 'When will you start work?' /the 5th/

Student: O ɪl ccɪm sicak-hamnita. — 'I begin work around the fifth.'

1. əlma tongan Səul e isskessɪmnikka? /han tal/ — Han tal ccɪm isskessɪmnita.
2. Musɪn yoil e pækhwacəm e kakessə yo? /Kɪmyoil/ — Kɪmyoil ccɪm (pækhwacəm e) kakessə yo.
3. Myəch tal tongan Hankuk mal ɪl pæwəssə yo? /yəsəs tal/ — Yəsəs tal ccɪm pæəssə yo.
4. Myəch-si e cip ɪl ttənamnikka? /ahop-si/ — Ahop-si ccɪm ttənamnita.
5. ənɪ tal e Hankuk mal kongpu ka kkɪth-namnikka? /taɪm tal/ — Taɪm tal ccɪm kkɪth-namnita.
6. Myəch sikan tongan il ɪl hamnikka? /tækæ ahop sikan/ — Tækæ ahop sikan ccɪm il ɪl hamnita.
7. Myəchil tongan hyuka lɪl patəssɪmnikka? /yəlhɪl/ — Yəlhɪl ccɪm (hyuka lɪl) patəssɪmnita.
8. Myəch-si e tapang e tɪllɪkessə yo? /cənyək ilkop-si/ — Cənyək ilkop-si ccɪm tɪllɪkessə yo.

V. Response Drill

Tutor: I tal i Sam-wəl iye yo. — 'This (month) is March.'

Student: Pəlssə Sam-wəl imnikka? — 'Is [it] already March?'

Tutor: Ne, kɪləhsɪmnita. — 'Yes, it is.'

1. Hakkyo ka sicak-hæssə yo. — Pəlssə sicak-hæssɪmnikka?
   Ne, kɪləhsɪmnita.
2. Il i kkɪth-nassə yo. — Pəlssə kkɪth-nassɪmnikka?
   Ne, kɪləhsɪmnita.
3. Cə nɪn kɪ il ɪl kkɪth-næssə yo. — Pəlssə kkɪth-næssɪmnikka?
   Ne, kɪləhsɪmnita.
4. Pihængki ka ttənassə yo. — Pəlssə ttənassɪmnikka?
   Ne, kɪləhsɪmnita.
5. Kicha ka han-si e tahassə yo. — Pəlssə tahassɪmnikka?
   Ne, kɪləhsɪmnita.

6. Cə nın pəlssə məkəssə yo.	Pəlssə məkəssımnikka?
Ne, kıləhsımnita.	
7. Onıl i Kımyoil iye yo.	Pəlssə Kımyoil imnikka?
Ne, kıləhsımnita.	
8. Hakkyo ka kkıth-nassə yo.	Pəlssə kkıth-nassımnikka?
Ne, kıləhsımnita.	

W. Response Drill

Tutor: Hakkyo ka pəlssə sicak-hæssımnikka?	'Has the school already started?'
Student: Aniyo, acik sicak-haci anhəssımnita.	'No, it hasn't started **yet**.'
1. Ppəsı ka pəlssə ttənassımnikka?	Aniyo, acik ttənaci anhəssımnita.
2. I tal i pəlssə Sa-wəl imnikka?	Aniyo, acik Sa-wəl i an imnita.
3. Pihængki ka pəlssə tahassımnikka?	Aniyo, acik tahci anhəssımnita.
4. Pəlssə məkəssımnikka?	Aniyo, acik məkci anhəssımnita.
5. Achim sinmun ıl pəlssə ilkəssımnikka?	Aniyo, acik ilkci anhəssımnita.
6. Hyuka lıl pəlssə patəssımnikka?	Aniyo, acik patci anhəssımnita.
7. Hankuk mal sənsæng ıl pəlssə mannassımnikka?	Aniyo, acik mannaci anhəssımnita.
8. Catongcha lıl pəlssə sassımnikka?	Aniyo, acik saci anhəssımnita.
9. Kı chæk ıl Ceimsı eke cuəssımnikka?	Aniyo, acik cuci anhəssımnita.
10. Kı yənphil ıl Kim Sənsæng eke tıliəssımnikka?	Aniyo, acik tılici anhəssımnita.

EXERCISES

1. Pak Sənsæng has asked what time it is. Give the following answers.

   a. It's 8 o'clock.
   b. It's 8:25.
   c. It's 5 after 9.
   d. It's 7:35.
   e. It's 20 before 10.
   f. It's a quarter to three.
   g. It's about 2:30.
   h. It's 6:28 in the morning.
   i. It's 4 in the afternoon.
   j. It's 7:43 in the evening.
   k. It's 2 minutes after 10 at night.

2. Using a paper clock, practice asking and answering questions on time.

3. Using a calendar, practice asking and answering questions pertaining to dates, months and days of the week.

4. Ask Kim Sənsæng the following questions:

   1. What time it is now.
   2. What date it is today.
   3. What day of the week it is today.
   4. What year this is.
   5. What year last year was.
   6. What month last month was.
   7. What month next month will be.
   8. What year next year will be.
   9. What month this month is.
   10. What day tomorrow will be.
   11. What time he starts working in the morning.
   12. How many hours he works a day.
   13. How long he has been in America.
   14. How long he has taught Korean.
   15. How many days a week he comes to school.
   16. How many weeks the students have studied Korean.
   17. How many months the students will be in Washington.
   18. How many years he has lived in Washington.

5. Instructor says that he bought things at the following prices; the student repeats after the instructor with the book closed.

1.	W 56	16.	W 813
2.	W 72	17.	W1,390
3.	W 69	18.	W2,917
4.	W 91	19.	W3,027
5.	W 35	20.	W4,014
6.	W 98	21.	W7,878
7.	W 79	22.	W3,427
8.	W126	23.	W4,592
9.	W254	24.	W4,760
10.	W348	25.	W8,352
11.	W473	26.	W7,265
12.	W627	27.	W6,327
13.	W565	28.	W5,279
14.	W758	29.	W9,822
15.	W893	30.	W6,789

End of Tape 5B

Tape 6A

제 7 과 시간(계속)

오셨읍니까

1. 박 : 제임스 선생, 언제 한국에 오셨읍니까?

이 년, 두 해

전에

이 년 전에, 두 해 전에

2. 제임스 : 이 년 전에 왔읍니다.

그 전

그 전에는

무슨 일

3. 박 : 아, 그러세요? 그 전에는 무슨 일을 했읍니까?

그 전에도

외교관으로

4. 제임스 : 그 전에도 외교관으로 있었읍니다.

이번

처음

5. 박 : 이번이 한국에 처음인가요?

두번

두 번째

왔었읍니다

UNIT 7. Time (Continued)

BASIC DIALOGUE FOR MEMORIZATION

Park

osiəssımnikka	did [you] come?
1. Ceimsı Sənsæng, ənce Hankuk e osiəssımnikka?	When did you come to Korea, Mr. James?

James

tu hæ / i nyən	two years
cən e	before; previously; ago
i nyən / tu hæ cən e	two years ago
2. I nyən cən e wassımnita.	(I came) two years ago.

Park

kı cən	before that; the previous time
kı cən e nın	before then
musın il	what kind of job
3. A kıləse yo? Kı cən e nın musın il ıl hæssımnikka?	(Oh, is that so?) What did you do before that? ('What kind of work did you do before then?')

James

kı cən e to	before that time also
wekyokwan ılo	as a diplomat
4. Kı cən e to wekyokwan ılo issəssımnita.	I was in the foreign service before, too. ('I exitsed as a diplomat before that time, too.')

Park

i pən	this time
chəım	first; the first time
5. I pən i Hankuk e chəım in ka yo?	Is the [your] first time in Korea?

6. 제임스 : 아니지요. 이번이 두번 째입니다.
전에도 왔었습니다.

그 때
그 때에
무엇하러

7. 박 : 그 때에는 무엇하러 왔었어요?

천 구백 오십 일 년
군 대

8. 제임스 : 그 때는 천 구백 오십 일 년이었습니다.
나는 그 때에 군 대에 있었습니다.

언제 쯤
돌아 가세요

9. 박 : 언제 쯤 미국에 돌아 가세요?

후에
한 달 후에
떠나려고 합니다

10. 제임스 : 한 달 후에 떠나려고 합니다.

무엇으로

11. 박 : 무엇으로 가시겠어요?

배
배로
갈까 합니다

James

tu pən	twice
tu pən ccæ	the second time; for the second time
wassəssɪmnita	[I] came; [I] had come
6. An ici yo. I pən i tu pən ccæ imnita. Cən e to wassəssɪmnita.	No, this is my second time. I've been here before. ('I came before, too.')

Park

kɪ ttæ	that time
kɪ ttæ e	at that time
muəs halə	to do what?; what for?
7. Kɪ ttæ e nɪn muəs halə wassəssə yo?	What were you doing here then? ('What for did you come at that time?')

James

chən-kupæk-osip-il nyən	the year 1951
kuntæ	military
8. Kɪ ttæ nɪn chən-kupæk-osip-il nyən iyəssɪmnita. Na nɪn kɪ ttæ e kuntæ e issəssɪmnita.	That was 1951. I was in the service. ('I was in the military at that time.')

Park

ənce ccɪm	about when
tola kase yo	do [you] go back?
9. ənce ccɪm Mikuk e tola kase yo?	When are [you] going back to America?

James

hu e	later; afterward
han tal hu e	one month later
ttənalyəko hamnita	[I]'m going to leave
10. Han tal hu e ttənalyəko hamnita.	I'm going to leave in a month (from now.)

Park

muəs ɪlo	by what means
11. Muəs ɪlo kasikessə yo?	How are you going? ('By what means will you go?')

12. 제임스 : 이번에는 배로 갈까 합니다.

지난 번
비행기

13. 박 : 지난 번에 비행기로 왔어요?

탔읍니다

14. 제임스 : 예, 비행기를 탔읍니다.

한국 에서
미국 까지
얼마나
걸립니까

15. 박 : 한국 에서 미국 까지 (시간이) 얼마나 걸립니까?

스므 날
설흔 시간 쯤

16. 제임스 : 배로는 대개 스므 날 걸립니다. 그리고, 비행기로는 설흔 시간 쯤 걸립니다.

James

pæ	ship; boat
pæ lo	by boat; by ship
kal kka hamnita	[I]'m thinking of going; ('[I] intend to go')
12. I pən e nın, pæ lo kal kka hamnita.	This time, I'm (thinking of) going by boat.

Park

cinan pən	last time
pihængki	airplane
13. Cinan pən e pihængki lo wassə yo?	Did you come by air (last time)?

James

thassımnita	[I] rode; [I] got on; [I] took
14. Ne, pihængki lıl thassımnita.	Yes, I flew. ('I got on airplane.')

Park

Hankuk esə	from Korea
Mikuk kkaci	as far as America; to America
əlma na	how long; how much
kəllimnikka	does it take?
15. Hankuk esə Mikuk kkaci (sikan i) əlma na kəllimnikka?	How long does it take to get to America (from Korea)?

James

sımu nal	twenty days
səlhın sikan ccım	about thirty hours
16. Pæ lo nın tækæ sımu nal kəllimnita. Kıliko, pihængki lo nın səlhın sikan ccım kəllimnita.	It usually takes 20 days by boat and (about) 30 hours by plane.

NUMERAL PHRASES

(a) 한 번
두 번
세 번
네 번
다섯 번
여섯 번
일곱 번
여덟 번
아홉 번
열 번

(b) 첫 째
둘 째
셋 째
넷 째
다섯 째
여섯 째
일곱 째
여덟 째
아홉 째
열 째

(c) 처음 - 첫 번째
두 번째
세 번째
네 번째
다섯 번째
여섯 번째
일곱 번째
아홉 번째
열 번째

(d) 이 배 - 두 배
삼 배 - 세 배
사 배 - 네 배
오 배 - 다섯 배
육 배 - 여섯 배
칠 배 - 일곱 배
팔 배 - 여덟 배
구 배 - 아홉 배
십 배 - 열 배

NUMERAL PHRASES

(a)

han pən	'once'
tu pən	'twice'
se pən	'three times'
ne pən	'four times'
tasəs pən	'five times'
yəsəs pən	'six times'
ilkop pən	'seven times'
yətəlp pən	'eight times'
ahop pən	'nine times'
yəl pən	'ten times'

(b)

chə(s) ccæ	'first' 'the first'
tu(l) ccæ	'second' 'the second'
se(s) ccæ	'third' 'the third'
ne(s) ccæ	'fourth' 'the fourth'
tasəs ccæ	'fifth' 'the fifth'
yəsəs ccæ	'sixth' 'the sixth'
ilkop ccæ	'seventh' 'the seventh'
yətəl(p) ccæ	'eighth' 'the eighth'
ahop ccæ	'ninth' 'the ninth'
yəl ccæ	'tenth' 'the tenth'

(c)

chəɪm chəs pən ccæ	'the first time'
tu pən	'the second time the second'
se pən ccæ	'the third time the third'
ne pən ccæ	'the fourth time the fourth'
tasəs pən ccæ	'the fifth time the fifth'
yəsəs pən ccæ	'the sixth time the sixth'
ilkop pən ccæ	'the seventh time the seventh'
yətəlp pən ccæ	'the eighth time the eighth'
ahop pen ccæ	'the ninth time the ninth'
yəl pən ccæ	'the tenth time' the tenth

(d)

i pæ tu pæ	'two times' 'twice'
sam pæ se pæ	'three times'
sa pæ ne pæ	'four times'
o pæ tasəs pæ	'five times'
yuk pæ yəsəs pæ	'six times'
chil pæ ilkop pæ	'seven times'
phal pæ yətəlp pæ	'eight times'
ku pæ ahop pæ	'nine times'
sip pæ yəl pæ	'ten times'

NOTES ON DIALOGUES

(Numbers correspond to the sentence numbers.)

2. Cən e without preceding any time epxression means 'previously' or 'before'; point in time + cən e means 'before the point in time'; period of time + cən e means 'period of time ago'. Compare:

a.	Kim Sənsæng ın cən e ttənnassımnita.	'Mr. Kim has left previously.'
b.	Il-wəl cən e ttənnassımnita.	'He left before January.'
c.	Han tal cən e ttənnassımnita.	'He left one month ago.'

3. Kı cən e (nın) 'before then', 'before that time', is an adverbial phrase which denotes 'the time previous to the mentioned one'.

10. Hu e not preceded by any time expression means 'later'; point in time + hu e means 'after + the point in time'; period of time + hu e means 'period of time later'. Compare:

a.	Hu e mannapsita.	'Let's meet later'.
b.	Han-si hu e mannapsita.	'Let's meet after 1 o'clock.'
c.	Han sikan hu e mannapsita.	'Let's meet one hour from now.'

11. Muəs ılo ('by what') refers to a means of transportation.

14. The verb stem tha- is a transitive verb which means 'to ride', 'to mount', 'to get on', 'to take (vehicle)'. Compare it with thæu- 'to give a ride (to someone)'. The antonym of tha- is næli- 'to get off', 'to descend'.

15. The adverbial question phrase əlma na 'how long?', 'how much', 'how?', occurs before description verbs, noun modifiers or other adverbs. The intransitive verb stem kəlli-, preceded by a time expression means 'to take' or 'to require'. Example:

Han sikan kəllimnita.	'It takes an hour.'

GRAMMAR NOTES

1. Numeral Phrases

In Unit 7 we have 4 series of mumeral phrases: (a) han pən 'once, tu pən 'twice', se pən 'three times'...; (b) chəs ccæ 'first' or 'the first', tu(l) ccæ 'second' or 'the second', se(s) ccæ 'third' or 'the third'...; (c) chəɪm or chəs pən ccæ 'the first time' or 'first', tu pən ccæ 'the second time' or 'second'...; (d) i pæ or tu pæ 'two times' or 'twice', sam pæ or se pæ 'three times', sa pæ or ne pæ 'four times'..., etc.

The numerals of series (a) occur as adverbial phrases and are used to denote the frequency of action of the subsequent inflected expressions; the numerals of series (b) occur before other nominals or by themselves and denote order within a sequence; the numerals of series (c) occur as noun or adverbial phrases and denote order within a sequence of occurences or points of time; the numerals of series (d) occur as noun or adverbial phrases and denote multiplication in quantity, quality, size or degree of the subsequent inflected expressions. Examples are provided in drills.

2. Particle lo/ɪlo 'as', 'in the capacity', 'by means of'

In Unit 2 we noticed that the particle lo/ɪlo after a place name indicates the direction of the following inflected expression. Lo/ɪlo occuring after other types of nominals denotes that the nominal is a capacity or means of subject or topic of the sentence. Examples:

a. Title names + lo/ɪlo 'as', 'in the capacity of'

sənsæng ɪlo	'as a teacher'
tæsa lo	'as an ambassador'
kongpokwan ɪlo	'an as information officer'

b. Transportation names + lo/ɪlo 'by means of'

ppəsɪ lo	'by bus'
kicha lo	'by train'
catongcha lo	'by automobile'
pihængki lo	'by airplane'
hapsɪng ɪlo	'by jitney'
cəncha lo	'by streetcar'

Other nominal + lo/ılo 'in', 'by', 'with'

Yəngə lo	'in English'
ınkhı lo	'in ink'
yənphil lo	'with pencil'
ton ılo	'with money'
hyənkım ılo	'in cash'

3. -n/ın/nın ka yo?

The construction -n/ın/nın ka yo? occurs only as the final form of a question sentence. This construction is a kind of informal polite speech which can be substituted for previously learned Formal or Informal Polite Speech question forms. -n/ın/nın is added to a verb stem or to a verb stem plus other suffixes: -n is added to a description verb stem ending in a vowel; -ın to a description verb stem ending in a consonant; -nın to an action verb stem. (For the selection of -n, -ın or -nın, see the rules for the formation of present noun-modifier ending, Unit 5.) Compare:

Cə yəca ka yeppın ka yo? Cə yəca ka yeppımnikka? Cə yəca ka yeppə yo?	'Is that woman pretty?'

4. -(ı)lyəko

The verb ending -(ı)lyəko is added to a verb stem or to a verb stem plus the honorific suffix -(ı)si-. Tense suffixes do not occur before the -(ı)lyəko ending. The inflected form ending in -(ı)lyəko (or simply the -(ı)lyəko form) occurs in two constructions:

(a) -(ı)lyəko + ha- 'be going to-', 'intend to-'

The construction -(ı)lyəko immediately followed by the verb ha- indicates that the subject or topic of the sentence intends a future action. Examples:

Hankuk e kalyəko hamnita.	'[I] intend to go to Korea.' '[I]'m going to go to Korea.'
Yəngə lıl kalıchilyəko hæssımnita.	'[I] was going to teach English.' '[I] intended to teach English.'
Kim Sənsæng ın næil ttənalyəko hamnikka?	'Is Mr. Kim going to leave tomorrow?'

(b) -(ɪ)lyəko + other than ha-

In the above construction, the -(ɪ)lyəko form which may be followed by a pause denotes that the following inflected expression in the same sentence occurs for the purpose of the action inflected by the -(ɪ)lyəko form. Compare this construction with the -(ɪ)lə form (Unit 6, G.N. 3). Examples:

Hankuk e kalyəko, Hankuk mal ɪl pæwə yo.	'In order to go to Korea, [I] am studying Korean.'
Chæk ɪl salyəko, sinæ chækpang e tɪlləssɪmnita.	'[I] stopped by a bookstore downtown to buy books.'

5. -(ɪ)l kka ha-

In Unit 3, we had the construction -(ɪ)l kka yo? as a sentence final question form. The construction -(ɪ)l kka immediately followed by ha- without a pause occurs in a statement sentence and denotes the speaker's intention for future action of the verb in the -(ɪ)l form. The English equivalent for -(ɪ)l kka ha- is either 'be thinking of doing something' or 'intend to do something'. The tenses and/or levels of speech for the whole construction are generated in ha-. Examples:

I pən e nɪn pæ lo kal kka hamnita.	'This time, I'm thinking of going by boat.'
Næil kkaci Səul e issɪl kka hæ yo.	'I intend to stay in Seoul until tomorrow.'
Na to kɪ ttæ e ttənal kka hæssɪmnita. Kɪlləna....	'I was thinking of leaving at that time, too, but....'

6. Particle kkaci 'to', 'as far as', 'until', 'till', 'by'.

Kkaci occurs either after a place name or a time name:

(a) Place name + kkaci denotes the destination or goal for the following inflected expression. Examples:

Pusan kkaci kakessə yo.	'I will go as far as Pusan.'
Səul esə Inchən kkaci əlma na mələ yo?	'How far is it from Seoul to Pusan?'

(b) Time name + kkaci denotes the final limit of action for the following inflected expressions.

næil kkaci	'until tomorrow' or 'by tomorrow'
onɪl kkaci	'till now' or 'by now'
han-si kkaci	'by one o'clock'

7. Inflected forms and Verb Phrases

We have noticed that each inflected form of a verb is used in certain ways. For example, the verb stem ka- 'to go' is inflected in many ways by adding endings to it. So far we have had the following types of inflections built on the stem ka- 'to go'. Note that a hyphen is inserted between the stem and the ending to distinguish them:

ka-mnita	ka-nin
ka-mnikka	ka-l
ka-psita	ka-lyəko
ka-sipsiyo	ka-lə
ka-ci	ka-ko

Each Korean verb is inflected in numerous forms. Many of these inflected forms are followed by other inflected forms. Some may be followed by other classes of words, namely nouns or particles. Therefore, it is important to know how each inflected form is used, e.g. whether as a verbal or as a modifier of another class of words. In Unit 4, we were introduced to the inflected form to which the particle yo can be added to make Informal Polite Speech. Remember that this form is called the Infinitive. An Infinitive is, then, distinguished from other inflected forms because it is not a verb stem + a certain ending, but instead is formed by a certain morphophonemic change in the final sound of the verb stem.

There are some verbs which occur without pause one after another. For example, mulə po-ta 'inquires', alə po-ta 'finds out', tola ka-ta 'goes back', tola o-ta 'comes back', etc. In such cases, the first verb occurs always in an infinitive form while the second verb may occur in any inflected form.

Such second verb is called the Auxiliary Verb and the first verb the Principal Verb. Any compound of principal verb + auxiliary verb is a Verb Phrase. Many of the principal verbs and auxiliary verbs that occur in verb phrases also occur independently or together with other principal or auxiliary verbs in other verb phrases, but some do not. Each verb phrase is not a simple combination of the separate meanings of its two parts: it is a compound deriving its unique indivisible meaning from both its parts. For instance, a(l)- means 'know', and po- means 'see', but alə po- means 'to find out'. Therefore, each verb phrase must be learned separately for its own unique meaning. Study the following examples:

mulə po-ta	'inquires'
alə po-ta	'finds out'
məkə po-ta	'tries (eating food)'

ipə po-ta	'tries on (clothes)'
na ka-ta	'goes out'
tɪlə ka-ta	'goes in'
olla ka-ta	'goes up'
tola ka-ta	'goes back'
næliə ka-ta	'goes down'
na o-ta	'comes out'
tɪlə o-ta	'comes in'
tola o-ta	'comes back'
olla o-ta	'comes up'
næliə o-ta	'comes down'
towa cu-ta	'gives help'
alə cu-ta	'recognizes (one's ability)'
pilliə cu-ta	'loans, lends'

DRILLS

A. Substitution Drill

1.	ənce Hankuk e osiəssımnikka?	When did you come to Korea?
2.	ənce Mikuk e osiəssımnikka?	When did you come to the United States?
3.	ənce Səul e osiəssımnikka?	When did you come to Seoul?
4.	ənce ce samusil e osiəssımnikka?	When did you come to my office?
5.	ənce yəki e osiəssımnikka?	When did you come here?
6.	Myəch-si e yəki e osiəssımnikka?	What time did you come here?
7.	Muəs ılo yəki e osiəssımnikka?	How ('by what means)' did you come here?
8.	Musın il lo yəki e osiəssımnikka?	On what business did you come here?
9.	Muəs halə yəki e osiəssımnikka?	Why ('to do what') did you come here?
10.	Nuku wa yəki e osiəssımnikka?	With whom did you come here?
11.	Myəch-si ccım yəki e osiəssımnikka?	Around what time did you come here?

B. Substitution Drill

1.	Il nyən cən e wassımnita.	[I] came [here] one year ago.
2.	Halu cən e wassımnita.	[I] came [here] yeaterday ('a day ago').
3.	Han sikan cən e wassımnita.	[I] came [here] one hour ago.
4.	Sam cuil cən e wassımnita.	[I] came [here] three weeks ago.
5.	Sək tal cən e wassımnita.	[I] came [here] three months ago.
6.	Yələ tal cən e wassımnita.	[I] came [here] several months ago.
* 7.	əlma cən e wassımnita.	[I] came [here] some time ago.
* 8.	Myəchil cən e wassımnita.	[I] came [here] some days ago.
* 9.	Myəch tal cən e wassımnita.	[I] came [here] some months ago.
*10.	Myəch nyən cən e wassımnita.	[I] came [here] some years ago.
*11.	Myəch cuil cən e wassımnita.	[I] came [here] some weeks ago.
12.	Myəch cuil cən e ttənassımnita.	[He] left [here] some weeks ago.
*13.	Myəch cuil cən e tahassımnita.	[He] arrived [here] some weeks ago.

C. Substitution Drill

1.	I nyən cən e yəki e wassə yo.	I came here two years ago.
2.	Ithıl cən e cip e wassə yo.	I came home two days ago.
3.	Tu sikan cən e samusil e wassə yo.	I came to my office two hours ago.
4.	I cuil cən e Səul e wassə yo.	I came to Seoul two weeks ago.
5.	Tu tal cən e Mikuk e wassə yo.	I came to America two months ago.
6.	Yələ nal cən e yəki e wassə yo.	I came here several days ago.
7.	I-sip il cən e Pusan e wassə yo.	I came to Pusan twenty days ago.
8.	Tu hæ cən e Wəsington e wassə yo.	I came to Washington two years ago.
*9.	Myəchil cən e sinæ e wassə yo.	I came to town some days ago.

D. Substitution Drill

1.	Cə nın wekyokwan ılo issımnita.	I am in the foreign service.('I exist as a diplomat.')
2.	Cə nın sənsæng ılo issımnita.	I am a teacher.
3.	Cə nın haksæng ılo issımnita.	I am a student.
* 4.	Cə nın tæsa lo issımnita.	I am an ambassador.
* 5.	Cə nın yəngsa lo issımnita.	I am a consul.
6.	Cə nın kongpokwan ılo issımnita.	I am a information officer.
* 7.	Cə nın kunin ılo issımnita.	I am in the military service.
* 8.	Cə nın kongmuwən ılo issımnita.	I am a {civil servant. / government employee.
9.	Cə nın cəmwən ılo issımnita.	I am a store clerk.
*10.	Cə nın samuwən ılo issımnita.	I am a clerk.
*11.	Cə nın pisə lo issımnita.	I am a secretary.
*12.	Cə nın pisə lo il-hamnita.	I work as a secretary.
*13.	Cə yəca nın pisə lo il-hamnita.	She ('that woman') works as a secretary.

E. Substitution Drill

1. I nyən cən kkaci wekyokwan ilo issəssimnita.	[I] was in the foreign service until two years ago.
2. Sahil cən kkaci sənsæng (ilo) issəssimnita.	[I] was a teacher until three days ago.
3. Se sikan cən kkaci haksæng (ilo) issəssimnita.	[I] was a student until three hours ago.
4. Ne cuil cən kkaci kunin (ilo) issəssimnita.	[I] was in the military service until 4 weeks ago.
5. Tasəs tal cən kkaci tæsa (lo) issəssimnita.	[I] was an ambassador until 5 months ago.
6. Sipo il cən kkaci yəngsa (lo) issəssimnita.	[I] was a consul until 15 days ago.
7. Yələ hæ cən kkaci pisə (lo) issəssimnita.	[I] was a secretary until several years ago.
8. əlma cən kkaci kongmuwən (ilo) issəssimnita.	[I] was a civil servant until some time ago.
9. Han tal cən kkaci cəmwən (ilo) issəssimnita.	[I] was a store clerk until one month ago.
10. Yəlhil cən kkaci wekyokwan (ilo) issəssimnita.	[I] was in the foreign service until 10 days ago.

F. Substitution Drill

1. I pən i Hankuk e cheim in ka yo?	Is this your first time in Korea?
2. I pən i Hankuk e tu pən ccæ in ka yo?	Is this your second time in Korea?
3. I pən i Hankuk e se pən ccæ in ka yo?	Is this your third time in Korea?
4. I pən i Hankuk e ne pən ccæ in ka yo?	Is this your fourth time in Korea?
5. I pən i Hankuk e tasəs pən ccæ in ka yo?	Is this your fifth time in Korea?
6. I pən i Hankuk e yəsəs pən ccæ in ka yo?	Is this your sixth time in Korea?
7. I pən i Hankuk e ilkop pən ccæ in ka yo?	Is this your seventh time in Korea?

8. I pən i Hankuk e yətəlp pən ccæ in ka yo?	Is this your eighth time in Korea?
9. I pən i Hankuk e myəch pən ccæ in ka yo?	How many times have you been in Korea?

G. Substitution Drill

1. Kim Sənsæng ıl han pən mannassımnita.	[I] met Mr. Kim once.
2. Pak Sənsæng ıl tu pən mannassımnita.	[I] met Mr. Pak twice.
3. I Sənsæng ıl se pən mannassımnita.	[I] met Mr. Lee three times.
4. Ceimsı Sənsæng ıl tasəs pən mannassımnita.	[I] met Mr. James five times.
5. Chwe Sənsæng ıl yələ pən mannassımnita.	[I] met Mr. Choe many times.
6. Kı salam ıl yələ pən pwassımnita.	[I] saw him many times.
7. Hankuk mal ıl yələ pən kalıchiəssımnita.	[I] taught Korean on many occasions.
8. Kil ıl yələ pən mulə pwassımnita.	[I] inquired about street directions many times.
9. Kı il ıl yələ pən hæssımnita.	[I] did the work many times.
10. Han-Yəng sacən ıl yələ pən wənhæssımnita.	[I] wanted a K-E dictionary many times.
11. Mikuk ıl yələ pən ttənassımnita.	[I] left America many times.
*12. Chą lıl yələ pən phalassımnita.	[I] sold cars many times.
*13. Catongcha lıl yələ pən sassımnita.	[I] bought many automobiles.
*14. Gungkuk ımsik ıl yələ pən məkəssımnita.	[I] have eaten Chinese food many times.

H. Substitutuon Drill

1. Kɪ ttæ e (na nɪn) kuntæ e issəssɪmnita.	At that time I was in the military.
2. Han sikan cən e (na nɪn) samusil e issəssɪmnita.	An hour ago I was in the office.
3. Sip pun cən e (na nɪn) cip e issəssɪmnita.	Ten minutes ago I was at home.
4. Han cuil cən e (na nɪn) Səul e issəssɪmnita.	One week ago I was in Seoul.
5. Tu(l) tal cən e (na nɪn) Wəsingthon e issəssɪmnita.	Two months ago I was in Washington.
6. Onɪl achim e (na nɪn) Mikuk Kongpowən e issəssɪmnita.	This morning I was at USIS.
*7. əce cənyək e (na nɪn) yəngsakwan e issəssɪmnita.	Last evening I was at the Consulate.
8. Kɪ nal pam e (na nɪn) kongwən e issəssɪmnita.	That night I was in the park.
9. Ilyoil ohu e (na nɪn) kɪkcang e issəssɪmnita.	Sunday afternoon I was at the theatre.
10. Kɪ ttæ e (na nɪn) siktang e issəssɪmnita.	At that time I was at a restaurant.

I. Substitution Drill

1. Han tal hu e ttənalyəko hamnita.	I'm going to leave one month from now.
2. Han cuil hu e ttənalyəko hamnita.	I'm going to leave one week from now.
3. Il nyən hu e ttənalyəko hamnita.	I'm going to leave one year from now.
4. Han sikan hu e ttənalyəko hamnita.	I'm going to leave in an hour.
5. Il pun hu e ttənalyəko hamnita.	I'm going to leave in a minute.
6. I pun hu e ttənalyəko hamnita.	I'm going to leave in two minutes.
* 7. I sam pun hu e ttənalyəko hamnita.	I'm going to leave in two or three minutes.
* 8. I sam il hu e ttənalyəko hamnita.	I'm going to leave in two or three days.
* 9. Sam sa il hu e ttənalyəko hamnita.	I'm going to leave in three or four days.

*10. Sa o il hu e ttənalyəko hamnita.	I'm going to leave in four or five days.
*11. I sam cuil hu e ttənalyəko hamnita.	I'm going to leave in two or three weeks.

J. Substitution Drill

1. Pihængki lo kal kka hamnita.	I'm thinking of going by airplane.
2. Pæ lo kal kka hamnita.	I'm thinking of going by ship.
* 3. Ppəsı lo kal kka hamnita.	I'm thinking of going by bus.
4. Cha lo kal kka hamnita.	I'm thinking of going by car.
* 5. Thækssi lo kal kka hamnita.	I'm thinking of going by taxi.
* 6. Kicha lo kal kka hamnita.	I'm thinking of going by train.
7. Catongcha lo kal kka hamnita.	I'm thinking of going by automobile.
* 8. Cəncha lo kal kka hamnita.	I'm thinking of going by streetcar.
9. Hapsıng ılo kal kka hamnita.	I'm thinking of going by jitney.

K. Substitution Drill

1. Pihængki lo Səul e kakessımnikka?	Will you go to Seoul by airplane?
2. Ppəsı lo Inchən e kakessımnikka?	Will you go to Inchon by bus?
3. Cha lo Pusan e kakessımnikka?	Will you go to Pusan by car?
4. Pæ lo Ilpon e kakessımnikka?	Will you go to Japan by ship?
5. Pihængki lo Mikuk e kakessımnikka?	Will you go to America by airplane?
6. Kicha lo Nyuyok e kakessımnikka?	Will you go to New York by train?
7. Catongcha lo sinæ e kakessımnikka?	Will you go to downtown by automobile?
8. Cəncha lo sicang e kakessımnikka?	Will you go to the market place by streetcar?

L. Substitution Drill

1. Hankuk esə Mikuk kkaci əlma na kəllimnikka?	How long does it take to go to America from Korea?
2. Səul esə Inchən kkaci əlma na kəllimnikka?	How long does it take to go to Inchon from Seoul?
3. Hakkyo esə cip kkaci əlma na kəllimnikka?	How long does it take from school to your house?

4. Sinæ esə cəngkəcang kkaci əlma na kəllimnikka? — How long does it take from downtown to the station?

5. Tæsakwan esə Mikuk Kongpowən kkaci əlma na kəllimnikka? — How long does it take from the Embassy to USIS?

6. Cip esə sichəng kkaci əlma na kəllimnikka? — How long does it take from your house to the City Hall?

7. Samusil esə siktang kkaci əlma na kəllimnikka? — How long does it take from your office to the restaurant?

8. Yəki esə kıkcang kkaci əlma na kəllimnikka? — How long does it take from here to the theatre?

9. Uphyənkuk esə tapang kkaci əlma na kəllimnikka? — How long does it take from the post office to the tearoom?

10. Yəki esə Mikuk kkaci əlma na kəllimnikka? — How long does it take from here to America.

M. Substitution Drill

1. Yəki esə Mikuk kkaci əlma (na) kəllimnikka? — How long does it take to go from here to America?

2. Yəki esə Mikuk kkaci myəchil (ina) kəllimnikka? — How many days does it take to go from here to America?

3. Yəki esə Mikuk kkaci myəch tal (ina) kəllimnikka? — How many months does it take to go from here to America.

4. Yəki esə Mikuk kkaci myəch cuil (ina) kəllimnikka? — How many weeks does it take to go from here to America?

5. Yəki esə Mikuk kkaci myəch sikan (ina) kəllimnikka? — How many hours does it take to go from here to America?

6. Yəki esə Mikuk kkaci myəch pun (ina) kəllimnikka? — How many minutes does it take to go from here to America?

7. Yəki esə Mikuk kkaci əlma (na) kəllimnikka? — How long does it take to go from here to America?

End of Tape 6A

Tape 6B

N. Transformation Drill (based on Grammar Note 4)

Tutor: Na nɪn pihængki lo kakessɪmnita.	'I'll go by airplane.'
Student: Na to pihængki lo kalyəko hæ yo.	'I'm also planning to go by airplane.'
1. Na nɪn næil tola kakessɪmnita.	Na to næil tola kalyəko hæ yo.
2. Na nɪn pæ lɪl thakessɪmnita.	Na to pæ lɪl thalyəko hæ yo.
3. Na nɪn i sam il hu e ttənakessɪmnita.	Na to i sam il hu e ttənalyəko hæ yo.
4. Na nɪn Mikuk yangpok ɪl sakessɪmnita.	Na to Mikuk yangpok ɪl salyəko hæ yo.
5. Na nɪn han cuil tongan Səul e isskessɪmnita.	Na to han cuil tongan Səul e issɪlyəko hæ yo.
6. Na nɪn taɪm tal e tto okessɪmnita.	Na to taɪm tal e tto olyəko hæ yo.
7. Na nɪn chinku lɪl mannakessɪmnita.	Na to chinku lɪl mannalyəko hæ yo.
8. Na nɪn hyuka lɪl patkessɪmnita.	Na to hyuka lɪl patɪlyəlo hæ yo.
9. Na nɪn cha lɪl phalkessɪmnita.	Na to cha lɪl phallyəko hæ yo.
10. Na nɪn tapang e tɪllɪkessɪmnita.	Na to tapang e tɪllɪlyəko hæ yo.
11. Na nɪn Ilyoil e swikessɪmnita.	Na to Ilyoil e swilyəko hæ yo.

O. Response Drill

Tutor: Pihængki lo kakessə yo?	'Will you go by airplane?'
Student: Ne, pihængki lo kalyəko hamnita.	'Yes, I'm planning (to go) by airplane.'
1. Næil tola kakessə yo?	Ne, næil tola kalyəko hamnita.
2. Pæ lɪl thakessə yo?	Ne, pæ lɪl thalyəko hamnita.
3. I sam il hu e ttənakessə yo?	Ne, i sam il hu e ttənalyəko hamnita.
4. Han tal tongan Səul e isskessə yo?	Ne, han tal tongan (Səul e) issɪlyəko hamnita.
5. Taɪm tal e tto okessə yo?	Ne, taɪm tal e tto olyəko hamnita.
6. Hyuka lɪl patkessə yo?	Ne, hyuka lɪl patɪlyəko hamnita.
7. Cha lɪl phalkessə yo?	Ne, phallyəko hamnita.
8. Tapang e tɪllɪkessə yo?	Ne, tɪllɪlyəko hamnita.
9. Ilyoil e swikessə yo?	Ne, swilyəko hamnita.
10. Cungkuk mal kongpu lɪl sicak-hakessə yo?	Ne, sicak-halyəko hamnita.

P. Response Drill (based on Grammar Note 5)

Tutor: Han tal hu e ttənalyəko hase yo?	'Are you going to leave in a month?'
Student: Ne, han tal hu e ttənal kka hamnita.	'Yes, I'm thinking of leaving in a month.'
1. I pən e nın pihængki lıl thalyəko hase yo?	Ne, (i pən e nın) pihængki lıl thal kka hamnita.
2. Cə kənmul aph esə nælilyəko hase yo?	Ne, cə kənmul aph esə nælil kka hamnita.
3. Nænyən e Wəsingthon e tola olyəko hase yo?	Ne, nænyən e (Wəsingthon e) tola ol kka hamnita.
4. Onıl cənyək e sinæ e na kalyəko hase yo?	Ne, (onıl cənyək e sinæ e) na kal kka hamnita.
5. Han tal hu e tola kalyəko hase yo?	Ne, han tal hu e tola kal kka hamnita.
6. Sichəng esə alə polyəko hase yo?	Ne, sichəng esə alə pol kka hamnita.
7. Taım cuil e hyuka lıl patılyəko hase yo?	Ne, taım cuil e hyuka lıl patıl kka hamnita.
8. Sənsæng ın catongcha lıl phalyəko hase yo?	Ne, (cə nın catongcha lıl) phal kka hamnita.

Q. Response Drill

Tutor: Muəs ıl sakessə yo? /kutu/	'What are you going to buy?' /shoes/
Student: Kutu lıl salyəko hamnita.	'I'm planning to buy shoes.'
1. ənce sicak-hakessə yo? /han cuil hu e/	Han cuil hu e sicak-halyəko hamnita.
2. Nuku lıl mannakessə yo? /Hankuk salam chinku/	Hankuk salam chinku lıl mannalyəko hamnita.
3. əncə kkaci kı il ıl kkıth-nækessə yo? /taım cuil/	Taım cuil kkaci kkıth-nælyəko hamnita.
4. əlma e sənsæng cha lıl phalkessə yo? /sam-man Wən/	Sam-man Wən e phallyəko hamnita.
5. Muəs ılo Hankuk e kakessə yo? /pihængki/	Pihængki lo kalyəko hamnita.

6. ənɪ tal e hyuka lɪl patkessə yo? /phal-wəl/	Phal-wəl e patɪlyəko hamnita.
7. əlma tongan Mikuk esə cinækessə yo? /i nyən ccɪm/	I nyən ccɪm Mikuk esə cinælyəko hamnita. ('I'm going to spend about two years in America.')
8. Taɪm pən e ənɪ ŋal ɪl pæukessə yo? /swiwn mal/	Swiwn mal ɪl pæulyəko hamnita.

R. Grammar Drill (Change -(ɪ)mnikka? to -n/in/nɪn ka yo? based on Grammar Note 3.)

Tutor: Hankuk e chəɪm imnikka?	'Is [this your] first time in Korea?'
Student: Hankuk e chəɪm in ka yo?	'Is [this your] first time in Korea?'
1. Kim Sənsæng ɪl asimnikka?	Kim Sənsæng ɪl asinɪn ka yo?
2. Ceimsɪ Sənsæng i Hankuk mal ɪl ilksɪmnikka?	Ceimsɪ Sənsæng i Hankuk mal ɪl ilknɪn ka yo?
3. ənce Mikuk e tola kasimnikka?	ənce Mikuk e tola kasinɪn ka yo?
4. Han tal hu e ttənamnikka?	Han tal hu e ttənanɪn ka yo?
5. Pæ lɪl thasimnikka?	Pæ lɪl thasinɪn ka yo?
6. Mikuk kkaci əlma na kəllimnikka?	Mikuk kkaci əlma na kəllinɪn ka yo?
7. Hakkyo ka məmnikka?	Hakkyo ka mən ka yo?
8. Cə yəca nɪn Mikuk salam imnikka?	Cə yəca nɪn Mikuk salam in ka yo?
9. Hankuk mal i philyo-hamnikka?	Hankuk mal i philyo-han ka yo?
10. Sənsæng ɪn mom i aphɪmnikka?	Sənsæng ɪn mom i aphɪn ka yo?
11. Cungkuk mal i swipsɪmnikka?	Cungkuk mal i swiun ka yo?
12. Kɪ kɪlim i alɪmtapsɪmnikka?	Kɪ kɪlim i alɪmtaun ka yo?
13. Mikuk yəca ka yeppɪmnikka?	Mikuk yəca ka yeppɪn ka yo?

S. Response Drill

Tutor: Hankuk e chəım in ka yo? /ne/	'Is [this your] first time in Korea? /yes/
Student: Ne, chəım iye yo.	'Yes, [this] is [my] first time [in Korea].'
1. Kim Sənsæng ıl asinın ka yo? /aniyo/	Aniyo, molla yo.
2. Ceimsı Sənsæng i Hankuk mal ıl ilknın ka yo? /ne/	Ne, ilkə yo.
3. ənce Mikuk e tola kasinın ka yo? /taım hæ/	Taım hæ e tola ka yo.
4. Han tal hu e Səul ıl ttənanın ka yo? /aniyo/	Aniyo, (han tal hu e) ttənaci anh yo.
5. Pæ lıl thanın ka yo? /ne/	Ne, pæ lıl tha yo.
6. Mikuk kkaci sahıl kəllinın ka yo? /ne/	Ne, sahıl kəllyə yo.
7. Hakkyo ka kakkaun ka yo? /aniyo/	Aniyo, kakkapci anhə yo.
8. Cə yəca nın Hankuk salam in ka yo? /ne/	Ne, Hankuk salam iye yo.
9. Ilpon mal to əlyəun ka yo? /aniyo/	Aniyo, əlyəpci anhə yo.
10. Tangsin ın mom i aphın ka yo? /ne/	Ne, (mom i) aphə yo.
11. Cungkuk mal i swiun ka yo? /aniyo/	Aniyo, swipci anhə yo.
12. I kılim i alımtaun ka yo? /ne/	Ne, (kı kılim i) alımtawə yo.

T. Response Drill

Tutor: Muəs ılo hakkyo e wassımnikka? /catongcha/	'How did you come to school?' /car/
Student: Catongcha lo wassımnita.	'I came by car.'
1. ənce Hankuk e wassımnikka? /chən-ku-pæk-yuk-sip nyən/	Chən-ku-pæk-yu-sip nyən e wassımnita.
2. Sənsæng ın əti esə il-hasimnikka? /Mikuk Kongpowən/	Mikuk Kongpowən esə il-hamnita.
3. Mikuk Tæsakwan e muəs ılo issımnikka? /yəngsa/	Yəngsa lo issımnita.

4. Cip esə samusil kkaci əlma na kəllimnikka? /i-sip-o pun/ — I-sip-o pun kəllimnita.
5. Han cuil e myəchil tongan il-haci yo? /tassæ/ — Tassæ tongan il-hamnita.
6. Halu e myəch sikan kongpu-haci yo? /yəsəs sikan/ — Yəsəs sikan kongpu-hamnita.
7. əlma tongan Hankuk mal ɪl pæwəssci yo? /tu tal/ — Tu tal tongan pæwəssɪmnita.
8. Muəs ɪlo yəki e wassɪmnikka? /pihængki/ — Pihængki lo wassɪmnita.

U. Response Exercise (Answer the questions in Informal Polite speech based on the fact.)

1. ənce Hankuk e wassə yo?
2. Muəs ɪlo wassə yo?
3. Cikɪm əti esə il-hase yo?
4. Kəki esə muəs ɪlo issɪse yo?
5. əlma tongan kəki esə il-hæssə yo?
6. Musɪn il ɪl hase yo?
7. Achim e muəs ɪlo il-halə ose yo?
8. Catongcha lo sikan i əlma na kəllyə yo?
9. Myəch-si e cip e kase yo?
10. Hankuk mal myəch tal tongan pæwəssə yo?
11. Halu e myəch sikan kongpu-haci yo?
12. Hakkyo esə sənsæng cip kkaci ppəsɪ lo əlma na kəllici yo?

EXERCISES

1. Tell the following story to Mr. Park once in Formal Polite and once in Informal Polite Speech.

You came to Korea two year ago. This is not your first time but second time in Korea. The first time was in 1951. At that time, you were in the military service. This time you have been here as a foreign service officer. Now, you're going to go back to America in one month. Last time you flew to Korea but you intend to go by boat this time. It usually takes 10 to 18 days (to go) to America by boat, and about 23 hours by plane.

2. Find out the following information from Mr. James (or Mr. Park)

a. When he came to Korea (or to America.)
b. How ('by what means of transportation') he came.
c. Where he is working.
d. In what capacity he works there.
e. How long he has been there.
f. What kind of work he does.
g. By what means he goes to work in the morning.
h. How long it takes.
i. How far it is from his house to the office.
j. What time he usually goes home.
k. How many hours a day he works.
l. How many days it takes to go to America (or Korea) by boat.
m. How many years he's going to live in Seoul (or Washington.)
n. How many weeks he has studied Korean.
o. What time he usually leaves home in the morning.

3. Using maps and/or a geometrical globe, practice asking and answering questions on how long it takes from one given geographical point to another by a given mode of transportation. The geographical points may include two place names within a city or building as well as countries.

4. Tell Mr. Park that:

   a. You have been to Korea several times.

   b. This is your third time in Seoul.

   c. Today is the fourth day of the week.

   d. Korean is your second foreign language.

   e. This week is your fifth week in Korean studies.

   f. Seoul is three times larger than Pusan.

   g. You were in the military service 8 years ago.

   h. Mr. Brown was an ambassador until three months ago.

   i. You are going to leave for America three weeks from now.

   j. You stayed in South Korea for five days.

   k. You came to work by streetcar this morning.

End of Tape 6B

Tape 7A

제 8 과 일에 관해서

(대화 A)

1. 이 : 선생은 요새 무엇(을) 하세요?

날
날마다
학교에 다닙니다

2. 제임스 : 날마다 학교에 다닙니다.

무엇(을) 배우러

3. 이 : 무엇을 배우러 (학교에) 다니세요?

배우려고

4. 제임스 : 한국 말을 배우려고 다닙니다.

배우기
쉽습니까

5. 이 : 한국 말을 배우기 쉽습니까?

그리
재미
재미 있읍니다

6. 제임스 : 아니요, 그리 쉽지 않습니다. 그러나, 재미 있읍니다.

UNIT 8. Talking About One's Work

BASIC DIALOGUES FOR MEMORIZATION

Dialogue A

Lee

1. Sənsæng ɪn yosæ muəs (ɪl) hase yo?	What are you doing these days?

James

nal	day
nal mata	everyday
hakkyo e tanimnita	[I]'m attending school
2. Nal mata hakkyo e tanimnita.	I go to school everyday.

Lee

muəs (ɪl) pæulə	('to learn what'); ('what to learn?')
3. Muəs (ɪl) pæulə (hakkyo) tanise yo?	What are you studying? ('What to learn do you go to school?')

James

pæulyəko	in order to learn
4. Hankuk mal ɪl pæulyəko tanimnita.	I'm studying Korean. ('I'm attending in order to learn Korean.')

Lee

pæuki	learning; to learn
swipsɪmnikka	is it easy?
5. Hankuk mal (ɪl) pæuki swipsɪmnikka?	Is Korean easy?' ('Is it easy to learn Korean?')

James

kɪli	so; in such a way; not so
cæmi	fun
cæmi issɪmnita	[it]'s interesting ('there's fun')
6. Aniyo, kɪli swipci ahhsɪmnita. Kɪləna, cæmi issɪmnita.	No, it's not very easy. But it's interesting.

7. 이 : 선생은 독일 말을 하세요?

조금
(말) 할 수 있읍니다
읽지 못 합니다

8. 제임스 : 예, 조금 (말) 할 수 있읍니다. 그러나, 읽지 못 합니다.

더
어렵습니까

9. 이 : 독일 말과 한국 말은 어느 말이 배우기(가) 더 어렵습니까?

독일 말보다

10. 제임스 : 한국 말이 독일 말보다 더 어렵습니다.

(대화 B)

오래간만입니다
이즘
재미가 어떻습니까

11. 김 : 오래간만입니다. 이즘 일에 재미가 어떻습니까?

덕분에

12. 제임스 : 덕분에 재미 있읍니다. 선생은 어떠세요?

분주합니다

13. 김 : 저는 요즘 좀 분주합니다.

Lee

7. Sənsæng ın Tokil mal ıl hase yo? — Do you speak German?

James

cokım — a little

(mal-)hal su issımnita — [I] can speak

i(l)kci mot hamnita — [I] cannot read

8. Ne, cokım (mal-)hal su issımnita. Kılena, ilkci mot hamnita. — Yes, I can speak [it] a little. I can't read [it], though.

Lee

tə — more

əlyəpsımnikka — is [it] difficult?

9. Tokil mal kwa Hankuk mal ın ənı mal i pæuki (ka) tə əlyəpsımnikka? — Which (language) is more difficult to learn, German or Korean?

James

Tokil mal pota — than German

10. Hankuk mal i Tokil mal pota tə əlyəpsımnita. — Korean is more difficult than German.

Dialogue B

Kim

olæ kan man imnita — long time no see

icım — these days

cæmi ka əttəhsımnikka — ('how is fun?')

11. Olæ kan man imnita. Icım il e cæmi ka əttəhsımnikka? — I haven't seen you for some time. How is your job coming along (these days)? ('How is fun at work these days?')

James

təkpun e — ('at your favor')

12. Təkpun e cæmi issımnita. Sənsæng ın əttəse yo? — I'm doing fine, thank you. And how about you?

그런데

근무

근무 하십니까

14. 제임스 : 그런데, 요새는 어데 근무 하십니까?

전에

말하지 않었읍니까

회사

15. 김 : 아, 제가 전에 말하지 않었읍니까? 지금 반도 회사에 근무 합니다.

주로

16. 제임스 : 무슨 일을 주로 하세요?

보통

사무

사무를 봅니다

17. 김 : 보통 사무를 봅니다.

오래

오래 동안

18. 제임스 : 아, 그러세요? 그 회사에서 오래 동안 일했읍니까?

한 삼 년

되었읍니다

19. 김 : 한 삼 년 되었읍니다.

Kim

punchuhamnita	[I]'m busy; [I]'m hectic
13. Cə nın yocım com puncuhamnita.	I'm a little busy these days.

James

kılən te	by the way
kınmu	('working')
kınmu-hasimnikka	do [you] work?
14. Kılən te, yosæ nın əte kınmu-hasimnikka?	Where do you work (these days), by the way?

Kim

cən e	previously
mal-haci anhəssınmikka	didn't [I] say?
hwesa	company; business firm
15. A, ce kan cən e mal-haci anhəssımnikka? Cikım Panto Hwesa e kınmu-hamnita.	Oh, didn't I tell you before? I work at the Bando Company (now).

James

culo	mainly; mostly
16. Musın il ıl culo hase yo?	What kind of work do you do mainly?

Kim

pothong	ordinary; ordinarily
samu	office work
samu lıl pomnita	[I] do office work
17. Pothong samu lıl pomnita.	I do ordinary office work.

James

olæ	a long time
olæ tongan	for a long time
18. A, kıləse yo? Kı hwesa esə olæ tongan il-hæssımnikka?	Is that so? Have you worked there ('at that company') for a long time?

Kim

han sam nyən	about 3 years; approximately 3 years
tweəssımnita	[it] has been; [it] became
19. Han sam nyən tweəssımnita.	I've been there for about three years.

NOTES ON DIALOGUES

(Numbers correspond to the sentence numbers.)

2. The verb tani- denotes the action of 'going and coming regularly'. Examples:

Na nın hakkyo e tanimnita.	'I am attending school.' / 'I go to school.'
Ppəsı ka tanimnita.	'Buses are running.'

4. Pæulyəko and pæulə mean the same. Their use is determined by environment: pæulyəko occurs before ha- and most other verbs, while pæulə occurs before only a few verbs (usually ka-, o-, and tani-). (See Grammar Note 3 of Unit 6 and Grammar Note 4 of Unit 7.)

6. Cæmi iss-ta 'is intersting' is a usage which literally means 'fun exists' or 'there is fun'. Cæmi (ka) issımnita which may precede a subject or a topic occurs as an intransitive expression with or without the particle ka after cæmi. Examples:

Hakkyo ka cæmi (ka) issımnita.	'I enjoy school.' ('School is interesting.')
I chæk i cæmi (ka) issımnikka?	'Is this book interesting?'

8. The negative equivalent of Hal su issımnita. 'is able to do' is Hal su əpsımnita.'is unable to do'. Haci mot hamnita '[I] cannot do' is a substitute for Hal su əpsımnita. (See Grammar Note 3.)

11. Olækan man imnita. ('It's only a long time.') is a standard expression used under the same circumstances as its English equivalent, 'I haven't seen you for some time.' or 'Long time no see.'.

14. Place name + e + kınmu-ha-ta and place name + esə + il-ha-ta both mean 'works at + place name'. Note that the verb kınmu-ha- takes the particle e when preceded by a place name while the verb il-ha- takes the particle esə when preceded by a place name.

17. Pothong is used either as a sentence adverb or as a noun, or as a determinative. When pothong is a free noun it means 'usual thing'; as determinative it means 'usual', 'average', 'ordinary'; as an adverb, is means 'usually', 'ordinarilly', 'generally'. Compare:

Kɨ kəs i pothong imnita.	'That's common. ('That is the usual thing.')
Kɨ pun ɨn pothong salam imnita.	{'He is an average person.' 'He is an ordinary man.'
Pothong, achim ɨl məkci anhsɨmnita.	'Generally, [I] don't eat breakfast.'

18. Olæ 'a long time' and olæ tongan 'for a long time' both occur either as a nominal or as an adverbial.

19. Han 'about' occurs before numerals and is a determinative which denotes approximation of the following numeral expressions. Compare han with ccɨm which occurs always after numeral expressions (Unit 6). The verb stem twe- is an intransitive verb which after a title name means 'to become' and after a period of time deontes elapsing.

Samu is a noun which means 'office work'; pothong samu 'general clerical office work'. Smau (lɨl) po-ta which literally means 'looks at office work' is an fixed usage, meaning 'does office work'.

GRAMMAR NOTES

1. -ki

The verb ending -ki is added to a verb stem, or to a verb stem plus other suffixes. An inflected form ending in -ki occurs only in the positions where nominals occur (e.g., in the positions of emphasized subject, topic or object). Since this form occupies only in nominal positions, we shall call it Nominalized Verb or simply the ki form, and the -ki ending Nominalizing Verb-Ending. Note that the ki form occurs mostly before description verbs and rarely before action verbs. Examples:

Hankuk mal (ɨl) pæuki (ka) cæmi issɨmnita.	'Learning Korean is interesting.'
Yəngə (lɨl) kalɨchiki (ka) əlyəpsɨmnikka?	'Is teaching English difficut?'
Nal i cohki (lɨl) palamnita.	'I hope that the weather is nice.'
Hankuk mal (ɨl) kongpu-haki (lɨl) wənhamnita.	'I want to study Korean.'

2. Particle mata

Mata 'every', 'each' occurs after a period of time or the name of an object, and means either 'each' or 'every'. A nominal + mata is used as an adverbial phrase. Examples:

Uli nın sikan mata suəp i issə yo.	'We have class every hour.'
Wəlyoil mata pi ka omnita.	'It rains every Monday.'
Hææ mata Nyuyok e kaci yo?	'You go to New York every year, don't you?'
Salam mata ilım i talımnita.	'Each man has a different name.'
Hakkyo mata Yəngə lıl kalıchimnita.	'All the schools teach English.' ('Each school teaches English.')

3. -(ı)l su iss- 'can' vs. -(ı)l su əps- 'cannot'

The construction -(ı)l su iss- ('[There] is a way to do.') is the Korean equivalent of English 'can' or 'is able to'. The verb stem to which -(ı)l is added is the equivalent of the English verb which occurs after either can or be able to. Tenses, levels and/or styles of speech are generated in the verb iss-. Compare:

Kal su issımnita.	'[I] can go.'
Kal su issəssımnita.	'[I] could go.'
Kal su issəssəssımnita.	'[I] could go.'
Kal su isskessə yo.	'[I] will be able to go.'
Kal su issə yo.	'[I] can go.'
Kal su issəssə yo.	'[I] could go.'

The negative equuvalent of -(ı)l su iss- is either -(ı)l su əps- or -ci mot ha-. Compare:

Kal su əpsımnita. Kaci mot hamnita.	'[I] cannot go.'

Note that mot 'cannot' is an adverb which occurs in the following two constructions (a) and (b) which are the same in meaning:

(a) mot + an inflected expression:

Mot without pause before an inflected expression is used to denote either 'inability' or 'impossibility' of an action or description of the subject or topic in the sentence for the following expression.

(b) -ci + mot + ha-:

The ci form of an action verb plus mot followed by ha- is used to denote either 'inability' or 'impossibility' of an action of the subject or topic in the sentence for the verb preceding mot. Compare:

1. Cə nın mot kamnita. Cə nın kaci mot hamnita.	'I cannot go.'
2. Cə nın Hankıl ıl mot ılkə yo. Cə nın Hankıl ıl ılkci mot hæ yo.	'I cannot read Hankıl.'
3. Kim Sənsæng i mot wassımnita. Kim Sənsæng i oci mot hæssımnita.	'Mr. Kim couldn't come.'

In either of the above two constructions, tenses and levels of speech are generated in the verb which occurs immediately after mot. Compare mot with the adverb an which is used before an inflected expression to denote simple negation of the following expression (See Unit 3). Note that the construction, the -ci form of a description verb + mot ha-, is synonymous with either -ci anh- or an + a description verb. We will learn more about this in further units.

4. Particle pota 'than', 'more than'

Pota follows a nominal X with which another nominal, Y, is being compared. Nominal Y may be followed by a description verb which may be preceded by tə 'more'. Examples:

Tokilə pota Hankukə ka tə əlyəpsımnita. Hankukə ka Tokilə pota tə əlyəpsımnita.	'Korean is more difficult than German.'
I chæk pota tə ssan chæk ın əpsımnita.	'We don't have a cheaper book than this (book).'
əce pota onıl ıl tə cohahamnita. Onıl ıl əce pota tə cohahamnita.	'[I] like today better than yesterday.'

DRILLS

A. Substitution Drill

1. Cə nɪn nal mata hakkyo e kamnita.	I go to school every day.
2. Cə nɪn Wəlyoil mata hakkyo e kamnita.	I go to school every Monday.
3. Cə nɪn achim mata hakkyo e kamnita.	I go to school every morning.
4. Cə nɪn cənyək mata hakkyo e kamnita.	I go to school every evening.
5. Cə nɪn tal mata hakkyo e kamnita.	I go to school every month.
6. Cə nɪn cuil mata hakkyo e kamnita.	I go to school every week.
7. Cə nɪn hæ mata hakkyo e kamnita.	I go to school every year.
8. Cə nɪn sikan mata hakkyo e kamnita.	I go to school every hour.
9. Cə nɪn pam mata hakkyo e kamnita.	I go to school every night.

B. Substitution Drill

1. Na nɪn nal mata hakkyo e kamnita.	I go to school everyday.
2. Na nɪn cuil mata Səul e kamnita.	I go to Seoul every week.
3. Na nɪn Ilyoil mata tapang e kamnita.	I go to a tearoom every Sunday.
4. Na nɪn pam mata siktang e kamnita.	I go to a restaurant every night.
5. Na nɪn cənyək mata kɪkcang e kamnita.	I go to the theatre every evening.
6. Na nɪn achim mata samusil e kamnita.	I go to the office every morning.
7. Na nɪn Thoyoil mata sicang e kamnita.	I go to the market place every Saturday.
8. Na nɪn sikan mata kyosil e kamnita.	I go to the classroom every hour.
9. Na nɪn tal mata ɪnhæng e kamnita.	I go to the bank every month.

C. Substitution Drill

1.	Salam mata Yəngə lıl pæulyəko hamnita.	Everybody intends to learn English.
2.	Salam mata Yəngə lıl kalıchilyəko hamnita.	Everybody intends to teach English.
3.	Salam mata Yəngə lıl alyəko hamnita.	Everybody intends to know English.
4.	Salam mata Yəngə lıl mal-halyəko hamnita.	Everybody intends to speak English.
5.	Salam mata Yəngə lıl ilkılyəko hamnita.	Everybody intends to read English.
*6.	Salam mata Yəngə lıl ssılyəko hamnita.	Everybody intends to write English.
7.	Salam mata Yəngə lıl kongpu-halyəko hamnita.	Everybody intends to study English.
8.	Salam mata Yəngə lıl mal-hal su issımnita.	Everybody can speak English.
9.	Salam mata Yəngə lıl mal-haci anhsımnita.	Not everybody speaks English.
10.	Salam mata Yəngə lıl kalıchil su əpsımnita.	Not everybody can teach English.
11.	Salam mata Yəngə lıl kalıchici mot hamnita.	Not everybody can teach English.

D. Substitution Drill

1.	Salam mata Yəngə lıl pæumnita.	Everybody learns English.
2.	Hakkyo mata Yəngə ıl kalıchimnita.	All the schools teach English.
3.	Sənsæng mata Yəngə lıl amnita.	All the teachers know English.
4.	Haksæng mata Yənge lıl kongpu-hamnita.	Each student studies English.
5.	Tæsa mata Yəngə lıl cal hamnita.	Every ambassador speaks good English.
6.	Wekyokwan mata Yəngə lıl ilksımnita.	Everyone in the foreign service reads English.
7.	Ai mata Yəngə lıl pæulyəko hamnita.	Every child intends to learn English.

8.	Sənsæng mata Yəngə lɪl (mal-)hal su issɪmnita.	All the teachers can speak English.
9.	Sənsæng mata Yəngə lɪl mal-haci mot hamnita.	Not every teacher can speak English.
10.	Sənsæng mata Yəngə lɪl kalɪchil su əpsɪmnita.	Not every teacher can teach English.
11.	Sənsæng mata Yəngə lɪl koŋpu-haci anhsɪmnita.	Not every teacher studies English.

E. Substitution Drill

1.	Hankuk mal pæuki swipsɪmnikka?	Is learning Korean easy?
2.	Hankuk mal kalɪchiki swipsɪmnikka?	Is teaching Korean easy?
3.	Hankuk mal (mal-)haki swipsɪmnikka?	Is speaking Korean easy?
4.	Hankuk mal i(l)kki swipsɪmnikka?	Is reading Korean easy?
5.	Hankuk mal ssɪki swipsɪmnikka?	Is writing Korean easy?
6.	Hankuk mal kongpu-haki swipsɪmnikka?	Is studying Korean easy?
7.	Hankuk mal kongpu-haki əlyəpsɪmnikka?	Is studying Korean difficult?
8.	Hankuk mal kongpu-haki cæmi issɪmnikka?	Is studying Korean interesting?
9.	Hankuk mal kongpu-haki kwænchanhsɪmnikka?	Is studying Korean all right?
10.	Hankuk mal kongpu-haki cohahamnikka?	Do you like studying Korean?
11.	Hankuk mal kongpu-haki consɪmnikka?	Is learning Korean, O.K.?
12.	Hankuk mal kongpu-haki əttəhsɪmnikka?	How do you like studying Korean?

F. Substitution Drill

1. Cə nɪn Panto Hwesa e kɪnmu-hamnita.	I work / I am employed } at Bando Company.
2. Cə nɪn Mikuk Tæsakwan e kɪnmu-hamnita.	I work at the US Embassy.
3. Cə nɪn Səul Sichəng e kɪnmu-hamnita.	I work at Seoul City Hall.
4. Cə nɪn Hankuk ɪnhæng e kɪnmu-hamnita.	I work at the Bank of Korea.
5. Cə nɪn Pusan Uphyənkuk e kɪnmu-hamnita.	I work at the Pusan Post Office.
6. Cə nɪn Panto Hothel e kɪnmu-hamnita.	I work at the Bando Hotel.
7. Cə nɪn Mikuk Cəngpu e kɪnmu-hamnita.	I work for the US Government.
8. Cə nɪn sinæ sangcəm e kɪnmu-hamnita.	I work at a store downtown.
9. Cə nɪn Səul pækhwacəm e kɪnmu-hamnita.	I work at Seoul Department Store.

G. Substitution Drill

1. Il i cæmi issɪmnita.	[My] work is interesting.
2. Hakkyo ka cæmi issɪmnita.	{School is interesting. / I enjoy school.
3. Kongpu ka cæmi issɪmnita.	{Studying is interesting. / I enjoy studying.
4. Chæk i cæmi issɪmnita.	This book is interesting.
5. Hankuk mal i cæmi issɪmnita.	Korean is interesting.
6. Cə salam i cæmi issɪmnita.	He ('that man') is interesting.
7. Il-haki ka cæmi issɪmnita.	{I enjoy working. ('It's interesting to to work.') / Working is interesting.
8. Kongpu-haki ka cæmi issɪmnita.	{I enjoy studying. / Studying is interesting.
9. Chæk i(l)kki ka cæmi issɪmnita.	{I enjoy reading books. / Reading books is interesting.
*10. Munce ka cæmi issɪmnita.	The problem is interesting.

H. Substitution Drill

1. Yəngə lɨl com (mal-)hal su issɨmnita.	I can speak a little English.
*2. Wekukə lɨl com (mal-)hal su issɨmnita.	I can speak foreign languages a little.
*3. Cungkukə lɨl com (mal-)hal su issɨmnita.	I can speak a little Chinese.
*4. Tokilə lɨl com (mal-)hal su issɨmnita.	I can speak a little German.
*5. Ilponə lɨl com (mal-)hal su issɨmnita.	I can speak a little Japanese.
*6. Pullansəə lɨl com (mal-)hal su issɨmnita.	I can speak a little French.
*7. Ssolyənə lɨl com (mal-)hal su issɨmnita.	I can speak a little Russian.
*8. Ithælliə lɨl com (mal-)hal su issɨmnita.	I can speak a little Italian.
*9. Səpanaə lɨl com (mal-)hal su issɨmnita.	I can speak a little Spanish.

I. Substitution Drill

1. Cə nɨn Yəngə lɨl ssɨci mot hamnita.	I can't write in English.
2. Cə nɨn ilɨm ɨl ssɨci mot hamnita.	I can't write [my] name.
3. Cə nɨn Hankɨl ɨl ssɨci mot ham ita.	I can't write Hankul.
4. Cə nɨn Tokilə lɨl ssɨci mot hamnita.	I can't write in German.
5. Cə nɨn Pullansəə lɨl ssɨci mot hamnita.	I can't wirte in French.
6. Cə nɨn Ssolyənə lɨl ssɨci mot hamnita.	I can't write in Russian.
7. Cə nɨn Ithælliə lɨl ssɨci mot hamnita.	I can't write in Italian.
8. Cə nɨn Hankukə lɨl ssɨci mot hamnita.	I can't write in Korean.
9. Cə nɨn Hakukə lɨl ilkci mot hamnita.	I can't read in Korean.

10. Cə nɪn Hankukə lɪl mal-haci mot hamnita.	I can't speak Korean.
11. Cə nɪn Hankukə lɪl pæuci mot hamnita.	I can't learn Korean.
12. Cə nɪn Hankukə lɪl kalɪchici mot hamnita.	I can't teach Korean.
*13. Cə nɪn Hankukə lɪl alci mot hamnita.	I don't know Korean. ('I can't know Korean.')
*14. Cə nɪn Hankukə lɪl ssɪci mot hamnita.	{I can't use Korean. / I can't write Korean.

J. Substitution Drill

1. Hankuk mal i Tokil mal pota tə əlyəpsɪmnita.	Korean is more difficult than German.
2. Cungkuk mal i Yəngə pota tə əlyəpsɪmnita.	Chinese is more difficult than English.
3. Pullansə mal i Ithæli mal pota tə əlyəpsɪmnita.	French is more difficult than Italian.
4. Ssolyən mal i Hankuk mal pota tə əlyəpsɪmnita.	Russian is more difficult than Korean.
5. Ilpon mal i Ssolyən mal pota tə əlyəpsɪmnita.	Japanese is more difficult than Russian.
6. Yəngə ka Tokil mal pota te əlyəpsɪmnita.	English is more difficult than German.
7. Yəngə ka Tokil mal pota tə swipsɪmnita.	English is easier than German.
8. Yəngə ka Tokil mal pota tə cæmi issɪmnita.	English is more interesting than German.
9. Yəngə ka Tokil mal pota tə pokcap-hamnita.	English is more complicated than German.
*10. Yəngə ka Tokil mal pota tə cæmi əpsɪmnita.	English is less interesting than German.
*11. Yəngə ka Tokil mal pota tə kantan-hamnita.	English is simpler than German.

K. Substitution Drill

1. Musın il ıl culo hase yo?	What (kind of work) do you do mainly?
2. Musın il ıl nal mata hase yo?	What (kind of work) do you do every-day?
3. Musın il ıl kıləhke hase yo?	{What are you working at so hard? What are you doing in such a way?
4. Musın il ıl pothong hase yo?	What do you usually do?
5. Musın il ıl kıli hase yo?	What are you doing so hard?
* 6. Musın il ıl manhi hase yo?	What do you do mostly?
7. Musın il ıl cənyək mata hase yo?	What do you do every evening?
8. Musın il ıl tækæ hase yo?	What do you usually do?
* 9. Musın il ıl cikım puthə hase yo?	What [are] you [going to] do from now on?
10. Musın il ıl næil kkaci hase yo?	What [are] you [going to] do until tomorrow?
11. Musın il ıl kı ttæ e hase yo?	What [are] you [going to] do at that time?

L. Substitution Drill

1. Cən e mal-haci anhəssımnikka?	Didn't [I] tell [you] before?
2. Cən e kaci anhəssımnikka?	Didn't [you] go [there] before?
3. Cən e saci anhəssımnikka?	Didn't [you] buy [it] before?
4. Cən e mannaci anhəssımnikka?	Didn't [we] meet before?
5. Cən e pæuci anhəssımnikka?	Didn't [you] learn [it] before?
6. Cən e ilkci anhəssımnikka?	Didn't [you] read [it] before?
7. Cən e cohci anhəssımnikka?	Wasn't [it] nice before?
*8. Cən e poci anhəssımnikka?	Didn't [you] see [it] before?
*9. Cən e kkıth-næci anhəssımnikka?	Didn't [you] finish [it] before?

M. Substitution Drill

1. (Han) sam nyən ccım tweəssımnita.	It's been about three years.
2. (Han) sam cuil ccım tweəssımnita.	It's been about three weeks.
3. (Han) se sikan ccım tweəssımnita.	It's been about three hours.
4. (Han) sək tal ccım tweəssımnita.	It's been about three months.
5. (Han) sam pun ccım tweəssımnita.	It's been about three minutes.
6. (Han) sa nyən pan ccım tweəssımnita.	It's been about four and a half years.
7. (Han) ne sikan pan ccım tweəssımnita.	It's been about four and a half hours.
8. (Han) nək tal pan ccım tweəssımnita.	It's been about four and a half months.

N. Substitution Drill

1. Kim Sənsæng ın wekyokwan (i) tweəssımnita.	Mr. Kim became a diplomat.
2. Kim Sənsæng ın kunin (i) tweəssımnita.	Mr. Kim became a soldier.
3. Kim Sənsæng ın tæsa (ka) tweəssımnita.	Mr. Kim became an ambassador.
4. Kim Sənsæng ın yəngsa (ka) tweəssımnita.	Mr. Kim became a consul.
*5. KiM Sənsæng ın Tæthongyəng (i) tweəssımnita.	Mr. Kim became the President.
*6. Kim Sənsæng ın hakca (ka) tweəssımnita.	Mr. Kim became a scholar.
*7. Kim Sənsæng ın tæhak kyosu (ka) tweəssımnita.	Mr. Kim became a college professor.
*8. Kim Sənsæng ın tæhak kangsa (ka) tweəssımnita.	Mr. Kim became a college instructor.
*9. Kim Sənsæng ın kongpokwan (i) tweəssımnita.	Mr. Kim became an information officer.
*10. Kim Sənsæng ın thongyəkkwan (i) tweəssımnita.	Mr. Kim became an interpreter.
*11. Kim Sənsæng ın sinmun kica (ka) tweəssımnita.	Mr. Kim became a journalist.
*12. Kim Sənsæng ın ıysa (ka) tweəssımnita.	Mr. Kim became a doctor.

*13. Kim Sænsæng ın sacang (i) tweəssımnita.	Mr. Kim became a president (of the company.
*14. Kim Sənsæng ın pyənhosa (ka) tweəssımnita.	Mr. Kim became a lawyer.
*15. Kim Sənsæng ın kyəngchal(kwan) (i) tweəssımnita.	Mr. Kim became a policeman.

O. Grammar Drill

Tutor: Hankuk mal i əlyəpsımnita. /Tokil mal/	'Korean is difficult.' /German/
Student: Tokil mal ın tə əlyəwə yo.	'German is more difficult.'
1. Tokil mal i swipsımnita. /Pullansə mal/	Pullansə mal ın tə swiwə yo.
2. Yəng-Han sacən i pissamnita. /Han-Yəng sacən/	Han-Yəng sacən ın tə pissa yo.
3. Səul i khımnita. /Nyuyok/	Nyuyok ın tə khə yo.
4. Səul e mulkən kaps i ssamnita. /Pusan/	Pusan e mulkən kaps ın tə ssa yo.
5. Kim Sənsæng cip i kakkapsımnita. /Pak Sənsæng cip/	Pak Sənsæng cip ın tə kakkawə yo.
*6. Catongcha ka copsımnita. /pihængki/	Pihængki nın tə copa yo.
7. Hankuk yəca ka yeppımnita. /Mikuk yəca/	Mikuk yəca nın tə yeppə yo.
8. Ilpon i cakın nala imnita. /Hankuk/	Hankuk ın tə cakın nala iye yo.

P. Expansion Drill

Tutor: Tokil mal i swipsımnita.. /Pullansə mal/	'German is easy.' /French/
Student: Tokil mal i Pullansə mal pota tə swipsımnita.	'German is easier than French.'
1. Hankuk i caksımnita. /Ilpon/	Hankuk i Ilpon pota tə caksımnita.
2. Pusan i məmnita. /Inchən/	Pusan i Inchən pota tə məmnita.
3. Kicha ka cal tanimnita. /pihængki/	Kicha ka pihængki pota tə cal tanimnita.
4. Yəngə ka əlyəpsımnita. /Hankuk mal/	Yəngə ka Hankuk mal pota tə əlyəpsımnita.
5. Hankuk yəca ka alımtapsımnita. /Cungkuk yəca/	Hankuk yəca ka Cungkuk yəca pota tə alımtapsımnita.
6. Kim Sənsæng i yəngə lıl cal hamnita. /Ceimsı Sənsæng/	Kim Sənsæng i Ceimsı Sənsæng pota Yəngə lıl tə cal hamnita.
7. Khın sacən ıl cohahamnita. /cakın sacən/	Khın sacən ıl cakın sacən pota tə cohahamnita.
8. Səul e salam i manhi issımnita. /Wəsingthon/	Səul e Wəsingthon pota tə salam i manhi issımnita.

Q. Response Drill

Tutor: Yəngə lıl mal-hal su issə yo?	'Can you speak English?'
Student: Ne, (Yəngə lıl) mal-hal su issımnita.	'Yes, I can (speak).'
1. Hankıl ıl ilkıl su issə yo?	Ne, (Hankıl ıl) ilkıl su issımnita.
2. Hakkyo e kal su issə yo?	Ne, (hakkyo e) kal su issımnita.
3. Yəngə lıl kalıchil su issə yo?	Ne, (Yəngə lıl) kalıchil su issımnita.
4. Onıl cip e issil su issə yo?	Ne, (onıl) cip e issil su issımnita.
5. Cikım kil ıl mulə pol su issə yo?	Ne, (cikım kil ıl) mulə pol su issımnita.
6. Næil il-hal su issə yo?	Ne, (næil) il-hal su issımnita.
7. Samusil e tıllil su issə yo?	Ne, (samusil e) tıllil su issımnita.
8. Kı catongcha lıl phal su issə yo?	Ne, (kı catongcha lıl) phal su issımnita.

9. Ohu e ttənal su issə yo?	Ne, (ohu e) ttənal su issɪmnita.
10. Ppəsɪ lɪl thal su issə yo?	Ne, (ppəsɪ lɪl) thal su issɪmnita.
11. Taɪm tal puthə hakkyo e tanil su issə yo?	Ne, (taɪm tal puthə hakkyo e) tanil su issɪmnita.
12. Næil kkaci il ɪl kkɪth-næl su i issə yo?	Ne, næil kkaci (il ɪl) kkɪth-næl su issɪmnita.
12. Kɪ il ɪl cikɪm sicak-hal su issə yo?	Ne, (kɪ il ɪl) cikɪm sicak-hal su issɪmnita.

R. Response Drill

Tutor: Hakkyo e kal su issɪmnikka?	'Can you go to school?'
Student: Aniyo, (hakkyo e) kal su əpsɪmnita.	'No, I cannot (go).'

1. Hankɪl ɪl ilkɪl su issɪmnikka?	Aniyo, (Hankɪl ɪl) ilkɪl su əpsɪmnita.
2. Yəngə lɪl kalɪchil su issɪmnikka?	Aniyo, (Yəngə lɪl) kalɪchil su əpsɪmnita.
3. Onɪl cip e issɪl su issɪmnikka?	Aniyo, (cip e) issɪl su əpsɪmnita.
4. Cikɪm kil ɪl mulə pol su issɪmnikka?	Aniyo, (kil ɪl) mulə pol su əpsɪmnita.
5. Næil il-hal su issɪmnikka?	Aniyo, il-hal su əpsɪmnita.
6. Samusil e tɪllɪl su issɪmnikka?	Aniyo, tɪllɪl su əpsɪmnita.
7. Kɪ catongcha lɪl phal su issɪmnikka?	Aniyo, phal su əpsɪmnita.
8. Ohu e ttənal su issɪmnikka?	Aniyo, ttənal su əpsɪmnita.
9. Mikuk esə hakkyo e tanil su issɪmnikka?	Aniyo, tanil su əpsɪmnita.

S. Response Drill

Tutor: Hakkyo e kal su əpsımnikka?	'Can't you go to school?'
Student: Ne, kaci mot hamnita.	'No, I can't (go).'
1. Yəngə lıl mal-hal su əpsımnikka?	Ne, mal-haci mot hamnita.
2. Hankıl ıl ilkıl su əpsımnikka?	Ne, ilkci mot hamnita.
3. Tokil mal ıl kalıchil su əpsımnikka?	Ne, kalıchici mot hamnita.
4. Onıl næ samusil e tıllil su əpsımnikka?	Ne, tıllıci mot hamnita.
5. Næil il-hal su əpsımnikka?	Ne, (næil) il-haci mot hamnita.
6. Cha lıl phal su əpsımnikka?	Ne, phalci mot hamnita.
7. Ohu e ttənal su əpsımnikka?	Ne, ttənaci mot hamnita.
8. Næil kkaci il ıl kkıth-næl su əpsımnikka?	Ne, (næil kkaci) khıth-næci mot hamnita.
9. Mikuk esə hakkyo e tanil su əpsımnikka?	Ne, (Mikuk esə hakkyo e) tanici mot hamnita.

T. Response Drill

Tutor: Hakkyo ka məmnikka?	'Is the school far?'
Student: Aniyo, kılı məlci anhsımnita.	'No, it's not so far.'
1. Haksæng i manhsımnikka?	Aniyo, kılı manhci anhsımnita.
2. Sicang e mulkən i pissamnikka?	Aniyo, kılı pissaci anhsımnita.
3. inhæng i kakkapsımnikka?	Aniyo, kılı kakkapci anhsımnita.
4. I kılim i alımtapsımnikka?	Aniyo, kılı alımtapci anhsımnita.
5. Kı pun i Ssolyən mal ıl cal hamnikka?	Aniyo, kılı cal haci anhsımnita.
6. Tangsin ın cə yəca lıl cohahamnikka?	Aniyo, kılı cohahaci anhsımnita.
7. Hankuk mal kyosil i khımnikka?	Aniyo, kılı khıci anhsımnita.
8. Sikan i manhi kəllimnikka?	Aniyo, kılı manhi kəllici anhsımnita.
9. Ssolyən mal i pæuki swipsımnikka?	Aniyo, kılı swipci anhsımnita.
10. Cə tokil yəca ka yeppımnikka?	Aniyo, kılı yeppıci anhsımnita.
11. Sənsæng ın cikım puncuhamnikka?	Aniyo, kılı puncuhaci anhsımnita.
12. Yəngə lıl kalıchiki əlyəpsımnikka?	Aniyo, kılı əlyəpci anhsımnita.
13. Yəng-Han sacən i philyo-hamnikka?	Aniyo, kılı philyo-haci anhsımnita.

U. Response Drill (Answer the question using /pəlssə/ in the proper place.)

Tutor: Kim Sənsæng i ttənassə yo?	'Has Mr. Kim left?'
Student: Ne, (Kim Sənsæng i) pəlssə ttənassɪmnita.	'Yes, he has laready left.'
1. Kɪ il ɪl kkɪth-næssə yo?	Ne, (kɪ il ɪl) pəlssə kkɪth-næssɪmnita.
2. Yəngə sənsæng ɪl mannassə yo?	Ne, (Yəngə sənsæng ɪl) pəlssə mannassɪmnita.
3. Han sam nyən ccɪm tweəssə yo?	Ne, pəlssə han sam nyən ccɪm tweəssɪmnita.
4. Haksæng i kicha e thassə yo?	Ne, (haksæng i) pəlssə (kicha e) thassɪmnita.
5. Hankuk mal kongpu lɪl sicak-hæssə yo?	Ne, (Hankuk mal kongpu lɪl) pəlssə sicak-hassɪmnita.
6. Onɪl i Suyoil iye yo?	Ne, (Onɪl i) pəlssə Suyoil imnita.
7. Pak Sənsæng ɪn il-halə kassə yo?	Ne, (Pak Sənsæng ɪn) pəlssə il-halə kassɪmnita.
8. Sənsæng ɪn hyuka lɪl patəssə yo?	Ne, pəlssə (hyuka lɪl) patəssɪmnita.
9. Com swiəssə yo?	Ne, pəlssə swiəssɪmnita.
10. Kicha ka cəngkəcang e tahassə yo?	Ne, pəlssə (cəngkəcang e) tahassɪmnita.

V. Response Drill (Answer the question using /acik/ in the proper place.)

Tutor: Kim Sənsæng i pəlssə ttənassɪmnikka?	'Has Mr. Kim left already?'
Student: Aniyo, (Kim Sənsæng i) acik ttənaci anhəssə yo?	'No, he's not left yet.'
1. Hakkyo ka pəlssə kkɪth-nassɪmnikka?	Aniyo, (hakkyo ka) acik kkɪth-naci anhəssə yo.
2. Yəngə sənsæng ɪl pəlssə mannassɪmnikka?	Aniyo, (Yəngə sənsæng ɪl) acik mannaci anhəssə yo.
3. Pəlssə sam nyən i tweəssɪmnikka?	Aniyo, acik (sam nyən i) tweci anhəssə yo.
4. Hankuk mal kongpu lɪl pəlssə sicak-hæssɪmnikka?	Aniyo, (Hankuk mal kongpu lɪl) aci sicak-haci anhəssə yo.

5. Pak Sənsæng ın pəlssə il-halə kassımnikka?
Aniyo, (Pak Sənsæng ın) acik (il-halə) kaci anhəssə yo.

6. Sənsæng ın pəlssə hyuka lıl patəssımnikka?
Aniyo, (Acik hyuka lıl) patci anhəssə yo.

7. Kicha ka pəlssə cəngkəcang e tahassımnikka?
Aniyo, (kicha ka) acik (cəngkəcang e) tahci anhəssə yo.

8. Pihængki ka pəlssə ttənassımnikka?
Aniyo, (pihængki ka) acik ttənaci anhəssə yo.

9. Kı il ıl pəlssə kkıth-næssımnikka?
Aniyo, (kı il ıl) acik kkıth-næci anhəssə yo.

10. Kim Sənsæng i pəlssə yəngsa ka tweəssımnikka?
Aniyo, (Kim Sənsæng i) acik yəngsa ka tweci anhəssə yo.

EXERCISES

1. Tell the following story to Mr. Park that:
   (a) You are attending school these days to study Korean. Learning Korean is not so easy but it is interesting. Foreign languages are necessary for you. You can speak German a little but cannot read it well. Korean is more difficult to study than German.
   (b) Mr. Lee is a little busy these days. He didn't tell you before, but he is employed at the Bando Company, where he does ordinary office work. And, he has lots of work everyday. He has been with the Company for about three months now. He likes his job very much.

2. James wants to know what Mr. Kim, you friend, is. Tell him that Mr. Kim has become a(n):

a. soldier
b. ambassador
c. the President
d. professor
e. journalist
f. (medical) doctor
g. lawyer
h. college professor
i. President of a company
j. Consul
k. clerk
l. scholar
m. interpreter
n. information officer
o. secretary
p. police(man)
Q. civil servant

3. Ask Mr. James in Korean:

a. Which (one) is more difficult to stydy, Korean or German.

b. Which (one) is more expensive, an English-Korean dictionry or a Korean-English dictionary.

c. Which is larger, Seoul or Pusan.

d. Which is nearer (or farther) from America, Japan or Korea.

e. Which is faster, an airplane or a train.

f. Which is needed more, a Korean-English dictionary or an English-Korean dictionary.

g. Which one he likes better, a pencil or a fountain pen.

h. Who speaks English better, Mr. Kim or Mr. James.

i. Which language is more complicated, French or German

j. Which is more interesting to learn, speaking or reading.

k. Which is less interesting, teaching or learning.

l. Which is simpler, to write or to read.

4.

Pak sənsæng asks:	You answer:
a. if Mr. Lee can write Hankɨl.	'No, he can't.'
b. if everybody knows English.	'Yes, everybody does.'
c. if you intend to leave tomorrow.	'No, I'm going to leave the day after tomorrow.'
d. if you go to the market place every Saturday.	'Yes, I do (go every Saturday).'
e. if you are employed by the Bank of America.	'No, I work for the Government.'
f. if every ambassador speaks good English.	'No, not every ambassador does.'
g. if teaching Korean is not easy.	'No, it's not that easy, but it's all right.'
h. how long you have worked for the Government.	'About three and a half years.'
i. how is it learning Korean.	'Oh, it's not so difficult.'
j. what kind of work you do mainly.	'Now I do consular work.'
k. if you have had a vacation.	'Not yet, but I'm going to get one next week.'
l. if the school already is over.	'No, it's not over yet.'

5. Make short statements in which the following expressions are included:

a. cuil mata

b. kɪli

c. tə

d. culo

e. pothong

f. olæ (tongan)

g. kɪləhke

h. cikɪm puthə

i. næil kkaci

k. pəlssə

k. acik

End of Tape 7A

Tape 7B

제 9 과 영화 구경

(대화 A)

영화

1. 미쓰 최 : 오늘 저녁에 영화 보러 안 가겠어요?

참

좋은 생각

2. 미쓰 부라운 : 아, 그것, 참 좋은 생각입니다. 어디에 좋은 영화가 있어요?

국제

국제 극장

(영화를) 상영합니다

상영하고 있읍니다

3. 미쓰 최 : 국제 극장에서 미국 영화를 상영하고 있읍니다.

보고 싶습니다

4. 미쓰 부라운 : 나는 한국 영화를 보고 싶습니다.

5. 미쓰 최 : 한국 영화를 좋아하세요?

가끔

6. 미쓰 부라운 : 예, 가끔 보러 가지요.

다

듣습니다, 들읍니다

알아 듣습니다

7. 미쓰 최 : 한국 말을 다 알아 듣습니까?

UNIT 9. Going to the Movies

BASIC DIALOGUES FOR MEMORIZATION

Dialogue A

(Miss Choi and Miss Brown work in the same office.)

Miss Choi

yənghwa	[the] movies
1. Onɪl cənyək e yənghwa polə an kakessə yo?	Wouldn't you like to go to see a movie tonight?

Miss Brown

cham	really; very
cohɪn sængkak	good idea; good thought
2. A, kɪ kəs, cham cohɪn sængkak imnita. əti e cohɪn yənghwa ka issə yo?	Oh, that's a very good idea. Is there a good movie on? ('Is there a good movie somewhere?')

Miss Choi

kukce	international
Kukce Kɪkcang	International Theatre
(yənghwa lɪl) sangyəng-hamnita	[they] show movies
sangyəng-hako issɪmnita	movies are being shown
3. Kukce Kɪkcang esə Mikuk yənghwa lɪl sangyəng-hako issɪmnita.	[They] are showing an American movie at the Interantional Theatre.

Miss Brown

poko siphsɪmnita/sipssɪmnita/	I want to see; I'd like to see
4. Na nɪn Hankuk yənghwa lɪl poko siphsɪmnita.	I want to see a Korean movie.

Miss Choi

5. Hankuk yənghwa lɪl cohahase yo?	Do you like Korean movies?

Miss Brown

kakkɪm	sometimes
6. Ne, kakkɪm polə kaci yo.	Yes, I go to see [them] sometimes.

알아 듣지 못 합니다
그렇지만
연습
연습합니다

8. 미스 브라운 : 아니요, 다 알아 듣지 못 합니다. 그렇지만, 좋은 연습입니다.

(대화 B)

틈

9. RA: 틈이 있읍니까?

바쁩니다

10. RB: 왜요? 좀 바쁩니다.

무슨 일로
그렇게
늘

11. RA: 무슨 일로 그렇게 늘 바빠요?

할 일
퍽
많습니다

12. RB: 오늘은 할 일이 퍽 많습니다.

그래서
나하고
구경
구경갑니다, 구경합니다

Miss Choi

	ta	all
	tıtsımnita / tılımnita	[I] hear; [I] listen to
	alə tıtsımnikka	do you comprehend?; do you understand?
7.	Hankuk mal ıl ta alə tıtsımnikka?	Do you understand Korean (language) thoroughly?

Miss Brown

	alə tıtci mot hamnita	I don't understand; I can't understand
	kıləchi man	however; nevertheless
	yənsıp	practice
	yənsıp-hamnita	[I] practice
8.	Aniyo, ta alə tıtci mot hamnita. Kıləhci man, cohın yənsıp imnita.	No, I don't understand it all. But it's good practice.

Dialogue B

Roommate A

	thım	free time; spare time
9.	Thım / Sikan i issımnikka?	Are you free now? ('Do you have spare time?')

Roommate B

	pappımnita	[I]'m busy
10.	Wæ yo? Com pappımnita.	I'm a little busy, why?

Roommate A

	musın il lo	why ('with what kind of business')
	kıləhke	so; that way; in such a way
	nıl	all the time; always
11.	Musın il lo kıləhke nıl pappə yo?	How come you are so busy all the time? ('With what business you are always busy?')

13. RA: 그래서, 나하고 구경 안 가겠어요?

미안하지만
나 갑니다
나 갈 수 없읍니다

14. RB: 미안하지만, 오늘은 나 갈 수 없읍니다.

15. RA: 그럼, 내일은 나와 같이 나 갈 수 있겠어요?

16. RB: 예, 내일은 바쁘지 않겠읍니다. 내일 같이 나 갑시다.

17. RA: 그러면, 내일까지 기다리겠어요.

Roommate B

hal il	work to do; something to do
phək	very; quite
manhsımnita	[there]'re many; [there]'re plenty
12. Onıl ın hal il i phək manhsımnita.	I have a lot of things to do today.

Roommate A

kılæ sə	therefore; so
na hako	with me
kukyəng	show; sightseeing
kukyəng kamnita kukyəng-hamnita }	[I] go to a show; [I] go sight-seeing; [I] look around
13. Kılæ sə, na hako kukyəng an kakessə yo?	Then, you won't go to a show with me?

Roommate B

mianhaci man	I'm sorry but...
na kamnita	[I] go out
na kal su əpsımnita	[I] cannot go out
14. Mianhaci man, onıl ın na kal su əpsımnita.	I'm sorry but I can't go out today.

Roommate A

15. Kıləm, næil ın na wa kathi na kal su isskessə yo?	Will you be able to go out with me tomorrow, then?

Roommate B

16. Ne, næil ıl pappıci anhkessımnita. Næil kathi na kapsita.	Yes, I will not be busy tomorrow. Let's go out together tomorrow.

Roommate A

kitalikessə yo	[I]'ll wait
17. Kıləmyən, næil kkaci kitalikessə yo.	Well, then, I'll wait until tomorrow.

NOTES ON DIALOGUES

(Numbers correspond to the sentence numbers in the dialogues.)

2. Cham 'really', 'very' is an adverb which occurs without pause before description verbs or other adverbs. It denotes intensification of the qualities of the following expression. Cham followed by a pause also occurs as a sentence adverb which means 'by the way'.

7. Ta 'all', 'in all', 'thoroughly' is an adverb which occurs before inflected expressions (mostly verbals or sentences) to denote either completion or entirety. Alə tıl- ~ alə tıl- 'to understand', 'to comprehend' is a verb phrase which implies that someone 'listens and understands through ears'. The second verb in the verb phrase occurs in an alternative form tıt- or tıl- which means 'listen to-' as an independent verb. In standard Korean, tıt- occurs only in the following inflected forms: tıtsımnita/tıtsımnikka and tıtkessımnita/tıtkessımnikka; tıl- occurs elsewhere. Note that there are a few verb stems which are called the t-l alternative stems to which tıt- ~ tıl- belongs. The inflections of this class of verbs are the same as tıt- ~ tıl-.

8. Yənsıp 'practice' is a noun. Its verb form yənsıp-ha- 'to practice' occurs as a transitive verb.

9. Thım 'spare time', 'free time' is a free noun.

11. Nıl 'always' is synonymous with hangsang 'all the time', ənce na 'all the time', ənce tınci 'all the time' and hangsi 'always'.

12. Phək 'quite', 'considerably', 'comparatively' is an adverb which occurs only before description verbs or other adverbs. It is used to imply that the degree of the following expression is more than the speaker's expectation.

GRAMMAR NOTES

1. -ko

The verb ending -ko may be added to a verb stem, or to a stem plus other suffixes. However, if either the verb iss- or siph- succeeds without pause immediately after it, tense suffixes do not occur before the -ko ending. Since the inflected form ending in -ko (or simply the ko form) occurs always before other inflected expressions it is often called the Korean Gerund. The ko form occurs in the following three constructions:

(a) -ko + iss- 'be ---ing'

An action verb ending in -ko + iss-, denotes that the action of the verb in the ko form is in the process of occuring, or in the state of being. Tenses and/or levels of speech may be generated in iss- but not in the ko form. Examples:

Cə nɨn kɨ yəca lɨl salang-hako issə yo.	'I am in love with her.' ('As for me, I'm in the process of loving that woman.')
Hankuk mal ɨl pæuko issɨmnita.	'[I] am studying Korean (now).'
Kɨ ttæ e Səul esə salko issəssə yo.	'[I] was living in Seoul at that time.'

(b) -ko + siph- and -ko siphə ha- 'want to-' and 'wants to-'

The verb siph- occurs only after the ko form. The construction -ko + siph- denotes the desire or hope of the sentence subject or topic for the action of the verb in the ko form. If the subject or topic in the sentence is other than the speaker or addressee -ko + siphə ha- is used. The tenses and/or levels of speech may be generated in the verb siph- or siphə ha-. Examples:

Cə nɨn yənghwa lɨl poko siphsɨmnita.	'I want to see a movie.'
Chinku lɨl mannako siphə yo?	'Do you want to meet a friend?'
Ceimsɨ ka Yəngə lɨl kalɨchiko siphə hamnita.	'James wants to teach English.'

(c) -ko + verbs other than iss- or siph-

The ko form which may be followed by a pause also occurs before another inflected expression. The honorific and tense suffixes may be added to the ko form, but if the subject or topic is the same for both verbs, tense suffixes occur only in the final verb. This construction (i.e. -ko followed by another verb) denotes that two actions and/or descriptions are expressed one after another with the one in the ko form occuring or being stated first. Examples:

Hankuk mal i əlyəpko, Yəngə nin swipsimnita.	'Korean is difficult and English is easy.'
Kim Sənsæng in tæsa ka tweəssko, na nin kyosu ka tweəssə yo.	'Mr. Kim became an ambassador, and I became a professor.'
Cə nin mal il pæuko, wekuk e kako siphsimnita.	'I want to study the language and then go to a foreign country.'

2. -ci man '...but'

Man is a particle which, preceded by a nominal or an adverbial, means simply 'only', i.e. N + man 'only N'. The ci form + man which may be followed by a pause occurs before another inflected expression to denote that some contradictory further explanation or remark will follow in the following inflected expression. Examples:

Kakkyo ka məlci man, sikan i kili manhi kəllici anhsimnita.	'The school is far, but it doesn't take much time.'
Cə nin Hankuk mal il pæuci man, ce chinku nin Ilpon mal il kalichiə yo.	'I am studying Korean, but my friend is teaching Japanese.'

3. -l/il

We called the inflected form ending in -n/in/nin before a nominal the Present Noun-Modifier Word. (See Unit 5, Grammar Note 1.) The inflected form ending in -(i)l also occurs as a modifier of the following nominal, to denote the future action or description of, or for, the nominal. We shall call such an inflected form the Prospective Noun-Modifier Word, and the ending -(i)l the Prospective Modifier Ending. -il is added to a consonant stem and -l to a vowel stem. The future tense suffix -kess- does not occur before -(i)l. Examples:

Ttənal kicha ka issimnita.	{'There is a train which will leave.' 'There is a train to leave.'

Nææ ka ilkil chæk i əpsə yo.	'There is no book which I will read.'
Onil mannal salam i nuku ici yo?	'Who is the man that [you] will meet today?'
Hal il i manhsimnita.	'[I] have a lot work to do.'

4. Particle hako 'with', 'as', 'and'

Hako is an one-shape particle which can be substituted for the particle wa/kwa. (See Grammar Note 4, Unit 4.) Like wa/kwa, hako occurs in two constructions:

(a) Nominal + hako 'with Nominal', 'as Nominal', 'with Nominal'

Nominal + hako, which may occur before an inflected expression, is an adverbial expression.

Kim Sənsæng hako (kathi) kakessə yo.	'I'll go with Kim.'
Chinku hako mal-hæssə yo.	'I talked with a friend.'
i kəs hako kathin chæk	'a book the same as this' ('the same book as this')

(b) Nominal 1 + hako + Nominal 2 = 'N1 and N2'

chæk hako yənphil	'a book and a pencil'
onil hako næil	'today and tomorrow'

DRILLS

A. Substitution Drill

1. Onɪl cənyək e yənghwa polə an kakessə yo?	Wouldn't you like to go to see movies this evening?
*2. Onɪl cənyək e mulkən salə an kakessə yo?	Wouldn't you like to go for shopping ('to buy goods') this evening?
3. Onɪl cənyək e kukyəng-halə an kakessə yo?	Wouldn't you like to go to see a show this evening?
4. Onɪl cənyək e chinku mannalə an kakessə yo?	Wouldn't you like to go to meet friends this evening?
5. Onɪl cənyək e Hankuk mal pæulə an kakessə yo?	Wouldn't you like to go to study Korean this evening?
6. Onɪl cənyək e Hankuk mal yənsɪp-halə an kakessə yo?	Wouldn't you like to go to practice Korean this evening?
*7. Onɪl cənyək e untong-halə an kakessə yo?	Wouldn't you like to go for exercise this evening?
*8. Onɪl cənyək e sanpo-halə an kakessə yo?	Wouldn't you like to take a walk this evening?
9. Onɪl cənyək e sinæ kukyəng-halə an kakessə yo?	Wouldn't you like to go sightseeing downtown this evening?
*10. Onɪl cənyək e chum chulə an kakessə yo?	Wouldn't you like to go for dancing this evening?
*11. Onɪl cənyək e sicang polə an kakessə yo?	Wouldn't you like to go for food shopping this evening?

B. Subsitution Drill

1. Kukce Kɪkcang esə Mikuk yənghwa lɪl sangyəng-hako issɪmnita.	American movies are being shown at the International Theatre.
2. Kukce Kɪkcang esə Hankuk yənghwa lɪl sangyəng-hako issɪmnita.	Korean movies are being shown at the International Theatre.
3. Kukce Kɪkcang esə Ilpon yənghwa lɪl sangyəng-hako issɪmnita.	Japanese movies are being shown at the International Theatre.
4. Kukce Kɪkcang esə Tokil yənghwa lɪl sangəng-hako issɪmnita.	German movies are being shown at the International Theatre.

5. Kukce Kıkcang esə <u>Ithæli yənghwa</u> lıl sangyəng-hako issımnita. — Italian movies are being shown at the International Theatre.

6. Kukce Kıkcang esə <u>Pullansə yənghwa</u> lıl sangyəng-hako issımnita. — French movies are being shown at the International Theatre.

7. Kukce Kıkcang esə <u>wekuk yənghwa</u> lıl sangyəng-hako issımnita. — Foreign movies are being shown at the International Theatre.

8. Kukce Kıkcang esə <u>Yəngkuk yənghwa</u> lıl sangyəng-hako issımnita. — British movies are being shown at the International Theatre.

9. <u>Səul Kıkcang esə</u> Yəngkuk yənghwa lıl sangyəng-hako issımnita. — British movies are being shown at the Seoul Theatre.

10. <u>Sinæ Kıkcang esə</u> Yəngkuk yənghwa lıl sangyəng-hako issımnita. — British movies are being shown at a theatre downtown.

C. Substitution Drill

1. Na nın Hankuk yənghwa lıl poko siphsımnita. — I want to see Korean movies.

2. Na nın <u>Səul sinæ</u> lıl poko siphsımnita. — I want to see downtown Seoul.

3. Na nın <u>wekuk yangpok</u> ıl poko siphsımnita. — I want to see foreign (made) suits.

4. Na nın <u>Han-Yəng sacən</u> ıl poko siphsımnita. — I want to see a Korean-English dictionary.

5. Na nın <u>Kukce Kıkcang</u> ıl poko siphsımnita. — I want to see the International Theatre.

6. Na nın <u>yələ kaci</u> lıl poko siphsımnita. — I want to see many kinds.

7. Na nın <u>Mikuk Tæsa</u> lıl poko siphsımnita. — I want to see the American Ambassador.

8. Na nın <u>Tokıl kunin</u> ıl poko siphsımnita. — I want to see German soldiers.

9. Na nın <u>hwesa sacang</u> ıl poko siphsımnita. — I want to see the president of the company.

10. Na nın <u>yəngsa pisə</u> lıl poko siphsımnita. — I want to see the secretary to the consul.

D. Substitution Drill

1. Na nın yənghwa lıl poko siphə yo. — I want to see a movie.
2. Na nın Hankuk e kako siphə yo. — I want to go to Korea.
3. Na nın i chæk ıl sako siphə yo. — I want to buy this book.
4. Na nın Yəngə lıl kalıchiko siphə yo — I want to teach English.
*5. Na nın Hankuk yəksa lıl ilkko siphə yo. — I want to read Korean history.
6. Na nın catongcha lıl phalko siphə yo. — I want to sell [my] car.
7. Na nın yəca chinku lıl mannako siphə yo. — I want to meet my girl friend.
8. Na nın tapang e tılliko siphə yo. — I want to stop by a tearoom.
9. Na nın sinæ lıl kukyəng-hako siphə yo. — I want to look around downtown.

E. Substitution Drill

1. Kakkım yənghwa (lıl) polə kaci yo. — Sometimes I go to see the movies.
2. Nıl yənghwa (lıl) polə kaci yo. — I always go to (see) the movies.
*3. Hangsang yənghwa (lıl) polə kaci yo. — I go to (see) the movies all the time.
*4. Ttæ ttæ lo yənghwa (lıl) polə kaci yo. — I go to (see) the movies occasionally.
5. Pam mata yənghwa (lıl) polə kaci yo. — I go to (see) the movies every night.
6. Cuil mata yənghwa (lıl) polə kaci yo. — I go to (see) the movies every week.
7. Han cuil e han pən yənghwa (lıl) polə kaci yo. — I go to (see) the movies once a week.
8. Han tal e tu pən yənghwa (lıl) polə kaci yo. — I go to (see) the movies twice a month.
9. Il nyən e se pən yənghwa (lıl) polə kaci yo. — I go to (see) the movies three times a year.
*10. Cacu yənghwa (lıl) polə kaci yo. — I go to (see) the movies frequently.

*11.	Cumal mata yənghwa (lıl) polə kaci yo.	I go to (see) the movies every weekend.
*12.	Mæil yənghwa (lıl) polə kaci yo.	I go to (see) the movies everyday.
*13.	Mæcu(ıl) yənghwa (lıl) polə kaci yo.	I go to (see) the movies every week.
*14.	Mæwəl yənghwa (lıl) polə kaci yo.	I go to (see) the movies every month.
*15.	Mænyən yənghwa (lıl) polə kaci yo.	I go to (see) the movies every year.

F. Substitution Drill

1.	Onıl ın hal il i manhsımnita.	I have a lot of things to do today.
2.	Onıl ın ilkıl chæk (i) manhsımnita.	I have a lot of books to read today.
3.	Onıl ın mannal salam (i) manhsımnita.	I have a lot of people to meet today.
4.	Onıl ın ol salam (i) manhsımnita.	There are a lot of people to come today.
5.	Onıl ın kitalil salam (i) manhsımnita.	There are a lot of people to wait for today.
6.	Onıl in ttənal pæ (ka) manhsımnita.	There are a lot of ships which will leave today.
7.	Onıl ıl sal mulkən (i) manhsımnita.	There are a lot of things to buy today.
8.	Onıl ın kalıchil haksæng (i) manhsımnita.	There are a lot of students to teach today.
9.	Onıl ın mulə pol mal (i) manhsımnita.	I have a lot of things to ask about today.
10.	Onıl ın tıllil sangcəm (i) manhsımnita.	There are many stores to stop by today.
11.	Onıl ın sicak-hal il (i) manhsımnita.	I have a lot of work to begin today.
*12.	Onıl ın ssıl phyənci (ka) manhsımnita.	I have a lot of letters to write today.

G. Substitution Drill

1. Mianhaci man, cikɪm nal kal su əpsɪmnita.	I'm sorry but I cannot go out now.
2. Mianhaci man, cikɪm hal su əpsɪmnita.	I'm sorry but I cannot do [it] now.
3. Mianhaci man, cikɪm kitalil su əpsɪmnita.	I'm sorry but I cannot wait for [you] now.
4. Mianhaci man, cikɪm ttənal su əpsɪmnita.	I'm sorry but I cannot leave now.
5. Mianhaci man, cikɪm (Hankuk mal ɪl) kalɪchil su əpsɪmnita.	I'm sorry but I cannot teach (Korean) now.
6. Mianhaci man, cikɪm kathi kal su əpsɪmnita.	I'm sorry but I cannot go with [you] now.
7. Mianhaci man, cikɪm (tangsin cip e) tɪllɪl su əpsɪmnita.	I'm sorry but I cannot stop by (your house) now.
8. Mianhaci man, cikɪm il ɪl sicak-hal su əpsɪmnita.	I'm sorry but I cannot start work now.
9. Mianhaci man, cikɪm kukyəng kal su əpsɪmnita.	I'm sorry but I cannot go sightseeing now.
10. Mianhaci man, cikɪm cip e issɪl su əpsɪmnita.	I'm sorry but I cannot be at home now.
11. Mianhaci man, cikɪm tola kal su əpsɪmnita.	I'm sorry but I cannot go back now.
*12. Mianhaci man, cikɪm tola ol su əpsɪmnita.	I'm sorry but I cannot come back now.
*13. Mianhaci man, cikɪm tɪlə ol su əpsɪmnita.	I'm sorry but I cannot come in now.
*14. Mianhaci man, cikɪm tɪlə kal su əpsɪmnita.	I'm sorry but I cannot go in now.
*15. Mianhaci man, cikɪm na ol su əpsɪmnita.	I'm sorry but I cannot come out now.
*16. Mianhaci man, cikɪm na kal su əpsɪmnita.	I'm sorry but I cannot go out now.
*17. Mianhaci man, cikɪm olla ol su əpsɪmnita.	I'm sorry but I cannot come up now.
*18. Mianhaci man, cikɪm olla kal su əpsɪmnita.	I'm sorry but I cannot go up now.

H. Substitution Drill

1.	Hankuk mal i cæmi issımnita.	Korean is interesting.
2.	Yəngə (ka) cæmi issımnita.	English is interesting.
3.	Chæk (ıl) i(l)kki (ka) issımnita.	Reading books is interesting.
4.	Səul e salki (ka) cæmi issımnita.	Living in Seoul is interesting.
5.	Mal pæuki (ka) cæmi issımnita.	Learning a language is interesting.
6.	Il-haki (ka) cæmi issımnita.	Working is interesting.
7.	Kalıchiki (ka) cæmi issımnita.	Teaching is interesting.
8.	Hakkyo e taniki (ka) cæmi issımnita.	Attending school is interesting.
9.	ınæng e kınmu-haki (ka) cæmi issımnita.	Working in a bank is interesting.
10.	Thipi poki (ka) cæmi issımnita.	Watching TV is interesting.

I. Substitution Drill

1.	Na wa kathi kakessə yo?	Will you go with me?
2.	Chinku (wa) kathi okessə yo?	Will you come with a friend?
3.	Sənsæng (kwa) kathi məkkessə yo?	Will you eat with [your] teacher?
4.	Cə yəca (wa) kathi na kakessə yo?	Will you go out with that girl?
5.	Puin (kwa) kathi tıllıkessə yo?	Will you stop by with your wife?
6.	Pisə (wa) kathi mal-hakessə yo?	Will you talk with your secretary?
*7.	Mikuk Tæsa (wa) kathi insa-hakessə yo?	Will you greet with the American Ambassador?
8.	Kunin (kwa) kathi nolkessə yo?	Will you play with a soldier?
9.	Yəngsa (wa) kathi ttənakessə yo?	Will you leave with the consul?
10.	Yəca chinku (wa) kathi kukyəng kakessə yo?	Will you go sightseeing with your girl friend?
11.	Uli (wa) kathi okessə yo?	Will you come with us?
12.	Yəhaksæng (kwa) kathi na kakessə yo?	Will you go out with a girl student?
13.	əməni (wa) kathi tola kakessə yo?	Will you go back with your mother?
14.	Tæthongyəng (kwa) kathi tola okessə yo?	will you come back with the President?

J. Substitution Drill

1. Kim Sənsæng kwa kathi mal-hasipsiyo.	Please talk with Mr. Kim.
2. Kim Sənsæng kwa kathi kongpu-hasipsiyo.	Please study with Mr. Kim.
3. Kim Sənsæng kwa kathi yəki esə kitalisipsiyo.	Please wait here with Mr. Kim.
4. Kim Sənsæng kwa kathi kı kəs ıl ilkısipsiyo.	Please read it with Mr. Kim.
5. Kim Sənsæng kwa kathi il-hasipsiyo.	Please work with Mr. Kim.
6. Kim Sənsæng kwa kathi sicak-hasipsiyo.	Please start with Mr. Kim.
7. Kim Sənsæng kwa kathi pæusipsiyo.	Please study with Mr. Kim.

K. Transformation Drill

Tutor: Uli nın Hankuk mal ıl kongpu-hamnita.	'We study Korean.'
Student: Uli nın Hankuk mal ıl kongpu-hako issımnita.	'We're studying Korean now.'
1. Cikım hakkyo e kamnita.	Cikım hakkyo e kako issımnita. ('[I]'m on [my] way to school now.')
2. Kıkcang esə Mikuk Yənghwa lıl sangyəng-hamnita.	Kıicang esə Mikuk Yənghwa lıl sangyəng-hako issımnita.
3. Ai ka thipi lıl pomnita.	Ai ka thipi lıl poko issımnita.
4. Sənsæng i kalıchimnita.	Sənsæng i kalıchiko issımnita.
5. Nal mata Hankuk mal ıl pæumnita.	Nal mata Hankuk mal ıl pæuko issımnita.
6. Cohın sacən ıl wənhamnita.	Cohın sacən ıl wənhako issımnita.
7. Kim Sənsæng ın wekuk salam ıl mannamnita.	Kim Sənsæng ın wekuk salam ıl mannako issımnita.
8. Na nın Kim Sənsæng cip ıl chacsımnita.	Na nın Kim Sənsæng cip ıl chacko issımnita.
9. Ceimsı Sənsæng ın Mikuk tæsakwan esə il-hamnita.	Ceimsı Sənsæng ın Mikuk tæsakwan esə il-hako issımnita.

L. Response Drill

Tutor: Pak Sənsæng ɪn Hankuk mal ɪl kalɪchyə yo?	'Does Mr. Park teach Korean?'
Student: Ne, cikɪm kalɪchiko issɪmnita.	'Yes, he's teaching [it] now.'
1. Ceimsɪ Sənsæng i tæsakwan esə il-hæ yo?	Ne, cikɪm tæsakwan esə il-hako issɪmnita.
2. Kicha ka ttəna yo?	Ne, cikɪm ttənako issɪmnita.
3. Salam tɪl i pihængki lɪl tha yo?	Ne, cikɪm thako issɪmnita.
4. Mikuk tæsa ka pihængki esə nælyə yo?	Ne, cikɪm næliko issɪmnita.
5. Tangsin ɪn hakkyo e tanyə yo?	Ne, cikɪm taniko issɪmnita.
6. Chinku lɪl kitalyə yo?	Ne, cikɪm kitaliko issɪmnita.
7. Səul yək e kanɪn kil ɪl alə yo?	Ne, cikɪm alko issɪmnita. ('Yes, I'm aware of it now.')
8. Hankuk mal ɪl manhi pæwə yo?	Ne, cikɪm manhi pæuko issɪmnita.
9. Kim Sənsæng ɪl chacə yo?	Ne, cikɪm chacko issɪmnita.
10. Kɪkcang esə Mikuk yənghwa lɪl sangyəng-hæ yo?	Ne, cikɪm sangyəng-hako issɪmnita.
11. Hankuk mal ɪl yənsɪp-hæ yo?	Ne, cikɪm yənsɪp-hako issɪmnita.

M. Response Drill

Tutor: Kɪ ttæ e Hankuk mal ɪl kongpu-hako issəssɪmnikka?	'Were you studying Korean at that time?'
Student: Ne, nɪ ttæ e Hankuk mal ɪl kongpu-hako issəssə yo.	'Yes, I was studying Korean at that time.'
1. Kɪ ttæ e hakkyo e kako issəssɪmnikka?	Ne, kɪ ttæ e hakkyo e kako issəssə yo.
2. Kɪ ttæ e Mikuk yənghwa lɪl sangyəng-hako issəssɪmnikka?	Ne, kɪ ttæ e Mikuk yənghwa lɪl sangyəng-hako issəssə yo.
3. Kɪ ttæ e Yengə lɪl kalɪchiko issəssɪmnikka?	Ne, kɪ ttæ e Yəngə lɪl kalɪchiko issəssə yo.
4. Kɪ ttæ e wekuk salam ɪl mannako issəssɪmnikka?	Ne, kɪ ttæ e wekuk salam ɪl mannako issəssə yo.
5. Kɪ ttæ e Kim Sənsæng cip ɪl chacko issəssɪmnikka?	Ne, kɪ ttæ e Kim Sənsæng cip ɪl chacko issəssə yo.

6. Kɪ ttæ e Mikuk tæsakwan esə il-hako issəssɪmnikka?	Ne, kɪ ttæ e Mikuk tæsakwan esə il-hako issəssə yo.
7. Kɪ ttæ e yənghwa lɪl poko issəssɪmnikka?	Ne, kɪ ttæ e yənghwa lɪl poko issəssə yo.
8. Kɪ ttæ e Mikuk esə hakkyo e taniko issəssɪmnikka?	Ne, kɪ ttæ e Mikuk esə hakkyo e taniko issəssə yo.
9. Kɪ ttæ e chinku lɪl kitaliko issəssɪmnikka?	Ne, kɪ ttæ e chinku lɪl kitaliko issəssə yo.
10. Kɪ ttæ e kicha esə næliko issəssɪmnikka?	Ne, kɪ ttæ e kicha esə næliko issəssə yo.

N. Response Drill

Tutor: Muəs ɪl salyəko hamnikka? /moca/	'What are you going to buy?' /hat/
Student: Moca lɪl sako siphsɪmnita.	'I want / 'I'd like } to buy a hat.'
1. Nuku lɪl mannalyəko hamnikka? /Ceimsɪ Sənsæng/	Ceimsɪ Sənsæng ɪl mannako siphsɪmnita.
2. əti esə il-halyəko hamnikka? /Mikuk Tæsakwan/	Mikuk Tæsakwan esə il-hako siphsɪmnita.
3. ənce Wəsingthon ɪl ttənalyəko hamnikka? /taɪm tal/	Taɪm tal e ttənako siphsɪmnita.
4. Musɪn yoil e sicang e kalyəko hamnikka? /Thoyoil/	Thoyoil e kako siphsɪmnita.
5. əlma tongan Hankuk mal ɪl pæulyəko hamnikka? /yəl tal/	Yəl tal tongan pæuko siphsɪmnita.
6. Musɪn yənghwa lɪl polyəko hamnikka? /Hankuk yənghwa/	Hankuk yənghwa lɪl poko siphsɪmnita.
7. Onɪl əte issɪlyəko hamnikka? /cip/	Cip e issko siphsɪmnita.
8. əti e tɪllɪlyəko hamnikka? /chinku samusil/	Chinku samusil e tɪllɪko siphsɪmnita.
9. ənɪ tal e hyuka lɪl patɪlyəko hamnikka? /Phal-wəl/	Phal-wəl e (hyuka lɪl) patko siphsɪmnita.
10. əti esə nælɪlyəko hamnikkə? /sichəng aph/	Sicheng aph esə næliko siphsɪmnita.

11. Muəs ılo Hankuk e kalyəko hamnikka? /pihængki/	Pihængki lo kako siphsımnita.
12. ənce ccım Mikuk e tola kalyəko hamnikka? /i nyən hu/	I nyən hu e tola kako siphsımnita.

O. Transformation Drill

Tutor: Ceimsı nın Səul esə sal(l)yəko hamnita.	'James intends to live in Seoul.'
Student: Cemisı nın Səul esə salko siphə hæ yo.	'James wants to live in Seoul.'
1. Kim Sənsæng ın onıl yənghwa lıl polyəko hamnita.	Kim Sənsæng ın onıl yənghwa lıl poko siphə hæ yo.
2. Hankuk haksæng i Mikuk hakkyo e tanilyəko hamnita.	Hankuk haksæng i Mikuk hakkyo e taniko siphə hæ yo.
3. Chwe Sənsæng ın Səul e halu tongan issılyəko hamnita.	Chwe Sənsæng ın Səul e halu tongan issko siphə hæ yo.
4. Haksæng ın næil sinæ e na kalyəko hamnita.	Hanksæng ın næil sinæ e na kako siphə hæ yo.
5. Salam tıl ın wekuk ıl kukyəng-halyəko hamnita.	Salam tıl ın wekuk ıl kukyəng-hako siphə hæ yo.
6. Pak Sənsæng ın Yəngə lıl kalıchilyəko hamnita.	Pak Sənsæng ın Yəngə lıl kalıchiko siphə hæ yo.
7. Kı salam ın Hankuk ınhæng esə il-halyəko hamnita.	Kı salam ın Hankuk ınhæng esə il-hako siphə hæ yo.
8. Cə e chinku nın hyuka lıl patılyəko hamnita.	Cə e chinku nın hyuka lıl patko siphə hæ yo.

P. Response Drill

Tutor: Kim Sənsæng ın Yəngə lıl pæuko siphə hæ yo?	'Does Mr. Kim want to study English?'
Student: Ne, phək pæuko siphə hamnita.	'Yes, [he] wants to study [it] very much.'
1. Kı chinku nın hyuka lıl patko siphə hæ yo?	Ne, phək patko siphə hamnita.
2. Kı salam ın Hankuk ınhæng e kınmu-hako siphə hæ yo?	Ne, (Hankuk ınhæng e) phək kınmu-hako siphə hamnita.
3. Pak Sənsæng ın Hankuk mal ıl kalıchiko siphə hæ yo?	Ne, phək kalıchiko siphə hamnita.
4. Chwe Sənsæng ın khəphi lıl masiko siphə hæ yo?	Ne, phək masiko siphə hamnita.
5. Kim Sənsæng ın tampæ lıl phiuko siphə hæ yo?	Ne, phək phiuko siphə hamnita.
6. Hankuk haksæng i Mikuk hakkyo e taniko siphə hæ yo?	Ne, phək taniko siphə hamnita.
7. Haksæng i Hankuk mal ıl yənsıp-hako siphə hæ yo?	Ne, phək yənsıp-hako siphə hamnita.
8. Cə ai ka lætiyo lıl tıtko siphə hæ yo?	Ne, phək tıtko siphə hamnita.

Q. Response Drill

Tutor: Kim Sənsæng ın Yəngə lıl kalıchiko siphə hamnikka?	'Does Mr. Kim want to teach English?'
Student: Aniyo, kalıchiko siphə haci anhə yo.	'No, he doesn't (want to teach).'
1. Kı yəca ka kıkcang e kako siphə hamnikka?	Aniyo, kako siphə haci anhə yo.
2. Kı chinku ka hyuka lıl patko siphə hamnikka?	Aniyo, patko siphə haci anhə yo.
3. Chwe Sənsæng ın khəphi lıl masiko siphə hamnikka?	Aniyo, masiko siphə haci anhə yo.
4. Hankuk haksæng tıl i Mikuk hakkyo e taniko siphə hamnikka?	Aniyo, (Mikuk hakkyo e) taniko siphə haci anhə yo.

5. Ceimsı Sənsæng i Mikuk tæsa ka tweko siphə hamnikka?	Aniyo, (Mikuk tæsa ka) tweko siphə haci anhə yo.
6. Kı salam i mal ıl mulə poko siphə hamnikka?	Aniyo, mulə poko siphə haci anhə yo.
7. Mikuk yəngsa ka Mikuk e tola kako siphə hamnikka?	Aniyo, tola kako siphə haci anhə yo.
8. Cə ai ka Yəngə chæk ıl ilkko siphə hamnikka?	Aniyo, ilkko siphə haci anhə yo.

R. Grammar Drill

Tutor: Hankuk mal i əlyəpsımnita. Kıləchi man, cæmi issımnita.	'Korean is difficult. However, it's interesting.'
Student: Hankuk mal i əlyəpci man, cæmi issımnita.	'Korean is difficult but it is interesting.'
1. Hankuk mal ıl pæumnita. Kıləhci man, swipci anhsımnita.	Hankuk mal ıl pæuci man, swipci anhsımnita.
2. Na nın pæ lo kamnita. Kıləhci man, Kim Sənsæng ın kicha lo kamnita.	Na nın pæ lo kaci man, Kim Sənsæng ın kicha lo kamnita.
3. Pihængki ka ttənamnita. Kıləhci man, ppəsı nın tahsımnita.	Pihængki ka ttənaci man, ppəsı nın tahsımnita.
4. Cə nın pappımnita. Kıləhci man, talın salam ın pappıci anhsımnita.	Cə nın pappıci man, talın salam ın pappıci anhsımnita.
5. Hankuk mal ıl alə tıtsımnita. Kıləhci man, ilkci mot hamnita.	Hankuk mal ıl alə tıtci man, ilkci mot hamnita.
6. I kılim ıl cohahamnita. Kıləhci man, phək pissamnita.	I kılim ıl cohahaci man, phək pissamnita.
7. Haksæng i manhsımnita. Kıləhci man, sənsæng ın əpsımnita.	Haksæng i manhci man, sənsæng ın əpsımnita.
8. Nal mata kı yəca lıl kitalimnita. Kıləhci man, kı yəca nın oci anhsımnita.	Nal mata kı yəca lıl kitalici man, kı yəca nın oci anhsımnita.
9. Pak Sənsæng ın Hankuk ınhæng e kınmu-hamnita. Kıləhci man, puncuhaci anhsımnita.	Pak Sənsæng ın Hankuk ınhæng e kınmu-haci man, puncuhaci anhsımnita.

10. Il e cæmi ka issımnita. Kıləhci man, hal il i phək manhsımnita.	Il e cæmi ka issci man, hal il i phək manhsımnita.

S. Transformation Drill

Tutor: Kicha ka ohu e ttənamnita.	'A train is leaving in the afternoon.'
Student: Ohu e ttənal kicha ka issımnita.	'There's a train which will leave in the afternoon.'
1. Onıl haksæng i omnita.	Onıl ol haksæng i issımnita.
2. Ohu e chinku lıl mannamnita.	Ohu e mannal chinku ka issımnita.
3. Chæk ıl samnita.	Sal chæk i issımnita.
4. Il ıl sicak-hamnita.	Sicak-hal il i issımnica.
5. Ppəsı lıl thamnita.	Thal ppəsı ka issımnita.
6. Hakkyo e tanimnita.	Tanil hakkyo ka issımnita.
7. Hankuk mal chæk ıl ilksımnita.	Ilkıl Hankuk mal chæk i issımnita.
8. Cip esə yəca lıl kitalımnita.	Cip esə kitalil yəca ka issımnita.
9. Han-si e kicha ka tahsımnita.	Han-si e tahıl kicha ka issımnita.

T. Completion Exercise

Tutor: Hankuk mal ıl əlyəpci man,	'Korean is difficult but...'
Student: Hankuk mal ıl əlyəpci man, cæmi issımnita.	'Korean is difficult but it's interesting.'

1. Yənghwa lıl cohahaci man,
2. Sikan i əpsci man,
3. Hankuk mal ıl pæuci man,
4. Kicha ka ttənaci man,
5. Pihængki nın tahci man,
6. Kı yəca lıl mannaci man,
7. Hakkyo e tanici man,
8. Yocım com puncuhaci man,
99. Hankuk mal ıl alə tıtci man,
10. Onıl hal il i issci man,
11. Cikım chinku lıl kitalici man,
12. Mikuk esə salko siphci man,
13. Hankıl ıl ilkci mot haci man,

14. Na nın Mikuk salam ici man,
15. Onıl mom i com aphıci man,

U. Combination Drill

Tutor: Kicha nın ttənassə yo. Ppəsı nın tahassə yo.	'The train has left. The bus has arrived.'
Student: Kicha nın ttənassko, ppəsı nın tahassə yo.	'The train has left and the bus has arrived.'
1. Cə nın Yəngə lıl pæwə yo. Ceimsı nın Hankuk mal ıl kongpu-hæ yo.	Cə nın Yəngə lıl pæuko, Ceimsı nın Hankuk mal ıl kongpu-hæ yo.
2. əce Hankuk ımsik ıl məkəssə yo. Onıl ın Cungkuk ımsik ıl məkkessə yo.	əce Hankuk ımsik ıl məkəssko, onıl ın Cungkuk ımsik ıl məkkəssə yo.
3. Na nın Hankuk yənghwa lıl cohahæ yo. Miss Chwe nın Ilpon yənghwa lıl poko siphə hæ yo.	Na nın Hankuk yənghwa lıl cohahako, Miss Chwe nın Ilpon yənghwa lıl poko siphə hæ yo.
4. Na nın puncuhæ yo. Ce chinku nın sikan i manhi issə yo.	Na nın puncuhako, ce chinku nın sikan i manhi issə yo.
5. Tæhak pyəngwən ın kakkawə yo. (The University hospital is near.) Cungang Tosəkwan ın com mələ yo. (The Central Library is a little far.)	Tæhak pyəngwən ın kakkapko, Cungang Tosəkwan ın com mələ yo.

EXERCISES

1. Tell Miss Choe: (Once in Formal Polite and once in Informal Polite Speech)

a. that you want to see Korean movies.
b. that you are practicing Korean now.
c. that you are not free now.
d. that you don't understand Korean well.
e. that you have lots of things to do.
f. that you are busy all the time.
g. that you have a friend to meet this afternoon.
h. that you can't go out tonight.
i. that you were waiting for Miss Brown at that time.
j. that learning a language is not interesting.
k. that you have many letters to write.
l. that you cannot finish the work by 4 o'clock.
m. that you go to see the Korean movies occasionally.
n. that American movies are shown at the International Theatre twice a month.
o. that you don't want to go out frequently.
p. that your girl friend doesn't want to take a walk.
q. that the students were eating in the dining hall.
r. that you cannot come out now.
s. that the children cannot come in the room now.
t. that you cannot go into the military (service).
u. that your wife cannot go up the building on foot.
v. that you are coming up the street.
w. that there are many students but not many teachers.
x. that German is easy and Korean is hard.
y. that you want to go out to see movies but you don't have time.
z. that the housing is expensive and is not good.
z1. You cannot go back to School now.
z2. Your Korean friend came back from the U.S.

2. You ask Miss Brown:	Miss Brown answers:
a. what she wants to see.	'I'd like to see your new car.'
b. what she would like to do today.	'I want to stay home.'
c. where the American movies are being shown.	'They are being shown at the Central Theatre.'
d. how she likes (<u>or</u> how it is) living in Seoul.	'Not too bad.'
e. how long she is going to stay in Korea (<u>or</u> in Washington).	'About three or four years.'
f. if she can go out with you tonight.	'I'd like to but I cannot go out tonight.'
g. if she wouldn't go dancing on the coming Saturday.	'I'm sorry but I'll be busy that day.'
h. if she goes for food shopping everyday.	'No, twice a week.'
i. if she likes sports.	'Yes, I do very much.'
j. if she doesn't want to sightsee downtown.	'I have already done some sightseeing downtown.'
k. if she can't wait for you.	'Why not. I'll wait for you.'

End of Tape 7B

Tape 8A

제 10 과 시내구경

먼저
가고 싶습니까
1. 김 : 어디에 먼저 가고 싶습니까?

2. 스미스 : 다방에 먼저 들릅시다.

누구
(누구) 만날 사람
3. 김 : 누구 만날 사람이 있읍니까?

커피 한 잔
마시면
마셨으면 좋겠읍니다
4. 스미스 : 커피 한 잔 마셨으면 좋겠읍니다.

가면
5. 김 : 먼저 시내로 갑시다. 시내에 가면 좋은 다방이 많이 있읍니다.

이 부근
6. 스미스 : 이 부근에는 다방이 없어요?

있어도
그리 좋지 않습니다
7. 김 : 이 부근에 다방이 있어도 그리 좋지 않습니다.

UNIT 10. Going Around the Town

BASIC DIALOGUE FOR MEMORIZATION

Kim

mәncә	first; above all
kako siphsɪmnikka	do you want to go
1. әti e mәncә kako sipsɪmnikka?	Where do you want to go first?

Smith

2. Tapang e mәncә tɪllɪpsita.	Let's stop by a tearoom first.

Kim

nuku	anybody; somebody; who?
(nuku) mannal salam	somebody to meet
3. Nuku mannal salam i issɪmnikka?	Are you meeting anyone? ('Do you have anyone to meet?')

Smith

khәphi han can	a cup of coffee
masimyәn	if [I] drink
masyәssɪmyәn cohkessɪmnita	(if [I] drank, [it]'ll be nice)
4. Khәphi han can masyәssɪmyәn cohkessɪmnita.	I'd like to have a cup of coffee. ('If I drank a cup of coffee, it would be nice.')

Kim

kamyәn	if [we] go
5. Mәncә sinæ lo kapsita. Sinæ e kamyәn, cohɪn tapang i manhi issɪmnita.	Let's go downtown first. There are good tearooms downtown. ('If [we] go downtown there are a lot of tearooms.')

Smith

i pukɪn	this area; this vicinity
6. I pukɪn e nɪn tapang i әpsә yo?	Aren't there any tearooms in this area?

얼마나
얼마나 멉니까
시내까지

8. 스미스 : 여기에서 시내까지 얼마나 멉니까?

아주
걸어서

9. 김 : 아주 가깝습니다. 걸어서 십 오 분 쯤 걸립니다.

빠스나 전차
다닙니다

10. 스미스 : 빠스나 전차는 다니지 않습니까?

합승

11. 김 : 왜요? 빠스, 전차, 택시, 그리고 합승도 있읍니다.

그것들
그(것들) 중 에서
어느 편
제일
편리
편리합니다
제일 편리합니다

12. 스미스 : 그(것들) 중 에서 어느 편이 제일 편리합니까?

Kim

issə to	even though there are; there are but...
kıli cohci anhsımnita	[it] is not so good
7. I pukın e tapang i issə to, kıli cohci anhsımnita.	[Yes], there are [some], but they are not very good.

Smith

əlma na	how; how much
əlma na məmnikka	how far is [it]?
sinæ kkaci	as far as downtown
8. Yəki esə sinæ kkaci əlma na məmnikka?	How far is downtown from here?

Kim

acu	really; very; extremely
kələ sə	on foot
9. Acu kakkapsımnita. Kələ sə sip-o pun ccım kəllimnita.	It is very close. It only takes about fifteen minutes to walk.

Smith

ppəsı na cəncha	bus or streetcar
tanimnita	('[I] go and come regularly.')
10. Ppəsı na cəncha nın tanici anhsımnikka?	Aren't there any buses or streetcars running?

Kim

hapsıng	jitney
11. Wæ yo? Ppəsı, cəncha, thæksi, kıliko hapsıng to issımnita.	Yes, there are. ('Why?') There are buses, streetcars, taxes and even jitneys.

빠릅니다
가장 빠릅니다
빠르고 편리합니다

13. 김 : 합승이 가장 빠르고 (가장) 편리합니다.

자주
얼마나 자주
다니는가요

14. 스미스 : 예, 그렇습니까? 합승은 얼마나 자주 다니는가요?

십 오 분에 한 번
번잡합니다

15. 김 : 대개 십 오 분에 한 번 있지만, 아침과 저녁에는 좀 번잡합니다.

Smith

kɪ kəs tɪl	they; those (things)
kɪ (kəs tɪl) cung esə	among them; among those
ənɪ phyən	which side; which way
ceil	number one
phyəlli	convenience
phyəlli-hamnita	[it]'s convenient
ceil phyəlli-hamnita	[it]'s most convenient
12. Kɪ (kəs tɪl) cung esə ənɪ phyən i ceil phyəlli-hamnikka?	Which is the most convenient (among them)? ('Among those things which one is the most convenient?')

Kim

ppalɪmnita	[it]'s fast ; [it]'s quick
kacang ppalɪmnita	[it]'s fastest
ppalɪko phyəlli-hamnita	[it]'s fast and convenient
13. Hapsɪng i kacang ppalɪko, (kacang) phyəlli-hamnita.	A jitney is the fastest and the most convenient.

Smith

cacu	frequently; often
əlma na cacu	how often?
tanɪnɪn ka yo	does [it] run?
14. Ne, kɪləhsɪmnikka? Hapsɪng ɪn əlma na cacu tanɪnɪn ka yo?	Is that right? How often do the jitneys run?

Kim

sip-o pun e han pən	every fifteen minutes ('once at 15 minutes')
pəncap-hamnita	[it]'s crowded
15. Tækæ sip-o pun e han pən issci man, achim kwa cənyək e nɪn com pəncap-hamnita.	They usually run every fifteen minutes but they are rather crowded in the morning and in the evening.

NOTES ON DIALOGUES

(Numbers correspond to the sentence numbers in the dialogue.)

1. Mәncә 'first', 'ahead', is an adverb which occurs before verbs and denotes priority for the following inflected expressions. Mәncә followed by a pause also occurs as a sentence adverb, meaning 'in the first place', 'above all'.

3. Nuku mannal salam i issimnikka? 'Are you meeting somebody?' ('Is there anybody to meet?') ends in a rising intonation with a stress on the first syllable of mannal.

4. Khәphi han can masyәssimyәn cohkessimnita. ('If [I] drank a cup of coffee, [it] will be good.') occurs with or without a pause after the -(i)myәn form. The pattern -(a, ә)ssimyәn cohkessimnita, which is the -(i)myәn form with the past tense suffix plus the verb coh- in the future tense, is used to express the desire of the speaker or the addressee (See Grammar Note 1).

6. Pukin 'vicinity' is a post-noun which, together with the preceeding noun, makes a noun phrase:

i pukin	'this area', 'this vicinity'
hakkyo pukin	'the vicinity of the school'

9. Acu 'very', 'extremely' is an adverb which occurs before description verbs or other adverbs, and denotes the extreme degree of the following inflected expressions. Kәlә sә 'on foot' is an adverbial phrase. Kәlә is the infinitive of the verb kәl- 'to walk'; sә is a particle. (We will learn more about the particle sә later.) Kәlә sә here should be memorized as it is as the Korean equivalent of the English phrase 'on foot'.

12. Til is a post-noun which occurs after a countable nominal and denotes plurality. Til does not occur after a numeral expression and/or a numeral + counter. In other words, if the nominal is specified by number, til is not used. Cung is a post-noun which occurs in the following types of adverbial phrases.

(a) Name of time + cung + e 'during / 'in + the name of time'

Il-wəl cung e	'in January' / 'during January'
onɪl cung e	'within today'
kɪmnyən cung e	'in this year' / 'within this year'

(b) Countable Noun + cung + esə 'among + Countable Noun'

hakkyo tɪl cung esə	'among the schools'
nala cung esə	'among the countries'

15. Pəncap-ha-ta 'is crowded' is an intransitive verb which may be preceded by a place name or a mode of transportation as the subject or topic of the sentence.

Kil i pəncap-hamnita.	'The street is crowded.'
Kɪkcang i pəncap-hæ yo?	'Is the theatre crowded?'
Kyothong i pəncap-hamnita.	'There is a traffic jam.'

GRAMMAR NOTES

1. -myən/ɪmyən 'if (when) X does something', 'if (when) X is such and such'

The inflected form ending in -(ɪ)myən (or simply the -(ɪ)myən form) which may be followed by a pause occurs before another inflected expression. The honorific and/or tense suffixes may occur in the -(ɪ)myən form; -myən is added to a stem ending in a vowel and -ɪmyən to a stem ending in a consonant. The -(ɪ)myən form indicates that the condition or time of the action or description takes place for the following inflected expression. Examples:

Pi ka omyən, cip e isskessə yo.	'If it rains, I will be home.'
Hankuk e kamyən, Səul esə kɪnmu-hako siphsɪmnita.	'If I go to Korea / 'When I go to Korea I'd like to work in Seoul.'
Wəsington e omyən, ce cip e to ose yo.	'If you come to Washington, come to my house, too.'

Remember that the pattern -(a,ə)ssɪmyən cohkessɪmnita. ('If [I] did..., [it] will be good.') is used to express the speaker's wish or desire.

2. Infinitive + to 'even though___,' 'although___,'

In Unit 5 we learned that the particle to after a nominal means 'also', 'too', 'even'. To occurs not only after nominals but also after a small number of inflected forms. Most Korean particles occur after nominals, but note that there also is a small class of particles which occur after other classes of words (e.g. inflected words). The construction Infinitive + to, followed by a pause occuring before another inflected expression, denotes concession to the following inflection expression. The tense suffixes may occur in the Infinitive which precedes to. Compare Infinitive + to with the construction -ci man 'but' for its meaning. Note that the pattern Infinitive + to + cohsımnikka?/ Inf. + to + kwænchanhsımnikka? ('Even if [I] do.., is it o.k.?') is used to get permission or consent from the addressee. In English the pattern 'May I...?' is usually used as the equivalent of the above Korean pattern. The usual 'yes' response to Infinitive + to + cohsımnikka? is Ne, Infinitive + to + cohsımnita. 'Yes, you man...'. 'No' response is either -ci masipsiyo or -ci anhın kəs i cohkessımnita. (See Grammar Notes, Unit 11.) Examples:

Sinæ e tapang i issə to, kılı cohci anhsımnita.	'Even though there are tearooms, [they) are not very good.'
Pi ka wa to, hakkyo e kakessə yo.	'Even if it rains, I will go to school.'
Cə yəca lıl han pən mannassə to, ilım ıl molımnita.	'Although I met her once I don't know [her] name.'
Hwesa ka com mələ to, kələ sə il-halə tanimnita.	'My office is a little far, but I go to work on foot.'
Kyosil esə khəphi lıl masiə to cohsımnikka?	'May I drink coffee in the classroom?'

3. Ceil / Kacang } 'the most___'

The adverb ceil (or its equivalent kacang) occurs before a verbal, noun-modifier word or another adverb, and denotes the superative degree of the following expression. Compare:

(a) Hapsıng i phyəlli-hamnita.	'Jitney is convenient.'
Hapsıng i tə phyəlli-hamnita.	'Jitney is more convenient.'
Hapsıng i {kacang / ceil} phyəlli-hamnita.	'Jitney is most convenient.'

(b)	yeppɨn yəca	'(a) pretty woman'
	tə yeppɨn yəca	'prettier woman'
	ceil / kacang } yeppɨn yəca	'the prettiest woman'
(c)	Ceimsɨ ka Hankuk mal ɨl cal hamnita.	'James speaks Korean well.'
	Ceimsɨ ka Hankuk mal ɨl tə cal hamnita.	'James speaks Korean better.'
	Ceimsɨ ka Hankuk mal ɨl ceil / kacang } cal hamnita.	'James speaks Korean best.'

4. Particle <u>na/ina</u>

<u>Na</u> occurs after a nominal ending in a vowel; <u>ina</u> after a nominal ending in a consonant. <u>Na/ina</u> occurs in the following constructions:

(a) <u>Nominal 1 + na/ina + Nominal 2</u> 'N 1 or N 2', 'either N 1 or N 2'

Between two nominals <u>na/ina</u> denotes <u>selection</u> of one of the two, N 1 or N 2.

Yənphil ina mannyənphil ɨl cusipsiyo.	'Give me a pencil or pen.'
Onɨl ina næil i cohsɨmnita.	'Either today or tomorrow is O.K.'
Wəlyoil ina Hwayoil e tola osipsiyo.	'Please come back either Monday or Tuesday.'

(b) <u>Question Nominal + na/ina</u> = adverbial phrases

muəs ina	'anything' / 'whatever [it] may be'
nuku na	'anybody' / 'whoever [he] may be'
ənce na	'anytime' / 'whenever [it]may be'
əti na	'ánywhere' / 'no matter where [it] may be'
əlma na	'how much' / 'how long'
əlma na cacu	'how often'

(c) Nominal + na/ina, followed by an inflected expression, denotes choice of the nominal among others for the following inflected expression.

Onıl ın yənghwa na polə kapsita.	'Let's go to see, say, movies.'
Khəphi ka əpsımyən, hongcha na hal kka yo?	'If they don't have coffee, shall we have, say, black tea?'
Ca, onıl ın kukyəng ina kaci yo.	'Say, how about going to a show today.'

DRILLS

A. Substitution Drill

1. Məncə tapang e tıllıpsita.	Let's stop by a tearoom first.
2. Məncə næ samusil e tıllıpsita.	Let's stop by my office first.
3. Məncə Kukuce Uphyənkuk e tıllıpsita.	Let's stop by the International Post Office first.
4. Məncə hakkyo chækpang e tıllıpsita.	Let's stop by the campus bookstore first.
*5. Məncə Cungkuk ımsikcəm e tıllıpsita.	Let's stop by a Chinese restaurant first.
*6. Məncə Səul Tæhakkyo e tıllıpsita.	Let's stop by Seoul University first.
*7. Məncə pakmulkwan e tıllıpsita.	Let's stop by the museum first.
*8. Məncə kyəngchalsə e tıllıpsita.	Let's stop by the police station first.
*9. Məncə Səul Kotıng Hakkyo e tıllıpsita.	Let's stop by the Seoul High School first.
*10. Məncə pyəngwən e tıllıpsita.	Let's stop by the hospital first.
*11. Məncə tosəkwan e tıllıpsita.	Let's stop by the library first.
*12. Məncə yakpang e tıllıpsita.	Let's stop by the drugstore first.
*13. Məncə tongmul-wən e tıllıpsita.	Let's stop by the zoo first.
*14. Məncə kyohwe e tıllipsita.	Let's stop by the church first.

B. Substitution Drill

1. Mannal salam i issımnikka?	Are you meeting anyone? ('Do you have anyone to meet?')
2. Hal il (i) issımnikka?	Do you have any work to do?
3. Pol yənghwa (ka) issımnikka?	Are there any movies to see?
4. Tıllıl tapang (i) issımnikka?	Is there a tearoom to stop by?
5. Sal kəs (i) issımnikka?	Is there anything to buy?
6. Ilkıl chæk (i) issımnikka?	Do you have a book to read?
7. Masil khəphi (ka) issımnikka?	Is there any coffee to drink?
8. Tanil hakkyo (ka) issımnikka?	Is there a school for you to attend?
9. Kitalil salam (i) issımnikka?	Are you waiting for anyone? ('Do you have anyone to wait for?')
*10. Kukyəng-hal te (ka) issımnikka?	Is there any place for sightseeing?

C. Substitution Drill

1.	Kyəphi han can masyəssımyən cohkessımnita.	I'd like to have a cup of coffee. ('[It]'ll be nice if [I] drank coffee.')
2.	Hakkyo e kassımyən cohkessımnita.	I'd like to go to school.
3.	Ceimsı lıl mannassımyən cohkessımnita.	I'd like to meet James.
4.	Tapang e tılləssımyən cohkessımnita.	I'd like to stop by a tearoom.
5.	Yənghwa lıl pwassımyən chokessımnita.	I'd like to see a movie.
6.	Tapang i issəssımyən cohkessımnita.	I wish there were tearooms.
7.	Kim Sənsæng i wassımyən cohkessımnita.	I wish Mr. Kim came.
8.	Onıl ttənassımyən cohkessımnita.	I'd like to leave today.
9.	Səul Tæhakkyo e taniəssımyən cohkessımnita.	I'd like to attend Seoul University.
10.	Pullansə mal ıl pæwəssımyən cohkessımnita.	I'd like to study French.
11.	Hankuk ıl kukyəng-hæssımyən cohkessımnita.	I'd like to see Korea.
12.	Cip i kakkawəssımyən cohkessımnita.	I wish my house were near.
13.	Cip kaps i ssassımyən cohkessımnita.	I wish the rent were cheap.

D. Substitution Drill

1.	Sinæ e cohın tapang i manhi issə yo.	There are many nice tearooms downtown.
2.	Səul e cohın hakkyo ka manhi issə yo.	There are many good schools in Seoul.
3.	Hankuk e cohın pækhwacəm i manhi issə yo.	There are many good department stores in Korea.
4.	Nyuyok e cohın kıkcang i manhi issə yo.	There are many good theatres in New York.
5.	Wəsingthon e cohın tosəkwan i manhi issə yo.	There are many good libraries in Washington.
6.	Yəki e cohın pakmulkwan i manhi issə yo.	There are many good museums here.
7.	Kəkı e cohın ımsikcəm i manhi issə yo.	There are many good restaurants there.

8.	<u>I pukın</u> e cohın <u>yakpang</u> i manhi issə yo.	There are many good drug stores in this vicinity.
9.	<u>Səul pukın</u> e cohın <u>kotıng hakkyo</u> ka manhi issə yo.	There are many good high schools in Seoul area.
10.	<u>Nyuyok pukın</u> e cohın <u>pyəngwən</u> i manhi issə yo.	There are many good hospitals in New York area.
11.	<u>Pusan pukın</u> e cohın <u>tæhakkyo</u> ka manhi issə yo.	There are many good universities in Pusan area.
*12.	<u>Tæku pukın</u> e cohın <u>cunghakkyo</u> ka manhi issə yo.	There are many good junior high Schools in Taeku area.
*13.	<u>Səul Tæhak pukın</u> e cohın <u>sohakkyo</u> ka manhi issə yo.	There are many good elementary schools in the vicinity of Seoul College.

E. Substitution Drill

1.	I pukın e tapang i əpsə yo?	Aren't there any tearooms in this area?
2.	<u>Tæsakwan pukın</u> e <u>ımsikcəm</u> i əpsə yo?	Aren't there any restaurants around the Embassy?
3.	<u>Cəngkəcang pukın</u> e <u>kyohwe</u> ka əpsə yo?	Aren't there any churches around the station?
4.	<u>Yakpang pukın</u> e <u>pyəngwən</u> i əpsə yo?	Aren't there any clinics around the drug store?
*5.	<u>Kyəngchalsə pukın</u> e <u>cæphanso</u> ka əpsə yo?	Aren't there any courts around the police station?
6.	<u>Səul Tæhakkyo pukın</u> e <u>pakmulkwan</u> i əpsə yo?	Aren't there any museums around Seoul University?
7.	<u>Tosəkwan pukın</u> e <u>cunghakkyo</u> ka əpse yo?	Aren't there any middle schools around the library?
8.	<u>Pakmulkwan pukın</u> e <u>kotıng hakkyo</u> ka əpsə yo?	Aren't there any high schools around the museum?
9.	<u>Pyəngwən pukın</u> e <u>sohakkyo</u> ka əpsə yo?	Aren't there any elementary schools around the hospital?

F. Substitution Drill

1. Hakkyo pukɪn e nɪn tapang i əpsɪmnita.	There are no tearooms around the school.
2. Pyəngwən pukɪn e nɪn yakpang i əpsɪmnita.	There are no drug stores around the hospital.
3. Səul Tæhakkyo pukɪn e nɪn chækpang i əpsɪmnita.	There are no bookstores around Seoul University.
4. Hwesa pukɪn e nɪn ɪmsikcəm i əpsɪmnita.	There are no restaurants around the company.
5. Kotɪng hakkyo pukɪn e nɪn sohakkyo ka əpsɪmnita.	There are no elementary schools around the high school.
6. Sohakkyo pukɪn e nɪn cunghakkyo ka əpsɪmnita.	There are no middle schools around the elementary schools.
7. Pakmulkwan pukɪn e nɪn kongwən i əpsɪmnita.	There are no parks around the museum.
8. Mikuk Tæsakwan pukɪn e nɪn sangcəm i əpsɪmnita.	There are no stores around the U.S. Embassy.
9. Mikuk Yəngsakwan pukɪn e nɪn ɪnhæng i əpsɪmnita.	There are no banks around the U.S. Consulate.
10. Mikuk Kongpowən pukɪn e nɪn uphyənkuk i əpsɪmnita.	There is no post office around USIS.
*11. Uphyənkuk pukɪn e nɪn cæphanso ka əpsɪmnita.	There are no courts around the post office.

G. Substitution Drill

1. Sinæ kkaci əlma na məmnikka?	How far is downtown [from here]?
2. Səul yək kkaci əlma na məmnikka?	How far is it to Seoul Station?
3. Cungkuk ɪmsikcəm kkaci əlma na məmnikka?	How far is it to a Chinese restaurant?
4. Hankuk ɪnhæng kkaci əlma na məmnikka?	How far is it to the Bank of Korea?
5. Panto Kwesa kkaci əlma na məmnikka?	How far is it to the Bando Company?
6. Kukce Kɪkcang kkaci əlma na məmnikka?	How far is it to the International Theatre?

7.	Səul Tæhakkyo tosəkwan kkaci əlma na məmnikka?	How far is it to the Seoul University library?
8.	Tæhak Pyəngwən kənmul kkaci əlma na məmnikka?	How far is it to the University Hospital building?
9.	Ceil kakkaun kongwən kkaci əlma na məmnikka?	How far is it to the nearest park?

H. Substitution Drill

1.	Hakkyo ka əlma na məmnikka?	How far is the school?
2.	Cip i əlma na kakkapsımnikka?	How near is the house?
3.	Pihængki ka əlma na ppalımnikka?	How fast is the airplane?
4.	Cəncha ka əlma na nilimnikka?	How slow is the streetcar?
5.	Hapsıng i əlma na phyəlli-hamnikka?	How convenient is the jitney?
6.	Kil i əlma na pəncap-hamnikka?	How crowded is the street?
*7.	Munce ka əlma na kantan-hamnikka?	How simple is the problem?
*8.	Munpəp i əlma na pokcap-hamnikka?	How complicated is the grammar?
*9.	ıyca ka əlma na phyənhamnikka?	How comfortable is the chair?
*10.	Kyothong i əlma na pulphyən-hamnikka?	How inconvenient is the transportation (or traffic)?
*11.	San i əlma na nophsımnikka?	How high is the mountain?
*12.	Kənmul i əlma na nacımnikka?	How low is the building?
*13.	Tali ka əlma na ki(l)mnikka?	How long (length) is the bridge?
*14.	Mul i əlma na kiphsımnikka?	How deep is the water?
*15.	Hakki ka əlma na cca(l)psımnikka?	How short is the semester?
*16.	Muke ka əlma na mukəpsımnikka?	How heavy is the weight?
*17.	Chæksang i əlma na kapyəpsımnikka?	How light (weight) is the table?
*18.	Pang i əlma na pa(l)ksımnikka?	How light is the room?
*19.	Kyosil i əlma na ətupsımnikka?	How dark is the classroom?
*20.	Tosi ka əlma na nəlpsımnikka?	How large is the city?

I. Substitution Drill

1.	Sinæ kkaci kələ sə sip-o pun ccɨm kəllimnita.	It takes about 15 minutes to walk downtown.
2.	Sinæ kkaci catongcha lo sip-o pun ccɨm kəllimnita.	It takes about 15 minutes to go downtown by car.
*3.	Siwe kkaci catongcha lo sip-o pun ccɨm kəllimnita.	It takes about 15 minutes to go to the suburb by car.
4.	Siwe kkaci catongcha lo i-sip-o pun ccɨm kəllimnita.	It takes about 25 minutes to go to the suburb by car.
5.	Siwe kkaci cəncha lo i-sip-o pun ccɨm kəllimnita.	It takes about 25 minutes by streetcar to go to the suburb.
6.	Sinmunsa kkaci cəncha lo i-sip-o ccɨm kəllimnita.	It takes about 25 minutes by streetcar to go to the newspaper publishing company.
7.	Sinmunsa kkaci cəncha lo pan sikan ccɨm kəllimnita.	It takes about half an hour by streetcar to go to the newspaper publishing company.
8.	Sinmunsa kkaci kələ sə pan sikan ccɨm kəllimnita.	It takes about half an hour on foot to go to the newspaper publisher.
9.	Mikuk Kongpowən tosəkwan kkaci kələ sə pan sikan ccɨm kəllimnita.	It takes about half an hour on foot to go to the USIS library.
10.	Mikuk Kongpowən tosəkwan kkaci kələ sə pan sikan ccɨm twemnita.	It's about half an hour (walk) to the USIS library.
11.	Mikuk Kongpowən tosəkwan kkaci kələ sə pan sikan ccɨm kamnita.	You [have to] go about half an hour on foot to get to the USIS library.

J. Substitution Drill

1.	Ppəsɨ na cəncha nɨn tanici anhsɨmnikka?	Aren't there any buses or streetcars running?
2.	Hapsɨng ina thækssi nɨn tanici anhsɨmnikka?	Aren't there any jitneys or taxis running?
3.	Pæ na pihængki nɨn tanici anhsɨmnikka?	Aren't there any ships or airplanes running?
4.	Kicha na catongcha nɨn tanici anhsɨmnikka?	Aren't there any trains or automobiles running?
*5.	Catongcha na hwamulcha nɨn tanici anhsɨmnikka?	Aren't there any cars or cargo trains running?

*6.	Hwamulcha na hwamulsən ın tanici anhsımnikka?	Aren't there any cargo trains or cargo ships running?
*7.	Hwamulsən ina kisən ın tanici anhsımnikka?	Aren't there any cargo ships or steamships running?
*8.	Kisən ina kæksən ın tanici anhsımnikka?	Aren't there any steamships or passenger ships running?
*9.	Hwamulcha na hwamul catongcha nın tanici anhsımnikka?	Aren't there any cargo trains or trucks running?
*10.	Kæksən ina kækcha nın tanici anhsımnikka?	Aren't there any passenger ships or passenger trains running?
*11.	Kıphæng (cha) na Wanhæng (cha) nın tanici anhsımnikka?	Aren't there any express (trains) or local (trains) running?

K. Substitution Drill

1.	Hapsıng i cacu tanimnita.	Jitneys run frequently.
2.	Hapsıng i kakkım tanimnita.	Jitneys run sometimes.
3.	Hapsıng i nıl tanimnita.	Jitneys run all the time.
4.	Hapsing i hangsang tanimnita.	Jitneys run all the time.
5.	Hapsıng i ənce na tanimnita.	Jitneys run {any time. / all the time.
6.	Hapsıng i manhi tanimnita.	Jitneys run a lot.
*7.	Hapsıng i ttæ ttæ lo tanimnita.	Jitneys run {occasionally. / from time to time.
*8.	Hapsıng i ittakım tanimnita.	Jitneys run {off and on. / once in a while.
9.	Hapsıng i han sikan e han pən tanimnita.	Jitneys run every hour.
10.	Hapsıng i halu e tu pən tanimnita.	Jitneys run twice a day.

L. Substitution Drill

1. əlma na cacu hapsıng i tanimnikka? — How often do the jitneys run?
2. əlma na cacu tapang e kamnikka? — How often do you go to a tearoom?
3. əlma na cacu pækhwacəm e tıllımnikka? — How often do you stop by the department store?
4. əlma na cacu yəca chinku lıl mannamnikka? — How often do you meet your girl friend?
5. əlma na cacu ppəsı lıl thamnikka? — How often do you take the bus?
6. əlma na cacu mom i aphımnikka? — How often are you sick?
7. əlma na cacu hyuka lıl patsımnikka? — How often do you take leave?
8. əlma na cacu cip esə swimnikka? — How often do you stay home ('rest home')?
9. əlma na cacu yənghwa lıl pomnikka? — How often do you see movies?
10. əlma na cacu yənghwa polə kamnikka? — How often do you go to see movies?
11. əlma na cacu Mikuk yənghwa lıl sangyəng-hamnikka? — How often do [they] show American movies?
*12. əlma na cacu sæ waisyassı ka philyo-hamnikka? — How often do you need new (dress) shirt?
13. əlma na cacu yangpok ıl samnikka? — How often do you buy suits?

M. Substitution Drill

1. Ppəsı (ka) Pəncap-hamnita. — Buses are crowded.
2. Cəncha (ka) pəncap-hamnita. — Streetcars are crowded.
3. Kıkcang (i) pəncap-hamnita. — Theatres are crowded.
4. Kicha (ka) pəncap-hamnita. — Trains are crowded.
5. Tapang (i) pəncap-hamnita. — Tearooms are crowded.
6. Siktang (i) pəncap-hamnita. — Restaurants are crowded.
7. Cəngkəcang (i) pəncap-hamnita. — The station is crowded.
8. Kil (i) pəncap-hamnita. — The streets are crowded.
*9. Kyothong (i) pəncap-hamnita. — {Traffic is heavy. / There is a traffic jam.}
*10. Kyothong (i) pokcap-hamnita. — {Transportation is complicated. / There is a traffic jam.}
*11. Munce (ka) pokcap-hamnita. — The problem is complicated.
*12. Munpəp i pokcap-hamnita. — The grammar is complicated.

N. Combination Drill (based on Grammar Note 1)

Tutor: Hankuk e kamnita. Səul esə il-hakessımnita.	'I go to Korea.' 'I'll work in Seoul.'
Student: Hankuk e kamyən, Səul esə il-hakessımnita.	'When/If I go to Korea I'll work in Seoul.'
1. Kim Sənsæng ıl mannamnita. Kıləhke mal-hakessımnita.	Kim Sənsæng ıl mannamyən, kıləhke mal-hakessımnita.
2. Sikan i issımnita. Kıkcang e kakessımnita.	Sikan i issımyən, kıkcang e kakessımnita.
3. Sinæ e kamnita. Khəphi lıl masikessımnita.	Sinæ e kamyən, khəphi lıl masikessımnita.
4. Tapang i əpsımnita. Tæsakwan esə mannakessımnita.	Tapang i əpsımyən, tæsakwan esə mannakessımnita.
5. I pukın e tapang i issımnita. Tıllıkessımnita.	I pukın e tapang i issımyən, tıllıkessımnita.
6. Kicha ka phyənhamnita. Kicha lo Səul e kakessımnita.	Kicha ka phyənhamyən, kicha lo Səul e kakessımnita.
7. Hakkyo ka kakkapsımnita. Kələ sə kakessımnita.	Hakkyo ka kakkaumyən, kələ sə kakessımnita.
8. Sinæ ka məmnita. Hapsıng ıl thakessımnita.	Sinæ ka məlmyən, hapsıng ıl thakessımnita.
9. Səul e tto omnita. Səul Tæhakkyo e tanikessımnita.	Səul e tto omyən, Səul Tæhakkyo e tanikessımnita.
10. Ppəsı ka phyəlli-hamnita. Ppəsi lo ttənakessımnita.	Ppəsi ka phyəlli-hamyən, ppəsi lo ttənakessımnita.
11. Cəncha e salam i manhsımnita. Tnæksi lo okessımnita.	Cəncha e salam i manhımyən, thæksi lo okessımnita.

O. Completion Exercise

Tutor: Hankuk e kamyən,	'When I go to Korea' / 'If I go to Korea' ,...
Student: Hankuk e kamyən, Səul esə il-hakessımnita.	'When / If I go to Korea I'll work in Seoul.'

1. Sikan i issımyən,
2. Sinæ e kamyən,
3. Tapang e tıllımyən,
4. Tapang i issımyən,
5. Chinku lıl mannamyən,
6. Hakkyo ka əpsımyən,
7. Kicha lıl thamyən,
8. Onıl yəki esə ttənamyən,
9. Nal i cohımyən,
10. Səul e cip kaps i pissamyən,
11. Sinæ ka məlmyən,
12. Kı yəca ka yeppımyən,
13. Cohın Hankuk mal sənsæng ıl chacımyən,
14. Yəng-Han sacən ıl samyən,
15. Hankuk mal ıl pæumyən,
16. Ilpon mal i swiumyən,
17. Yəngə ka əlyəumyən,
18. Hankuk mal i cæmi issımyən,
19. Tokil mal ıl hal su issımyən,
20. Hankuk e kaci anhımyən,
21. Khəphi lıl masiko siphımyən,
22. Næil an pappımyən,
23. Hankuk mal ıl alə tılımyən,
24. Hankuk mal ıl alə tıtci mot hamyən,

<u>End of Tape 8A</u>

Tape 8B

P. Grammar Drill (based on Grammar Note 2)

Tutor: Hankuk mal i əlyəpci man, cæmi issımnita.	'Korean is difficult but it's interesting.'
Student: Hankuk mal i əlyəwə to, cæmi issə yo.	'Even though Korean is difficult, it's interesting.'
1. Sinæ e tapang i issci man, cohci anhsımnita.	Sinæ e tapang i issə to, cohci anhə yo.
2. Nal mata hakkyo e kaci man, kongpu-haci anhsımnita.	Nal mata hakkyo e ka to, kongpu-haci anhə yo.
3. Com pappıci man, sinæ e kakessımnita.	Com pappə to, sinæ e kakessə yo.
4. Hankuk mal ıl alə tıtci man, mal-haci mot hamnita.	Hankuk mal ıl alə tılə to, mal-haci mot hæ yo.
5. Kı salam ıl kitalıci man, oci anhsımnita.	Kı salam ıl kitalyə to, oci anhə yo.
6. Cə yəca lıl mannassci man, ilım ıl molımnita.	Cə yəca lıl mannassə to, ilım ıl molla yo.
7. Sənsæng ın əpsəssci man, haksæng ın manhəssımnita.	Sənsæng ın əpsəssə to, haksæng ın manhəssə yo.
8. Hwesa ka mələssci man, kələ sə taniəssımnita.	Hwesa ka mələssə to, kələ sə taniəssə yo.
9. Pihængki ka phyəlli-hæssci man, com pissassımnita.	Pihængki ka phyəlli-hæssə to, com pissassə yo.
10. Kim Sənsæng ın Yəngə lıl mal-hæssci man, ssıci mot hæssımnita.	Kim Sənsæng ın Yəngə lıl mal-hæssə to, ssıci mot hæssə yo.
11. Hankuk mal ıl pæuko siphci man, sikan i əpsımnita.	Hankuk mal ıl pæuko siphə to, sikan i əpsə yo.
12. Səul e kalyəko haci man, Hankuk mal ıl molımnita.	Səul e kalyəko hæ to, Hankuk mal ıl molla yo.

Q. Completion Exercise (based on Grammar Note 2)

Tutor: I pukɪn e tapang i issə to, — 'Even though there are tearooms in this area,...'

Student: I pukɪn e tapang issə to, cohci anhsɪmnita. — 'Even though there are tearooms in this area, they're not good.'

1. Hankuk mal i əlyəwə to,
2. Nal mata Hankuk mal ɪl pæwə to,
3. Yəngə lɪl alə tɪlə to,
4. Pihængki ka phyəlli-hæ to,
5. Sənsæng ɪn əpsə to,
6. Cə yəca lɪl mannassə to,
7. Hakkyo ka mələ to,
8. Hankuk mal ɪl pæuko siphə to,
9. Səul e kalyəko hæ to,

R. Response Drill

Tutor: Cip e ka to cohsɪmnikka? — 'May I go home? ('Is it all right even if I go home?')

Student: Ne, ka to cohsɪmnita. — 'Yes, you may (go).'

1. I chæk ɪl ilkə to cohsɪmnikka?	Ne, ilkə to cohsɪmnita.
2. Sənsæng cip e tɪllə to cohsɪmnikka?	Ne, tɪllə to cohsɪmnita.
3. Sənsæng e cha lɪl tha to cohsɪmnikka?	Ne, tha to cohsɪmnita.
4. Cə kɪlim ɪl pwa to cohsɪmnikka?	Ne, pwa to cohsɪmnita.
5. Yəki esə tangsin ɪl kitaliə to cohsɪmnikka?	Ne, yəki esə kitaliə to cohsɪmnita.
6. Onɪl ttəna to cohsɪmnikka?	Ne, onɪl ttəna to cohsɪmnita.
7. Kyosil esə khəphi lɪl masyə to cohsɪmnikka?	Ne, masyə to cochɪmnita.
8. Onɪl cip esə swiə to cohsɪmnikka?	Ne, swiə to cohsɪmnita.
9. Mikuk yənghwa lɪl pwa to cohsɪmnikka?	Ne, pwa to cohsɪmnita.
10. Hankuk mal lo mal-hæ to cohsɪmnikka?	Ne, Hankuk mal lo mal-hæ to cohsɪmnita.

S. Response Drill (based on Grammar Note 3)

Tutor: I chæk i pissamnikka?	'Is this book expensive?'
Student: Ne, i chæk ceil pissamnita.	'Yes, this (book) is the most expensive.'
1. Hankuk mal i əlyəpsımnikka?	Ne, Hankuk mal i ceil əlyəpsımnita.
2. Hapsıng i phyəlli-hamnikka?	Ne, hapsıng i ceil phyəlli-hamnita.
3. Kim Sənsæng i (Hankuk mal ıl) cal kalıchimnikka?	Ne, Kim Sənsæng i (Hankuk mal ıl) ceil cal kalıchimnita.
4. Pihængki ka ppalımnikka?	Ne, pihængki ka ceil ppalımnita.
5. Cəncha ka nılimnikka?	Ne, cəncha ka ceil nılimnita.
6. Hapsıng i cacu tanimnikka?	Ne, hapsıng i ceil cacu tanimnita.
7. Səul i khın tosi imnikka?	Ne, Səul i ceil khın tosi imnita.
8. Cə yəca lıl cohahamnikka?	Ne, cə yəca lıl ceil cohahamnita.
9. Yəng-Han sacən i philyo-hamnikka?	Ne, Yəng-Han sacən i ceil philyo-hamnita.

T. Response Drill

Tutor: Muəs i ceil phyəlli-hamnikka? /hapsıng/	'What is most convenient?' /jitney/
Student: Hapsıng i kacang phyelli-hamnita.	'A jitney is the most convenient.'
1. Nuka ceil Yəngə lıl cal hamnikkə? /Kim Sənsæng/	Kim Sənsæng i Yəngə lıl kacang cal hamnita.
2. ənı mal i ceil əlyəpsımnikka? /Ssolyən mal/	Ssolyən mal i kacang əlyəpsımnita.
3. Mikuk esə ənı tosi ka ceil khımnikka? /Nyuyok/	Nyuyok i kacang khımnita.
4. Musın catongcha ka ceil pissamnikka? /khyatalæk/	Khyatalæk i kacang pissamnita.
5. Hankuk esə əti e Mikuk salam i ceil manhi samnikka? /Səul pukın/	Səul pukın e kacang manhi samnita.
6. Muəs i ceil ppalımnikka? /kicha/	Kicha ka kacang ppalımnita.
7. ənı phyən i ceil nılimnikka? /cəncha/	Cəncha phən i kacang nılimnita.

8. əti lıl ceil mencə kukyəng-hako siphsımnikka? /sinæ kongwən/ — Sinæ kongwən ıl kacang mencə kukyəng-hako siphsımnita.

9. ənı phyən i ceil cacu tanimnikka? /hapsıng/ — Hapsıng (phyən) i kacang cacu tanimnita.

U. Expansion Drill

Tutor: I chæk i pissamnita. /Yəng-Han sacən/ — 'This book is expensive.' /English-Korean dicationary/

Student: Yəng-Han sacən cung esə i chæk i kacang pissamnita. — 'Of the English-Korean dictionaries this book is the most expensive.'

1. Mikuk i cohsımnita. /nala tıl/ — Nala tıl cung esə Mikuk i kacang cohsımnita.

2. Mikuk catongcha ka phyənhamnita. /yələ nala cha/ — Yələ nala cha cung esə Mikuk catongcha ka kacang phyənhamnita.

3. Səul i khın tosi imnita. /Hankuk e yələ tosi/ — Hankuk e yələ tosi cung esə Səul i kacang khın tosi imnita.

4. Kicha ka ppalımnita. /catongcha wa ppəsı wa kicha/ — Catongcha wa ppəsı wa kicha cung esə kicha ka kacang ppalımnita.

5. Cungkuk ımsik ıl cohahamnita. /yələ kaci ımsik/ — Yələ kaci ımsik cung esə Cungkuk ımsik ıl kacang cohahamnita.

6. Hankuk mal i əlyəpsımnita. /mal tıl/ — Mal tıl cung esə Hankuk mal i kacang əlyəpsımnita.

7. Cho Sənsæng i cal kalıchimnita. /sənsæng tıl/ — Sənsæng tıl cung esə Cho Sənsæng i kacang cal kalıchimnita.

EXERCISES

1. Kim Sənsæng asks you what you want to see first. Propose that you go together to see the following places:

   a. Seoul University
   b. Seoul High School
   c. a girls' middle school
   d. the nearest elementary school
   e. a library
   f. a hospital
   g. the zoo
   H. a museum
   i. a drug store
   j. the central police station
   k. the British consulate
   l. a church
   m. the International Post Office
   n. the dormitory

2. Mr. James asks: / You respond:

Mr. James asks:	You respond:
a. how far the school is from your house.	'It's about three miles.'
b. how long your car is.	'It's 5 and a half meters (long).'
c. how long it takes to come to work.	'It usually takes 25 minutes by car.'
d. how high the mountain is.	'It is low but is about 850 feet high.'
e. which is slower, the bus or the train.	'The bus is a little slower than the train.'
f. which way is the most convenient of them all.	'The airplane is the most convenient of them all.'
g. if Korean is complicated.	'No, it's not so complicated and the writing is simple.'
h. if you came to school early /ilcciki/.	'No, I came a little late /nicke/.'
i. if the chair is very heavy.	'It's quite heavy but it is lighter than a table.'
j. if the chair is comfortable.	'It's not bad.'
k. if the room is dark.	'No, it's quite light.'
l. if the Han bridge is longer than the other one.	'No, it's shorter.'
m. if the street is always crowded.	'No, not always. Only in the morning and afternoon.'
n. if the Korean grammar is simple.	'No, it's very complicated.'
o. if you want to study Korean.	'I have no time even though I would like to.'
p. if he may get off in front of the building.	'Yes, you may.'
q. if he may use your car.	'I'm sorry but you can't.'
r. if he may ask you a question.	'Yes, please do.'
s. if he may drink coffee in the classroom.	'Yes, please if you want to.'

3. Find out the following information at the travel bureau:

a. if there are any passenger ships running between Inchon and Pusan.

b. if so, whether they are steamships.

c. if any cargo ships go to Tokyo.

d. if it is more expensive to ship /puchi-ta/ things by airplane.

e. how often express trains are running between Seoul and Pusan, and how much is a round-traip ticket /wangpok phyo/.

f. how much longer it takes to go to Suwon by a local train.

제 11 과 시내구경 (계속)

(대화 A)

타고 갑시다

1. 스미스 : 시내까지 합승을 타고 갑시다.

타지 맙시다

2. 김 : 뻐스나 합승은 타지 맙시다. 지금은 합승에도 사람이 많습니다.

걸어 갑시다

3. 스미스 : 그럼, 걸어 갈까요?

택시를 탑시다.
여보세요! 택시!

가 드릴까요

5. 운전수 : 어서 타십시요. 어디로 가 드릴까요?

중앙
중앙 우편국
가 주십시요

6. 김 : 서울 중앙 우편국으로 가 주십시요.

거의
다
거의 다
내립니다

UNIT 11. Going Around the Town (Continued)

BASIC DIALOGUE FOR MEMORIZATION

Smith

thako kapsita — ('let's ride and go')

1. Sinæ kkaci hapsıng ıl thako kapsita. — Let's take a jitney downtown.

Kim

thaci mapsita — let's not ride

2. Ppəsı na hapsıng ın thaci mapsita. Cikım ın hapsıng e to salam i manhsımnita. — Let's not take the bus or a jitney. Jitneys are (also) crowded at this time (of day).

Smith

kələ kamnita — [I] walk; [I] go on foot

3. Kıləm, kələ kal kka yo? — Shall we walk, then?

Kim

4. Thækssi lıl thapsita. — Let's take a taxi.

(... to a taxi)

Yəpose yo! Thækssi! — Hey! Taxi!

Driver

ka tılil kka yo — (shall I go (for you)?)

5. əsə thasipsiyo. əti lo ka tılil kka yo? — Please get in. Where shall I take you? ('Where shall I go for you?')

Kim

cungang — center; central

Cungang Uphyənkuk — Central Post Office

ka cusipsiyo — please for (for me)

6. Səul Cungang Uphyənkuk ılo ka cusipsiyo. — Please go to the Seoul Central Post Office.

7. 운전수 : 중앙 우편국에 거의 다 왔습니다.
어디에서 내리시겠습니까?

앞 문
가까이에서
내려 주십시요

8. 김 : 앞 문 가까이에서 내려 주십시요.

(대화 B)

잠간
들를 일

9. 김 : 저는 잠간 우편국에 들를 일이 있습니다.
선생은 먼저 다방으로 가시겠어요?

10. 스미스 : 무슨 일이 있습니까?

편지
부칩니다
부쳐야
부쳐야 합니다

11. 김 : 예, 편지 한 장 부쳐야 하겠습니다.

12. 스미스 : 저도 같이 갈까요?

기다리는 것
기다리는 것이 좋겠습니다

13. 김 : 선생은 다방에서 기다리는 것이 좋겠습니다.

(... a little later)

Driver

kəi	almost; nearly
kəi ta	most; almost; almost all; almost everyone
nælimnita	[I] get off; [it] falls down
7. Cungang Uphyənkuk e kəi ta wassımnita. əti esə nælisikessımnikka?	We've almost come to the Central Post Office. Where would you like to get off?

Kim

aph mun/ammun/	the front door
kakkai esə	near; at the near place
nælyə cusipsiyo	drop [me] off
8. Aph mun kakkai esə nælyə cusipsiyo.	Please drop [us] off at the front door.

(...They got off the taxi.)

Kim

camkan	a little while
tıllıl il/tılyılyil/	something to stop by for
9. Cə nın camkan uphyənkuk e tıllıl il i issımnita. Sənsæng ın məncə tapang ılo kasikessə yo?	I have some business at the post office for a moment. Would you [like to] go to the tearoom first?

Smith

10. Musın il i issımnikka?	What do you have [to do]?

Kim

phyənci	letter
puchimnita	[I] mail
puchiə ya	('only if [I] mail'); ('only when [I] mail')
puchiə ya hamnita	[I] have to mail; [I] must mail
11. Ne, phyənci han cang puchiə ya hakessımnita.	Well, I have to mail a letter.

아마

시간이 걸릴 것입니다

14. 아마, 시간이 좀 걸릴 것입니다.

너무

늦습니다, 늦읍니다

늦지 마십시요

15. 스미스 : 그럼, 너무 늦지 마십시요.

곧

돌아 옵니다

16. 김 : 아니요, 곧 돌아 오겠어요.

이따

17. 스미스 : 그럼, 이따 만납시다.

Smith

12. Cə to kathi kal kka yo? — Shall I also go with you?

Kim

kitalinın kəs — ('the waiting thing')

kitalinın kəs i cohkessımnita — you'd better wait ('that you wait will be good')

13. Sənsæng ın tapang esə kitalinın kəs i cohkessımnita. — You'd better wait in the tearoom.

ama — perhaps; probably

sikan i kəllil kəs imnita — it will take time

14. Ama, sikan i com kəllil kəs imnita. — It may take a little time. ('Probably time will take a little.')

Smith

nəmu — too

nıcsımnita / nıcımnita — [it]'s late; [it] delays

nıcci masipsiyo — don't be late; don't be long

15. Kıləm, nəmu nıcci masipsiyo. — Don't be too long, then.

Kim

kot — soon; immediately

tola omnita — [I] come back

16. Aniyo, kot tola okessə yo. — No, I'll be soon back.

Smith

itta — later; after a while

17. Kıləm, itta mannapsita. — See you in a few minutes, then.

NOTES ON DIALOGUES

(Numbers correspond to the sentence numbers)

1. 3. Thako kapsita. ('Let's ride and go.') is a fixed expression used in contrast to Kələ (sə) kapsita 'Let's go on foot.' Thako ka- with or without specifying a mode of transportation before it (as an object) is used to denote going by some means of transportation (e.g. car, taxi, bus, streetcar, etc.)

5. əti lo ka tɪlil kka yo? ('Where shall I go for you?') is the politer equivalent of əti lo ka cul kka yo?. The verb cu- or its politer equivalent tɪli- is used as an auxiliary verb. (See Grammar Note 2.)

6. Cungang 'central', 'center' occurs either as a determinative or a free-noun. As a determinative it forms a noun phrase with the following noun; as a free-noun it denotes geographical location. Compare (a) and (b):

(a)	Cungang Kɪkcang	'Central Theatre'
	Cungang Cəngkəcang	'Central Station'
(b)	Sinæ cungang e samnita.	[I] live in the center of the city.

7. Kəi 'almost', 'most of them' and kəi ta 'almost (all)', 'most of all' both occur either nominals or adverbials. Kəi ta is a two-word phrase. As a nominal, either one of them occurs in the subject, topic or object position in a sentence.

8. Næli- 'to get off', 'to descend' is an intransitive verb which may precede a place or transportation name + esə. Tha- 'to ride', 'to get on' is antonymous with næli- (See Notes on Dialogues 14, Unit 7.) The verb phrase næliə cu- 'to drop somebody off' occurs as a transitive verb phrase which may precede a direct object with or without a place or transportation name + esə. The antonymous verb for mæliə cu- is either thæu- or thæwə cu-, both of which mean 'to give someone a ride' or 'to load'. Kakkai 'near', 'at the near place', 'the near place' occurs either as an adverb or a noun. The antonym for the adverb kakkai is məlli 'far away'.

14. Ama 'perhaps', 'probably' occurs as a sentence adverb which is usually followed by either an inflected form with the suffix -kess- in it or the construction -(ɪ)l kəs i-. It denotes the speaker's presumption for the probable action or description of the subject or topic in the sentence.

15. Nəmu 'too' is an adverb which, without being followed by a pause immediately before verbals, noun-modifier words, or other adverbs, denotes excessive degree of the following descriptive expressions.

16. Kot 'soon', 'right away', 'immediately' which may be followed by a pause occurs as a sentence adverb. It denotes immediate time for the following inflected expression.

17. Itta 'later', 'after a while' which may be followed by a pause, occurs as a sentence adverb, and denotes later point of time on the same day for the following inflected expression. The antonym of itta is akka 'a little while ago' which is also a sentence adverb.

GRAMMAR NOTES

1. -ci + ma(l)-

We learned in Unit 4 that the ci form plus the verb anh- was used to negate the verb in the ci form in a statement or question sentence. Remember that anh- does not occur alone but is always preceded by the ci form without a pause. Like anh-, the verb ma(l)- does not occur without being preceded by the ci form. -ci + ma(l)- is used to indicate negation of the verb in the ci form in either propositative or imperative sentences. Note that in the construction -ci + anh- tenses and/or levels of speech may be generated in the verb anh-, but in the construction -ci + ma(l)-, tense suffixes do not occur in the inflected form of the stem ma(l)-: the verb ma(l) takes only -(ɪ)psita and -(ɪ)sipsiyo endings in Formal Polite Speech, and the infinitive form of ma(l)- is malə, making the informal polite speech present form malə yo. Compare:

GROUP 1

a.	Hankukə lo (mal-)hapsita.	'Let's speak in Korean.'
	Hankukə lo (mal-)haci mapsita.	'Let's not speak in Korean.'
b.	Kələ kapsita.	'Let's go on foot.'
	Kələ kaci mapsita.	'Let's not go on foot.'

c Kyosil esə tampæ (lıl) phiupsita. — 'Let's smoke in the classroom.'
Kyosil esə tampæ (lıl) phiuci mapsita. — 'Let's not smoke in the classroom.'

GROUP 2

a. I chæk ıl ilkısipsiyo. — 'Read this book.'
I chæk ıl ilkci masipsiyo. — 'Don't read this book.'

b. Hankuk mal lo mal-hasipsiyo. — 'Speak in Korean.'
Hankuk mal lo mal-haci masipsiyo. — 'Don't speak in Korean.'

c. Kimchi lıl məkısipsiyo. — 'Eat Kimchi.'
Kimchi lıl məkci masipsiyo. — 'Don't eat Kimchi.'

2. Infinitive + cu-

In Unit 7, we were introduced to a verb phrases (i.e. infinitive + auxiliary verb). The verb cu- preceded by an infinitive without a pause occurs as an auxiliary verb. As an independent verb cu- means 'to give', and the construction Infinitive + cu- which may be preceded by a Personal Nominal + {eke / hanthe} 'to + Personal Nominal' means literary something like 'do and give to someone'. But the auxiliary verb cu- is generally used either to denote 'rendering service to someone' by the subject or topic, or simply to mean nothing but to make the speech politer in an imperative sentence. The politer or honorific equivalent of cu- is an irregular form tıli- which occurs also either as an independent verb or as an auxiliary verb. Observe the following examples:

1. a. Chæk ıl ilkısipsiyo. — 'Read the book.'
b. Chæk ıl ilkə cusipsiyo. — {'Please read the book.' / 'Please read me the book.'}
c. Chæk ıl na eke ilkə cusipsiyo. — {'Please read me the book.' / 'Please read the book {for / to} me.'}

2. a. Kim Sənsæng i khəphi lıl sassımnita. — 'Mr. Kim bought coffee.'
b. Kim Sənsæng ı khəphi lıl sa cuəssımnita. — 'Mr. Kim bought [me] coffee.'
c. Kim Sənsæng i cə eke khəphi lıl sa cuəssımnita. — {'Mr. Kim bought me coffee.' / 'Mr. Kim bought coffee for me.'}

3. a. Cə yəca ka Yəngə lıl kalıchiəssımnita. — 'That woman taught English.'

b. Cə yəca ka Yəngə lıl kalıchiə cuəssımnita. — 'That woman taught [me] English.'

c. Cə yəca ka na hanthe Yənge lıl kalıchiə cuəssımnita. — 'That woman taught me English.'

4. a. Sənsæng kwa kathi kal kka yo? — 'Shall I go with you?'

b. Sənsæng kwa kathi ka tılil kka yo? — { 'Shall I go with you (for you)?' / 'Shall I accompany you?' / 'Would you like me to go with you?' }

c. Ne, na wa kathi ka cusiɒsiyo. — 'Yes, please go with me.'

3. Particle ya

Ya belongs to a small class of particles which occur without a pause immediately after inflected forms (e.g. Infinitives). Infinitive + ya occurs in the following two constructions:

a. Infinitive + ya + ha- 'must..', 'have (or has) to__'

Infinitive + ya followed by the verb ha- without a pause is used to denote obligation of the action or description of the verb in the infinitive for the subject or topic in the sentence. In this construction the tenses and/or levels of speech is generated only in ha-. Examples:

Wekyokwan ın wekuk mal ıl alə ya hamnita. — 'Diplomats must know foreign languages.'

Cə to Hankuk mal ıl pæwə ya hæ yo. — 'I have to study Korean, too.'

Chinku lıl manna ya hakessə yo? — 'Do [you] have to meet a friend?'

Hakkyo e ka ya hæssımnita. — 'I had to go to school.'

Note that the pattern -ci ahhımyən an twemnita. ('If [one] doesn't do... [it] doesn't become.') is often interchangeably used with Infinitive + ya ha-. Thus, the Yes response to either Infinitive + ya hamnikka? or -ci anhımyən an twemnikka? is either Ne, Infinitive + ya hamnita. or Ne, -ci anhımyən an twemnita. The most usual No response to either of the above questions is Aniyo, -ci anhə to {cohsımnita. / kwænchansımnita.} 'No, [you] don't have to...' ('Even if [one] does not do... [it]'s O.K.')

b. Infinitive + ya + verbs other than ha- 'only when,.', 'only if..', 'must...to...'

Infinitive + ya, which may be followed by a pause before another inflected expression, occurs to denote obligatory condition of action or description of the subject or topic for the following inflected expression. In this construction, the tense suffixes may also occur in the infinitive form which precedes ya, while tenses and/or levels of speech are generated in the following inflected expression. Examples:

Hankuk mal ıl alə ya, il-haki swipsımnita.	'It is easy to work only when [you] know Korean.' 'You have to know Korean to make it easy to work.'
Ton i issə ya, cha lıl sal su issımnita.	'Only if [I] have money, I can buy a car.' '[I] have to have money to buy a car.'
Chæk kaps i ssa ya, sakessə yo.	'Only if the book is cheap, I will buy it.'
Pam e cal ca ya, kongpu cal hal su issımnita.	'[You] have to have a goodnight sleep to study well.' 'Only when [you] sleep well, you can study well.'
Kı ttæ e Səul e issəssə ya, kı kəs ıl pol su issəssıl kəs imnita.	'Only if [you] had been in Seoul at that time [you] could have seen it.' '[You] should have been in Seoul at that time to have seen it.'

4. -n/ın/nın + kəs

Remember that the Nominalized verb (i.e. the ki form) occurs in a nominal position in a sentence, e.g. subject, topic, object (See Unit 8). Just like the ki form, the phrase -n/ın/nın + kəs (which is the present noun-modifier word plus the post-noun kəs) often occurs in the nominal positions. Any English verbal expression which occurs in nominal positions can be compared with the above Korean construction. Observe the following examples:

Wekuk mal ıl pæunın kəs ın swipci anhsımnita.	'Learning foreign languages is not easy.'
Ceimsı ka Yəngə lıl kalıchinın kəs ıl amnita.	'[I] know that James is teaching English.'
Kim Sənsæng i hakkyo e kanın kəs ıl pwassə yo.	'I saw that Mr. Kim was going to school.'

Thækssi lɨl thanɨn kəs i əttəhsɨmnikka? — 'How would you like to take a taxi?'

Səul esə sanɨn kəs ɨl cohahamnikka? — 'Do you like to live in Seoul?'

Note, however, that the expression -n/ɨn/nɨn kəs i coh(kess)sɨmnita '[You] had better do..' ('It (will) be good to do such-and-such' or 'That [you] do.. will be good.') occurs as a fixed expression to indicate the speaker's recommendation, suggestion or wishes.

5. -(ɨ)l kəs i-

We learned about the inflected forms which include the suffix -kess- (Grammar Note 2, Unit 3). Like the inflected forms including -kess-, the construction -(ɨ)l kəs i- is also used to indicate either the future action or description, or the speaker's presumption, about the subject or the topic in the sentence. Study the following formula:

	Subject/Topic	Form	Denotation
a.	Speaker	-kess-	Speaker's positive intention for the future
b.	Addressee (in a question sentence)	-kess-	Addressee's positive intention for the future
c.	Other than speaker or addressee (in a question sentence)	-kess-	Addressee's opinion or presumption for the future
d.	Other than speaker or addressee (in a statement sentence)	-kess-	Speaker's presumption
e.	Speaker	-(ɨ)l kəs i-	Speaker's passive future
f.	Addressee (in a question sentence)	-(ɨ)l kəs i-	Addressee's passive future
g.	Addressee (in a statement sentence)	-(ɨ)l kəs i-	Speaker's presumption for the future
h.	Other than the speaker or addressee (in a statement sentence)	-(ɨ)l kəs i-	Speaker's belief or knowledge for the future
i.	Other than the speaker or addressee (in a question sentence)	-(ɨ)l kəs i-	Addressee's opinion, presumption or knowledge for the future

Note that if the subject/topic in the sentence is other than the speaker or addressee, and if the speaker simply states his knowledge about the action or description of the subject/topic for the future, the construction -(ɨ)l kəs i-is usually used instead of the -kess- form. However, -(ı)l kəs i- is also used occasionally to denote the speaker's presumption about the subject/topic. Compare the following pairs:

a. Onıl pi ka okessımnita.	'It is going to rain today (I suppose).'
Onıl pi ka ol kəs imnita.	'It will rain today.'
b. Kı cha ka pissakessımnita.	'That car must be expensive.'
Kı cha ka pissal kəs imnita.	'That car will be expensive.'
c. Onıl Thoyoil ini kka, haksæng tıl i hakkyo e əpskessımnita.	'Because today is Saturday, I presume there are not students at school.'
Onıl Thoyoil ini kka, haksæng tıl i hakkyo e əpsıl kəs imnita.	'Because today is Saturday, there (will) be no students at school.' / 'Probably there (will) be no students at school because today is Saturday.'
d. Pak Sənsæng i onıl ttənakessımnita.	'I believe Mr. Park will leave today.'
Pak Sənsæng i onıl ttənal kəs imnita.	'Mr. Park will leave today.'

6. Further Notes on Honorifics

In Unit 3, we noticed that when the subject, topic or the person acted upon in a sentence is honored, the honorific suffix -(ı)si- is added to the verb stem. While most Korean verb stems take -(ı)si- to form honorifics there is a small class or verb stems of which honorifics have irregular shapes. Examples:

Stem	Honorific or Humble form	
ca-	cumusi-	'to sleep'
iss-	kyesi-	'to exist'
mək-	capsusi-	'to eat'
cu-	tıli(si)-	'to give'
cuk-	tola kasi-	'to die', 'to pass away (H)'

Remember that the speaker does not honor himself regardless of age, status or other factors. That is, the honorific suffix -(ı)si- should not occur in the verb in a sentence where the speaker himself is the subject, topic or the person acted upon.

DRILLS

A. Substitution Drill

1.	Sinæ kkaci hapsıng ıl thako kapsita.	Let's take a jitney as far as the downtown area.
2.	Səul Yək kkaci cəncha lıl thako kapsita.	Let's take a streetcar as far as Seoul Station.
3.	Cungang Uphyənkuk kkaci ppəsı lıl thako kapsita.	Let's take a bus as far as the Central Post Office.
4.	Hankuk ınhæng kkaci catongcha lıl thako kapsita.	Let's take a car as far as the Bank of Korea.
5.	Tæsakwan aph kkaci thækssi lıl thako kapsita.	Let's take a taxi as far as the front of U.S. Embassy.
6.	Kukce Kıkcang kkaci hapsıng ıl thako kapsita.	Let's take a jitney as far as the International Theatre.
7.	Cungkuk ımsikcəm kkaci cha lıl thako kapsita.	Let's take a car as far as the Chinese restaurant.
8.	Yəngsakwan pukın kkaci hapsıng ıl thako kapsita.	Let's take a jitney as far as the vicinity of the consulate.
*9.	Pihængcang kkaci kələ kapsita.	Let's walk as far as the airport.

B. Substitution Drill

1.	Cungang Uphyənkuk ılo ka cusipsiyo.	Please go to the Central Post Office.
2.	Cungang Sicang ılo ka cusipsiyo.	Please go to the Central Market.
3.	Cungang Kıkcang ılo ka cusipsiyo.	Please go to the Central Theatre.
4.	Cungang Tosəkwan ılo ka cusipsiyo.	Please go to the Central Library.
5.	Cungang Kyəngchalsə lo ka cusipsiyo.	Please go to the Central Police Station.
6.	Cungang Kongwən ılo ka cusipsiyo.	Please go to the Central Park.
7.	Cungang Pakmulkwan ılo ka cusipsiyo.	Please go to the Central Museum.
8.	Səul Sinmunsa lo ka cusipsiyo.	Please go to the Seoul Newspaper Co.
9.	Pihængcang ılo ka cusipsiyo.	Please go to the airport.
10.	Pyəngwən ılo ka cusipsiyo.	Please go to the hospital.
*11.	Mun ılo ka cusipsiyo.	Please go to the door.
*12.	Cali lo ka cusipsiyo.	Please go to the seat.

C. Substitution Drill

1. Mun kakkai esə nælio cusipsiyo.	Please drop [me] off near the door.
2. Mun yəph esə nælio cusipsiyo.	Please drop [me] off beside the door.
3. ınhæng aph esə nælio cusipsiyo.	Please drop [me] in front of the bank.
4. Tosəkwan twi esə nælio cusipsiyo.	Please drop [me] behind the library.
5. Cə kənmul kakkai esə nælio cuispsiyo.	Please drop [me] near that building.
6. Pækhwacəm olın ccok esə nælio cusipsiyo.	Please drop [me] on the right side of the department store.
*7. Sopangsə wen ccok esə nælio cusipsiyo.	Please drop [me] on the left side of the fire station.
8. Kyəngchalsə yəph esə nælio cusipsiyo.	Please drop [me] next to the police station.
9. Munpangkucəm aph esə nælio cusipsiyo.	Please drop [me] in front of the stationery shop.
10. Cungkuk siktang twi esə nælio cusipsiyo.	Please drop [me] behind the Chinese restaurant.
*11. Cungkuk siktang twi esə məmchuə cusipsiyo.	Please stop behind the Chinese restaurant.
*12. Cungkuk siktang twi esə sə cusipsiyo.	Please stop (or stand) behind the Chinese restaurant.
*13. Cungkuk siktang twi esə sewə cusipsiyo.	Please park behind the Chinese restaurant.

D. Substitution Drill

1. Uphyənkuk ılo ka cusimyən, kamsahakessımnita.	I would appreciate it if you'd go to the post office for me.
2. Hankuk mal ıl kalıchiə cusimyən, kamsahakessımnita.	I would appreciate it if you would teach [me] Korean.
3. Cə lıl kitalyə cusimyən, kamsahakessımnita.	I would appreciate it if you would wait for me.
4. Yəki esə nælio cusimyən, kamsahakessımnita.	I would appreciate it if you would drop me off here.
5. Kı sacən ıl poyə cusimyən, kamsahakessımnita.	I would appreicate it if you would show me the dictionary.

*6. Mun ɪl tatə cusimyən, kamsahakessɪmnita.	I would appreciate it if you would close the door.
*7. Mun ɪl yələ cusimyən, kamsahakessɪmnita.	I would appreciate it if you would open the door.
*8. Kɪ chæk ɪl pillyə cusimyən, kamsahakessɪmnita.	I would appreciate it if you would lend me that book.
*9. Cali e ancə cusimyən, kamsahakessɪmnita.	I would appreciate it if you would take a seat.
*10. Catongcha lɪl ponæ cusimyən, kamsahakessɪmnita.	I would appreciate it if you would send [me] a car.
*11. Mun aph esə sə cusimyən, kamsahakessɪmnita.	I would appreciate it if you would stop in front of the door.

E. Substitutuion Drill

1. Camkan uphyənkuk e tɪllɪl il i issɪmnita.	I have to stop by the post office for a few minutes. ('I have something to stop by the post office for.')
2. Camkan chækpang e tɪllɪl il i issɪmnita.	I have to stop by a bookstore for a few minutes.
3. Camkan yakpang e tɪllɪl il i issɪmnita.	I have to stop by the drugstore for a few minutes.
4. Camkan pyəngwən e tɪllɪl il i issɪmnita.	I have to stop by the hospital for a few minutes.
5. Camkan kyəngchalsə e tɪllɪl il i issimnita.	I have to stop by the police station for a few minutes.
*6. Camkan pangsongkuk e tɪllɪl il i issɪmnita.	I have to stop by the radio station for a few minutes.
7. Camkan kyohwe e tɪllɪl il i issɪmnita.	I have to stop by the church for a few minutes.
8. Camkan hwesa e tɪllɪl il i issɪmnita.	I have to stop by the office for a few minutes.
9. Camkan hwesa e kal il i issɪmnita.	I have to go ('something to go for') to the office for a few minutes.
10. Camkan hwesa e hal il i issɪmnita.	I have something to do at the office for a few minutes.
*11. Camkan hwesa e pol il i issɪmnita.	I have some business at the office for a few minutes.

F. Substitution Drill

1. Sənsæng ɪn tapang esə kitalinɪn kəs i cohkessɪmnita.	You'd better wait at the tearoom.
2. Sənsæng ɪn hakkyo e kanɪn kəs i cohkessɪmnita.	You'd better go to school.
3. Sənsæng ɪn Yəngə lɪl kalɪchinɪn kəs i cohkessɪmnita.	You'd better teach English.
4. Sənsæng ɪn cip e issnɪn kəs i cohkessɪmnita.	You'd better stay home.
5. Sənsæng ɪn hyuka lɪl patnɪn kəs i cohkessɪmnita.	You'd better take a vacation.
6. Sənsæng ɪn com swinɪn kəs i cohkessɪmnita.	You'd better take a little rest.
7. Sənsæng ɪn kɪ yəca lɪl mannanɪn kəs i cohkessɪmnita.	You'd better meet her.
8. Sənsæng ɪn Ceimsɪ eke mulə ponɪn kəs i cohkessɪmnita.	You'd better ask James.
*9. Sənsæng ɪn kɪmantunɪn kəs i cohkessɪmnita.	You'd better stop doing [it].
10. Sənsæng ɪn tæhak ɪl kɪth-nænɪn kəs i cohkessɪmnita.	You'd better finish college.
11. Sənsæng ɪn məncə ttənanɪn kəs i cohkessɪmnita.	You'd better leave first (before me).
12. Sənsæng ɪn yəki esə nælinɪn kəs i cohkessɪmnita.	You'd better get off here.
13. Sənsæng ɪn yəki e cha lɪl seunɪn kəs i cohkessɪmnita.	You'd better park [your] car here.

End of Tape 8B

Tape 9A

G. Substitution Drill

1. (Sənsæng ɪn) hakkyo e kaci anhnɪn kəs i cohkessɪmnita.	[You]'d better not go to school.
2. (Sənsæng ɪn) Yəngə lo mal-haci anhnɪn kəs i cohkessɪmnita.	[You]'d better not speak in English.
3. (Sensæng ɪn) kɪ salam ɪl kitalici anhnɪn kəs i cohkessɪmnita.	[You]'d better not wait for him.

4. (Sənsæng ın) ki yənghwa lıl poci anhnın kəs i cohkessımnita. — [You]'d better not see the movie.

5. (Sənsæng ın) i catongcha lıl saci anhnın kəs i cohkessımnita. — [You]'d better not buy this automobile.

6. (Sənsæng ın) onıl tola oci anhnın kəs i cohkessımnita. — [You]'d better not go back today.

7. (Sənsæng ın) yəki esə nælici anhnın kəs i cohkessımnita. — [You]'d better not get off here.

8. (Sənsæng ın) yəki e cha lıl seuci anhnın kəs i cohkessımnita. — [You]'d better not park the car here.

*9. (Sənsæng ın) i phyənci lıl ponæci anhnın kəs i cohkessımnita. — [You]'d better not send this letter.

H. Response Drill

Tutor: Hapsıng ıl thal kka yo? — 'Shall we take a jitney?'
Student: Aniyo, thaci mapsita. — 'No, let's not (take).'

1. Kələ kal kka yo? 'Shall we walk?'	Aniyo, kələ kaci mapsita. 'No, let's not (walk).'
2. Mun aph esə nælil kka yo?	Aniyo, mun aph esə nælici mapsita.
3. Hankuk yənghwa lıl pol kka yo?	Aniyo, (Hankuk yənghwa lıl) poci mapsita.
4. Onıl cip e issıl kka yo?	Aniyo, cip e issci mapsita.
5. Cənghkəcang esə kı pun ıl kitalil kka yo?	Aniyo, (cəngkəcang esə) kitalici mapsita.
6. I phyənci lıl puchil kka yo?	Aniyo, puchici mapsita.
7. Kathi tapang e tıllil kka yo?	Aniyo, (tapang e) tıllici mapsita.
8. Uli kot tola ol kka yo?	Aniyo, kot tola oci mapsita.
9. Itta mannal kka yo?	Aniyo, (itta) mannaci mapsita.
10. Kı yəca eke i kılim ıl poyə cul kka yo?	Aniyo, poyə cuci mapsita.
11. Cikım il ıl sicak-hal kka yo?	Aniyo, cikım sicak-haci mapsita.
12. Cokım swil kka yo?	Aniyo, swici mapsita.

I. Response Drill

Tutor: Hapsıng ıl thal kka yo?	'Shall we take a jitney?'
Student: Aniyo, hapsıng ıl thaci anhnın kəs i cohkessımnita.	'No, we'd better not take a jitney.'
1. Tapang e tıllıl kka yo?	Aniyo, (tapang e) tıllıci anhnın kəs i cohkessımnita.
2. Kı yəca lıl kitalil kka yo?	Aniyo, (kı yəca lıl) kitalici anhnın kəs i cohkessımnita.
3. Səul e tola kal kka yo?	Aniyo, (Səul e) tola kaci anhnın kəs i cohkessımnita.
4. Ppəsı lıl thako kal kka yo?	Aniyo, (ppəsı lıl) thako kaci anhnın kəs i cohkessımnita.
5. Taım cuil e hyuka lıl patıl kka yo?	Aniyo, taım cuil e (hyuka lıl) patci anhnın kəs i cohkessımnita.
6. Ləetiyo lıl tılıl kka yo?	Aniyo, (ləetiyo lıl) tıtci anhnın kəs i cohkessımnita.
7. Hankuk mal ıl pæul kka yo?	Aniyo, (Hankuk mal ıl) pæuci anh ın kəs i cohkessımnita.

J. Response Drill

Tutor: Cikım hakkyo e ka to cohsımnikka?	'May I go to school now?'
Student: Aniyo, kaci masipsiyo.	'No, please don't go.'
1. Phyənci lıl puchyə to cohsımnikka?	Aniyo, puchici masipsiyo.
2. Hapsıng ıl thako ka to cohsımnikka?	Aniyo, thako kaci masipsiyo.
3. Sənsæng e samusil e tıllə to cohsımnikka?	Aniyo, tıllıci masipsiyo.
4. Sichəng aph esə næliə to cohsımnikka?	Aniyo, (sichəng aph esə) nælici masipsiyo.
5. Sənsæng ıl tapang esə kitaliə to cohsımnikka?	Aniyo, (na lıl) kitalici masipsiyo.
6. Cip e tola ka to cohsımnikka?	Aniyo, tola kaci masipsiyo.
7. Cokım swiə to cohsımnikka?	Aniyo, swici masipsiyo.
8. Cikım ttəna to cohs mnikka?	Aniyo, cikım ttənaci masipsiyo.
9. Hankuk mal lo mal-hæ to cohsımnikka?	Aniyo, Hankuk mal lo mal-haci masipsiyo.

10. Kyosil esə khəphi lıl masiə to cohsımnikka? — Aniyo, (kyosil esə khəphi lıl) masici masipsiyo.

11. Malssım com mulə pwa to cohsımnikka? — Aniyo, mulə poci masipsiyo.

K. Grammar Drill

Tutor: Na nın phyənci lıl puchikessımnita. — 'I'll mail a letter.'

Student: Na to phyənci lıl puchiə ya hæ yo. — 'I have to mail a letter, too.'

1. Na nın kicha lıl thakessımnita. — Na to kicha lıl tha ya hæ yo.
2. Na nın Mikuk Tæsakwan e tıllıkessımnita. — Na to Mikuk Tæsakwan e tıllə ya hæ yo.
3. Na nın cohın tæhakkyo e tanikessımnita. — Na to cohın tæhakkyo e tanniə ya hæ yo.
4. Na nın Ceimsı lıl kitalikessımnita. — Na to Ceimsı lıl kitaliə ya hæ yo.
5. Na nın næil Səul ıl ttənakessımnita. — Na to næil Səul ıl ttəna ya hæ yo.
6. Na nın nal mata Hankuk mal ıl yənsıp-hakessımnita. — Na to nal mata Hankuk mal ıl yənsıp-hæ ya hæ yo.
7. Na nın cənyək e cip e isskessımnita. — Na to cənyək e cip e issə ya hæ yo.
8. Na nın khəphi lıl masikessımnita. — Na to khəphi lıl masiə ya hæ yo.
9. Na nın wekyokwan i twekessımnita. — Na to wekyokwan i tweə ya hæ yo.
10. Na nın taım cuil e Səul e tola okessımnita. — Na to taım cuil e Səul e tola wa ya hæ yo.

L. Response Drill

Tutor: Hankuk mal ıl pæwəssə yo? — 'Have you studied Korean?'

Student: Ne, (Hankuk mal ıl) pæwə ya hæssə yo. — 'Yes, I had to (study Korean).'

1. Phyənci lıl puchiəssə yo? — Ne, phyənci lıl puchiə ya hæssə yo.
2. Kicha lıl thako kassə yo? — Ne, kicha lıl thako ka ya hæssə yo.
3. Cohın tæhakkyo e taniəssə yo? — Ne, cohın tæhakkyo e taniə ya hæssə yo.
4. Mun aph esə næliəssə yo? — Ne, mun aph esə næliə ya hæssə yo.

5. Kim Sənsæng ın Səul ıl ttənassə yo?	Ne, (Kim Sənsæng ın Səul ıl) ttəna ya hæssə yo.
6. Tosəkwan esə Ceimsı lıl kitaliəssə yo?	Ne, (tosəkwan esə Ceimsı lıl) kitaliə ya hæssə yo.
7. əce Pusan esə tola wassə yo?	Ne, (əce Pusan esə) tola wa ya hæssə yo.
8. Kı pun ın hakkyo sənsæng i tweəssə yo?	Ne, (kı pun ın) hakkyo sənsæng i tweə ya hæssə yo.
9. Kı il ıl əce kkaci kkıth-næssə yo?	Ne, (kı il ıl) əce kkaci kkıth-næ hæssə yo.
10. Pəlssə hyuka lıl patəssə yo?	Ne, pəlssə hyuka lıl patə ya hæssə yo.

M. Grammar Drill (based on Grammar Note 2)

Tutor: Sinæ lo kal kka yo? — 'Shall I go downtown?' / 'Do you want me to go downtown?'

Student: Sinæ lo ka tılil kka yo? — 'Shall I go downtown (for you)?' / 'Would you like me to go downtown (for you)?'

1. Chæk ıl ilkıl kka yo?	Chæk ıl ilkə tılil kka yo?
2. Tapang esə kitalil kka yo?	Tapang esə kitaliə tılil kka yo?
3. Khəphi lıl sal kka yo?	Khəphi lıl sa tılil kka yo?
4. I cha lıl phal kka yo?	I cha lıl phala tılil kka yo?
5. Hankuk mal ıl kalıchil kka yo?	Hankuk mal ıl kalıchiə tılil kka yo?
6. Kathi cip e issıl kka yo?	Kathi cip e issə tılil kka yo?
7. Kil ıl mulə pol kka yo?	Kil ıl mulə pwa tılil kka yo?
8. Kı chæk ıl chacıl kka yo?	Kı chæk ıl chacə tılil kka yo?
9. Yəki esə nælil kka yo?	Yəki esə næliə tılil kka yo?
10. Kim Sənsæng ıl mannal kka yo?	Kim Sənsæng ıl manna tılil kka yo?

N. Response Drill

Tutor: Chæk ɪl ilkə tɪlikessə yo.	'I will read the book for you.'
Student: Ne, (chæk ɪl) ilkə cusipsiyo.	'Yes, please read it for me.'
1. Tapang esə kitaliə tɪlikessə yo.	Ne, tapang esə kitaliə cusipsiyo.
2. Khəphi lɪl sa tɪlikessə yo.	Ne, khəphi lɪl sa cusipsiyo.
3. Kil ɪl mulə pwa tɪlikessə yo.	Ne, kil ɪl mulə pwa cusipsiyo.
4. Kɪ chæk ɪl chacə tɪlikessə yo.	Ne, kɪ chæk ɪl chacə cusipsiyo.
5. Cip e {isskessə yo. / issə tɪlikessə yo.}	Ne, cip e issə cusipsiyo.
6. Hankuk mal ɪl kalɪchiə tɪlikessə yo.	Ne, (Hankuk mal ɪl) kalɪchiə cusipsiyo.
7. Wen ccok ɪlo ka tɪlikessə yo.	Ne, wen ccok ɪlo ka cusipsiyo.
8. Mikuk Yəngsakwan esə næliə tɪlikessə yo.	Ne, Mikuk Yəngsakwan esə næliə cusipsiyo.
9. Onɪl ohu e samusil e tɪllə tɪlikessə yo.	Ne, onɪl ohu e samusil e tɪllə cusipsiyo.

O. Response Drill

Tutor: əti lo ka tɪlil kka yo? /sichəng ccok/	'Where shall I go?' /the direction of the City Hall/
Student: Sichəng ccok ɪlo ka cusipsiyo.	'Please go to (the direction of) the City Hall.'
1. əti esə næliə tɪlil kka yo? /pækhwacəm mun/	Pækhwacəm mun esə næliə cusipsiyo.
2. Muəs ɪl sa tɪlil kka yo? /khəphi/	Khəphi lɪl sa cusipsiyo.
3. ənce sənsæng e cip e tɪllɪl kka yo? /Suyoil/	Suyoil e tɪllə cusipsiyo.
4. əti esə sənsæng ɪl kitalil kka yo? /tosəkwan aph/	Tosəkwan aph esə (na lɪl) kitaliə cusipsiyo.
5. ənɪ sinmun ɪl ilkə tɪlil kka yo? /Səul Sinmun/	Səul Sinmun ɪl ilkə cusipsiyo.
6. ənce kkaci i il ɪl kkɪth-næ tɪlil kka yo? /mole kkaci/	Mole kkaci i il ɪl kkɪth-næ cusipsiyo.
7. ənɪ mal ɪl kalɪchiə tɪlil kka yo? /Cungkuk Mal/	Cungkuk Mal ɪl kalɪchiə cusipsiyo.
8. Myəch-si e tasi wa tɪlil kka yo? /tasəs-si/	Tasəs-si e tasi wa cusipsiyo.

P. Expansion Drill (Use /kəi ta/ in the proper place.)

Tutor: Uphyənkuk e wassımnita.	'[We] have come to the post office.'
Student: Uphyənkuk e kəi ta wassımnita.	'[We] have come to the post office almost.'
1. Haksæng tıl i Səul esə ttənassımnita.	Haksæng tıl i Səul esə kəi ta ttənassımnita.
2. Onıl il i kkıth-nassımnita.	Onıl il i kəi ta kkıth-nassımnita.
3. Hakkyo kal sikan i tweəssımnita.	Hakkyo kal sikan i kəi ta tweəssımnita.
4. Hankuk mal sənsæng tıl ıl mannassımnita.	Hankuk mal Sənsæng tıl ıl kəi ta mannassımnita.
5. Salam tıl i kicha e thassımnita.	Salam tıl i kicha e kəi ta thassımnita.
6. Ceimsı Sənsæng ın Hankuk mal ıl alə tıtsımnita.	Ceimsı Sənsæng ın Hankuk mal ıl kəi ta alə tıtsımnita.
7. Uli nın Səul ıl kukyəng-hæssımnita.	Uli nın Səul ıl kəi ta kukyəng-hæssımnita.
8. Ai tıl i cip e tola wassımnita.	Ai tıl i cip e kəi ta tola wassımnita.

Q. Response Drill

Tutor: Sinæ lo ka tılil kka yo?	'Shall I go downtown (for you)?'
Student: Ne, sinæ lo ka cuse yo.	'Yes, please (go downtown for me).'
1. I chæk ıl ilkə tılil kka yo?	Ne, ilkə cuse yo.
2. Khəphi lıl sa tılil kka yo?	Ne, sa cuse yo.
3. Hankuk mal ıl kalıchyə tılil kka yo?	Ne, kalıchyə cuse yo.
4. Kil ıl mulə pwa tılil kka yo?	Ne, mulə pwa cuse yo.
5. Yəki esə nælyə tılil kka yo?	Ne, yəki esə nælyə cuse yo.
6. Sənsæng e cip e tillə tılil kka yo?	Ne, tillə cuse yo.
7. Sənsæng ıl kitalyə tılil kka yo?	Ne, kitalyə cuse yo.
8. Kı chæk ıl chacə tılil kka yo?	Ne, chacə cuse yo.

R. Response Drill

Tutor: Khəphi lıl sa tılil kka yo?	'Shall I buy you coffee?'
Student: (Ne), sa cusimyən komapkessımnita.	'I would appreciate [it] if you buy me [coffee].'
1. I chæk ıl ilkə tılil kka yo?	Ne, ilkə cusimyən komapkessımnita.
2. Hankuk mal ıl kalıchiə tılil kka yo?	Ne, kalıchiə cusimyən kompakessımnita.
3. Sənsæng e cip e tıllə tılil kka yo?	Ne, tıllə cusimyən komapkessımnita.
4. Tangsin ıl kitaliə tılil kka yo?	Ne, kitaliə cusimyən komapkessımnita.
5. Yənphil ıl chacə tılil kka yo?	Ne, chacə cusimyən komapkessımnita.
6. Kil ıl mulə pwa tılil kka yo?	Ne, mulə pwa cusimyən komapkessımnita.
7. Cəngkəcang e kathi ka tılil kka yo?	Ne, kathi ka cusimyen komapkessımnita.
8. Mun ıl tatə tılil kka yo?	Ne, tatə cusimyən komapkessımnita.
9. Mun ıl yələ tılil kka yo?	Ne, yələ cusimyən komapkessımnita.

S. Grammar Drill (based on Grammar Note 3)

Tutor: Hankuk mal ıl alə ya hamnita.	'I have to know Korean.'
Student: Hankuk mal ıl alci anhımyən an twemnita.	'I have to know Korean.('If I don't know Korean, it does not become.')
1. Kicha lıl thako ka ya hamnita.	Kicha lıl thako kaci anhımyən an twemnita.
2. Yəki esə næliə ya hamnita.	Yəki esə nælici anhımyən an twemnita.
3. Mikuk tæsa lıl kitaliə ya hamnita.	Mukuk tæsa lıl kitalici anhımyən an twemnita.
4. Mun aph esə məmchuə ya hamnita.	Mun aph esə məmchuci anhımyən an twemnita.
5. Mun ıl tatə ya hamnita.	Mun ıl tatci anhımyən an twemnita.
6. Catongcha mun ıl yələ ya hamnita.	Catongcha mun ıl yəlci anhımyən an twemnita.
7. Cali e ancə ya hamnita.	Cali e ancci anhımyən an twemnita.
8. Phyənci lıl ponæ ya hamnita.	Phyənci lıl ponæci anhımyən an twemnita.

T. Response Drill

Tutor: (Sənsæng ın) Ceimsı lıl kitaliə ya hæ yo?	'Do you have to wait for James?'
Student: Ne, Ceimsı lıl kitalici anhımyən an twe yo.	'Yes, I have to wait for James.'
1. (Sənsæng ın) wekuk mal ıl cal hæ ya hæ yo?	Ne, wekuk mal ıl cal haci anhımyən an twe yo.
2. (Sənsæng ın) kot tola wa ya hæ yo?	Ne, kot tola oci anhımyən an twe yo.
3. Catongcha mun ıl tatə ya hæ yo?	Ne, (catongcha mun ıl) tatci anhımyən an twe yo.
4. Kı sacən i coha ya hæ yo?	Ne, kı sacən i cohci anhımyən an twe yo.
5. Yəki esə Sənsæng ıl kitaliə ya hæ yo?	Ne, yəki esə (na lıl) kitalici anhımyən an twe yo.
6. Næil achim e ttəna ya hæ yo?	Ne, næil achim e ttənaci anhımyən an twe yo.
7. Cha lıl kil yəph e sewə ya hæ yo?	Ne, (cha lıl kil yəph e) seuci anhımyən an twe yo.

U. Response Drill

Tutor: Onıl hakkyo e kaci anhımyən an twemnikka?	'Do you have to go to school today?'
Student: Aniyo, (onıl hakkyo e) kaci anhə to kwænchanhə yo.	'No, I don't have to go (to school today).' ('Even though I don't go to school, it is O.K.')
1. Yəki esə thaci anhımyən an twemnikka?	Aniyo, yəki esə thaci anhə to kwænchanhə yo.
2. Pyəngwən e tıllıci anhımyən an twemnikka?	Aniyo, tıllıci anhə to kwænchanhə yo.
3. Kıləhke mal-haci anhımyən an twemnikka?	Aniyo, kıləhke mal-haci anhə to kwænchanhə yo.
4. ıyca e ancci anhımyən an twemnikka?	Aniyo, ıyca e ancci anhə to kwænchanhə yo.
5. Inchən kkaci kələ kaci anhımyən an twemnikka?	Aniyo, kələ kaci anhə to kwænchanhə yo.
6. Tæhak kyosu ka tweci anhımyən an twemnikka?	Aniyo, tæhak kyosu ka tweci anhə to kwænchanhə yo.

V. Combination Drill

Tutor: Hankuk mal ıl alə ya hamnita. Chinku lıl mantıl su issımnita.	'[You] have to know Korean.' '[You] can make friends in Korea.'
Student: Hankuk mal ıl alə ya, chinku lıl mantıl su issımnita.	'[You] have to know Korean to make friends.' ('Only when you know Korean you can make friends in Korea.')
1. Səul e salə ya hamnita. Yələ kaci lıl kukyəng-hal su issə yo.	Səul e salə ya, yələ kaci lıl kukyəng-hal su issə yo.
2. Sikan i issə ya hamnita. Sinæ e na kakessə yo.	Sikan i issə ya, sinæ e na kakessə yo.
3. Cal swiə ya hamnita. Taım nal il-hal su issə yo.	Cal swiə ya, taım nal il-hal su issə yo.
4. Ppəsı ka əpsə ya hamnita. Kələ sə il-halə ka yo.	Ppəsı ka əpsə ya, kələ sə il-halə ka yo.
5. Ton i issə ya hamnita. Cha lıl saci yo.	Ton i issə ya, cha lıl saci yo.
6. Yəngə lıl alə tılə ya hamnita. Mal i cæmi issə yo.	Yəngə lıl alə tılə ya, mal i cæmi issə yo.

W. Response Drill (the use of nəmu)

Tutor: Səul e kil i pencap-haci yo?	'The streets in Seoul are crowded, aren't they?'
Student: Ne, kılæ yo. Nəmu pəncap-hæ yo.	'That's right. [They] are too crowded.'
1. Sənsæng ın yosæ puncuhaci yo?	Ne, kılæ yo. Nəmu puncuhæ yo.
2. I kyosil i com copci yo?	Ne, kılæ yo. Com nəmu copa yo.
3. Hankuk mal i əlyəun mal ici yo?	Ne, kılæ yo. Nəmu əlyəun mal iye yo.
4. Kim Sənsæng i Səul pukın ıl cal alci yo?	Ne, kılæ yo. Nəmu cal alə yo.
5. Onıl achim cəncha ka nılici yo?	Ne, kılæ yo. Nəmu nıliə yo.
6. Səul esə Inchən kkaci kicha ka cacu tanici yo?	Ne, kılæ yo. Nəmu cacu taniə yo.
7. Sənsæng ın achim e nıcəssci yo?	Ne, kılæ yo. Nəmu nıcəssə yo.
8. Yosæ nın sikan i ppalli kaci yo?	Ne, kılæ yo. Nəmu ppalli ka yo.

X. Response Drill (the use of itta)

Tutor: Cikɪm ka to cohsɪmnikka? 'May I go now?'

Student: Aniyo, cikɪm kaci masipsiyo. Com itta kase yo. 'No, don't go now. [You'd better] go a little later.'

1. Cikɪm puchiə to cohsɪmnikka? Aniyo, cikɪm puchici masipsiyo. Com itta puchise yo.
2. Cikɪm sicak-hæ to cohsɪmnikka? Aniyo, cikɪm sicak-haci masipsiyo. Com itta sicak-hase yo.
3. Cikɪm tola wa to cohsɪmnikka? Aniyo, cikɪm tola oci masipsiyo. com itta tola ose yo.
4. Cikɪm næliə to cohsɪmnikka? Aniyo, cikɪm nælici masipsiyo. Com itta nælise yo.
5. Cikɪm yəki esə Sənsæng ɪl kitaliə to cohsɪmnikka? Aniyo, cikɪm (na lɪl) kitalici masipsiyo. Com itta kitalise yo.
6. Cikɪm cha e tha to cohsɪmnikka? Aniyo, cikɪm thaci masipsiyo. Com itta thase yo.
7. Cikɪm mun ɪl yələ to cohsɪmnikka? Aniyo, cikɪm yəlci masipsiyo. Com itta yə(lɪ)se yo.
8. Cikɪm mun ɪl tatə to cohsɪmnikka? Aniyo, cikɪm tatci masipsiyo. Com itta tatɪse yo.
9. Cikɪm yəki esə næliə tɪliə to cohsɪmnikka? Aniyo, cikɪm næliə cuci masipsiyo. Com itta næliə cuse yo.

Y. Grammar Drill (the use of kot)

Tutor: Tola osipsiyo. 'Come back.'

Student: Kot tola osipsiyo. 'Come back soon.'

1. Cə nɪn ttənalyəko hamnita. Cə nɪn kot ttənalyəko hamnita.
2. Sicak-hanɪn kəs i cohkessɪmnita. Kot sicak-hanɪn kəs i cohkessɪmnita.
3. Il ɪl kɪmantusipsiyo. Il ɪl kot kɪmantusipsiyo.
4. Hal su issɪmyən, ce cip e tɪllɪsipsiyo. Hal su issɪmyən, kot ce cip e tɪllɪsipsiyo.
5. I catongcha nɪn phalci anhkessə yo. I catongcha nɪn kot phalci anhkessə yo.
6. Hankuk mal kongpu lɪl kɪmantuəssɪmnita. Hankuk mal kongpu lɪl kot kɪmantuəssɪmnita.

7. Kı il ıl kkıth-næl su əpsımnita. — Kı il ıl kot kkıth-næl su əpsımnita.

8. Kukce Kıkcang esə Mikuk yənghwa lıl sangyəng-hal kəs imnita. — Kukce Kıkcang esə Mikuk yənghwa lıl kot sangyəng-hal kəs imnita.

Z. Response Drill

Tutor: Kim Sənsæng i onıl ttənal kka yo? — 'Will Mr. Kim leave today (do you think)?'

Student: Ne, ama onıl ttənal kəs imnita. — 'Yes, probably [he]'ll leave today.'

Aniyo, ama onıl ttənaci anhıl kəs imnita. — 'No, probably [he]'ll not leave today.'

1. Pak Sənsæng i cip e issıl kka yo?

Ne, ama (cip e) {issıl / kyesil} kəs imnita.

Aniyo, ama (cip e) {əpsıl / an kyesil / kyesici anhıl} kəs imnita.

2. Hakkyo ka məl kka yo?

Ne, ama məl kəs imnita.

Aniyo, ama məlci anhıl kəs imnita.

3. Næil nal i cohıl kka yo?

Ne, ama cohıl kəs imnita.

Aniyo, ama cohci anhıl kəs imnita.

4. Ceimsı ka kot tæsa ka twel kka yo?

Ne, ama kot (tæsa ka) twel kəs imnita.

Aniyo, ama kot (tæsa ka) tweci anhıl kəs imnita.

5. Onıl kı il i kəi ta kkıth-nal kka yo?

Ne, ama kəi ta kkıth-nal kəs imnita.

Aniyo, ama kəi ta kkıth-naci anhıl kəs imnita.

6. Kı salam i kil e cha lıl seul kka yo?

Ne, ama seul kəs imnita.

Aniyo, ama seuci anhıl kəs imnita.

7. Miss Brown i Hankuk mal ıl ta alə tılıl kka yo?

Ne, ama ta alə tılıl kəs imnita.

Aniyo, ama ta alə tıtci ahhıl kəs imnita.

8. Sikan i manhi kəllil kka yo?

Ne, ama (sikan i) manhi kəllil kəs imnita.

Aniyo, ama (sikan i) manhi kəllici anhıl kəs imnita.

EXERCISES

1. You are in the taxi. Ask the taxi driver to:
    a. go to the airport.
    b. hurry to the International Broadcasting Station.
    c. go a little faster.
    d. go a little slowly /chənchənhi/.
    e. close the window /chang-mun/ on his left.
    f. turn /tol-ta/ left at the next corner /kolmok/.
    g. turn right at the second crossroad /ne-kəli/.
    h. tell you when you come to the downtown area.
    i. let you know /allyə cu-ta/ if he sees the fire station.
    j. park the car across the street /kil kənnə/.
    k. stop the car at the gate /tæmun/ of the playground /utongcang/.
    l. wait for you for a little while.
    m. not go too fast.
    n. not take on other passengers.
    o. not stop on the street.
    p. not park on the street.

2. Make short dialogues so that the second party uses the following expressions in his speech:
    a. kələ sə
    b. thako kamyən
    c. com tə ppalli
    d. kakkai esə
    e. camkan man
    f. pol il
    g. tillil il
    h. itta
    i. kot
    j. nəmu
    k. ama
    l. kəi ta
    m. palssə
    n. acik

3. Tell Mr. Smith that you would appreciate it if he would:
    a. show you the dictionary.
    b. teach you Korean.
    c. give you a ride.
    d. drop you off at the door.
    e. buy you a cup of coffee.
    f. stop the car.
    g. park his car straight.
    h. wait for you.
    i. mail this letter for you.
    j. correct /kochi-ta/ your Korean.
    k. loan you some money.
    l. send you a book.
    m. let you know the time.
    n. come a little early /ilcciki/.
    o. go a little slowly.

4. Tell the following stories to Pak Sənsæng that:

(a) Messrs. Smith and Kim are going downtown. Mr. Smith wants to stop by a tearoom first. He is not going to meet anyone there, but he'd like to have a cup of coffee. Mr. Kim wants to go downtown first and stop by a tearoom. There are lots of nice tearooms downtown. Even though there are tearooms in this area, they are not so good.

(b) Messrs. Kim and Smith took a taxi and went to the Central Post Office first. They got off near the front door. Mr. Kim had some business to take care of for a while. He had to mail a letter. And it took him a little time. So, Mr. Smith went to the tearoom first and waited there. Mr. Kim came to the tearoom a little later but was not too late.

End of Tape 9A

Tape 9B

제 12 과 음식

(대화 A)

배
배가 고픕니다
1. 부라운 : 나는 좀 배가 고픕니다.

점심
먹으러
점심 먹으러 안 가겠읍니까?

점심 시간
되었읍니까
시간이 되었읍니다
2. 이 : 벌써 점심 시간이 다 되었읍니까?

3. 부라운 : 예, 점심 먹을 시간입니다. 점심 먹으러 (나) 갑시다.

잡수십니까
4. 이 : 오늘 점심은 무엇을 잡수시겠어요?

한식, 한국 음식
먹어 볼까요
5. 부라운 : 오늘은 한식을 먹어 볼까요?

아무 것이나
음식점

UNIT 12. Eating and Drinking

BASIC DIALOGUES FOR MEMORIZATION

Dialogue A

Brown

pæ	stomach
pæ ka kophimnita	I'm hungry
1. Na nin com pæ ka kophimnita.	I'm a little hungry.
cəmsim	lunch
məkilə	to eat
Cəmsim məkilə an kakessimnikka?	Wouldn't you like to go to eat (lunch)?'

Lee

cəmsim sikan	lunch hour
sikan i tweəssimnita	time is up ('time became')
2. Pəlssə cəmsim sikan i ta tweəssimnikka?	Is it already lunch time? ('Has the lunch hour already become?')

Brown

3. Ne, cəmsim məkil sikan imnita. Cəmsim məkilə (na) kapsita.	Yes, it is (lunch time). ('It's time to eat lunch.) Let's go (out) for lunch.

Lee

capsusimnikka	do [you] eat (honored)?
4. Onil cəmsim in muəs il capsusikessə yo?	What will you have for lunch today?

Brown

Hankuk imsik } Hansik }	Korean food
məkə pol kka yo	shall we try eating?
5. Onil in Hansik il məkə pol kka yo?	Shall we try Korean food today?

6. 이 : 저는 아무 것이나 좋습니다. 어디에 좋은 음식점이 있어요?

가까운 곳, 가까운 데
한식점

7. 부라운 : 예, 여기에서 가까운 곳에 한식점이 하나 있습니다.

음식

8. 김 : 거기 음식은 어떻습니까?

잘 합니다, 잘 만듭니다

9. 부라운 : 예, 거기 음식을 잘 합니다.

싸니까
언제든지

10. 그리고, 음식 값도 싸니까, 언제든지 사람이 많습니다.

(대화 B)

주문
들겠읍니까, 드시겠읍니까

11. 웨이트레스: 아직 주문 안 하셨읍니까? 무엇을 드시겠어요?

메뉴

12. 이 : 메뉴를 좀 보여 주세요. 한식은 무엇이 있어요?

Lee

amu kəs (ina)	anything; whatever it may be
ımsikcəm	restaurant
6. Cə nın amu kəs ina cohsımnita. əti e cohın ımsikcəm i issə yo?	Anything is O.K. Do you know of a good restaurant? ('Is there a good restaurant somewhere?')

Brown

kakkaun te kakkaun kos }	some place near
Hansikcəm	Korean restaurant
7. Ne, yəki esə kakkaun kos e Hansikcəm i hana issımnita.	Yes, there is a Korean restaurant near here. ('At the nearby place from here, there's one Korean restaurant.')

Lee

ımsik	food (cooked)
8. Kəki ımsik ın əttəhsımnikka?	How is the food there?

Brown

cal hamnita cal mantı(lı)mnita	([they] do well) ([they] make well)
9. Ne, kəki ımsik ıl cal hamnita.	Oh, the food is good.
ssani kka	because [it]'s cheap
ənce tınci	anytime; all the time
10. Kıliko, ımsik kaps to ssani kka, ənce tınci salam i manhsımnita.	And because it ('food price') is cheap, it is always crowded.

Dialogue B

(..in the restaurant..)

Waitress

cumun	order
tılkessımnikka	[I] lift; [I] have ('eat; drink')
tılkessımnikka tı(lı)sikessımnikka }	will you have ('eat; drink')?
11. Acik cumun an hasyəssımnikka? Muəs ıl tılısikessə yo?	Haven't you ordered, yet? What would you like to have, sir?

잡수시려면
불고기
곰탕
냉면 등

13. 웨이트레스: 여러 가지가 있읍니다. 한식을 잡수시려면 불고기와 곰탕, 그리고 냉면 등이 있읍니다.

14. 이 : 선생은 무엇을 하시겠어요?

불고기하고 밥

15. 부라운 : 나는 불고기하고 밥을 먹겠읍니다.

해 보겠읍니다

16. 이 : 저는 곰탕을 해 보겠읍니다.

또
가져 옵니다

17. 웨이트레스: 다른 것은 또 무엇을 가져 올까요?

목
마릅니다
목이 마릅니다
마실 것

18. 이 : 아, 나는 목이 마릅니다. 마실 것은 무엇이 있지요?

맥주
사이다

Lee

menyu	menu
12. Menyu (lɪl) com poyə cuse yo. Hansik ɪn muəs i issə yo?	Please let me see the menu. What kinds of Korean food do you have?

Waitress

capsusilyəmyən	if you are going to eat
Pul-koki	(a kind of barbecue beef) ('fire-meat')
Komthan	(soup with rice and meat)
Nængmyən tɪng	(cold noodle) and so on
13. Yələ kaci ka issɪmnita. Hansik ɪl capsusilyəmyən, Pul-koki wa Komthang, kɪliko, Nængmyən tɪng i issɪmnita.	We have several kinds. If you're going to have Korean food, there are Pul-koki, Komthang, Nængmyən and other things.

Lee

14. Sənsæng ɪn muəs ɪl hasikessə yo?	What will you have?

Brown

pap	(cooked) rice; meal
Pul-koki hako pap	Pul-koki and rice
15. Na nɪn Pul-koki hako pap ɪl məkkessɪmnita.	I'll have Pul-koki and rice.

Lee

16. Cə nɪn Komthang ɪl hæ pokessɪmnita.	I'll try Komthang.

Waitress

tto	also; besides; again
kacə omnita	[I] bring (thing)
17. Talɪn kəs (ɪn) tto muəs (ɪl) kacə ol kka yo?	Would you like anything else? ('What other things shall I also bring?')

19. 웨이트레스: 맥주와 사이다가 있읍니다.

안주
병
병마
콩

20. 이 : 그럼, 맥주 두병과 안주로 콩을 좀 가져 오세요.

Lee

mok	neck; throat
malımnita	[it] dries
mok i malımnita	[I]'m thirsty ('throat dries')
masil kəs	something to drink
18. A, na nın mok i malımnita. Masil kəs ın muəs i issci yo?	Oh, I'm thirsty. What do you have to drink?

Waitress

mækcu	beer
Saita	(a kind of soft drink)
19. Mækcu wa Saita ka issımnita.	We have beer and Saita.

Lee

ancu	relish [taken with wine]; snacks
pyəng	bottle
pyəng man	bottle only; just bottle
khong	beans
20. Kıləm, mækcu tu pyəng kwa ancu lo khong ıl com kacə ose yo.	Well, bring us just two bottles of beer and some beans for snacks.

NOTES ON DIALOGUES

(Numbers correspond to the sentence numbers.)

1. Pæ ka kophımnita. ('Stomach is empty.') is the Korean equivalent of 'I'm hungry'. The intransitive verb kophı- may be preceded by pæ 'stomach' as its subject or topic, but never by other nominals.

2. Sikan i (ta) tweəssımnita. ('Time (all) became.') is a fixed expression which is used as the equivalent of 'time is up'. The intransitive verb twe-, occuring usually in the past tense form /tweəssımnita/ after a point in time, denotes arriving at a certain point in time, and after a period of time denotes elasping of a certain period of time. Compare:

Han-si ka tweəssımnita.	'It is one o'clokc now.'
Han sikan i tweəssımnita.	'It has been an hour.'

4. Capsusi- is the honorific or polite equivalent of mək- 'to eat'.

6. Amu 'any-' is a determinative which occurs before (a nominal +) na/ina, making an adverbial phrase: amu kəs ina 'anything', amu salam ina 'anybody', amu ımsik ina 'any food', amu ttæ na 'any time', amu nal ina 'any day', amu cip ina 'any house', amu na 'anyone'. The construction amu + Nominal + na/ina = Question Nominal + na/ina (See Grammar Note 4, Unit 10). -cəm is a bound form which occurs as a part of certain place nouns, meaning 'store' or 'shop': sangcəm 'store', pækhwacəm 'department store', ımsikcəm 'restaurant', Hansikcəm 'Korean restaurant', etc.

7. Both te 'place' and kos 'place' are synonyms and both are post-nouns. However, te occurs only after noun-modifier words, whereas kos occurs after either determinatives or noun-modifier words. Compare Group 1 with Group 2:

GROUP 1

cohın te	'a good place'
pissan te	'an expensive place'
kongpu-hanın te	'the place of studying'
sanın te	'a living place'

GROUP 2

ənɪ kos	'which place'
i kos	'this place'
cə kos	'that place'
kakkaun kos	'the place which is near'
mən kos	'the faraway place'

9. In Kəki ɪmsik ɪl cal hamnita. ('There [they] do food well.'), cal hamnita is the substitute for cal mant(ɪl)ɪmnita. ('[They] make well.').

11. Tɪ(l)- 'to lift', 'to hold' is either a transitive or an intransitive verb. When the situation is clear, with or without being preceded by the name of food and/or beverage, tɪ(l)- is used as a substitute for mək- 'to eat', or masi- 'to drink'.

13. Tɪng 'and so forth', 'etc.' is a post—noun which occurs after two or more nominals. It singles out the preceding nominals to be the subject, the topic or the object for the following inflected expression.

14. (Sənsæng ɪn) muəs ɪl hasikessə yo? ('What will you do?') in an eating and/or drinking situation is used as a substitute for Muəs ɪl məkkessə yo? 'What will you eat?' or Muəs ɪl masikessə yo? 'What will you drink?'. This is like the English expression, What will you have? Ha- and tɪ(l)- are interchangeably used in such a situation.

17. The principal verb stem kaci- in the phrase kacə o- 'to bring' means 'to possess', 'to have', 'to hold', or 'to take'. Observe the following verb phrases:

kacə o-	=	kaciko o-	'to bring [something]' ('to have and come')
kacə ka-	=	kaciko ka-	'to take away [something]'
taliə o-	=	taliko o-	'to bring [someone]'
taliə ka-	=	taliko ka-	'to take [someone]'

18. Mok i malımnita. ('Throat is dry.') is the Korean equivalent of 'I'm thirsty'. The noun mok means either 'throat' or 'neck'. The verb malı- is either an action verb or a description verb, meaning 'to dry' and 'to be dry' respectively.

19. Saita is a kind of soft drink which is commonly used in Korea during warm seasons. The taste of it is similar to that of Seven-ups.

GRAMMAR NOTES

1. -(ı)ni kka 'because...', 'since...'

The inflected form ending in -(ı)ni plus kka which may be followed by a pause occurs before another inflected expression. The ending -(ı)ni is added to a verb stem, or to a verb stem plus other suffixes: -ni to a stem ending in a vowel and -ıni to a stem ending in a consonant. The construction -(ı)ni kka denotes the cause or basis of the action or description of the verb in the (ı)ni form for the succeeding inflected expressions. Examples:

Cip i kakkauni kka, kələ sə il-halə omnita.	'I come to work on foot because my home is near.'
Ton i əpsıni kka, na kaci anhkessə yo.	'Because I don't have money, I wont't go out.'
Hankuk mal ıl mal-hani kka, Hankuk esə il-haki phyəlli-hamnita.	'Because I speak Korean, it is very convenient to work in Korea.'

Note: In the above construction kka may be dropped with the same meaning.

2. -(ı)lyəmyən 'if [you] are going to...', 'if [you] intend to...'

The inflected form ending in -(ı)lyəmyən which may be followed by a pause denotes the conditional desire or intention of the subject for the future for the following inflected expression. The ending -(ı)lyəmyən may be added to a verb stem with or without the honorific suffix, but with no tense suffixes. Examples:

Wekyokwan i twelyəmyən, wekuk mal ıl cal hæ ya hamnita.	'If [you] intend to be a diplomat, [you] have to speak foreign languages.'
Hankuk mal ıl cal halyəmyən, Yəngə lıl ssıci anhnın kəs i cohkessımnita.	'If [you]'re going to speak Korean well, [you]'d better not use English.'

Mikuk yənghwa lıl polyəmyən, Kukce Kıkcang ılo kapsita.	'If you {want / intend} to see American movies, let's go to the International Theatre.'

Note: -lyəmən is added to a vowel stem and -ılyəmən to a consonant stem.

3. Infinitive + po-

The verb po- preceded by an infinitive without a pause occurs as an auxiliary verb. The construction Infinitive + po- literally means something like 'does something and see', but the denotation of the auxiliary po- is 'try doing something to see the result'. Some verb phrases of this construction have unique meanings and the two verbs (i.e. principal and auxiliary verbs) are inseparable from each other. Thus, each verb phrase of this kind should be memorized as a unit. Examples:

mulə po-ta	'inquires'
tola po-ta	'looks back'
hılkiə po-ta	'steers'
pala po-ta	'looks over' (from the distance)
hæ po-ta	'tries (doing)'
manna po-ta	'tries meeting'
alə po-ta	'finds out'
chiəta po-ta	'looks up to', 'beholds'
ipə po-ta	'tries on (clothes)'
məkə po-ta	'tries (eating) food'
tılə ka po-ta	'goes in to see'

4. Particle tınci/itınci

Tınci occurs after a nominal ending in a consonant; itınci after a nominal ending in a vowel. The particle tınci/itınci which is synonymous with na/ina can be interchangeable only in the following two constructions (See (a) and (b) of Grammar Note 4, Unit 10).

(a) Nominal 1 + tınci/itınci + Nominal 2 = 'N1 or N2', 'either N1 or N2'

hakkyo tınci cip	'either school or house'
Yəngə tınci Tokilə	'either English or German'
onıl itınci næil	'either today or tomorrow'

(b) Question Nominal + tınci/itınci = adverbial phrase

muəs itınci	'anything'
əti tınci	'anywhere'
ənce tınci	'any time'

nuku tınci	'anybody'
myəchil itınci	'any date'

5. Particle man 'only'

In Unit 9, we noticed the construction -ci man (i.e. the ci form + the Particle man) means '-but'.

A nominal X + man occurs as an adverbial phrase for the following inflected expressions, meaning 'only X' or 'just X'. Examples:

Mækcu tu pyəng man kacə ose yo.	'Bring [us] just two bottles of beer.'
Na nın kı yəca man salang-hamnita.	'I love only her.'
Kim Sənsæng ın nal mata Yəngə man mal-hæ yo.	'Mr. Kim speaks only English everyday.'
Kı nal, Kim ın əpsəssko, na man Tæthongyəng ıl mannassə yo.	'Kim was not [there] that day, and only I met Mr. President.'

DRILLS

A. Substitution Drill

1. Cəmsim məkılə an kakessımnikka?	Wouldn't you like to go to eat lunch?
2. Sinæ kukyəng-halə an kakessımnikka?	Wouldn't you like to go to see around downtown?
3. Capci ilkılə an kakessımnikka?	Wouldn't you like to go to read magazines?
*4. Sanpo-halə an kakessımnikka?	Wouldn't you like to go to take a walk?
5. Mækcu masilə an kakessımnikka?	Wouldn't you like to go for beer?
*6. Sicang polə an kakessımnikka?	Wouldn't you like to go for food shopping?
7. Yənghwa polə an kakessımnikka?	Wouldn't you like to go to see a movie?
*8. Chum chulə an kakessımnikka?	Wouldn't you like to go for dancing?

B. Substitution Drill

1. Cəmsim məkıl sikan i ta tweəssımnita.	It's time for lunch now. ('Lunch time is all up.')
2. Hakkyo kal sikan i ta tweəssımnita.	It's time to go to school now.
3. Kongpu-hal sikan i ta tweəssımnita.	It's time for studying now.
4. Kicha thal sikan i ta tweəssımnita.	It's time to get on the train now.
5. Ttənal sikan i ta tweəssımnita.	It's time to leave now.
6. Sicak-hal sikan i ta tweəssımnita.	It's time to begin now.
7. Ppəsı ka tahıl sikan i ta tweəssımnita.	It's time for bus to arrive now.
8. Swil sikan i ta tweəssımnita.	It's time to take a break ('rest') now.
9. (Cam) cal sikan i ta tweəssımnita.	It's time to go to bed now.
10. Kımantul sikan i ta tweəssımnita.	It's time to quit [it] now.
*11. Ilənal sikan i ta tweəssımnita.	It's time to get up now.
*12. Il i kkıth-nal sikan i ta tweəssımnita.	It's time to end the work.
*13. Sicang polə kal sikan i ta tweəssımnita.	It's time to go for food shopping.

C. Substitution Drill

1. Cəmsim ın muəs ıl capsusikessə yo?	What will you have for lunch?
*2. Achim ın muəs ıl capsusikessə yo?	What will you have for breakfast?
*3. Cənyək ın muəs ıl capsusikessə yo?	What will you have for supper?
*4. Achim siksa nın muəs ıl capsusikessə yo?	What will you have for breakfast ('morning meal')?
*5. Cəyək siksa nın muəs ıl capsusikessə yo?	What will you have for dinner ('evening meal')?
6. Onıl cəmsim ın muəs ıl capsusikessə yo?	What will you have for lunch today?
7. Onıl cəmsim ın musın ımsik ıl capsusikessə yo?	What kind of food will you have for lunch today?
8. Onıl cəmsin ın Cungkuk ımsik ıl capsusikessə yo?	Will you have Chinese food for lunch today?
*9. Onıl cəmsim ın Yangsik ıl capsusikessə yo?	Will you have Western food for lunch today?
*10. Onıl cəmsim ın Wæsik ıl capsusikessə yo?	Will you have Japanese food for lunch today?
11. Onıl cəmsim ın Hansik ıl capsusikessə yo?	Will you have Korean food for lunch today?

D. Grammar Drill (based on Grammar Note 3)

Tutor: Hansik ıl məkıl kka yo?	'Shall we eat Korean food?'
Student: Hansik ıl məkə pol kka yo?	'Shall we try (eating) Korean food?'

1. Hakkyo e kal kka yo?	Hakkyo e ka pol kka yo?
2. Il ıl sicak-hal kka yo?	Il ıl sicak-hæ pol kka yo?
3. Wekuk mal ıl pæul kka yo?	Wekuk mal ıl pæwə pol kka yo?
4. Kicha lıl thal kka yo?	Kicha lıl tha pol kka yo?
5. Mækcu lıl masil kka yo?	Mækcu lıl masiə pol kka yo?
6. Samusil e tıllıl kka yo?	Samusil e tıllə pol kka yo?
7. Komthang ıl hal kka yo?	Komthang ıl hæ pol kka yo?
8. Hankuk mal ıl yənsıp-hal kka yo?	Hankuk mal ıl yənsıp-hæ pol kka yo?
9. Mun aph esə nælil kka yo?	Mun aph esə nælið pol kka yo?
10. Tapang esə kı salam ıl kitalil kka yo?	Tapang esə kı salam ıl kitaliə pol kka yo?

E. Response Drill (based on Grammar Note 3)

Tutor: Hansik ıl məkə pol kka yo?	'Shall we try Korean food?'
Student: Ne, Hansik ıl məkə popsita.	'Yes, let's try (Korean food).'

1.	Hakkyo e tıllə pol kka yo?	Ne, hakkyo e tıllə popsita.
2.	Kyosil e tılə ka pol kka yo?	Ne, kyosil e tılə ka popsita.
3.	Cikım sicak-hæ pol kka yo?	Ne, cikım sicak-hæ popsita.
4.	Yəki esə Kim Sənsæng ıl kitaliə pol kka yo?	Ne, Yəki esə kitaliə popsita.
5.	Mun aph esə næliə pol kka yo?	Ne, mun aph esə næliə popsita.
6.	Hankuk mal lo mal-hæ pol kka yo?	Ne, Hankuk mal lo mal-hæ popsita.
7.	Hankuk mækcu lıl masiə pol kka yo?	Ne, Hankuk mækcu lıl masiə popsita.

F. Subsitutuion Drill

1.	Amu kəs ina cohsımnita.	Anything is O.K.
2.	Muəs ina cohsımnita.	Anything is O.K.
3.	Amu salam ina cohsımnita.	Anyone is O.K.
4.	əti na cohsımnita.	Any place is O.K.
5.	Nuku na cohsımnita.	Anybody is O.K.
6.	Amu haksæng ina cohsımnita.	Any student is O.K.
7.	Amu {te na / kos ina} cohsımnita.	Any place is O.K.
8.	Amu kıkcang ina cohsımnita.	Any theatre is O.K.
*9.	Amu ttæ na cohsımnita.	Any time is O.K.
10.	ənce na cohsımnita.	Any time is O.K.
11.	ənı nal ina cohsımnita.	Any day is O.K.
12.	Musın yoil ina cohsımnita.	Any day of the week is O.K.
13.	Amu ımsik ina cohsımnita.	Any kind of food is O.K.
*14.	ənı cumal ina cohsımnita.	Any weekend is O.K.

G. Subsitution Drill

1. Menyu (lɨl) com poyə cusipsiyo.	Please show me the menu.
2. Kɨ kɨlim (ɨl) com poyə cusipsiyo.	Please show me that picture.
3. Nolan syassɨ (lɨl) com poyə cusipsiyo.	Please show me a yellow shirt.
4. Kkaman yangpok (ɨl) com poyə cusipsiyo.	Please show me the black suit.
5. Phalan sukən (ɨl) com poyə cusipsiyo.	Please show me a blue towel.
6. Hayan congi (lɨl) com poyə cusipsiyo.	Please show me the white paper.
7. Han-Yəng sacən (ɨl) com poyə cusipsiyo.	Please show me a Korean-English dictionary.
8. Menyu (lɨl) com poyə cusipsiyo.	Please show me the menu.
9. Menyu (lɨl) com kacə osipsiyo.	Please bring [me] the menu.
10. Menyu (lɨl) com kacə kasipsiyo.	Please take (away) the menu.

H. Substitution Drill

1. Na nɨn mækcu lɨl masiko siphsɨmnita.	I'd like to drink beer.
2. Na nɨn saita lɨl masiko siphsɨmnita.	I'd like to drink saita.
3. Na nɨn mul ɨl masiko siphsɨmnita.	I'd like to drink water.
4. Na nɨn khəphi lɨl masiko siphsɨmnita.	I'd like (to drink) coffee.
5. Na nɨn khokhoa lɨl masiko siphsɨmnita.	I'd like (to drink) cocoa.
6. Na nɨn cha lɨl masiko siphsɨmnita.	I'd like (to drink) tea (green).
*7. Na nɨn hongcha lɨl masiko siphsɨmnita.	I'd like (to drink) tea (black).
*8. Na nɨn chan mul ɨl masiko siphsɨmnita.	I'd like (to drink) cold water.
*9. Na nɨn əlɨm mul ɨl masiko siphsɨmnita.	I'd like to drink ice water.
*10. Na nɨn khokhakholla lɨl masiko siphsɨmnita.	I'd like to drink coca cola.
*11. Na nɨn uyu lɨl masiko siphsɨmnita.	I'd like to drink milk.
*12. Na nɨn sul ɨl masiko siphsɨmnita.	I'd like to have (some) {wine / liquor}.

I. Grammar Drill (Make one sentence out of two as in the example.)

Tutor: Hakkyo ka məmnita. Catongcha lo kamnita.	'The school is far. I go by car.'
Student: Hakkyo ka məni kka, catongcha lo kamnita.	'Because the school is far, I go by car.'
1. I siktang e nın ımsik kaps i ssamnita. Salam i manhsımnita.	I siktang e nın ımsik kaps i ssani kka, salam i·manhsımnita.
2. Hankuk e kamnita. Hankuk mal ıl pæwə ya hamnita.	Hankuk e kani kka, Hankuk mal ıl pæwə ya hamnita.
3. Yəki e siktang i əpsımnita. Sinæ kkaci kamnita.	Yəki e siktang i əpsıni kka, sinæ kkaci kamnita.
4. Mok i malımnita. Mækcu lıl masikessımnita.	Mok i malıni kka, mækcu lıl masikessımnita.
5. Cəmsim sikan i ta twemnita. Na nın pæ ka kophımnita.	Cəmsim sikan i ta tweni kka, na nın pæ ka kophımnita.
6. Na nın Hansik ıl cohahamnita. Hansikcəm e kakessımnita.	Na nın Hansik ıl cohahani kka, Hansikcəm e kakessımnita.
7. Ppəsi ka manhci anhsımnita. Nıl salam i manhsımnita.	Ppəsı ka manhci anhıni kka, nıl salam i manhsımnita.
8. Samusil i cip esə kakkapsımnita. Kim Sənsæng ın kələ sə tanimnita.	Samusil i cip esə kakkauni kka, Kim Sənsæng ın kələ sə tanimnita.
9. Hankuk mal ıl amnita. Hankuk salam kwa il-haki cæmi issımnita.	Hankuk mal ıl ani kka, Hankuk salam kwa il-haki cæmi issımnita.

J. Response Drill

Tutor: Wæ catongcha lo kamnikka? /Hakkyo ka məmnita./	'Why do you go by car?' /School is is far./
Student: Hakkyo ka məni kka, catongcha lo kamnita.	'Because the school's far, I go by car.'
1. Wæ Hankuk mal ıl pæumnikka? /Hankuk e kamnita./	Hankuk e kani kka, Hankuk mal ıl pæumnita.
2. Wæ nal mata Səul Tæhakkyo e na kamnikka? /Yəngə lıl kalıchimnita./	Yəngə lıl kalıchini kka, nal mata Səul Tæhakkyo e na kamnita.

3. Wæ yətəlp-si pan kkaci samusil e wa ya hamnikka. /Yətəlp-si pan e il i sicak-hamnita./	Yətəlp-si pan e il i sicak-hani kka, yətəlp-si pan kkaci wa ya hamnita.
4. Wæ əce nın swiəssımnikka? /Mom i aphəssımnita./	Mom i aphəssıni kka, əce nın swiəssımnita.
5. Wæ Hankuk mal kongpu-haki e kıləhke sikan i kəllimnikka? /Hankuk mal i əlyəpsımnita./	Hankuk mal i əlyəuni kka, kongpu-haki e kıləhke sikan kəllimnita.
6. Wæ kələ sə hakkyo e tanimnikka? /Cip esə məlci anhsımnita./	Cip esə məlci anhıni kka, kələ sə hakkyo e tanimnita.
7. Wæ kıləhke puncuhamnikka? /Yosæ nın hal il i manhsımnita./	Yosæ nın hal il i manhıni kka, kıləhke puncuhamnita.
8. Wæ kıləhke pæ ka kophımnikka? /Achim ıl məkci anhəssımnita./	Achim ıl məkci anhəssıni kka, kıləhke pæ ka kophımnita.
9. Wæ kı salam cip e tıllə ya hamnikka? /Na lıl kitaliko issımnita./	Na lıl kitaliko issıni kka, kı salam cip e tıllə ya hamnita.

K. Completion Exercise (Complete the sentence using the given expression based on your own experiences.)

Tutor: Na nın Hankuk e kani kka,...	'Because I go to Korea...'
Student: Na nın Hankuk e kani kka, Hankuk mal ıl kongpu-hamnita.	'Because I go to Korea I'm studying Korean.'

1. Hankuk mal ın Yəngə wa talıni kka,
2. Hankuk mal ıl cal mal-haci mot hani kka,
3. Na nın mok i malıni kka,
4. Cəmsim sikan i tweəssıni kka,
5. Hakkyo kal sikan i nıcəssıni kka,
6. Hapsıng i ceil phyəllihani kka,
7. Na nın Yəngə lıl alə tılıl su issıni kka,
8. Na nın mom i aphəssıni kka,
9. Səul ıl kukyəng-hako siphıni kka,
10. Taım tal e Mikuk e tola kani kka,

L. Response Exercise (Answer the questions based on the reality.)

Tutor: Wæ Hankuk mal ɨl kongpu-hase yo? 'Why do you study Korean?'

Student: Hankuk e kanɨ kka,. Hankuk mal ɨl Kongpu-hæ yo. 'Because I go to Korea, (I'm studying Korean)'.

1. Wæ kələ sə hakkyo e tanɨse yo?
2. Wæ Hankuk mal ɨ kɨləhke əlyəwə yo?
3. Wæ yosæ kɨləkhe pappɨse yo?
4. Wæ Hankuk yənghwa lɨl poko siphɨse yo?
5. Wæ Mikuk Tæsakwan e tɨllə ya hæ yo?
6. Wæ Thoyoil mata sicang e kase yo?
7. Wæ cip esə hakkyo kkaci sikan ɨ manhɨ kəllyə yo?
8. Wæ əce nɨn cip esə swiəssə yo?
9. Wæ Hankuk mal ɨ philyo-hase yo?

M. Completion Exercise

Tutor: Hankuk e kalyəmyən, 'If [you]'re going to go to Korea,.'

Student: Hankuk e kalyəmyən, Hankuk mal ɨl pæwə ya hamnita. 'If [you]'re going to go to Korea, [you] have to learn Korean.'

1. Hansik ɨl capsusilyəmyən,
2. Cə lɨl kitalilyəmyən,
3. Catongcha lɨl phallyəmyən,
4. Mikuk yənghwa lɨl polyəmyən,
5. Hakkyo e ppəsɨ lo kalyəmyən,
6. Kil ɨl mulə polyəmyən,
7. Mækcu lɨl masilyəmyən,
8. Chinku lɨl mannalyəmyən,
9. Hankuk e olæ tongan issɨlyəmyən,
10. Mikuk e tola kalyəmyən,

N. Expansion Drill

Tutor: Pul-koki wa Komthang, Nængmyən i issımnita.	'We have Pul-koki, Komthang and Nængmyən.'
Student: Pul-koki wa Komthang, kıliko, Nængmyən tıng i issımnita.	'We have Pul-koki, Komthang and Nængmyən and others (so forth).'
1. Yəngə wa Pullansə mal, Tokil mal ıl kalıchimnita.	Yəngə wa Pullansə mal, kıliko, Tokil mal tıng ıl kalıchimnita.
2. Yəki esə moca wa kutu, yangpok ıl phamnita.	Yəki esə moca wa kutu, kıliko, yangpok tıng ıl phamnita.
3. Ppəsı wa cəncha, hapsıng i tanimnita.	Ppəsı wa cəncha, kıliko, hapsıng tıng i tanimnita.
4. Hansikcəm kwa Yangsikcəm, Cungkuk siktang ıl pol su issımnita.	Hansikcəm kwa Yangsikcəm, kıliko, Cungkuk siktang tıng ıl pol su issımnita.
5. Pækhwacəm kwa pakmulkwan, sicang ıl kukyənghako siphsımnita.	Pækhwacəm kwa pakmulkwan, kıliko, sicang tıng ıl kukyəng-hako siphsımnita.
6. Mannyənphil kwa congi, khal ıl sassımnita.	Mannyənphil kwa congi, kıliko, khal tıng ıl sassımnita.
7. Cip kaps kwa mulkən kaps, ımsik kaps ıl alə ya hakessımnita.	Cip kaps kwa mulkən kaps, kıliko, ımsik kaps tıng ıl alə ya hakessımnita.

O. Grammar Drill

Tutor: Hankuk mal ıl pæuko siphımyən, hakkyo e tanisipsiyo.	'If you want to learn Korean, (please) go to school.'
Student: Hankuk mal ıl pæulyəmyən, hakkyo e tanisipsiyo.	'If you're going to learn Korean (please) go to school.'
1. Hansik ıl məkko siphımyən, Hansikcəm e kasipsiyo.	Hansik ıl məkılyəmhən, Hansikcəm e kasipsiyo.
2. Mikuk moca lıl sako siphımyən, pækhwacəm e tıllısipsiyo.	Mikuk moca lıl salyəmyən, pækhwacəm e tıllısipsiyo.
3. Hankuk sinmun ıl ilkko siphımyən, il nyən tongan ilkki lıl pæwə ya hamnita.	Hankuk sinmun ıl ilkılyəmyən, il nyən tongan ilkki lıl pæwə ya hamnita.

4. Səul kanɪn kicha lɪl thako siphɪmyən, han-si kkaci yək e kasipsiyo.
   Səul kanɪn kicha lɪl thalyəmyən, han-si kkaci yək e kasipsiyo.
5. Tæsakwan aph esə næliko siphɪmyən, məncə mal-hasipsiyo.
   Tæsakwan aph esə nælilyəmyən, məncə mal-hasipsiyo.
6. Catongcha lɪl phalko siphɪmyən, cə eke com poyə cusipsiyo.
   Catongcha lɪl phallyəmyən, cə eke com poyə cusipsiyo.
7. Hyuka lɪl patko siphɪmyən, taɪm tal e patɪsipsiyo.
   Hyuka lɪl patɪlyəmyən, taɪm tal e patɪsipsiyo.
8. Tæhak kyosu ka tweko siphɪmyən, kongpu lɪl manhi hæ ya hamnita.
   Tæhak kyosu ka twelyəmyən, kongpu lɪl manhi pæ ya hamnita.
9. Kil ɪl mulə poko siphɪmyən, catongcha esə nælisipsiyo.
   Kil ɪl mulə polyəmyən, catongcha esə nælisipsiyo.
10. Na lɪl kitaliko siphɪmyən, tapang e issɪsipsiyo.
   Na lɪl kitalilyəmyən, tapang e issɪsipsiyo.

P. Grammar Drill

Tutor: Hankuk mal ɪl pæukessə yo? Hakkyo e tanisipsiyo.
'Will you study Korean? Go to (<u>or</u> attend) school.'

Student: Hankuk mal ɪl pæulyəmyən, hakkyo e tanisipsiyo.
'If you intend (<u>or</u> are going) to study Korean, go to school.'

1. Hansik ɪl capsusikessə yo? Pul-koki ka issɪmnita.
   Hansik ɪl capsusilyəmyən, Pul-koki ka issɪmnita.
2. Hankuk e kakessə yo? Mal ɪl pæwə ya hamnita.
   Hankuk e kalyəmyən, mal ɪl pæwə ya hamnita.
3. Tapang e tɪllɪkessə yo? Na wa kathi kapsita.
   Tapang e tɪllɪlyəmyən, na wa kathi kapsita.
4. Yənghwa lɪl pokessə yo? Kukce Kɪkcang i cohsɪmnita.
   Yənghwa lɪl polyəmyən, Kukce Kɪkcang i cohsɪmnita.
5. Mækcu lɪl masikessə yo? Tapang e kaci masipsiyo.
   Mækcu lɪl masilyəmyən, tapang e kaci masipsiyo.
6. Wekyokwan i twekessə yo? Yələ nala mal ɪl pæwə ya hamnita.
   Wekyokwan i twelyəmyən, yələ nala mal ɪl pæwə ya hamnita.
7. Kil ɪl mulə pokessə yo? Catongcha esə nælisipsiyo.
   Kil ɪl mulə polyəmyən, catongcha esə nælisipsiyo.
8. Mikuk yangpok ɪl sakessə yo? Pækhwacəm e manhi issə yo.
   Mikuk yangpok ɪl salyəmyən, pækhɪacəm e manhi issə yo.

EXERCISES

A. Tell Mr. Lee that:

1. You are hungry.
2. It is time to eat lunch; time to go to bed; time to get up.
3. It has already been two hours.
4. Any food is O.K. with you.
5. You would like to try Chinese food.
6. You are thirsty.
7. The food at the nearby restaurant is very good.
8. They serve Pul-koki, Nængmyən, Komthang, and so forth.
9. You have not ordered (food) yet.
10. You haven't had breakfast (or supper) yet.
11. It's time to go for food shopping.

B. Order from the waitress the following:

1. two bottles of beer
2. Pulkoki for two people /tu salam pun/
3. three cups of coffee afterward
4. one glass of cold water and one ice tea
5. milk for the baby
6. Chinese food
7. Japanese food
8. Komthang for only one person /han salam pun man/

C. Make short dialogues so that the second party responds using the following phrases:

1.	muəs itıncı	'anything'	7.	amu yoil itıncı	'any day of the week'
2.	əti tıncı	'any place'	8.	ənı cumal itıncı	'any weekend'
3.	ənce tıncı	'any time'	9.	amu kos itıncı	'any place'
4.	nuku tıncı	'anybody'	10.	amu nal itıncı	'any day'
5.	myəchil itıncı	'any date'	11.	amu ttæ tıncı	'any time'
6.	amu ımsik itıncı	'any food'	12.	amu te tıncı	'any place'

D. Jones Sənsæng explains the reasons when you ask him:

1. Why he is studying Korean.
2. Why he hasn't had breakfast yet.
3. Why the nearby restaurant is always crowded.
4. Why he is busy all the time.
5. Why he didn't come to school yesterday.
6. Why he has to speak Korean.
7. Why he's going to sell his car.
8. Why the traffic is so thick.
9. Why he joined the foreign service.
10. Why he wants to take a vacation.
11. Why he intends to walk.
12. Why he doesn't take the bus.
13. Why he doesn't take his wife to the movies.
14. Why he tries to find out Mr. Kim's telephone number /cənhwa pənho/.
15. Why he doesn't want to try Korean food.

End of Tape 9B

Tape 10A

제 13 과 음식 (계속)

자

1. 부라운 : 자, 어서 드십시요.

시작합시다

2. 이 : 예, 같이 시작합시다.

소금

고추

고추 가루

저에게

3. 부라운 : 거기 소금과 고추 가루 좀 저에게 주시겠읍니까?

4. 이 : 예, 여기 있읍니다. 나도 소금이 좀 필요합니다.

맛

5. 부라운 : 곰탕 맛이 어떻습니까?

6. 이 : 맛(이) 있읍니다. 선생의 불고기는요?

맛은 좋으나

고기가 질깁니다

7. 부라운 : 맛은 좋으나, 고기가 좀 질깁니다.

맵습니다

매운 음식

8. 이 : 선생은 매운 음식이 좋습니까?

UNIT 13. Eating and Drinking (Continued)

BASIC DIALOGUE FOR MEMORIZATION

Brown

ca	well; now
1. Ca, əsə tı(lı)sipsiyo.	(Now) Please help yourself.

Lee

sicak-hapsita	let's start
2. Ne, kathi sicak-hapsita.	Thank you. ('Let's begin together.')

Brown

sokım	salt
kochu	red pepper
kochu kalu	(pepper powder)
cə eke	to me
3. Kəki sokım kwa kochu kalu com cə eke cusikessımnikka?	May I have the salt and pepper, please? ('Will you give me the salt and red pepper there?')

Lee

4. Ne, yəki issımnita. Na to sokım i com philyo-hamnita.	Here you are! I need a little salt, too.

Brown

mas	taste
5. Komthang mas i əttəhsımnikka?	How does the Komthang taste?

Lee

6. Mas i issımnita. Sənsæng e Pul-koki nın yo?	It tastes good. ('Taste exists.') And how about your Pul-koki?

Brown

cohına	[it]'s good but...
mas ın cohına	it's tasty but...
koki ka cilkimnita	the meat is tough
7. Mas ın cohına, koki ka com cilkimnita.	It's tasty but the meat is a little tough.

싫어합니다

9. 부라운 : 예, 그리 싫어하지 않습니다.

먹은 일, 먹어 본 일, 먹어 본 적

먹어 본 일(적)이 있읍니다

10. 이 : 선생은 중국 음식을 먹어 본 일이 있읍니까?

11. 부라운 : 예, 여러 번 먹어 본 적이 있읍니다.

12. 이 : 아, 그래요? 어디에서요?

13. 부라운 : 미국에도 중국 음식점이 많습니다.

양식

별로

별로 먹지 않었읍니다

14. 이 : 나도 중국 음식은 많이 먹었지만, 양식은 별로 많이 먹지 않었읍니다.

양식 집

15. 부라운 : 그럼, 내일은 양식 집에 갑시다.

있는지

있는지 아십니까

16. 이 : 그것, 좋습니다. 양식점이 어디에 있는지 아십니까?

Lee

mæpsımnita	(food) is spicy
mæun ımsik	spicy (hot) food
8. Sənsæng ın mæun ımsik i cohsımnikka?	Do you like spicy food? ('Is spicy food good for you?')

Brown

silhəhamnita	[I] dislike
9. Ne, kıli silhəhaci anhsımnita.	It's all right. ('I don't dislike it so much.')

Lee

məkın il məkə pon il məkə pon cək	('the experience of eating')
məkə pon il i issımnita	[I] have an experience of eating
10. Sənsæng ın Cungkuk ımsik ıl məkə pon il i issımnikka?	Have you ever eaten Chinese food?

Brown

11. Ne, yələ pən məkə pon cək i issımnita.	Yes, I have (eaten) many times.

Lee

12. A, kılæ yo? əti esə yo?	Oh, you have? Where?

Brown

13. Mikuk e to Cungkuk ımsikcəm i manhsımnita.	There are many Chinese restaurants in the U.S., too.

Lee

Yangsik	Western food
pyəllo	not particularly; not so much
pyəllo məkci anhəssımnita	[I] didn't eat so much
14. Na to Cungkuk ımsik ın manhi məkəssci man, Yangsik ın pyəllo manhi məkci anhəssımnita.	I also have eaten Chinese food a lot but I haven't had much Western food.

17. 부라운 : 예, 압니다.

어느 곳
몰라도
이 부근에

18. 어느 곳이 더 좋은지 몰라도, 이 부근에 두 개 있읍니다.

Brown

15. Kɪləm, næil ɪn Yangsik cip e kapsita. — Let's go to a Western restaurant tomorrow, then.

Lee

issnɪn ci/innɪnci/ — if there is; that there is
issnɪn ci asimnikka — do [you] know if there is?
əti e issnɪn ci asimnikka — do [you] know where [it] is?

16. Kɪ kəs, cohsɪmnita. Yangsikcəm i əti e issnɪn ci asimnikka? — Fine. Do you know where there is a Western restaurant?

Brown

17. Ne, amnita. — Yes, I do (know).

ənɪ kos — which place
molla to — even though [I] do not know
i pukɪn e — in this vicinity

18. ənɪ kos i tə cohɪn ci molla to, i pukɪn e tu kæ issɪmnita. — There are two in this area but I don't know which one is better. ('Even though I don't know which place is better, there are two in this vicinity.')

ADDITIONAL VOCABULARY AND PHRASES

1. a. Mom i aphɪmnita. — I'm sick. ('Body hurts.')
   b. əlkul i aphɪmnita. — My face hurts.
   c. Nun i aphɪmnita. — My eyes hurt.
   d. Ppyam i aphɪmnita. — My cheek hurts.
   e. Son i aphɪmnita. — My hand hurts.
   f. Son-kalak i aphɪmnita. — My finger aches.
   g. Pal i aphɪmnita. — My foot hurts.
   h. Pal-kalak i aphɪmnita. — My toes are aching.
   i. Tali ka aphɪmnita. — My leg hurts.
   j. Phal i aphɪmnita. — My arm hurts.
   k. əkkæ ka aphɪmnita. — My shoulder hurts.
   l. Ip i aphɪmnita. — My mouth is sore.
   m. Mok i aphɪmnita. — I have a sore throat.
   n. Thək i aphɪmnita. — My chin hurts.

Additional Vocabulary and Phrases

A. 1. 몸이 아픕니다.
2. 얼굴이 아픕니다.
3. 눈이 아픕니다.
4. 뺨이 아픕니다.
5. 손이 아픕니다.
6. 손가락이 아픕니다.
7. 발이 아픕니다.
8. 발가락이 아픕니다.
9. 다리가 아픕니다.
10. 팔이 아픕니다.
11. 어깨가 아픕니다.
12. 입이 아픕니다.
13. 목이 아픕니다.
14. 턱이 아픕니다.
15. 머리가 아픕니다.
16. 가슴이 아픕니다.
17. 귀가 아픕니다.
18. 코가 아픕니다.
19. 이(빨)가/이 아픕니다.
20. 등이 아픕니다.
21. 허리가 아픕니다.

B. 1. 소금이 좀 필요합니다.
2. 설탕이 좀 필요합니다.
3. (간)장이 좀 필요합니다.
4. 양념이 좀 필요합니다.
5. 물이 좀 필요합니다.

o.	Məli ka aphımnita.	I have a headache.
p.	Kasım i aphımnita.	I have a pain on my chest.
q.	Kwi ka aphımnita.	My ear aches.
r.	Kho ka aphımnita.	My nose hurts.
s.	{I ka / Ippal i} aphımnita.	My teeth ache.
t.	Tıng i aphımnita.	I have a backache.
u.	Həli ka aphımnita.	My waist aches.
2. a.	Sokım i com philyo-hamnita.	I need some salt.
b.	Səlthang i com philyo-hamnita.	I need some sugar.
c.	(Kan)cang i com philyo-hamnita.	I need some soy sauce.
d.	Yangyəm/yangnyəm/ i com philyo-hamnita.	I need some seasoning.
e.	Mul i com philyo-hamnita.	I need some water.
f.	Kılıs i com philyo-hamnita..	I need some containers.
g.	Koppu ka com philyo-hamnita.	I need some {cups. / glasses.}
h.	Cho ka com philyo-hamnita.	I need some vinegar.
i.	Huchu kalu ka com philyo-hamnita.	I need some black pepper (powder).
j.	Sut-kalak i com philyo-hamnita.	I need a spoon.
k.	Cəs-kalak i com philyo-hamnita.	I need chopsticks.
3. a.	(Hong)cha lıl hakessımnita.	I'll have tea.
b.	Khəphi lıl hakessımnita.	I'll have coffee.
c.	Sul ıl hakessımnita.	I'll have {wine. / liquor.}
d.	Ppilu lıl hakessımnita.	I'll have beer.
e.	Mækcu lıl hakessımnita.	I'll have beer.
f.	Yachæ lıl hakessımnita.	I'll have vegetables.
g.	Chæso lıl hakessımnita.	I'll have vegetables.
h.	Kwail ıl hakessımnita.	I'll have fruits.
i.	Kwasil ıl hakessımnita.	I'll have fruits.
j.	Silkwa lıl hakessımnita.	I'll have fruits.
k.	Koki lıl hakessımnita.	I'll have [some] meat.
l.	Sængsən ıl hakessımnita.	I'll have fish.
m.	So koki lıl hakessımnita.	I'll have beef ('cow meat').

6. 그릇이 좀 필요합니다.
7 고뿌가 좀 필요합니다.
8. 초가 좀 필요합니다.
9. 후추 가루가 좀 필요합니다.
10. 숟가락이 좀 필요합니다.
11. 젓가락이 좀 필요합니다.

C. 1. (홍)차를 하겠읍니다.
2. 커피를 하겠읍니다.
3. 술을 하겠읍니다.
4. 맥주를 하겠읍니다.
5. 야채를 하겠읍니다.
6. 채소를 하겠읍니다.
7. 과일을 하겠읍니다.
8. 과실을 하겠읍니다.
9. 고기를 하겠읍니다.
10. 생선을 하겠읍니다.
11. 소 고기를 하겠읍니다.
12. 닭 고기를 하겠읍니다.
13. 돼지 고기를 하겠읍니다.
14. 도야지 고기를 하겠읍니다.
15. 겨란을 하겠읍니다.
16. 달걀을 하겠읍니다.
17. 국을 하겠읍니다.

D. 1. 잠이 옵니다.
2. 잠을 잡니다.
3. 좀 피곤합니다.
4. 좀 고단합니다.
5. 좀 피로합니다.

n.	Ta(l)k koki lɪl hakessɪmnita.	I'll have chicken ('chicken meat').
o.	Tweci koki lɪl hakessɪmnita.	I'll have pork ('pig meat').
p.	Toyaci koki lɪl hakessɪmnita.	I'll have pork.
q.	Kyəlan ɪl hakessɪmnita.	I'll have eggs.
r.	Talkyal ɪl hakessɪmnita.	I'll have eggs.
s.	Kuk ɪl hakessɪmnita.	I'll have soup.
4. a.	ɪmsik i nəmu ccamnita.	[This] food is too salty.
b.	ɪmsik i nəmu tamnita.	[This] food is too sweet.
c.	ɪmsik i nəmu singkəpsɪmnita.	[This] food is too bland.
d.	ɪmsik i nəmu mæpsɪmnita.	[This] food is too hot (spicy).
e.	ɪmsik i nəmu chamnita.	[This] food is too cold.
f.	ɪmsik i nəmu simnita.	[This] food is too sour.
g.	ɪmsik i nəmu ttɪkəpsɪmnita.	[This] food is too hot (temperature).
h.	ɪmsik i nəmu təpsɪmnita.	[This] food is too hot (temperature).
i.	ɪmsik i nəmu ssɪmnita.	[This] food is too bitter.
5. a.	(ɪmsik) mas i cohsɪmnita.	It tastes good. ('(Food) taste is good.') It's delicious.
b.	(ɪmsik) mas i issɪmnita.	It's tasty; It tastes good.
c.	(ɪmsik) mas i əpsɪmnita.	It's tasteless.
d.	(ɪmsik) mas i kwænchanhsɪmnita.	It tastes all right.
e.	(ɪmsik) mas i hullyunghamnita.	It tastes very good. ('Taste is excellent.')
6. a.	Kipun i cohsɪmnita.	I feel well. ('Feeling is good.')
b.	Kipun i com nappɪmnita.	I don't feel very well. ('Feeling is a little bad.')
c.	Kipun i əttəhsɪmnikka?	How are you feeling?
7. a.	Pæ ka kophɪmnita.	I'm hungry. ('Stomach is empty.')
b.	Pæ ka pulɪmnita.	I'm full.
c.	Pæ ka aphɪmnita.	I have a stomach-ache.
d.	Pæ ka pulphyənhamnita.	My stomach is uncomfortable.
8. a.	Cam i omnita.	I'm sleepy. ('Sleep comes.')
b.	(Cam ɪl) camnita.	I'(m) sleep(ing).
c.	(com) phikonhamnita.	I'm (a little) tired.

6. 목이 마릅니다.
7. 음식이 넉넉합니다.
8. 음식이 충분 합니다.
9. 음식이 부족합니다.
10. 음식이 모자랍니다.
11. 음식이 많습니다.

E. 1. 음식이 너무 짭니다.
2. 음식이 너무 답니다.
3. 음식이 너무 싱겁습니다.
4. 음식이 너무 맵습니다.
5. 음식이 너무 찹니다.
6. 음식이 너무 십니다.
7. 음식이 너무 뜨겁습니다.
8. 음식이 너무 덥습니다.
9. 음식이 너무 쓥니다.

F. 1. (음식)맛이 좋습니다.
2. (음식)맛이 있습니다.
3. (음식)맛이 없습니다.
4. (음식)맛이 괜찮습니다.
5. (음식)맛이 훌륭합니다.

G. 1. 기분 이 좋습니다.
2. 기분 이 좀 나쁩니다.
3. 기분 이 어떻습니까?

H. 1. 배가 고픕니다.
2. 배가 부릅니다.
3. 배가 아픕니다.
4. 배가 불편합니다.

d. (com) kotanhamnita. — I'm (a little) tired.

e. (com) philohamnita. — I'm (rather) fatigued.

f. Mok i malımnita. — I'm thirsty. ('Throat dries.')

9. a. ımsik i {nəknəkhamnita / /nəngnəkhamnita/}. — The food is sufficient.

b. ımsik i chungpun-hamnita. — The food is enough.

c. ımsik i pucok-hamnita. — The food is not enough.

d. ımsik i mocalamnita. — {The food is not enough. / We are short of food.}

e. ımsik i manhsımnita. — The food is plenty.

NOTES ON DIALOGUES

(Numbers correspond to the sentence numbers.)

1.2. Ca, əsə tı(lı)sipsiyo. ('Well, lift [it] please.', 'Well, please have [it].') is a fixed expression in the eating or drinking situation to have your guest or company start eating or drinking. The usual response to Ca, əsə tı(lı)sipsiyo. is Ne, kathi sicak-hapsita. ('Yes, let's begin together.').

6. Mas i iss-ta. ('Taste exists.') and Mas i coh-ta. ('Taste is good.') are the two common fixed expressions, both of which are used as the Korean equivalents of 'It's tasty.' or 'It's delicious.'

10. Məkə pon il (or məkə pon cək) ('The experience of having eaten') and məkın il (or məkın cək) can be interchangeably used (See Grammar Note 3.)

12. In Kılæ yo? ('Is that so?') kılæ is the infinitive form of the verb kıləh- 'to be so'. Thus, Kılæ yo? is the informal polite equivalent of the formal polite Kıləhsımnikka?; Kılæ yo. of the formal polite Kıləhsımnita.

13. Cungkuk ımsikcəm 'Chinese restaurant' is often substituted by Cungkuk cip ('Chinese house'). In Korea, Cungkuk cip is usually referred to Cungkuk ımsikcəm.

14. Pyəllo '(not) particularly', is an adverb which occurs before an negative inflected expression, and denotes mildness or less being positive in negating the following expression.

15. Yangsik cip ('Western food house.') is a substitute for Yangsikcəm.

GRAMMAR NOTES

1. -(ɪ)na

The inflected form ending in -(ɪ)na (or simply the -(ɪ)na form) which may be followed by a pause occurs before another inflected expression. The honorific and/or tense suffixes may occur in the -(ɪ)na form: -na is added to a vowel stem; -ɪna to a consonant stem. The -(ɪ)na form denotes that some contradictory further explanation or remark will follow in the following inflected expression. (Compare the -(ɪ)na form with -ci + man, Grammar Note 2, Unit 9.) Examples:

Mas ɪn cohɪna, koki ka com cilkimnita.	'It's tasty, but the meat is a little tough.'
Hankuk mal i əlyəuna, cæmi issə yo.	'Korean is difficult but is interesting.'
Kim Pyənhosa e əlkul ɪn molɪna, ilɪm ɪn tɪləssɪmnita.	'I don't know Lawyer Kim's face, but I've heard of his name.'

2. $\left.\begin{matrix}\text{-n/ɪn}\\ \text{Infinitive + pon}\end{matrix}\right\} + \left\{\begin{matrix}\text{il}\\ \text{cək}\end{matrix}\right\}$ i + iss- 'has an experience of having done something'

The construction -n/ɪn il i issɪmnita is used to mean 'have, sometime up to the present, done so-and-so'. The question form, -n/ɪn il i issɪmnikka?, is the Korean equivalent of 'Have [you] ever done so-and-so?'. In the above construction il meaning'work' or 'act' or 'experience' is snyonymous with cək and they are interchangeable with each other. The first word in the construction ending in -n/ɪn (-n is added to a vowel stem; -ɪn to a consonant stem) can be substituted by the verb phrase Infinitive + pon. The negation for the whole expression is made by replacing əps- 'not exit' in place of iss-. Thus, -n/ɪn il i əpsɪmnita. means '[Someone] has, some time up to the present, never done so-and-so.' and -n/ɪn il i əpsɪmnikka? 'Haven't [you] ever done so-and-so?'. Examples:

Cungkuk ɪmsik ɪl məkɪn il i issɪmnikka?	'Have you ever eaten Chinese food?'
Hankuk e kasin cək i issna yo?	'Have you ever been ('gone') to Korea?'
Cə nɪn Nyuyok esə cihachəlto lɪl than il i issci yo.	'I have an experience of riding a subway in New York.'
Cən e catongcha lɪl uncənhæ pon il i issci man, cikɪm ɪn uncənhanɪn kəs ɪl icə pəliəssɪmnita.	'I drove an automobile before, but I have forgotten how to drive (now).'

Ne, Hankuk e olæ cən e kan cək i issımnita. — 'Yes, I've gone to Korea long time ago.'

Note that the ending -n/ın is distinguished from the present noun-modifier ending -n/ın/nın since -n/ın which is added only to an action verb stem indicates the past action of the following nominal. We shall call the ending -n/ın Past Noun-Modifier Ending. We will learn more about the ending -n/ın as well as the description verb past noun-modifier forms in the further units. For the time being, observe the following examples:

a.	kanın salam	'the person who (is) go(ing).'
	kan salam	'the person who has gone'
b.	næ ka mannanın yəca	'the woman (or girl) whom I'(m) meet(ing)'
	næ ka mannan yəca	'the woman whom I've met'
c.	atıl i sanın chæk	'the book that my son is buying'
	atıl i san chæk	'the book that my son bought'
d.	məknın ımsik	'the food that [we] eat'
	məkın ımsik	'the food that [we] ate'

3. Interrogative + -n/ın/nın ci

An interrogative (i.e. what, who, where, why, etc.) followed by a present noun-modifier word + ci, occurs as a nominal expression with or without a particle after it before another inflected expression, and denotes the present action or description of the verb for the subject or topic in the same nominal expression. When the phrase interrogative + -n/ın/nın ci is followed by the verb a(l)- 'know' or molı- 'not know', it is always the object of the verb. Examples:

Cə salam i nuku in ci alə yo.	'[I] know who that man is.'
I chæk i əlma in ci alko siphə yo?	'Do you want to know how much this book is?'
Kim Sənsæng i əti e sanın ci asici yo?	'You know where Mr. Kim lives, don't you?'
Sənsæng i muəs ıl wənhanın ci molımnita.	'I don't know what you want.'

Note that the present noun-modifier word in the same construction may be replaced by the form -(a,ə)ssnın for the past and the form -(ı)l for the future, if the equivalent English noun clause is in the past or future tense respectively.

Observe the following:

GROUP 1

Kɪ salam i əti e kassnɪn ci amnita.	'[I] know where he went.'
Hakkyo ka ənce sicak-hæssnɪn ci molla yo.	'[I] don't know when the school began.'
Næ ka Yəngə lɪl əttəhke pæwəssnɪn ci ase yo?	'Do you know how I have learned English?'

GROUP 2

Sip nyən hu e muəs ɪl hal ci acik molɪmnita.	'[I] don't know what [I] will do after ten years from now.'
Sikan i əlma na kəllil ci alki əlyəpsɪmnita.	'It's difficult to know how long it will take.'
Kɪ i ka əlma tongan Səul esə kɪnmu-hal ci molla yo?	'Don't you know how long he will work in Seoul?'

4. Particles eke 'to' and ekesə 'from'

A personal nominal + eke and a personal nominal + ekesə before an inflected expression mean 'to + P.N.' and 'from + P.N.' respectively. Remember that the particles e and esə preceded by a place name before an inflected expression mean also 'to' and 'from' respectively (Units 2 and 3). Do not use e and esə after a personal nominal to mean the same. Examples:

GROUP 1 (eke)

I chæk ɪl Kim Sənsæng eke tɪlisipsiyo.	'Please give this book to Mr. Kim.'
Halapəci eke mulə pwassci man, mollassə yo.	'I asked (to) my grandfather but he didn't know.'
Onɪl ɪn chinku eke phyənci lɪl ssə ya hakessə yo.	'[I think] I've got to write a letter to my friend today.'

GROUP 2 (ekesə)

Pak Sənsæng ekesə kɪ mal ɪl tɪtko, nollassɪmnita.	'I was surprised to hear that from Mr. Park. ('I heard that word from Mr. Park and was surprised.')'
əməni ekesə sængil sənmul ɪl patəssɪmnita.	'I have received a birthday present from my mother.'

5. Dependent Nouns

There is a small class of Korean nouns which occur only as bound forms in certain constructions but are neither Determinatives nor Post-Nouns (Unit 3). We shall call the words of this class Dependent Nouns. Remember that a determinative is a word which occurs before another noun (free or bound), and that a post-noun occurs either after other nouns or after modifier categories of inflected words. In both cases, they form nominal phrases. However, a dependent noun also occurs after the modifier categories of inflected words, but is followed by a certain expression to form a phrase. Thus, it is not necessary to learn the meaning of an individual dependent noun separately. Instead, you should learn the meaning of the whole phrase where such a dependent noun is included as if it were one word. For example, in Kal kka yo? 'Shall [we] go?', Ttənal kka hamnita. '[I]'m thinking of leaving.', Anın ka yo? 'Do [you] know?', Kal su issımnita. '[I] can go.', Muəs in ci amnita. '[I] know what [it] is.', əti e sanın ci molımnita. 'I don't know where [he] lives.', Pi ka ol tıt hamnita. 'It looks like rain.', Kəki kan cək i issə yo? 'Have you ever been there?', kka, ka, su, ci, tıt, cək, etc. are Dependent Nouns.

DRILLS

A. Substitution Drill

1.	Cə nɨn pæ ka kophɨmnita.	I'm hungry.
2.	Cə nɨn pæ ka pulɨmnita.	I'm full.
3.	Cə nɨn mok i malɨmnita.	I'm thirsty.
4.	Cə nɨn (com) phikonhamnita.	I'm (a little) tired.
5.	Cə nɨn (com) kotanhamnita.	I'm (rather) fatigued.
6.	Cə nɨn cam i omnita.	I'm sleepy.
7.	Cə nɨn mom i aphɨmnita.	I'm sick.
8.	Cə nɨn kipun i cohsɨmnita.	I'm feeling well.
9.	Cə nɨn kipun i nappɨmnita.	I'm not feeling well.

B. Substitution Drill

1.	Na nɨn mom i com aphɨmnita.	I'm a little sick. ('My body aches a little.')
2.	Na nɨn məli ka com aphɨmnita.	I have a little headache.
3.	Na nɨn tali ka com aphɨmnita.	My leg hurts a little.
4.	Na nɨn nun i com aphɨmnita.	My eyes hurt a little.
5.	Na nɨn pal i com aphɨmnita.	My foot hurts a little.
6.	Na nɨn son i com aphɨmnita.	My hand hurts a little.
7.	Na nɨn i ka com aphɨmnita.	My tooth aches a little.
8.	Na nɨn ip i com aphɨmnita.	My mouth is a little sore.
9.	Na nɨn əkkæ ka com aphɨmnita.	My shoulder hurts a little.
10.	Na nɨn mok i com aphɨmnita.	I have a little sore throat. ('My throat is a little sore.')

C. Substitution Drill

1.	Kəki sokɨm com (cə eke) cusikessɨmnikka?	Please pass me the salt. ('Will you give me the salt there?')
2.	Kəki səlthang com (cə eke) cusikessɨmnikka?	Please pass me the sugar.
3.	Kəki kochu kalu com (cə eke) cusikessɨmnikka?	Please pass me the pepper. ('red-pepper powder')
4.	Kəki huchu kalu com (cə eke) cusikessɨmnikka?	Please pass me the pepper. ('black-pepper powder')

5.	Kəki (kan)cang com (cə eke) cusikessımnikka?	Please pass me the soy sauce.
*6.	Kəki ccæm com (cə eke) cusikessımnikka?	Please pass me the jam.
*7.	Kəki ppata com (cə eke) cusikessımnikka?	Please pass me the butter.
*8.	Kəki ppang com (cə eke) cusikessımnikka?	Please pass me the bread.
*9.	Kəki Kimchi com (cə eke) cusikessımnikka?	Please pass me Kimchi.
*10.	Kəki næphıkhin com (cə eke) cusikessımnikka?	Please pass me the napkins.

D. Substitution Drill

1.	Kı chæk ıl na eke cusipsiyo.	Give me that book.
2.	Kı chæk ıl Kim Sənsæng eke cusipsiyo.	Give that book to Mr. Kim.
3.	Kı chæk ıl Ceimsı eke cusipsiyo.	Give that book to James.
4.	Kı chæk ıl apəci eke cusipsiyo.	Give that book to your father.
5.	Kı chæk ıl cə haksæng eke cusipsiyo.	Give that book to the student.
6.	Kı chæk ıl Mikuk chinku eke cusipsiyo.	Give that book to your American friend.
7.	Kı chæk ıl Kim Sənsæng puin eke cusipsiyo.	Give that book to Mrs. Kim.

E. Substitution Drill

1.	Chinku ekesə sikye lıl patəssımnita.	I received a watch from a friend.
2.	Ceimsı ekesə moca lıl patəssımnita.	I received a hat from James.
3.	Kim Sənsæng ekesə kapang ıl patəssımnita.	I received a briefcase from Mr. Kim.
*4.	əməni ekesə phyənci lıl patəssımnita.	I received a letter from my mother.
*5.	Tæsa ekesə cənhwa lıl patəssımnita.	I received a telephone call from the ambassador.

*6.	Apəci ekesə sənmul ıl patəssımnita.	I received a present from my father.
*7.	Hankukə kangsa ekesə Yəng-Han sacən ıl patəssımnita.	I received an English-Korean dictionary from the Korean instructor.
*8.	Yəngsa ekesə cənpo lıl patəssımnita.	I received a {telegram / cable} from the consul.
*9.	Sangkwan ekesə myəngnyəng ıl patəssımnita.	I received an order from [my] {boss. / supervisor.}
*10.	Sonnim ekesə cumun ıl patəssımnita.	I received an order from [my] {customer. / guest.}
*11.	Tæthongyəng ekesə chotæ lıl patəssımnita.	I received an invitation from the President.
*12.	Haksæng tıl ekesə cilmun ıl patəssımnita.	I received questions from the students.
*13.	Tongyo ekesə puthak ıl patəssımnita.	I was asked of a favor from a colleague.
*14.	Sacang ekesə sıngkıp ıl patəssımnita.	I received a promotion from the president (of the company).
*15.	Insakwacang ekesə pongkıp ıl patəssımnita.	I've got my pay from the personnel officer.

F. Substitution Drill

1.	Sənsæng ın mæun ımsik i cohsımnikka?	Do you like hot (spicy) food?
2.	Sənsæng ın Cungkuk ımsik i cohsımnikka?	Do you like Chinese food?
3.	Sənsæng ın Yangsik i cohsımnikka?	Do you like Western food?
4.	Sənsæng ın Wæsik i cohsımnikka?	Do you like Japanese food?
5.	Sənsæng ın Hankuk mækcu ka cohsımnikka?	Do you like Korean beer?
6.	Sənsæng ın musın ımsik i cohsımnikka?	What kind of food do you like?
7.	Sənsæng ın ənı siktang i cohsımnikka?	Which restaurant do you like?
8.	Sənsæng ın ənı sənsæng i cohsımnikka?	Which teacher do you prefer?

G. Substitution Drill

1.	I ımsik ın com mæpsımnita.	This food is a little spicy.
2.	I ımsik ın com ccamnita.	This food is a little salty.
3.	I ımsik ın com chamnita.	This food is a little cold.
4.	I ımsik ın com təpsımnita.	This food is a little warm.
5.	I ımsik ın com simnita.	This food is a little sour.
6.	I ımsik ın com tamnita.	This food is a little sweet.
7.	I ımsik ın com ssımnita.	This food is a little bitter.

H. Substitution Drill

1.	I koki nın com cilkimnita.	This meat is a little tough.
2.	I Pul-koki nın com cilkimnita.	This Pul-koki is a little tough.
3.	I sængsən ın com cilkimnita.	This fish is a little tough.
4.	I ta(l)k koki nın com cilkimnita.	This chicken is a little tough.
5.	I so koki nın com cilkimnita.	This beef is a little tough.
6.	I toyaci koki nın com cilkimnita.	This pork is a little tough.
7.	I tweci koki nın com cilkimnita.	This pork is a little tough.
*8.	I tweci koki nın putıləpsımnita.	This pork is {tender. / soft.}
*9.	I tweci koki nın yənhamnita.	This pork is tender (for meat).

I. Substitution Drill

1.	Yangsikcəm i əti e issnın ci asimnikka?	Do you know where a restaurant for Western food is.
2.	Hansikcəm i əti e issnın ci asimnikka?	Do you know where a Korean restaurant is?
3.	Wæsikcəm i əti e issnın ci asimnikka?	Do you know where a Japanese restaurant is?
4.	Cungkuk ımsikcəm i əti e issnın ci asimnikka?	Do you know where a Cinese restaurant is?
5.	Pakmulkwan i əti e issnın ci asimnikka?	Do you know where the museum is?
*6.	Tongmulwən i əti e issnın ci asimnikka?	Do you know where the zoo is?

*7.	Kukhwe ka əti e issnın ci asimnikka?	Do you know where the {National Assembly / Congress} is?
*8.	Wemupu ka əti e issnın ci asimnikka?	Do you know where the Ministry of Foreign Affairs is?
*9.	Sopangsə ka əti e issnın ci asimnikka?	Do you know where the fire station is?
*10.	Kukmusəng i əti e issnın ci asimnikka?	Do you know where the State Department is?
*11.	Kukpangpu ka əti e issnın ci asimnikka?	Do you know where the Ministry of Defense is?
*12.	Kukpansəng i əti e issnın ci asimnikka?	Do you know where the Defense Department is?
*13.	Kisuksa ka əti e issnın ci asimnikka?	Do you know where the dormintory is?

J. Transformation Drill

Tutor: Sənsæng ın cən e Hankuk e kassımnikka? — 'Did you go to Korea before?'

Student: Sənsæng ın cən e Hankuk e kan il i issımnikka? — 'Have you ever been to Korea before?'

1.	Sənsæng ın cən e Ilpon mal ıl pæwəssımnikka?	Sənsæng ın cən e Ilpon mal ıl pæun il i issımnikka?
2.	Sənsæng ın cən e Yəngə lıl kalıchiəssımnikka?	Sənsæng ın cən e Yəngə lıl kalıchin il i issımnikka?
3.	Sənsæng ın cən e wekuk tæhakkyo e taniəssımnikka?	Sənsæng ın cən e wekuk tæhakkyo e tanin il i issımnikka?
4.	Sənsæng ın cən e Mikuk tæsa lıl mannassımnikka?	Sənsæng ın cən e Mikuk tæsa lıl mannan il i issımnikka?
5.	Sənsæng ın cən e Səul esə il-hæssımnikka?	Sənsæng ın cən e Səul esə il-han il i issımnikka?
6.	Sənsæng ın cən e pihængki lıl thassımnikka?	Sənsæng ın cən e pihængki lıl than il i issımnikka?
7.	Sənsæng ın cən e Hankuk esə phyənci lıl patəssımnikka?	Sənsæng ın cən e Hankuk esə phyənci lıl patın il i issımnikka?
8.	Sənsæng ın cən e Mikuk chinku eke sacən ıl puchiəssımnikka?	Sənsæng ın cən e Mikuk chinku eke sacən ıl puchin il i issımnikka?

9. Sənsæng ın cən e Hankuk ımsik ıl məkəssımnikka?	Sənsæng ın cən e Hankuk ımsik ıl məkın il i issımnikka?
10. Sənsæng ın cən e kı yəca lıl kitaliəssımnikka?	Sənsæng ın cən kı yəca lıl kitalin il i issımnikka?

K. Response Drill

Tutor: Cən e Hankuk ımsik ıl məkın il i issımnikka?	'Have you ever eaten Korean food before?'
Student: Ne, məkə pon cək i issımnita.	'Yes, I have (eaten).'
1. Cən e Ilpon mal ıl pæun il i issımnikka?	Ne, pæwə pon cək i issımnita.
2. Cən e Yəngə lıl kalıchin il i issımnikka?	Ne, kalıchiə pon cək i issımnita.
3. Cən e Hankuk mækcu lıl masin il i issımnikka?	Ne, masyə pon cək i issımnita.
4. Cən e kuntæ e kan il i issımnikka?	Ne, ka pon cək i issımnita.
5. Talın salam eke i chæk ıl poyə cun il i issımnikka?	Ne, poyə cuə pon cək i issımnita.
6. Cən e mok i aphın il i issımnikka?	Ne, aphə pon cək i issımnita.
7. Hankuk salam chinku ekesə phyənci lıl patın il i issımnita.	Ne, patə pon cək i issımnita.
8. Wəlyoil e cip esə swin il i issımnikka?	Ne, (Wəlyoil e) swiə pon cək i issımnita.
9. Cip esə hakkyo kkaci tu sikan i kəllin il i issımnikka?	Ne, tu sikan i kəlliə pon cək i issimnikka?

L. Transformation Drill

Tutor: Siktang i əti e issımnikka?	'Where is the restaurant?'
Student: Siktang i əti e issnın ci asimnikka?	'Do you know where the restaurant is?'
1. Kim Sənsæng i muəs ıl hamnikka?	Kim Sənsæng i muəs ıl hanın ci asimnikka?
2. Kı sikye ka əlma imnikka?	Kı sikye ka əlma in ci asimnikka?
3. Cə Mikuk yəca ka nuku imnikka?	Cə Mikuk yəca ka nuku in ci asimnikka?
4. Hakkyo ka myəch-si e sicak-hamnikka?	Hakkyo ka myəch-si e sicak-hanın ci asimnikka?
5. Cungkuk mal i əlma na əlyəpsımnikka?	Cungkuk mal i əlma na əlyəun ci asimnikka?
6. Onıl i myəchil imnikka?	Onıl i myəchil in ci asimnikka?
7. I catongcha lıl əlma e phamnikka?	I catongcha lıl əlma e pha(lı)nın ci asimnikka?
8. ənce ppəsı ka ttənamnikka?	ənce ppəsı ka ttənanın ci asimnikka?
9. Cə Mikuk kunin i muəs ıl wənhamnikka?	Cə Mikuk kunin i muəs ıl wənhanın ci asimnikka?
10. Ceimsı Sənsæng i musın yoil e hyuka lıl patsımnikka?	Ceimsı Sənsæng i musın yoil e hyuka lıl patnın ci asimnikka?

M. Response Drill

Tutor: Siktang i əti e issnın ci asimnikka?	'Do you know where the restaurant is?'
Student: Ne, (siktang i) əti e issnın ci alə yo.	'Yes, I know where it is.'
1. I catongcha ka əlma in ci asimnikka?	Ne, (i catongcah ka) əlma in ci alə yo.
2. Sımisı Sənsæng i əti esə il-hanın ci asimnikka?	Ne, (Sımisı Sənsæng i) əti esə il-hanın ci alə yo.
3. Kicha ka myəch-si e ttənanın ci asimnikka?	Ne, (kicha ka) myəch-si e ttenanın ci alə yo.
4. ənce Hankuk ılo kanın ci asimnikka?	Ne, ənce (Hankuk ılo) kanın ci alə yo.

5. Cə salam i əlma na Hankuk mal ıl cal hal su issnın ci asimnikka? — Ne, (cə salam i) əlma na (Hankuk mal ıl) cal hal su issnın ci alə yo.

6. Ppəsı ka ənce ttənassnın ci asimnikka? — Ne, (ppəsı ka) ənce ttənassnın ci alə yo.

7. Ceimsı Sənsæng i myəch sal e Hankuk e wassnın ci asimnikka? — Ne, (Ceimsı Sənsæng i) myəch sal e Hankuk e wassnın ci alə yo.

8. Næ ka tæhakkyo esə muəs ıl kongpu-hæssnın ci asimnikka? — Ne, (tangsin i tæhakkyo esə) muəs ıl kongpu-hæssnın ci alə yo.

9. Cip esə cəngkəcang kkaci əlma na mən ci asimnikka? — Ne, (cip esə cəngkəcang kkaci) əlma na mən ci alə yo.

10. Səul e mulkən kaps i əlma na pissan ci asimnikka? — Ne, (Səul e mulkən kaps i) əlma na pissan ci alə yo.

11. Næ ka nuku lıl mannako siphın ci asimnikka? — Ne, (sənsæng i) nuku lıl mannako siphın ci alə yo.

12. Mikuk esə Hankuk kkaci myəchil i kəllinın ci asimnikka? — Ne, (Mikuk esə Hankuk kkaci) myəchil i kəllinın ci alə yo.

N. Response Drill

Tutor: I kəs i muəs in ci ase yo? — 'Do you know what this is?'
Student: Aniyo, (muəs in ci) molımnita. — 'No, I don't know (what is it).'

1, Pak Sənsæng i musın ımsik ıl cohahanın ci ase yo? — Aniyo, (musın ımsik ıl cohahanın ci) molımnita.

2. Hwesa samu ka myəch-si e sicak-hanın ci ase yo? — Aniyo, (myəch-si e sicak-hanın ci) molımnita.

3. Næ ka hwesa esə han tal e əlma patnın ci ase yo? — Aniyo, (əlma patnın ci) molımnita.

4. əlma tongan Yəngə lıl pæwəssnın ci ase yo? — Aniyo, (əlma tongan Yəngə lıl pæwəssnın ci) molımnita.

5. Mikuk tæsa ka əlma cən e yəki e wassnın ci ase yo? — Aniyo, (əlma cən e yəki e wassnın ci) molımnita.

6. Nuka na eke Hankuk mal ıl kalıchiə cuəssnın ci ase yo? — Aniyo, (nuka kalıchiə cuəssnın ci) molımnita.

7. Kim Sənsæng i myəch-si e samusil e tola onın ci ase yo? — Aniyo, (myəch-si e tola onın ci) molımnita.

8. Cə yəca ka nuku lıl salang-hanın ci ase yo?	Aniyo, (nuku lıl salang-hanın ci) molımnita.
9. Səul e Mikuk salam i myəch salam i issnın ci ase yo?	Aniyo, (myəch salam i issnın ci) molımnita.

O. Response Drill

Tutor: Pæ ka kophımnikka?	'Are you hungry?'
Student: Ne, (pæ ka) com kophımnita.	'Yes, (I'm) a little.'
1. Mok i malımnikka?	Ne, (mok i) com malımnita.
2. (Mom i) phikon-hamnikka?	Ne, com phikon-hamnita.
3. Cam i omnikka?	Ne, (cam i) com omnita.
4. Kipun i cohsımnikka?	Ne, (kipun i) com cohsımnita.
5. Mom i aphımnikka?	Ne, (mom i) com aphımnita.
6. Kotanhamnikka?	Ne, com kotanhamnita.
7. Pæ ka pulımnikka?	Ne, (pæ ka) com pulımnita.
8. Mas i issımnikka?	Ne, (mas i) com issımnita.
9. Koki ka cilkimnikka?	Ne, (koki ka) com cilkimnita.

P. Response Drill

Tutor: Pæ ka kophımnikka?	'Are you hungry?'
Student: Aniyo, kıli kophıci anhə yo.	'No, (I'm) not very much (hungry).'
1. Mok i malımnikka?	Aniyo, kıli malıci anhə yo.
2. Phikon-hamnikka?	Aniyo, kıli phikon-haci anhə yo.
3. Cam i omnikka?	Aniyo, kıli oci anhə yo.
4. Kipun i cohsımnikka?	Aniyo, kıli cohci anhə yo.
5. Kipun i nappımnikka?	Aniyo, kıli nappıci anhə yo.
6. Mom i aphımnikka?	Aniyo, kıli aphıci anhə yo.
7. Kotanhamnikka?	Aniyo, kıli kotanhaci anhə yo.
8. Pæ ka pulımnikka?	Aniyo, kıli pulıci anhə yo.
9. Mas i issımnikka?	Aniyo, kıli issci anhə yo.
10. Mas i cohsımnikka?	Aniyo, kıli cohci anhə yo.
11. Koki ka cilkimnikka?	Aniyo, kıli cilkici anhə yo?

Q. Response Drill

Tutor: Pæ ka kophımnikka? — 'Are you hungry?'

Student: Aniyo, pyəllo kophıci anhsımnita. — 'No, not particularly. ('I'm not particularly hungry.')

1. Mom i aphımnikka? — Aniyo, pyəllo aphıci anhsımnita.
2. Sokım i philyo-hamnita. — Aniyo, phəllo philyo-haci anhsımnita.
3. ımsik i ccamnikka? — Aniyo, pyəllo ccaci anhsımnita.
4. (ımsik) mas i issımnikka? — Aniyo, pyəllo issci anhsımnita.
5. Kipun i cohsımnikka? — Aniyo, pyəllo cohci anhsımnita.
6. Cam i omnikka? — Aniyo, pyəllo oci anhsımnita.
7. Mok i malımnikka? — Aniyo, pyəllo malıci anhsımnita.
8. Phikon-hamnikka? — Aniyo, pyəllo phikon-haci anhsımnita.
9. Kotanhamnikka? — Aniyo, pyəllo kotanhaci anhsımnita.
10. Koki ka cilkimnikka? — Aniyo, pyəllo cilkici anhsımnita.
11. Hankuk mal ıl cal hamnikka? — Aniyo, pyəllo cal haci anhsımnita.

EXERCISES

A. Ask Kim Sənsæng the following questions: (Mr. Kim answers beginning once with Ne, and once with Aniyo, both in Informal Polite Speech.)

1. if he is hungry.
2. if he is tired.
3. if he is sleepy.
4. if he is sick.
5. if he is feeling well.
6. if he is not feeling well.
7. if his stomach is uncomfortable.
8. if the meat is too tough.
9. if the pork is tender.
10. if the chicken is delicious.
11. if the food is spicy (hot).
12. if the soup is too salty.
13. if the coffee is too sweet (sugary).
14. if he needs salt and pepper.
15. if he has ever eaten Chinese food.
16. if he has ever taught Korean before.
17. if he knows what time the school ends.
18. if he knows who taught you Korean.
19. if he knows how you have studied Korean.
20. if he doesn't like Chinese food.
21. if the food is enough.
22. if the food is insufficient
23. if the food is plenty.

B. Tell the waitress to bring the following:

1. two bottles of O.B. beer
2. wine (or liquor)
3. vegetables
4. fruits
5. fish
6. seasoning
7. salt and pepper

8. spoon and chop sticks
9. soy sauce and a bowl
10. bread, butter and jam.
11. chicken and eggs.
12. three bowls of beef soup.
13. Pul-koki for two people.

C. Ask Pak Sənsəng whether he likes the following kinds of food:

1. salty food
2. sweet food
3. bland food
4. spicy (hot) food
5. cold food
6. sour food
7. bitter food
8. dry food
9. western food
10. hot (in temperature) food

D. Make a short simple statement using each of the following words:

1. face
2. head
3. neck
4. throat
5. eye
6. nose
7. cheek
8. chin
9. mouth
10. tooth
11. hair
12. ear
13. shoulder
14. arm
15. hand
16. finger
17. foot
18. toe
19. leg
20. knee/mulɪp/
21. waist
22. chest
23. back
24. wrist/son-mok/

E. Pak Sənsæng wants to know what have happened to you; answer as follows:

1. that you received a letter from your mother.
2. that you received questions from the student.
3. that you received a promotion from your boss.
4. that you received your pay from the personnel officer /insa kwacang/.
5. that your bookstore received an order from the customers.
6. that your colleague asked a favor of you.
7. that you have received an order from the Ambassador.
8. that you've received a dinner invitation from the (company) president.
9. that you've received a birthday present from your girl friend.
10. that you received a telephone call from your father.

End of Tape 10A

Tape 10B

제 14 과 개인의 일생과 가족 이야기

고향

1. 제임스 : 박 선생은 고향이 어디이세요?

원래

거의

2. 박 : 제 고향은 원래 인천이었으나 거의 서울에서 살았읍니다.

어립니다

어릴 때에, 어렸을 때에

3. 제임스 : 그럼, 어렸을 때에 서울로 왔읍니까?

세 살

세 살 때에

이사

이사했읍니다

4. 박 : 예, 그렇습니다. 제가 세 살 때에 우리 가족이 서울로 이사했읍니다.

계십니까

5. 제임스 : 지금, 가족은 몇 분이나 계십니까?

결혼

결혼했읍니다

결혼해서

아내, 처

아이들

UNIT 14. Talking About One's Life and Family

BASIC DIALOGUE FOR MEMORIZATION

James

kohyang	native place; home town
1. Pak Sənsæng ɪn, kohyang i əti ise yo?	Where do you come from, Mr. Park?

Park

wəllæ	originally; formerly
kəi	almost; mostly
2. Ce kohyang ɪn wəllæ Inchən iəssɪna, kəi Səul esə saləssɪmnita.	I am originally from Inchon but I have lived mostly in Seoul.

James

əlimnita	[I]'m young
əlil ttæ (e) / əlyəssɪl ttæ (e)	when [I] was young ('at the time of being young')
3. Kɪləm, əlyəssɪl ttæ e Səul lo wassɪmnikka?	Then, did you come to Seoul when you were young?

Park

se sal	three years old
se sal ttæ e	at the age of three
uli kacok	my family ('our family')
isa	moving (house, office, etc.)
isa-hæssɪmnita	[we] moved
4. Ne, kɪləhsɪmnita. Ce ka se sal ttæ e uli kacok i Səul lo isa-hæssɪmnita.	That's right. When I was three years old, my family moved to Seoul.

James

kyesimnikka	do you have?; are there? (H)
5. Cikɪm, kacok ɪn myəch pun ina kyesimnikka?	How many are there in your family now?

6. 박 : 지금은 결혼해서 아내와 아이들이 둘
있읍니다.

아들

7. 제임스 : 아이들은 다 아들인가요?

큰 아이

딸

8. 박 : 아닙니다. 큰 아이는 딸이고 둘 째 아이가
아들입니다.

부모, 부모님

살아 계십니다

9. 제임스 : 부모님도 살아 계십니까?

아버지

어머니

형님, 형

돌아 가셨읍니다

댁

10. 박 : 아버지는 돌아 가셨고, 어머니는 형님 댁에서
삽니다.

형제

모두, 전부

11. 제임스 : 형제는 모두 몇 분이나 됩니까?

형님 외에

누이 (동생)

Park

kyəlhon	marriage
kyəlhon-hæssımnita	[I]'m married; [I] got married
kyəlhon-hæ sə	[I]'m married and..; [I] got married and...
anæ	wife
ai tıl	children; babies

6. Cikım ın kyəlhon-hæ sə, anæ wa ai tıl i tul issımnita. — I'm married now and have a wife and two children.

James

atıl	son

7. Ai tıl ın ta atıl in ka yo? — Are your children both sons?

Park

khın ai	the eldest child ('big child')
ttal	daughter

8. An imnita. Khın ai nın ttal iko, tul ccæ ai ka atıl imnita. — No. The elder child is a daughter, and the second is a son.

James

pumo / pumo nim	parents
sala issımnita / sala kyesimnita	[he] is alive; [he] is living

9. Pumo nim to sala kyesimnikka? — Are your parents still living?

Park

apəci	father
əməni	mother
hyəng / hyəng nim	(man's) older brother
tola kasyəssımnita	[they] passed away ('went back')
tæk	house; home (H)

10. Apəci nın tola kasyəssko, əməni nın hyəng nim tæk esə samnita. — My father is dead but my mother lives at my older brother's home.

(남) 동생

하나 씩

12. 박 : 형님 한 분 외에 누이 동생과 남 동생이 하나 씩 있읍니다.

다 들

13. 제임스 : 다 들 결혼했나요?

얼마 전에

혼자

14. 박 : 누이 동생은 얼마 전에 결혼했지만, 남 동생은 아직 혼자입니다.

몇 살

15. 제임스 : 남 동생은 몇 살입니까?

나이

나이가 많습니다

나이가 작습니다

16. 박 : 아직 나이가 그렇게 많지 않습니다. 에 금년에 스무 살입니다.

17. 제임스 : 학교에 다니는 가요?

고등학교

대학

대학교

졸업

졸업하고

삼 학년

James

hyəngce	brothers and sisters; siblings
motu } cənpu }	in all; all together
11. Hyəngce nɪn motu myəch pun ina twemnikka?	How many brothers and sisters do you have in all? ('As for your siblings how many persons do they become in all?')

Park

hyəng nim we e/weye/	beside an older brother
nui (tongsæng)	(younger) sister
(nam) tongsæng	younger brother
hana ssik	one each; one at one time
12. Hyəng nim han pun we e, nui tongsæng kwa nam tongsæng i hana ssik issɪmnita.	Besides an older brother, I have a younger sister and a younger brother.

James

ta tɪl	all; everybody
kyəlhon-hæssna yo/kyəlhonhænnayo/	did [he] get married?
13. Ta tɪl kyəlhon-hæssna yo?	Are they all married? ('Did they all get married?')

Park

əlma cən e	sometime ago
honca	single; alone
14. Nui tongsæng ɪn əlma cən e kyəlhon-hæssci man, nam tongsæng ɪn acik honca imnita.	My younger sister got married sometime ago, but my younger brother is still single.

James

myəch sal/myəssal/	how old?; what age?
15. Nam tongsæng ɪn myəch sal imnikka?	How old is your younger brother?

18. 박 : 예, 삼 년 전에 고등 학교를 졸업하고, 지금은 서울 대학교 삼 학년에 다니고 있읍니다.

Park

nai	age
nai ka manhsımnita	[he] is old ('age is much')
nai ka cəksımnita	[he] is young ('age is little')
16. Acik nai ka kıləhke manhci anhsımnita. Kımnyən e sımu sal imnita.	He is still quite young. He is twenty years old (this year).

James

17. Hakkyo e tanının ka yo?	Does he go to school?

Park

kotıng hakkyo	high school
tæhakkyo	university
coləp	graduation
coləp-hako	[he] graduated and...
sam haknyən/hangnyən/	3rd grade
18. Ne, sam nyən cən e kotıng hakkyo lıl coləp-hako, cikım ın Səul Tæhakkyo sam haknyən e taniko issımnita.	Yes, he finished high school three years ago and is attending Seoul University in the junior class.

NOTES ON DIALOGUES

(Numbers correspond to the sentence numbers.)

1. (Sənsæng ɪn) kohang i əti i(si)mnikka? ('What place is your native place?') is the fixed expression of which English equivalent is 'Where do you come from?' or 'Where are you from?'. The noun kohyang refers to either 'one's birth-place' or 'the place of his family origin'.

3. əli- 'to be young' is a description verb which usually means someone 'is in or before his boyhood'. It is also used to the grownups in somewhat cynical sense, implying 'immaturity' for the age. Ttæ 'time', 'occasion', 'when', is a noun. (See Grammate Note 1.)

4. isa 'moving' is a noun which refers to only moving one's residence and/or office from one place to another, and isa-ha- 'to move' is its verb. For 'moving something' other than one's residence, the verb o(l)mki- (transitive verb) is used. Uli 'we' which includes the speaker is a personal noun which occurs in the nominal positions: uli ka 'we (as subject)', uli lɪl 'us (as object)', uli eke 'to us', uli e 'our', uli nɪn 'we (as topic)', etc. However, before certain nouns uli occurs without accompanying any particle to make up noun phrases: uli kacok 'my family', uli əməni 'my mother', uli apəci 'my father', uli nala 'my country', uli cip 'my home', uli hakkyo 'our school', uli cip salam 'my wife ('our house person')', etc.

5. Kacok means either 'family' or 'a family member'. So, Kacok i manhsɪmnita. means '[I] have a large family.' but not '[I] have many families.'

6. Kyəlhon means either 'marriage' or 'wedding'; Kyəlhon-hæssɪmnikka? means either 'Are [you] married?' or 'Did [you] get married?'

8. Khɪn atɪl ('big son') refers to 'the first son', and khɪn ttal 'the first daughter'. Mat atɪl and khɪn atɪl are synonymous, so are mat ttal and khɪn ttal. Regardless of sex, the last child is called mangnæ. Mangnæ + atɪl (or ttal) = the last child who is a son (or daughter). An imnita. ('No, [it]'s not.') is synonymous with aniyo.

9. Pumo refers always to 'both parents'. Nim is either a free noun or a post-noun. As a free noun it is a poetic word, meaning 'sweetheart' or 'lover'. As a post-noun occuring after a title or kindship name, nim makes up a noun phrase: Title (or kinship name) + nim = Title or kinship name (honored). Examples:

Regular	Honored	
sənsæng	sənsæng	'teacher' 'you'
Pak Sənsæng	Pak Sənsæng nim	'Mr. Park'
pumo	pumo nim	'parents'
hyəng	hyəng nim	'older brother'
tæsa	tæsa nim	'Mr. Ambassador' 'ambassador'
sacang	sacang nim	'the president of the company'
apəci	apənim	'father'
əməni	əmənim	'mother'
nui	nunim	'older sister'
atıl	atınim	'your son'
ttal	ttanim	'your daughter'

Note: apənim, əmənim, nunim, atınim, ttanim are irregular one-word expressions.

10. Tola ka(siə)ssımnita. ('[They] went back.', '[They] returned.') is a Korean euphemism for 'died'. Tæk is the polite equivalent of cip 'house', 'home'. Used directly to the addressee tæk also means 'your home' or sometimes 'you'.

11. Motu and its synonym cənpu 'in all', 'all' occurs either as an adverb or as a noun.

12. Nui means 'female sibling' which is used by a male sibling. Nunim is one-word term specifically for 'older sister' and nui tongsæng is a noun phrase which means 'younger sister'. Tongsæng is used for any 'younger sibling' of either sex. Nui, nunim, nui tongsæng are words for males only.

14. Honca 'single','alone' occurs either as a noun or as an adverb. As a noun it denotes 'a single person with no family' which is often the synonym of toksin 'an unmarried single person.'

16. Nai ka manh-ta. ('Age is plenty.') and Nai ka cək-ta. ('Age is little.') are most commonly used for the single verb expressions nılkəss-ta 'is aged'; cə(l)məss-ta 'is young', 'is youthful'. The stems of nılkəss-ta and cəlməss-ta, both of which occur usually in the past tense to describe the present state, are nılk- and cəlm- respectively. Sal ('the age counter') never occurs with the numerals of Chinese character origin, but always preceded by the numerals of Korean origin.

18. Haknyən/hangnyən/ ('learning year') is a counter which occurs only after the numerals of Chinese character origin, and means either 'grader' or 'school grade':

il haknyən	'1st grader' or '1st grade'
i haknyən	'2nd grader' or '2nd grade'
sam haknyən	'3rd grader' or '3rd grade'

GRAMMAR NOTES

1. ttæ 'time', 'occasion', 'when'

The noun ttæ bound to other forms occurs in the following constructions:

(a.1.) A (certain) nominal + ttæ = a nominal phrase 'such-and-such time'

Examples:

hakkyo ttæ	'the school days'
cəmsim ttæ	'the lunch time'
se sal ttæ	'the age of three'
kuntæ ttæ	'the time of military service'
ai ttæ	'childhood'

(a.2.) A nominal + ttæ + e = an adverbial phrase

hakkyo ttæ e	'in the school days'
cəmsim ttæ e	'during the lunch time'
ai ttæ e	'in [my] childhood', 'when I was child'
se sal ttæ e	'at the age of three'

(b.1.) -(ɪ)l + ttæ = a nominal phrase 'the time of doing so-and-so'

The honorific and/or the past tense suffixes may occur in the -(ɪ)l form. Examples:

Cal ttæ lɪl kitalimnita.	'[I]'m waiting for the bed-time ('sleeping time').'
Səlo ssaul ttæ ka issɪmnita.	'There are times of fighting each other.'
Thipi lɪl pol ttæ ka ceil cæmi issnɪn sikan ici yo.	'When I watch TV is the most interesting time.' ('The time of watching TV is the most interesting time.')

(b.2.) -(ɪ)l + ttæ + e = an adverbial phrase 'at the time of doing so-and so', 'when [someone] does so-and-so'

The construction -(ɪ)l ttæ e which may be followed by a pause occurs as a time adverbial expression before another inflected expression to indicate that the second action/description takes place at the time of the first action/description. Examples:

Hakkyo e kal ttæ e, tækæ ttwiə kamnita.	'When [we] go to school, [we] usually run.'
Tæhak e tanil ttæ e, cikim anæ wa kyəlhon-hæssci yo.	'When [I] was in college, [I] married my present wife.'
Achim e ilənassɪl ttæ e, pi ka oko issəssɪmnita.	'When [I] got up in the morning, it was raining.'
Chəɪm Hankuk e wassɪl ttæ e, cə nɪn chongkak iəssə yo.	'When [I] first came to Korea, I was a bachelor.'

2. Infinitive + sə, 'and...', 'and so...'

Sə like the particles to (Unit 10) and ya (Unit 11), belongs to a small class of particles which occur after inflected words. Infinitive + sə which may be followed by a pause occurs before another inflected expression, and denotes the cause, reason or sequence of the first action or description for which the following inflected expression follows. Examples:

Cikim ɪn kyəlhon-hæ sə, anæ wa ai tɪl i tul issɪmnita.	'Now, I'm married, and have a wife and two children.'
əce nɪn mom i aphə sə, il-halə kaci anhəssə yo.	'I was sick yesterday, so I didn't go to work.'
Pi ka wa sə, kil i nappɪkun yo.	'Because it rained, the roads are bad.'

Tosəkwan e ka sə, tasəs sikan tongan kongpu-hæssımnita.	'I went to the library and studied for five hours.'

3. A nominal + {we / pakk} e 'beside + the nominal', 'except the nominal'

We ('outside') is a noun which with the preceeding nominal makes up a nominal phrase. A nominal + we + e which may be followed by a pause occurs as an adverbial phrase for the following inflected affirmative expression, meaning 'beside the nominal' or 'except the nominal'.

We and pakk are synonymous and are interchangeable each other. Examples:

Hyəng nim han salam we e, nui tongsæng i issə yo.	'Beside one older brother, [I] have a sister.'
Səul we e Pusan esə to kınmu-hæssə yo.	'Not only in Seoul, [I] also worked in Pusan.'

Note that a nominal {we / pakk} e + negative inflected expression means either 'only the nominal + affirmative inflected expression' or 'except the nominal + negative expression'. Observe the following:

Na nın Hankuk mal pakk e molımnita.	'I know only Korean.' ('Except Korean, I don't know.')
Yəngə pakk e pæuci anhəssımnita.	'I learned only English.' ('Except English, I didn't learn.')
Phyo lıl tu cang pakk e saci mot hæssə yo.	'I could buy only two tickets.' ('Except two tickets, I couldn't buy.')

Also note that kı we e, (or kı pakk e) 'Besides', 'Beside that' followed by a pause at the beginning of a sentence occurs as a sentence adverbial.

4. ssik 'each', 'at one time'

A numeral expression + ssik occurs as an adverbial phrase for the following inflected expression, denoting distribution for each separate action. Examples:

Nunim kwa nui tongsæng i hana ssik issə yo.	'I have one older sister and one younger sister each.'
Tu salam ssik tılə osipsiyo.	'Please come in, two at a time.'
Hankuk ımsik ıl han kaci ssik məkə pokessə yo.	'I will try (eating) Korean food one by one.'
Han tal e han pən ssik əməni eke phyənci-haci yo.	'I write my mother once a month.'

5. Infinitive + iss-

The verb iss- preceded by a small class of action verbs in the infinitive form, occurs as an auxiliary verb.. It deontes the state of being. Compare the following:

sal-	'to live'	{salə issımnita salə kyesimnita}	'is alive'; 'is living'
anc-	'to sit'	ancə issımnita	'is seated'
kac-	'to possess'	kacə issımnita	'has'; 'possess'
sə-	'to stand'	sə issımnita	'is standing'
seu-	{'to erect' 'to park'}	sewə issımnita	'is being erected'; 'is being parked'
tu-	{'to put' 'to place'}	tuə issımnita	'is being placed'
noh-	{'to put' 'to place'}	noha issımnita	'is being left'; 'is being placed'
yəlli-	'to be open'	yəlliə issımnita	'is being open'; 'is left open'

DRILLS

A. Substitution Drill

1.	Pak Sənsæng ın kohyang i əti ise yo?	Where is Mr. Park from? Where do you come from, Mr. Park?
2.	Ceimsı Sənsæng ın kohyang i əti ise yo?	Where's Mr. James from?
3.	Sənsæng puin ın kohyang i əti ise yo?	Where's your wife from?
4.	Sənsæng əməni nın kohyang i əti ise yo?	Where was your mother born?
5.	Mikuk tæsa nın kohyang i əti ise yo?	Where's the U.S. Ambassador from?
6.	Hankuk mal sənsæng ın kohyang i əti ise yo?	Where's the Korean teacher from?
7.	Yəngə sənsæng ın kohyang i əti ise yo?	Where's the English teacher from?
8.	Yəngə sənsæng ın kohyang i əti isimnikka?	Where's the English teacher from?
9.	Yəngə sənsæng ın kohyang i əti imnikka?	Where's the English teacher from?
10.	Yəngə sənsæng ın kohyang i əti iye yo?	Where's the English teacher from?

B. Substitution Drill

1.	Ce ka se sal ttæ Səul lo isa-hæssımnita.	[We] moved to Seoul when I was 3 years old.
2.	Ce ka se sal ttæ (e) Səul lo wassımnita.	[We] camed to Seoul when I was 3 years old.
3.	Ce ka tasəs sal ttæ (e) Səul lo wassımnita.	[We] came to Seoul when I was 5 years old.
4.	Ce ka ilkop sal ttæ (e) Səul lo wassımnita.	[We] came to Seoul when I was 7 years old.
5.	Ce ka ahop sal ttæ (e) Səul lo wassımnita.	[We] came to Seoul when I was 9 years old.

6.	Ce ka yəl sal ttæ (e) Səul lo wassımnita.	[We] came to Seoul when I was 10 years old.
7.	Ce ka yəl han sal ttæ (e) Səul lo wassımnita.	[We] came to Seoul when I was 11 years old.
8.	Ce ka sımul tu sal ttæ (e) Səul lo wassımnita.	[We] came to Seoul when I was 22 years old.
9.	Cə ka səlhın se sal ttæ (e) Səul lo wassımnita.	[We] came to Seoul when I was 33 years old.
10.	Ce ka mahın ne sal ttæ (e) Səul lo wassımnita.	[We] came to Seoul when I was 44 years old.

C. Substitution Drill

1.	Cə nın kəi Səul esə saləssımnita.	I have lived mostly in Seoul.
2.	Cə nın kəi Səul esə il-hæssımnita.	I have worked mostly in Seoul.
3.	Cə nın kəi Səul esə kongpu-hæssımnita.	I have studied mostly in Seoul.
4.	Cə nın kəi Səul esə hakkyo e taniəssımnita.	I attended school mostly in Seoul.
5.	Cə nın kəi Səul esə issəssımnita.	I have stayed mostly in Seoul.
*6.	Cə nın kəi Səul esə hakkyo lıl na wassımnita.	I finished most of schools in Seoul.
7.	Cə nın kəi Səul esə hakkyo lıl coləp-hæssımnita.	I graduated most of schools in Seoul.
*8.	Cə nın kəi Səul esə calassımnita.	I have grown up mostly in Seoul.
9.	Cə nın kəi Səul esə Hankuk mal ıl pæwəssımnita.	I have learned Korean mostly in Seoul.

D. Substitution Drill

1.	Hyəng nim i kyesımnikka?	Do you have an older brother? (to male)
*2.	Nunim i kyesımnikka?	Do you have an older sister? (to male)
*3.	Oppa ka kyesımnikka?	Do you have an older brother? (to female)
*4.	ənni ka kyesımnikka?	Do you have an older sister? (to female)

*5. Acəssi ka kyesimnikka? — Do you have an uncle?

*6. Acuməni ka kyesimnikka? — Do you have an aunt?

*7. Ttanim i kyesimnikka? — Do you have a daughter (H)?

*8. Chinchək i kyesimnikka? — Do you have relatives?

9. Hyəngce (tɪl) i kyesimnikka? — Do you have brothers and sisters?

10. Puin i kyesimnikka? — Do you have a wife?

*11. Cangmo (nim) i kyesimnikka? — Do you have mother-in-law ('wife's mother)?

*12. Cangin i kyesimnikka? — Do you have father-in-law ('wife's father')?

*13. Sipumo (nim) i kyesimnikka? — Do you have your husband's parents?

E. Substitution Drill

1. Cə e anæ nɪn Mikuk e issɪmnita. — My wife is in America.

2. Cə e kacok ɪn Mikuk e issɪmnita. — My family is in America.

3. Cə e atɪl ɪn Mikuk e issɪmnita. — My son is in America.

4. Cə e ttal ɪn Mikuk e issɪmnita. — My daughter is in America.

5. Cə e (nam) tongsæng ɪn Mikuk e issɪmnita. — My younger brother is in America.

*6. Cə e sachon ɪn Mikuk e issɪmnita. — My cousin is in America.

*7. Cə e cokha nɪn Mikuk e issɪmnita. — My nephew is in America.

*8. Cə e cokha ttal ɪn Mikuk e issɪmnita. — My niece is in America.

*9. Cə e chinchək ɪn Mikuk e issɪmnita. — My relatives are in America.

*10. Uli cuin ɪn Mikuk e issɪmnita. — My husband ('our master') is in America.

*11. Cə e namphən ɪn Mikuk e issɪmnita. — My husband is in America (to older people).

*12. Uli sawi nɪn Mikuk e issɪmnita. — My son-in-law is in America.

*13. Uli myənuli nɪn Mikuk e issɪmnita. — My daughter-in-law is in America.

F. Substitution Drill

1. Pumo nim i sala kyesimnikka? — Are [your] parents living?

2. Apəci ka sala kyesimnikka? — Is [your] father living?

3. əməni ka sala kyesimnikka? — Is [your] mother living?

*4. Halapəci ka sala kyesimnikka? — Is [your] grandfather living?

*5. Halməni ka sala kyesimnikka?	Is [your] grandmother living?
6. Acəssi ka sala kyesimnikka?	Is [your] uncle living?
7. Acuməni ka sala kyesimnikka?	Is [your] aunt living?
8. Nunim i sala kyesimnikka?	Is [your] older sister living? (to male
9. Cangmo (nim) i sala kyesimnikka?	Is [your] mother-in-law ('wife's mother') living?
10. Cangin i sala kyesimnikka?	Is [your] father-in-law ('wife's father') living?

G. Substitution Drill

1. Uli kacok i Səul lo isa-hæssimnita.	My family moved to Seoul.
2. Uli kacok i Səul lo kassimnita.	My family went to Seoul.
3. Uli kacok i Səul lo ttənassimnita.	My family left for Seoul.
4. Uli kacok i Səul lo wassimnita.	My family came to Seoul.
5. Uli kacok i Səul lo olla wassimnita.	My family came up to Seoul.
6. Uli kacok i Səul lo olla kassimnita.	My family went up to Seoul.
7. Uli kacok i Səul lo nælyə kassimnita.	My family went down to Seoul.
8. Uli kacok i Səul lo kələ kassimnita.	My family walked to Seoul.
9. Uli kacok i Səul lo thako kassimnita.	My family rode to Seoul.

H. Substitution Drill

1. Kacok in myəch pun ina kyesimnikka?	How many are there in your family?
2. Sənsæng in myəch pun ina kyesimnikka?	How many teachers are there?
3. Hyəng nim in myəch pun ina kyesimnikka?	How many older brothers do you have? (to male)
4. Nunim in myəch pun ina kyesimnikka?	How many older sisters do you have? (to male)
5. Acəssi nin myəch pun ina kyesimnikka?	How many uncles do you have?
6. Acuməni nin myəch pun ina kyesimnikka?	How many aunts do you have?

7. Mikuk chinku nɨn myəch pun ina kyesimnikka?	How many American friends do you have?
8. Hyəngce nɨn myəch pun ina kyesimnikka?	How many brothers and sisters do you have?
9. Ttanim ɨn myəch pun ina kyesimnikka?	How many daughters do you have?
10. ənni nɨn myəch pun ina kyesimnikka?	How many older sisters do you have? (to female)
11. Oppa nɨn myəch pun ina kyesimnikka?	How many older brothers do you have? (to female)
12. Oppa nɨn myəch pun ina twesimnikka?	How many older brothers do you have? ('As for your older brothers, how many do they become?')

I. Substitution Drill

1. Apəci nɨn tola kasyəssımnita.	My father passed away.
2. əməni nɨn tola kasyəssɨmnita.	My mother passed away.
3. Halapəci nɨn tola kasyəssɨmnita.	My grandfather passed away.
4. Halməni nɨn tola kasyəssɨmnita.	My grandmother passed away.
5. Acəssi nɨn tola kasyəssɨmnita.	My uncle passed away.
6. Acuməni nɨn tola kasyəssɨmnita.	My aunt passed away.
*7. Khɨn hyəng nim ɨn tola kasyəssɨmnita.	My oldest brother passed away.
*8. Khɨn nunim ɨn tola kasyəssɨmnita.	My oldest sister passed away.
*9. Khɨn nunim ɨn cukəssɨmnita.	My oldest sister {is dead. / died.}
10. Khɨn nunim ɨn kyəlhon-hæssɨmnita.	My oldest sister is married.
11. Khɨn nunim ɨn honca imnita.	My oldest sister is single.
12. Khɨn nunim ɨn honca samnita.	My oldest sister lives alone.
13. Khɨn nunim ɨn nai ka manhsɨmnita.	My oldest sister is old.
14. Khɨn nunim ɨn nai ka cəksɨmnita.	My oldest sister is young.

J. Substitution Drill

1. əməni nɨn hyəng nim tæk esə samnita.	[My] mother lives at my older brother's home.
2. Ceimsɨ nɨn Kim Sənsæng tæk esə samnita.	James lives at Mr. Kim's home.

3. Apəci nın Mikuk esə samnita. — [My] father lives in America.
4. Halapəci nın kohyang esə samnita. — [My] grandfather lives in the home town.
5. Acəssi nın Kulapha esə samnita. — [My] uncle lives in Europe.
6. Hyəng nim ın Inchən pukın esə samnita. — [My] older brother lives in the vicinity of Inchon.
7. Nunim ın Pusan sinæ esə samnita. — [My] older sister lives in downtown Pusan.
8. Cangin kwa cangmo nın sikol esə samnita. — [My] wife's father and mother live in the country.
9. Siapəci wa siəməni nın kohyang esə samnita. — [My] husband's father and mother live in the home town.

K. Substitution Drill

1. Ai ka tul issımnita. — I have two children.
2. Atıl i hana issımnita. — I have one son.
3. Ttal i ses issımnita. — I have three daughters.
*4. Sonca ka tul issımnita. — I have two grandsons.
*5. Sonnyə ka nes issımnita. — I have four granddaughters.
6. Hyəng nim i ne(s) (salam) issımnita. — I have four older brothers.
7. Nunim i tasəs (salam) issımnita. — I (male) have five older sisters.
8. Acəssi ka yəsəs pun issımnita. — I have six uncles.
9. Acuməni ka ilkop pun issımnita. — I have seven aunts.
10. Oppa ka han pun issımnita. — I (female) have one older brother.
11. Yətongsæng i tul issımnita. — I have two younger sisters.
*12. Chənam i yələs issımnita. — I have several brothers-in-law ('wife's brothers').
*13. Chəce ka myəch issımnita. — I have some wife's younger sisters.
*14. Chəhyəng i tu-sə-nəs issımnita. — I have a couple of wife's older sisters.

L. Substitution Drill

1. Tongsæng ın myəch sal imnikka? — How old is your younger brother?
2. Sənsæng ın myəch sal imnikka? — How old is the teacher?
3. Punin ın myəch sal imnikka? — How old is your wife?
4. Nunim ın myəch sal imnikka? — How old is your older sister?

5.	Hyəng nim ın myəch sal imnikka?	How old is your older brother? (to male)
6.	Ttanim ın myəch sal imnikka?	How old is your daughter?
7.	Atıl ın myəch sal imnikka?	How old is your son?
8.	Khın ai nın myəch sal imnikka?	How old is your first child?
9.	Chəs ccæ atıl ın myəch sal imnikka?	How old is your first son?
10.	Chənam ın myəch sal imnikka?	How old is your wife's brother?
11.	Chəce ın myəch sal imnikka?	How old is your wife's younger sister?
12.	Sitongsæng ın myəch sal imnikka?	How old is your husband's younger brother?

M. Substitution Drill

1.	Hyəng nim we e nunim to issımnita.	I have an older sister as well as an older brother.
2.	Namtongsæng we e yətongsæng to issımnita.	I have a younger sister as well as a younger brother.
3.	Səul Tæhakkyo we e Kolyə Tæhakkyo to issımnita.	There is Korea University as well as Seoul University.
4.	Panto Hothel we e Cosən Hothel to issımnita.	There is Chosen Hotel as well as Bando Hotel.
5.	Mikuk Tæsakwan we e Yəngkuk Yəngsakwan to issımnita.	There is British Consulate as well as American Embassy.
6.	Ilpon chinku we e Cungkuk chinku to issımnita.	I have a Chinese friend as well as a Japanese friend.
7.	Atıl hana we e ttal tul to issımnita.	I have two daughters as well as a son.
8.	Kicha wa ppəsı we e pihængki wa pæ to issımnita.	There are airplanes and ships as well as trains and buses.
9.	Kukce Kıkcang we e Cungang Kıkcang to issımnita.	There is Central Theatre as well as International Theatre.

N. Expansion Drill

Tutor: Hyəng nim i issımnita. /nunim/ — 'I have an older brother.' /older sister/

Student: Hyəng nim we e nunim to issımnita. — 'Beside an older brother I also have an older sister.'

1. Pullansə mal ıl pæwəssımnita. /Tokil mal/ — Pullansə mal we e Tokil mal to pæwəssımnita.
2. Na nın Səul esə salassımnita. /Pusan/ — Na nın Səul we e Pusan esə to salassımnita.
3. Uli hakkyo esə Hankuk mal ıl kalıchimnita. /Ssolyən mal/ — Uli hakkyo esə Hankuk mal we e Ssolyən mal to kalıchimnita.
4. Səul sinæ lıl kukyəng-hæssımnita. /Cungang Pakmulkwan/ — Səul sinæ we e Cungang Pakmulkawan to kukyəng-hæssımnita.
5. Kicha wa ppəsı lo kal su issımnita. /pihængki/ — Kicha wa ppəsı we e pihængki lo to kal su issımnita.
6. Kı yəca wa kathi kako siphsımnita. /Kim Kisu/ — Kı yəca we e Kim Kisu wa to kathi kako siphsımnita.
7. Səul pukın ıl kukyəng-halyəko hamnita. /Pusan/ — Səul pukın we e Pusan to kukyəng-halyəko hamnita.
8. Kacok tıl ıl pwa ya hakessımnita. /yələ chinku/ — Kacok tıl we e yələ chinku to pwa ya hakessımnita.
9. Hankuk ınhæng e kal il i issımnita. /Cungang Sicang/ — Hankuk ınhæng we e Cungang Sicang e to kal il i issımnita.

O. Substitution Drill

1. Cə nın cangnyən e kotıng hakkyo lıl coləp-hæssımnita. — I graduated from the high school last year.
2. Cə nın cangnyən e <u>cunghakkyo</u> lıl coləp-hæssımnita. — I graduated from the junior high school ('middle school') last year.
3. Cə nın cangnyən e <u>tæhakkyo</u> lıl coləp-hæssımnita. — I graduated from the university last year.
4. Cə nın cangnyən e <u>sohakkyo</u> lıl coləp-hæssımnita. — I graduated from the elementary school last year.
5. Cə nın cangnyən e <u>Səul Tæhak</u> ıl coləp-hæssımnita. — I graduated from Seoul University last year.

6. Cə nın cangnyən e Səul Tæhak ıl na wassımnita.	I graduated from Seoul University last year
7. Cə nın cangnyən e Səul Tæhak ıl taniəssımnita.	I attended Seoul University last year.
*8. Cə nın cangnyən e Səul Tæhak ıl tılə kassımnita.	I entered Seoul University last year.
*9. Cə nın cangnyən e Səul Tæhak ıl kkıth-machiəssımnita.	I finished Seoul University last year.
10. Cə nın cangnyən Səul Tæhak ıl kımantuəssımnita.	I quit Seoul University last year.
11. Cə nın cangnyən e Səoul Tæhak ıl sicak-hæssımnita.	I began Seoul University last year.

P. Grammar Drill

Tutor: Hakkyo e kamnita. Ppəsi lıl thamnita.	'[I] go to school. [I] take the bus.'
Student: Hakkyo e kal ttæ (e), ppəsi lıl thamnita.	'When I go to school I take the bus.'
1. Mok i malımnita. Mul ıl masimnita.	Mok i malıl ttæ (e), mul ıl masimnita.
2. Pæ ka kophımnita. Cəmsim ıl məksımnita.	Pæ ka kophıl ttæ (e), cəmsim ıl məksımnita.
3. Catongcha lıl samnita. Ton i philyo-hamnita.	Catongcha lıl sal ttæ (e), ton i philyo-hamnita.
4. Phyənci lıl puchimnita. Uphyənkuk e ka ya hamnita.	Phyənci lıl puchil ttæ (e), uphyənkuk e ka ya hamnita.
5. Hankuk yənghwa lıl sangyənghamnita. Hangsang polə kamnita.	Hankuk yənghwa lıl sangyənghal ttæ (e), hangsang polə kamnita.
6. Səul esə il-hamnita. Kukyəng-hakessımnita.	Səul esə il-hal ttæ (e), kukyəng-hakessımnita.
7. Kələ sə hwesa e kamnita. Kim Sənsæng cip e tıllıkessımnita.	Kələ sə hwesa e kal ttæ (e), Kim Sənsæng cip e tıllıkessımnita.
8. Isa-hamnita. Sæ cha lıl sakessımnita.	Isa-hal ttæ (e), sæ cha lıl sakessımnita.
9. Na nın pappımnita. Məkılə na kal su əpsımnita.	Na nın pappıl ttæ (e), məkılə na kal su əpsımnita.

11. Tæhak e taniəssımnita. Hankuk mal ıl pæwəssımnita.
Tæhak e taniəssıl ttæ (e), Hankuk mal ıl pæwəssımnita.

12. Hankuk mal ıl sicak-hæssımnita. Chəım e nın əlyəwəssımnita.
Hankuk mal ıl sicak-hæssıl ttæ (e), chəım e nın əlyəwəssımnita.

13. Kı yəca ekesə phyənci lıl patəssımnita. Na to kot ssəssımnita.
Kı yəca ekesə phyənci lıl patəssıl ttæ (e), na to kot ssəssımnita.

14. Tæhak ıl kkıth-machiəssımnita. Cikım anæ lıl mannassımnita.
Tæhak ıl kkıth-machiəssıl ttæ (e), cikım anæ lıl mannassımnita.

15. Ppəsı esə næliəssımnita. Anæ ka kitaliko issəssımnita.
Ppəsı esə næliəssıl ttæ (e), anæ ka kitaliko issəssımnita.

Q. Grammar Drill

Tutor: ənce ppəsı lıl thamnikka? /Hakkyo e kamnita./
'When do you take the bus?' /[I] go to school./

Student: Hakkyo e kal ttæ (e), ppəsı lıl thamnita.
'When I go to school, I take the bus.'

1. ənce phyənci lıl ssımmikka? /Sikan i issımnita./
Sikan i issıl ttæ (e), phyənci lıl ssımnita.

2. ənce mækcu lıl masimnikka? /Mok i malımnita./
Mok i malıl ttæ (e), mækcu lıl masimnita.

3. ənce hapsıng ıl thamnikka? /Salam i manhci anhsımnita./
Salam i manhci anhıl ttæ (e), hapsıng ıl thamnita.

4. ənce Yəngə lıl kalıchikessımnikka? /Yəngə sənsæng i əpsımnita./
Yəngə səngsæng i əpsıl ttæ (e), yəngə lıl kalıchikessımnita.

5. ənce tæk e kyesikessımnikka? /Cənyək ıl məksımnita./
Cənyək ıl məkıl ttæ (e), cip e isskessımnita.

6. ənce kyəlhon-hakessımnikka? /Cohahanın yəca lıl mannamnita./
Cohahanın yəca lıl mannal ttæ (e), kyəlhon-hakessımnita.

7. ənce halapəci ka tola kasyəssımnikka? /Næ ka yəl sal tweəssımnita./
Næ ka yəl sal tweəssıl ttæ (e), halapəci ka tola kasyəssımnita.

8. ənce kkaci honca saləssımnikka? /Tæhak ıl coləp-hæssımnita./
Tæhak ıl coləp-hæssıl ttæ kkaci, honca saləssımnita.

9. ənce Yəngə lıl pæwəssımnikka? /Cunghakkyo e taniəssımnita./
Cunghakkyo e taniəssıl ttæ (e), Yəngə lıl pæwəssımnita.

R. Response Exercise

Tutor: Hakkyo e kal ttæ (e), muəs ɪlo kase yo? — 'What do you ride when you go to school?'

Student: Hakkyo e kal ttæ e, ppəsi lo kamnita. — 'I take the bus when I go to school.'

1. Cəmsim ɪl məkɪl ttæ e, nuku wa kathi kase yo?
2. Cip e issɪl ttæ e, muəs ɪl hase yo?
3. Sikan i issɪl ttæ e, tækæ muəs (ɪl) hase yo?
4. Hankuk ɪl ttənal ttæ e, muəs ɪlo okessə yo?
5. Səul esə saləssɪl ttæ e, musɪn cip e saləssə yo?
6. Mom i aphɪl ttæ e, muəs ɪl capsuse yo?
7. Tæhakkyo e taniəssɪl ttæ e, muəs ɪl kongpu-hæssə yo?
8. Kotɪng hakkyo lɪl coləp-hæssɪl ttæ e, myəch sal iyəssə yo?
9. Khəphi lɪl masiko siphɪl ttæ e, əti e kase yo?
10. Mok i malɪl ttæ e, muəs ɪl masise yo?
11. Mikuk e tola kal ttæ e, nuku wa kathi kakessə yo?
12. Phyənci lɪl puchil ttæ e, muəs i philyo-hæ yo?

EXERCISES

A. Tell the following story to the class that:

You are originally from Inchon but you have lived most of your life in in Seoul. When you were three years old, your family moved to Seoul, and you began elementary school there at six. You went to junior high, senior high and college, all in Seoul. You are employed by a big company. You are married and have a wife and two children. Your first child is a daughter but the second one is a son. Your parents are not with your family. Your mother is still living but your father passed away a few years ago, and your mother lives at your brother's home. Besides one older brother, you have one (each) younger sister and one younger brother but you don't have any older sisters. Your sister got married sometime ago, but your younger brother is still single. He is now 20 years old and is still too young to get married. After finishing high school 3 years ago, he entered Seoul University. Since he is a junior this year he will be graduated in a year and a half, but probably he will have to go into military service for two years after that.

B. Prepare a short biography of yourself and tell the class. The information in your autobiography may include your home town, your schools, your immediate family, your parents, brothers and sisters if any; what they are doing; their ages; their marital status, and so forth.

C. Make a short statement or question using each of the following kinship terms:

1. grandfather
2. grandmother
3. parents
4. father
5. mother
6. uncle
7. aunt
8. older sister (for male and female)
9. older brother (for male and female)
10. daughter
11. son
12. cousin (male, female)
13. nephew
14. niece
15. grandson
16. granddaughter
17. my wife
18. my husband
19. your wife
20. your husband
21. your daughter
22. relatives
23. parents-in-law ('husband's parents')
24. father-in-law ('husband's father')
25. mother-in-law ('husband's mother')
26. father-in-law ('wife's father')
27. mother-in-law ('wife's mother')
28. sister-in-law ('wife's older sister')
29. sister-in-law ('wife's younger sister')
30. sister(s)-in-law ('husband's sister(s)')
31. brother(s)-in-law ('wife's brother(s)') /chənam/
32. son-in-law /sawi/
33. daughter-in-law
34. brother-in-law ('male's sister's husband') /mæpu/
35. brother-in-law ('female's older sister's husband') /hyəngpu/

End of Tape 10B

Tape 11A

제 15 과 개인의 일생과 가족 이야기 (계속)

1. 이 : 제임스 선생은 미국 어디에서 오셨읍니까?

뉴욕 주
낳았읍니다
아이를 낳았읍니다
아이가 낳았읍니다
자랐읍니다

2. 제임스 : 저의 집은 시카고에 있읍니다. 그러나, 저는 뉴욕 주에서 낳아서 거기에서 자랐읍니다.

3. 이 : 그럼, 학교도 뉴욕 주에서 다녔읍니까?

대학

4. 제임스 : 대학 말입니까? 대학은 보스톤에서 다녔읍니다.

나 왔읍니다

5. 이 : 언제 대학은 나 왔읍니까?

팔 년 전에

6. 제임스 : 팔 년 전에 나 왔읍니다.

그 후에

7. 이 : 그 후에는 무엇을 했읍니까?

졸업합니다
졸업한 후에

UNIT 15. Talking About One's Life and Family (Continued)

BASIC DIALOGUES FOR MEMORIZATION

Dialogue A

Lee

1. Ceimsɪ Sənsæng ɪn Mikuk əti esə osyəssɪmnikka?	Where in America are you from, Mr. James?

James

Nyuyok Cu	New York State
nahassɪmnita	[I] was born
ai lɪl nahassɪmnita	[she] gave birth to a child
ai ka nahassɪmnita	a child was born
calassɪmnita	[I] grew up
2. Cə e cip ɪn Sikhako e issɪmnita. Kɪləna, cə nɪn Nyuyok Cu esə naha sə kəki esə calassɪmnita.	My home is in Chicago. But I was born in New York State and grew up there.

Lee

3. Kɪləm, hakkyo to Nyuyok Cu esə tanyəssɪmnikka?	Well, did you go to school in New York State, too?

James

tæhak	college
4. Tæhak mal ɪmnikka? Tæhak ɪn Posɪthon esə tanyəssɪmnita.	You mean college? I went to college in Boston.

Lee

na wassɪmnikka	('did you come out?')
5. ənce tæhak ɪn na wassɪmnikka?	When did you graduate from college?

James

phal nyən cən e	8 years ago
6. Han phal nyən cən e na wassɪmnita.	I graduated about eight years ago.

얼마 동안
어느 회사에서

8. 제임스 : 대학을 졸업한 후에 얼마 동안 어느 회사에서 일했읍니다.

언제부터
외교관이 되었어요

9. 이 : 그럼, 언제부터 외교관이 되었어요?

들어 옵니다
들어 온지
국무성
꼭

10. 제임스 : 국무성에 들어 온지 꼭 육 년 되었읍니다.

오기 전에
여러 나라에서

11. 이 : 한국에 오기 전에 여러 나라에서 일했나요?

12. 제임스 : 예, 서울에 오기 전에(는) 구라파 여러 나라에서 한 사 년 동안 근무했었읍니다.

있는 동안
구라파에 있는 동안
여행
여행(을) 했읍니까

13. 이 : 구라파에 있는 동안 여행 많이 했읍니까?

Lee

kɪ hu e	after that
7. Kɪ hu e nɪn muəs ɪl hæssɪmnikka?	What did you do after that?

James

coləp	graduation
coləp-hamnita	[I] graduate
colәphan hu e	after graduating
əlma tongan	for some time
ənɪ hwesa	a certain firm
8. Tæhak ɪl coləp-han hu e, əlma tongan ənɪ hwesa esə il-hæssɪmnita.	After I graduated from college, I worked with a business firm for some time.

Lee

ənce puthə	since when
wekyokwan i tweəssə yo	have [you] become a diplomat?
9. Kɪləm, ənce puthə wekyokwan i tweəssə yo?	Then, when did you join the foreign service? ('Since when have you become a diplomat?')

James

tɪlə omnita	('I come in'); [I] join
tɪlə on ci	since I joined
Kukmusəng/kungmusəng/	State Department
kkok	just; without fail; exactly
10. Kukmusəng e tɪlə on ci, kkok yuk nyən tweəssɪmnita.	It has been excatly six years since I came into the State Department.

Dialogue B

Lee

oki cən e	before coming
yələ nala esə	in many countries
11. Hankuk e oki cən e, yələ nala esə il-hæssna/ilhænna/ yo?	Have you worked in many countries before coming to Korea?

14. 제임스 : 예, 많이 (여행)했읍니다.

기후
비슷합니까
15. 이 : 거기에 기후는 한국과 비슷했읍니까?

생각합니다
16. 제임스 : 예, 그렇게 생각합니다.

기후에 대해(서)
말씀 해 주십시요
17. 이 : 그 곳, 기후에 대해서 좀 말씀 해 주십시요.

봄
날씨
따뜻하지만
비
비가 옵니다
여름
덥지 않습니다
18. 제임스 : 봄 날씨는 따뜻하지만, 비가 좀 많이 오지요.
여름에는 그리 덥지 않어요.

가을
겨울
같습니다
19. 이 : 가을과 겨울 날씨도 한국과 같습니까?

James

12. Ne, Səul e oki cən e (nɪn), Kulapha yələ nala esə han sa nyən tongan kɪnmu-hæssəssɪmnita. — Yes, I worked in several countries in Europe for about four years before I came to Seoul.

Lee

issnɪn/innɪn/ tongan — while [I] stay; while [I] was (there)

Kulapha e issnɪn tongan — while [you] were in Europe

yəhæng — travelling; trip

yəhæng (ɪl) hæssɪmnikka — have you travelled?

13. Kulapha e issnɪn tongan, yəhæng manhi hæssɪmnikka? — Did you travel a lot while in Europe?

James

14. Ne, manhi (yəhæng-)hæssɪmnita. — Yes, I travelled a lot.

Lee

kihu — climate; weather

pisɪthamnikka — is [it] similar?

15. Kəki e kihu nɪn Hankuk kwa pisɪthæssɪmnikka? — Was the weather there similar to that of Korea?

James

sængkak-hamnita — [I] think

16. Ne, kɪləhke sængkak-hamnita. — Yes, I think so.

Lee

kihu e tæhæ (sə) — about the weather; concerning the weather

malssɪm-hæ cusipsiyo — please tell me

17. Kɪ kos kihu e tæhæ (sə) com malssɪm-hæ cusipsiyo. — Please tell me a little about the climate there.

James

pom — spring

nalssi — weather

ttattɪthaci man — [it]'s warm but

눈
눈이 오고
바람
바람이 붑니다

20. 제임스 : 예, 대개 가을 날씨는 같습니다. 그러나, 겨울에는 한국보다 눈이 많이 오고, 바람이 많이 붑니다.

pi	rain
pi ka omnita	it rains ('rain comes')
yəlɪm	summer
təpci anhsɪmnita	[it]'s not hot
18. Pom nalssi nɪn ttattɪthaci man, pi ka com manhi oci yo. Yəlɪm e nɪn kɪli təpci anhə yo.	Spring weather is warm but it rains a lot. It's not so hot in the summer.

Lee

kaɪl	autumn; fall
kyəul	winter
kathsɪmnikka/kassɪmnikka/	is [it] the same?
19. Kaɪl kwa kyəul nalssi to Hankuk kwa kathsɪmnikka?	Is the weather in the autumn and winter the same as in Korea?

James

nun	snow
nun i oko	it snows and ('snow comes and..')
palam	wind
palam i pu(lɪ)mnita	it's windy; wind blows
20. Ne, tækæ kaɪl nalssi nɪn kathsɪmnita. Kɪləna, kyəul e nɪn Hankuk pota nun i mahhi oko, palam i manhi pumnita.	Yes, the weather in the fall is about the same, but in the winter it is more snowy and windy than in Korea.

NOTES ON DIALOGUES

(Numbers correspond to the sentence numbers.)

5. (Hakkyo lɨl) na o- ('to come out (of school)') is more colloquial than colǝp-ha- 'to graduate'

8. ǝnɨ hwesa and ǝlma tongan in the statement sentences mean 'a (certain) company' and 'for some time' respectively. Some of the interrogative expressions in the sentences other than question sentences mean 'certain--' or 'some--': ǝnɨ hakkyo 'some school', nuku 'somebody', ǝti 'some place', ǝnɨ nal 'one-day' or 'someday', ǝnce 'sometime', myǝch pǝn 'several times', myǝchil tongan 'for some days', etc. (See Grammar Note 4b, Unit 10.)

10. Kkok 'exactly', 'just', 'without fail' is an adverb which occurs either before another adverbial expression or before an inflected expression. When it occurs before another adverbial expression kkok means 'exactly' or 'just'; before an inflected expression it means 'without fail'. Compare the following:

GROUP 1 'exactly'

Kkok han-si e ttǝnakessɨmnita.	'I will leave at 1 o'clock sharp.' ('I will leave exactly at 1 o'clock.')
Kkok kɨlǝhke hasipsiyo.	'Do [it] exactly like that.' ('Do exactly so.')
Na nɨn kkok han tal tongan Hankukǝ lɨl pæwǝssɨmnita.	'I have studied Korean just (for) a month.'

GROUP 2 'without fail'

Onɨl pam e kkok tola osipsiyo.	'Be sure to come back tonight.' ('Come back tonight without fail.')
Kɨ il ɨl kkok kkɨth-nækessɨmnita.	'I will finish the work without fail.'
Kkok yumyǝng-han salam i twee ya hamnita.	'[You] have to become a famous man by all means.'

15. Kihu 'weather', 'climate' and nalssi are synonymous.

16. Sængkak is a noun which means 'thought' or 'idea'. Sængkak-ha- is a transitive verb. Thus, N + ɨl/lɨl + sængkak-ha- means 'to think of N'.

GRAMMAR NOTES

1. hu (or taım) 'after', 'the later time', 'next'

Hu occurred previously as a noun. Hu e 'later', 'afterward', 'at a later time'; kı hu e 'after that'; a point in time + hu e 'after + the point in time'; a period of time + hu e 'the period of time + later', also occurred as adverbial phrases (See Unit 7).

The construction -n/ın hu e, (i.e. the inflected form of an action verb ending in -n/ın plus hu + e) which may be followed by a pause before another inflected expression, means 'after having done so-and-so' or 'after doing so-and-so'. Hu and taım are snyonymous and are interchangeable in all the above phrase constructions. Examples:

Tæhak ıl coləp-han hu e, ənı hwesa e kınmu-hæssımnita.	'After I graduated from college, I worked with a business firm.'
Kuntæ esə na on hu e, tæhakwən kongpu lıl sicak-hæssımnita.	'After [I] got out of the Army, [I] began my graduate studies.'
Kı hwesa lıl kımantun hu e, wekyokwan sihəm ıl pwassə yo.	'I took the foreign service examination after I had quit the company.'
Tul ccæ ai lıl nahın hu e, sæ cip ıl sassımnita.	'After the second child was born, [we] bought a new house.'
Hankuk mal ıl pæun hu e, Səul e kalyəko hamnita.	'I intend to go to Korea after I (have) studied Korean.'

2. cən 'before' 'the previous time'

Cən is a noun. Cən e 'previously', kı cən e 'before that', a point in time + cən e 'before + the point in time', a period of time + cən e 'the period of time + ago' occurred previously as adverbial phrases (See Unit 7).

The construction -ki cən e (i.e. the ki form + cən e) which may be followed by a pause before another inflected expression means 'before doing so-and-so' or 'before [someone] having done so-and-so'. Examples:

Hankuk e oki cən e, Tong Kulapha lıl yəhæng-hæssə yo.	'Before [I] came to Korea, [I] travelled in East Europe.'
Sənsæng ın Kukmusəng e tılə oki cən e, muəs ıl hæssə yo?	'What did you do before you joined the State Department?'
Nalssi ka chupki cən e, kyəul cunpi lıl hæ ya hamnita.	'Before the weather gets cold, I have to prepare for the winter.'

3. -n/ın ci + (period of time) + {twe- / cina-} 'It has been...(period of time) since..'

We noticed that the intransitive verb twe-, occuring after 'a period of time', denotes 'elapsing of a period of time', and after 'a point in time' denotes 'arriving at a point in time' (Units 8 and 12). Observe (a) and (b):

(a)

Pəlssə {sam nyən (i) / se hæ (ka)} tweəssımnita.	'It's been already three years.'
Panto·hwesa esə han tasəs tal (i) tweəssə yo.	'[I]'ve been with Bando Company about five months now.'

(b)

Yəl-tu-si ka tweyə sə, cəmsim məkılə kassımnita.	'It was 12 o'clock, so [we] went to eat lunch.'
Tasəs-si ka twemyən, ttənakessə yo.	'When it is 5 o'clock, I'll leave.'

The construction -n/ın ci + a period of time + twe- denotes that a period of time has elapsed since the action of the verb in -n/ın form took place. In the above construction twe- and cina- can be interchangeably used. Examples:

Kukmusəng e tılə on ci yuk nyən tweəssımnita.	'It has been six years since [I] came into the State Department.'
Ce ka kyəlhon-han ci sa nyən pan tweəssə yo.	'I have been married four and a half years.'
Kim Sənsæng ıl an ci phək olæ tweəssımnita.	'I have known Mr. Kim quite a long time now.'
Hankuk e osin ci əlma na tweəssna yo?	'How long have you been in Korea?' ('How long has it been since you came to Korea?').
Næil lo Hankuk mal kongpu sicak-han ci kkok nək tal i twekessımnita.	'It will be exactly 4 months by tomorrow since [I] began the Korean language studies.'

4. -nın + tongan, 'while doing so-and-so'

Tongan 'for', 'during' previously occurred as a post-noun which, preceded by a time expression, forms an adverbial phrase (Unit 6). The -nın form (i.e. the present Noun-Modifier word of an action verb) + tongan, which may be followed by a pause before another inflected expression, means 'while doing so-and-so' or 'while [someone] having done so-and-so'. Examples:

Kulapha e issnın tongan, yəhæng manhi hæssımnikka?	'Did you travel a lot while [you were] in Europe?'

Nææ ka cip e əpsnın tongan, ai ka pyəng i nassımnita.	'In my absence from home, the child has got sick.' ('While I was not home, the child has got sickness.')
Tæhak e tanının tongan, kisuksa esə saləssımnita.	'While I was attending college, I lived in the dormitory.'
Cə nın Səul esə il-hanın tongan, Hankuk phungsok ıl pæuko siphsımnita.	'I'd like to learn Korean customs while I work in Seoul.'

5. A nominal e + {tæhæ / kwanhæ} sə 'concerning + the nominal', 'about + the nominal'

The verb tæha- 'to face' or 'to confront' is an transitive verb. However, its infinitive form tæhæ (or tæhayə) + the particle sə occurs immediately after a nominal + e before an inflected expression to mean 'concerning the nominal' or 'about the nominal'. Examples:

Hankuk phungsok e tæhæ sə com mal-hæ cusipsioy.	'Please tell me a little about Korean customs.'
Sənsæng e tæhæ sə (iyaki) tılın il i issımnita.	'I have heard about you (before).'
Mikuk yəksa e tæhæ sə amu kəs to molımnikka?	'Don't [you] know anything about American history?'
Ceimsı ka na eke Hankuk sosik e tæhæ sə mulə pwassə yo.	'James asked me about news from Korea.'

DRILLS

A. Substitution Drill

1.	Cə nɨn Nyuyok Cu esə nahassɨmnita.	I was born in New York State.
2.	Cə e hyəng nim ɨn Sikhako esə nahassɨmnita.	My older brother was born in Chicago.
3.	Cə e anæ nɨn Kulapha esə nahassɨmnita.	My wife was born in Europe.
4.	Cə e tongsæng ɨn Puk-Han esə nahassɨmnita.	My younger brother was born in North Korea.
5.	Cə e ənni nɨn Inchən esə nahassɨmnita.	My older sister was born in Inchon.
6.	Cə e oppa nɨn Wəsingthon Cu esə nahassɨmnita.	My older borther was born in Washington State.
7.	Uli khɨn atɨl ɨn pyəngwən esə nahassɨmnita.	Our oldest son was born in the hospital.
8.	Cə e nui tongsæng ɨn wekuk esə nahassɨmnita.	My younger sister was born abroad.
*9.	Cə e ttal ɨn hæwe esə nahassɨmnita.	My daughter was born abroad.
10.	Cə e ttal ɨn hæwe esə calassɨmnita.	My daughter grew up abroad.
11.	Cə e ttal ɨn hæwe esə salassɨmnita.	My daughter has lived abroad.
12.	Cə e ttal ɨn hæwe esə hakkyo e tanyəssɨmnita.	My daughter went to school abroad.
*13.	Cə e ttal ɨn hæwe esə khəssɨmnita.	My daughter grew up abroad.

B. Substitution Drill

1.	Cə nɨn Nyuyok esə naha sə kəki esə calassɨmnita.	I was born in New York and grew up there.
2.	Cə nɨn Inchən esə naha sə Səul esə calassɨmnita.	I was born in Inchon and grew up in Seoul.
3.	Cə nɨn Puk-Han esə naha sə Nam-Han esə calassɨmnita.	I was born in North Korea and grew up in South Korea.
4.	Cə nɨn Kulapha esə naha sə Mikuk esə calassɨmnita.	I was born in Europe and grew up in the United States.
*5.	Cə nɨn Sikhako esə naha sə Tongpu esə calassɨmnita.	I was born in Chicago and grew up in the East.

*6. Cə nɪn <u>Tongpu</u> esə naha sə <u>Səpu</u> esə calassɪmnita. — I was born in the East and grew up in the West.

*7. Cə nɪn <u>Səpu</u> esə naha sə <u>Nampu</u> esə calassɪmnita. — I was born in the West and grew up in the South.

*8 Cə nɪn <u>Mikuk Nampu</u> esə naha sə <u>Nammi</u> esə calassɪmnita. — I was born in the Southern part of the U.S. and grew up in South America.

*9. Cə nɪn <u>Hawai</u> esə naha sə (Mikuk) <u>pontho</u> esə calassɪmnita. — I was born in Hawaii and grew up on the mainland (of the U.S.).

*10. Cə nɪn <u>səm</u> esə naha sə <u>yukci</u> esə calassɪmnita. — I was born on an island and grew up on the mainland.

*11. Cə nɪn <u>sikol</u> esə naha sə <u>tosi</u> esə calassɪmnita. — I was born in a village and grew up in the city.

*12. Cə nɪn <u>chon</u> esə naha sə <u>tohweci</u> esə calassɪmnita. — I was born in a village and grew up in a metropolitan area.

C. Substitution Drill

1. Tæhak ɪn Nyuyok Cu esə tanyəssɪmnita. — [I] went to college in New York State.

2. Tæhak ɪn Nyuyok Cu esə <u>na wassɪmnita</u>. — I finished college in New York State.

3. Tæhak ɪn Nyuyok Cu esə <u>tɪlə kassɪmnita</u>. — I was admitted to ('entered') college in New York State.

4. Tæhak ɪn Nyuyok Cu esə <u>coləp-hæssɪmnita</u>. — I graduated from college in New York State.

5. Tæhak ɪn Nyuyok Cu esə <u>sicak-hæssɪmnita</u>. — I began college in New York State.

6. Tæhak ɪn Nyuyok Cu esə <u>kkɪth-machiəssɪmnita</u>. — I finished college in New York State.

7. Tæhak ɪn Nyuyok Cu esə <u>taniko siphəssɪmnita</u>. — I wanted to attend college in New York State.

8. Tæhak ɪn Nyuyok Cu esə <u>tanilyəko hæssɪmnita</u>. — I intended to go to college in New York State.

9. Tæhak ɪn Nyuyok Cu esə <u>tanici mot hæssɪmnita</u>. — I could not attend college in New York State.

10. Tæhak ɪn Nyuyok Cu esə <u>taniə ya hæssɪmnita</u>. — I had to attend college in New York State.

D. Substitution Drill

1. Hakkyo lıl colǝp-han hu e, hwesa esǝ il-hæssımnita.	I worked for a company after graduating from school.
2. Hakkyo lıl colǝp-han hu e, Kukmusǝng e tılǝ wassımnita.	I joined the State Department after graduating from school.
3. Hakkyo lıl colǝp-han hu e, wekyokwan i tweyǝssımnita.	I joined the foreign service after graduating from school.
4. Hakkyo lıl colǝp-han hu e, Kulapha lıl yǝhæng-hæssımnita.	I travelled in Europe after graduating from school.
5. Hakkyo lıl colǝp-han hu e, kyǝlhon-hæssımnita.	I got married after graduating from school.
6. Hakkyo lıl colǝp-han hu e, kuntæ e tılǝ kalyǝko hæssımnita.	I intended to join the (military) service after graduating from school.
7. Hakkyo lıl colǝp-han hu e, chǝs ccæ ai lıl nahassımnita.	We had our first child after I graduated from school.
8. Hakkyo lıl colǝp-han hu e, cǝngpu e kınmu-hæssımnita.	I worked for the government after graduating from school.
9. Hakkyo lıl colǝp-han hu e, kılǝhke sængkak-hæssımnita.	I thought so after I graduated from school.

E. Substitution Drill

1. Mikuk Kongpowǝn e tılǝ on ci sam nyǝn tweǝssımnita.	It's been three years since I joined USIS.
2. I il (ıl) sicak-han ci sam nyǝn tweǝssımnita.	It's been three years since I began this job.
3. Kyǝlhon-han ci sam nyǝn tweǝssımnita.	I have been married for three years.
4. Wekyokwan i twen ci sam nyǝn tweǝssımnita.	It's been three years since I joined the foreign service.
5. I hwesa esǝ il-han ci sam nyǝn tweǝssımnita.	I have worked at this company for three years now.
6. Tæhak ıl colǝp-han ci sam nyǝn tweǝssımnita.	It's been three years since I graduated from college.
7. Hankuk esǝ san ci sam nyǝn tweǝssımnita.	I have lived in Korea for three years now.

8. Ceimsi Sənsæng il an ci sam nyən tweəssımnita. — I have known Mr. James for three years now.

9. Anæ lıl chəim mannan ci sam nyən tweəssımnita. — It's been three years since I first met my wife.

F. Substitution Drill

1. Səul e oki cən e, Kulapha esə il-hæssımnita. — Before I came to Seoul I worked in Europe.

2. Səul e oki cən e, tæhak ıl na wassımnita. — I graduated from college before I came to Seoul.

3. Səul e oki cən e, Hankuk mal ıl pæwəssımnita. — I studied Korean before I came to Seoul.

4. Səul e oki cən e, Kukmusəng e kınmu-hæssımnita. — I worked at the State Department before I came to Seoul.

5. Səul e oki cən e, kyəlhon-hæssımnita. — I got married before I came to Seoul.

6. Səul e oki cən e, kuntæ esə na wassımnita. — I got out of the army before I came to Seoul.

7. Səul e oki cən e, Ilpon ıl kukyəng-hæssımnita. — I went sightseeing in Japan before I came to Seoul.

8. Səul e oki cən e, uli ai ka nahassımnita. — Our child was born before we came to Seoul.

9. Səul e oki cən e, apəci ka tola kasiəssımnita. — My father passed away before I came to Seoul.

10. Səul e oki cən e, yələ nala lıl yəhæng-hæssımnita. — I travelled in many countries before I came to Seoul.

*11. Səul e oki cən e, ai ka cukəssımnita. — [Our] child died before [we] came to Seoul.

G. Combination Drill

Tutor: Tæhak ıl coləp-hæssımnita. ənı hwesa esə il-hæssımnita. — '[I] graduated from college. [I] worked for a (certain) company.'

Student: Tæhak ıl coləp-han hu e, ənı hwesa esə il-hæssımnita. — '[I] worked for a company after graduating from college.'

1. Wekyokwan i tweəssımnita. Yələ nala esə saləssımnita. — Wekyokwan i twen hu e, yələ nala esə saləssımnita.

2. Cəngpu e tılə wassımnita. Sam nyən tweəssımnita.	Cəngpu e tılə on hu e, sam nyən tweəssımnita.
3. Kuntæ esə na wassımnita. Tæhak ıl sicak-hæssımnita.	Kuntæ esə na on hu e, tæhak ıl sicak-hæssımnita.
4. Anæ ka ai lıl nahassımnita. Mom i aphəssımnita.	Anæ ka ai lıl nahın hu e, mom i aphəssımnita.
5. Na nın kyəlhon-hæssımnita. Səul e kassımnita.	Na nın kyəlhon-han hu e, Səul e kassımnita.
6. I nyən tongan ənı hwesa esə il-hæssımnita. Cəngpu e tılə wassımnita.	I nyən tongan ənı hwesa esə il-han hu e, cəngpu e tılə wassımnita.
7. Apəci ka tola kasiəssımnita. əməni ka hyəng nim tæk e samnita.	Apəci ka tola kasin hu e, əməni ka hyəng nim tæk e samnita.
8. Pihængki ka ttənassımnita. Kicha ka tahassımnita.	Pihængki ka ttənan hu e, kicha ka tahassımnita.
9. Kı yəca lıl han pən pwassımnita. Kı yəca lıl cohahæssımnita.	Kı yəca lıl han pən pon hu e, kı yəca lıl cohahæssımnita.
10. Kı yəca lıl mannassımnita. Il nyən hu e kyəlhon-hæssımnita.	Kı yəca lıl mannan hu e, il nyən hu e kyəlhon-hæssımnita.

H. Grammar Drill

Tutor: Hakkyo lıl coləp-hako kuntæ e kakessə yo.	'[I]'ll graduate from school and go to the army.'
Student: Hakkyo lıl coləp-han hu e, kuntæ e kakessə yo.	'After graduating from college [I]'ll go to the army.'
1. Hankuk mal ıl məncə pæuko, Hankuk e kalyəko hæ yo.	Hankuk mal ıl məncə pæun hu e, Hankuk e kalyəko hæ yo.
2. Cəmsim ıl məkko, Mikuk Tæsakwan e tıllıkessə yo.	Cəmsim ıl məkın hu e, Mikuk Tæsakwan e tıllıkessə yo.
3. Wekuk esə manhi kukyəng-hako, nænyən ccım e tola okessə yo.	Wekuk esə manhi kukyəng-han hu e, nænyən ccım e tola okessə yo.
4. Uphyənkuk esə phyənci lıl puchiko, kot tapang ılo okessə yo.	Uphyənkuk esə phyənci lıl puchin hu e, kot tapang ılo okessə yo.
5. Wekyokwan i tweko, kyəlhon-hakessə yo.	Wekyokwan i twen hu e, kyəlhon-hakessə yo.

6. Catongcha lıl phalko, wekuk ılo ttənakessə yo.	Catongcha lıl phan hu e, wekuk ılo ttənakessə yo.
7. Chinku eke i chæk ıl cuko, talın chæk ıl patkessə yo.	Chinku eke i chæk ıl cun hu e, talın chæk ıl patkessə yo.
8. Səul lo isa-hako, cip ıl sakessə yo.	Səul lo isa-han hu e, cip ıl sakessə yo.
9. I il ıl kkıth-næko, talın il ıl sicak-hakessə yo.	I il ıl kkıth-næn hu e, talın il ıl sicak-hakessə yo.
10. Com tə sængkak-hako, mal-hakessə yo.	Com tə sængkak-han hu e, mal-hakessə yo.

I. Grammar Drill (Use kkok in the proper place.)

Tutor: Sam nyən tweəssımnita.	'It has been three years.'
Student: Kkok sam nyən tweəssımnita.	'It has been exactly three years.'
1. Cikım han-si imnita.	Cikım kkok han-si imnita.
2. Cə nın kımnyən e səlhın sal imnita.	Cə nın kımnyən e kkok səlhın sal imnita.
3. Onıl pam e uli cip e osipsiyo.	Onıl pam e uli cip e kkok osipsiyo.
4. Kim Sənsæng eke kıləhke mal-hasipsiyo.	Kim Sənsæng eke kkok kıləhke mal-hasipsiyo.
5. Manhi capsusipsiyo.	Kkok manhi capsusipsiyo.
6. Pak Sənsæng eke mulə posipsiyo.	Pak Sənsæng eke kkok mulə posipsiyo.
7. I chæk i cohsımnita.	I chæk i kkok cohsımnita.
8. Han-Yəng sacən ın sakessımnita.	Han-Yəng sacən ın kkok sakessımnita.
9. Næil kkaci tola okessımnita.	Næil kkaci kkok tola okessımnita.
10. Kı il ıl kkıth-næ ya hamnita.	Kı il ıl kkok kkıth-næ ya hamnita.
11. Khəphi lıl masiko siphsımnita.	Khəphi lıl kkok masiko siphsımnita.

J. Transformation Drill

Tutor: Han tal cən e Səul e wassımnita.	'I came to Seoul one month ago.'
Student: Səul e on ci, han tal tweəssımnita.	'It's been one month since I came to Seoul.'
1. Sam nyən cən e tæhakkyo lıl coləp-hæssımnita.	Tæhakkyo lıl coləp-han ci, sam nyən tweəssımnita.

2. O nyən cən e kyəlhon-hæssımnita.	Kyəlhon-han ci, o nyən tweəssımnita.
3. Tu tal cən e Kim Sənsæng i yəki lıl ttənassımnita.	Kim Sənsæng i yəki lıl ttənan ci, tu tal tweəssımnita.
4. Sam-sip pun cən e hakkyo e wassımnita.	Hakkyo e on ci, sam-sip pun tweəssımnita.
5. Il nyən cən e Ceimsı Sənsæng ıl aləssımnita.	Ceimsı Sənsæng ıl an ci, il nyən tweəssımnita.
6. Ne cuil cən e Hankuk mal kongpu lıl sicak-hæssımnita.	Hankuk mal kongpu lıl sicak-han ci, ne cuil tweəssımnita.
7. Tassæ cən e Mikuk e tahassımnita.	Mikuk e tahın ci, tassæ tweəssımnita.
8. Yəlhıl cən e Səul lo isa-hæssımnita.	Səul lo isa-han ci, yəlhıl tweəssimnita.
9. Myəch tal cən e i sikye lıl sassımnita.	I sikye lıl san ci, myəch tal tweəssımnita.
10. Yələ hæ cən e Mikuk ıl ttənassımnita.	Mikuk ıl ttənan ci, yələ hæ tweəssımnita.

K. Response Drill

Tutor: ənce Hankuk e wassımnikka? /tasəs tal/	'When did you come to Korea?' /five months/
Student: Hankuk e on ci, tasəs tal tweəssımnita.	'I have been in Korea for five months.' ('It's been five months since I came to Korea.')
1. ənce Hankuk mal kongpu (lıl) sicak-hæssımnikka? /ne cuil/	Hankuk mal kongpu (lıl) sicak-han ci ne cuil tweəssımnita.
2. ənce kyəlhon-hæssımnikka? /sam nyən/	Kyəlhon-han ci, sam nyən tweəssımnita.
3. ənce wekyokwan i tweəssımnikka? /il nyən pan/	Wekyokwan i twen ci, il nyən pan tweəssımnita.
4. ənce catongcha lıl sassımnikka? /myəchil/	Catongcha lıl san ci, myəchil tweəssımnita.
5. ənce tæhak ıl coləp-hæssımnikka? /sa nyən ccım/	Tæhak ıl coləp-han ci, sa nyən ccım tweəssimnita.
6. ənce hyəng nim ekesə phyənci lıl patəssımnikka? /il cuil/	(Hyəng nim ekesə) phyənci lıl patın ci, il cuil tweəssımnita.

7. ənce halapəci ka tola kasiəssımnikka? /olæ/	Halapəci ka tola kasin ci, olæ tweəssımnita.
8. ənce Səul lo isa-hæssımnikka? /yələ hæ/	Səul lo isa-han ci, yələ hæ tweəssımnita.
9. ənce puthə kı yəca lıl aləssımnikka? /myəch nyən/	Kı yəca lıl an ci, myəch nyən tweəssımnita.
10. ənce hakkyo lıl kımantuəssımnikka? /myəch tal/	Hakkyo lıl kımantun ci, myəch tal tweəssımnita.

L. Response Exercise (Answer the question based on reality.)

Tutor: Hankuk mal ıl pæun ci, əlma na tweəssə yo?	'How long have you studied Korean (by now)?'
Student: Hankuk mal ıl pæun ci, tu tal tweəssımnita.	'I have studied Korean two months.'

1. Tæhakkyo lıl na on ci, əlma na tweəssə yo?
2. Wekyokwan i twen ci, myəch nyən ina tweəssə yo?
3. Kyəlhon-han ci, əlma na tweəssə yo?
4. Kohyang ıl ttənan ci, əlma na tweəssə yo?
5. Puin kwa mannan ci, myəch hæ na tweəssə yo?
6. Tæhak ıl coləp-han ci, myəch nyən ina tweəssə yo?
7. Cəngpu il e tılə on ci, əlma na tweəssə yo?
8. Yəki e san ci, əlma na tweəssə yo?
9. Kuntæ lıl kkıth-machin ci, əlma na tweəssə yo?
10. Mikuk Tæsakwan e kınmu-han ci, əlma na tweəssə yo?

M. Response Exercise (Answer the question based on the fact.)

1. Sənsæng ın kohyang i əti (i)ci yo?
2. Mikuk ənı cu esə osyəssci yo?
3. Sənsæng ın əti esə nahassci yo?
4. Sənsæng ın əti esə calassci yo?
5. Tæhak ın musın tæhak ıl taniəssci yo?
6. Tæhak ın ənce na wassci yo?
7. Kotıng hakkyo nın myəch sal e tılə kassci yo?
8. Kacok ın motu myəch salam ina twesici yo?

9. Ai tıl ın musın hakkyo e tanici yo?
10. Khın ai nın myəch sal ici yo?

N. Grammar Drill (Use acik in the proper place.)

Tutor: Sikye ka ppalımnita.	'The watch is fast.'
Student: Sikye ka acik ppalımnita.	'The watch is still fast.'
1. Hankuk mal pæuki ka əlyəpsımnita.	Hankuk mal pæuki ka acik əlyəpsımnita.
2. Ce tongsæng ın honca imnita.	Ce tongsæng ın acik honca imnita.
3. Kim Sənsæng i samusil esə il-hako issımnita.	Kim Sənsæng i acik samusil esə il-hako issımnita.
4. Na nın cə yəca e ilım ıl molımnita.	Na nın cə yəca e ilım ıl acik molımnita.
5. Kıkcang e salam i manhsımnita.	Kıkcang e acik salam i manhsımnita.
6. Pak Sənsæng ın kimchi lıl cohahamnita.	Pak Sənsæng ın acik kimchi lıl cohahamnita.
7. Cə nın cohın il ıl chacko issımnita.	Cə nın acik cohın il ıl chacko issımnita.
8. Uli hwesa esə nın yosæ to pappımnita.	Uli hwesa esə nın yosæ to acik pappımnita.
9. Apəci nın nai ka kıli manhci anhsımnita.	Apəci nın nai ka acik kıli manhci anhsımnita.
10. Cə e nunim ın cikım to yeppımnita.	Cə e nunim in cikım to acik yeppımnita.

O. Response Drill (Answer the question using acik.)

Tutor: Kulapha e ka pon il i issımnikka?	'Have you ever been in Europe?'
Student: Aniyo, acik (ka pon il i) əpsımnita.	'No, not yet.'
1. Cəmsim ıl capsusyəssımnikka?	Aniyo, acik məkci anhəssımnita.
2. Cip e kal sikan i tweəssımnikka?	Aniyo, acik tweci anhəssımnita.
3. Nui tongsæng ın kyəlhon-hæssımnikka?	Aniyo, acik kyəlhon-haci anhəssimnita.
4. Tongsæng ın tæhak ıl coləp-hæssımnikka?	Aniyo, acik coləp-haci anhəssimnita
5. Samu sikan i kkıth-nassımnikka?	Aniyo, acik kkith-naci anhəssımnita.
6. Səul kanın kicha ka ttənassımnikka?	Aniyo, acik ttənaci anhəssımnita.

7. Yəltu-si ppəsı ka pəlssə tahassımnikka?	Aniyo, acik tahci anhəssımnita.
8. Kulapha lıl yəhæng-han il i issımnikka?	Aniyo, acik yəhæng-han il i əpsımnita.
9. Səul Cungang Kongwən ıl kukyəng-hæssımnikka?	Aniyo, acik kukyəng-haci anhəssımnita.
10. Sæ il ıl chacəssımnikka?	Aniyo, acik chacci anhəssımnita.

P. Response Drill

Tutor: Hankuk e oki cən e, əti esə il-hæssə yo? /Ilpon/	'Where did you work before you came to Korea? /Japan/
Student: Hankuk e oki cən e, Ilpon esə il-hæssımnita.	'I worked in Japan before I came to Korea.'
1. Kyəlhon-haki cən e nuku e·cip esə salassə yo? /pumo nim cip/	Kyəlhon-haki cən e, pumo nim cip esə salassımnita.
2. Kuntæ e kaki cən e, muəs ıl hæssə yo? /tæhak/	Kuntæ e kaki cən e, tæhak e taniəssımnita.
3. Cəmsim ıl məkki cən e, muəs ıl masil kka yo? /mækcu/	Cəmsim ıl məkki cən e, mækcu lıl masipsita.
4. Cikım puin ıl alki cən e, nuku lıl aləssə yo? /talın yəca/	Cikım anæ lıl alki cən e, talın yəca lıl aləssımnita.
5. Wekyokwan i tweki cən e, muəs i tweko siphəssə yo? /tæhak kyosu/	Wekyokwan i tweki cən e, tæhak kyosu ka tweko siphəssımnita.
6. Səul Tæhakkyo e tılə kaki cən e, ənı hakkyo e taniəssə yo? /kotıng hakkyo/	Səul Tæhakkyo e tılə kaki cən e, kotıng hakkyo e taniəssımnita.
7. Phyənci lıl puchiki cən e, muəs ıl sassə yo? /uphyo/	Phyənci lıl puchiki cən e, uphyo lıl sassımnita.

Q. Response Drill (Give a negative answer using /kıləhke/.)

Tutor: Nai ka manhsımnikka?	'Is [he] old?'
Student: Aniyo, kıləhke manhci anhə yo.	'No, not so old.'
1. Nai ka cəksımnikka?	Aniyo, kıləhke cəkci anhə yo.

2. Nal mata pappımnikka?	Aniyo, kılәhke pappıci anhә yo.
3. Sәul cip kaps i pissamnikka?	Aniyo, kilәhke pissaci anhә yo.
4. Kı yәca lıl cohahamnikka?	Aniyo, kilәhke cohahaci anhә yo.
5. Kim Sәnsæng i Yәngә lıl cal hamnikka?	Aniyo, kilәhke cal haci anhә yo.
6. Catongcha ka philyo-hamnikka?	Aniyo, kılәhke philyo-haci anhә yo.
7. Mәli ka aphımnikka?	Aniyo, kilәhke aphıci anhә yo.

EXERCISES

A. Tell the following story about Mr. James to Pak Sәnsæng in Korean:

Mr. James' home is in Chicago but he was born in New York State and grew up there. Until he finished high school he lived in his home town with his parents and brothers and sisters, but he went to college in Boston, Massachusetts. He enjoyed his college life/sænghwal/ very much. After he graduated from the college he worked for a while with a business firm but his work was not very enjoyable. He wanted to become a diplomat, so he took examinations/sihәm ıl pwassımnita/. After that, he was able to join the foreign service right away. It was six years ago. For the first four years he worked in two countries in Europe. While he was in Europe, he could travel in several countries, and saw many interesting places. Since then, Mr. James has been in Korea almost two years now. The weather in Europe is more or less similar to that of Korea. The spring climate in Europe is warm but it rains more than in Korea. The autumn weather there is the same as that of Korea, but in winter it is more snowy and windy. Before he came to Korea, he didn't know much about Korea and the Korean people, but he has been enjoying his work here. He made many Korean friends and learned many Korean customs/phungsok/.

B. Conduct short conversations so that the following expressions are included in the second partner's responses.

1. әnı hwesa	'a (certain company)'
2. әlma tongan	'for some time'
3. kkok	'without fail', 'exactly', 'at all cost'
4. Hankuk e {tæhæ / kwanhæ} sә	'about Korea'
5. tæhak e tanının tongan	'while [I was] attending college'

6. Səul e oki cən e — 'before [I] came to Seoul'
7. wekyokwan i twen hu e — 'since [I] joined the foreign service'

C. Find out from Brown Sənsæng the following information.

1. where he was born.
2. where he grew up.
3. what schools he went to.
4. when he finished college.
5. where he worked first after he graduated from college.
6. why he quit the first job.
7. how long he has been married.
8. how many years he has been with the government.
9. what country he served in before he came to Seoul.
10. how many countries he has travelled in so far.

D. Pak Sənsæng wants to know where you were born and grew up; tell him that you were born at (A) and grew up at (B) :

	(A)	(B)
1.	farm/nongcang/	city
2.	island	mainland
3.	country (or village)	metropolitan area
4.	the East	the South
5.	the Mid-west	the West
6.	North America	South America
7.	overseas	home country/ponkuk/
8.	North Korea	South Korea

E. Prepare a ten-minute narrative autobiography of yourself based on Units 14 and 15 for a fluency drill and tell it to the class, giving such information as your hometown, your schools, some of your experiences, your parents, brothers and sisters, relatives, your immediate family members, their ages, your immediate plans, etc.

End of Tape 11A

Tape 11B

제 16 과 전화

(대화 A)

전화
전화 번호
찾는데

1. 제임스 : 이 선생의 전화 번호를 찾는데 찾을 수(가) 없습니다.

걸읍니다
전화(를) 걸겠읍니다

2. 김 : 전화를 걸려고 하십니까?

전화 걸 일

3. 제임스 : 예, 좀 전화 걸 일이 있읍니다.

전화 번호책

4. 김 : 전화 번호책에 없읍니까?

보입니다
보이지 않습니다
혹, 혹시

5. 제임스 : 보이지 않습니다. 혹시 아세요?

잠간만
수첩
적습니다
적어 두었읍니다

UNIT 16. Telephoning

BADIC DIALOGUES FOR MEMORIZATION

Dialogue A

James

cənhwa	telephone
cənhwa pənho	telephone number
chacnɪn te/channɪnte/	[I]'m looking for [it] and...
1. I Sənsæng e cənhwa pənho lɪl chacnɪn te, chacɪl su (ka) əpsɪmnita.	I'm looking for Mr. Lee's telephone number but I cannot find it.

Kim

kə(lɪ)mnita	('[I] hang [it]')
cənhwa (lɪl) kəlkessɪmnita	[I]'ll make a telephone call
2. Cənhwa kə(l)lyəko hasimnikka?	Are you going to make a phone call?

James

cənhwa kəl il	something to call for
3. Ne, com cənhwa kəl il i issɪmnita.	Yes, I have something to ask him about.

Kim

cənhwa pənho chæk	telephone book
4. Cənhwa pənho chæk e əpsɪmnikka?	Can't you find it in the telephone book? ('Isn't it in the telephone book?')

James

poimnita	I see [it] ('it is seen'); [it] is visible
poici anhsɪmnita	I can't see [it]; [it] is not visible
hok } hoksi }	by any chance?
5. Poici anhsɪmnita. Hoksi ase yo?	I can't find it. Do you happen to know it?

6. 김 : 잠간만 기다리세요. 내 수첩에 적어 두었읍니다.

다행입니다, 다행합니다

7. 제임스 : 아, 다행입니다. 좀 찾아 주십시요.

8. 김 : 예, 여기 이 선생의 회사 번호만 있읍니다.

몇 번

9. 제임스 : 몇 번이지요?

공, 영

10. 김 : 삼의 육 오 공 삼입니다.

(대화 B)

-전화기에서-

11. S : 여보세요.

12. 제임스 : 여보세요. 반도 회사입니까?

예?
들립니다
안 들립니다
크게

13. S : 예? 잘 안 들립니다. 좀 더 크게 말씀 해 주십시요.

Kim

camkan man	just a while; only a short time
suchəp	address book
næ suchəp	my address book
cəksɪmnita	[I] write [it] down
cəkə tuəssɪmnita	[I] wrote [it] down (for future use)
6. Camkan man kitalise yo. Næ suchəp e cəkə tuəssɪmnita.	Just a minute. I wrote it down in my address book.

James

tahæng imnita / tahæng-hamnita	[it] is fortunate
7. A, tahæng imnita. Com chacə cusipsiyo.	Oh, that's lucky. Please look it up for me.

Kim

8. Ne, yəki I Sənsæng (e) hwesa pənho man issɪmnita.	I have only his office number, here.

James

myəch pən/myəppən/	what number
9. Myəch pən ici yo?	What is it? ('What number is it?')

Kim

kong / yəng	zero
10. Sam e yuk o kong sam imnita.	It is 3-6503.

Dialogue B
(..on the telephone..)

S

11. Yəpose yo.	Hello.

James

12. Yəpose yo. Panto Hwesa imnikka?	Hello, is this the Bando Company?

14. 제임스 : 아, 거기 반도 회사이지요?

15. S : 예, 그렇습니다.

바꿉니다
바꿔 주십시요

16. 제임스 : 거기에 이 기수 선생 계시면 좀 바꿔 주십시요.

17. S : 거기는 어데(이)시지요?

18. 제임스 : 미국 대사관의 제임스입니다.

계시는지 보겠읍니다
틈이 계시는지 보겠읍니다

19. S : 잠간만 계십시요. 지금 틈이 계시는지 보겠읍니다.

20. 제임스 : 고맙습니다.

(대화 C)

-전화기에서-

21. 교환수 : 한국 은행입니다.

외환과
부탁
부탁합니다

S

	ne?	(I beg your pardon.)
	tıllimnita	I hear [it] ('[it] is heard'); [it] is audible
	an tıllimnita	I can't hear [you]; [it] is not audible
	khıke	loudly; to be big
13.	Ne? Cal an tıllimnita. Com tə khıke malssım-hæ cusipsiyo.	I beg your pardon! I can't hear you very well. Please speak a little louder.

James

14.	A, kəki Panto Hwesa ici yo?	Oh, isn't this the Bando Company?

S

15.	Ne, kıləhsımnita.	Yes, it is.

James

	pakkumnita	[I] exchange; [I] change
	pakkwə cusipsiyo	please let me talk to.. ('please change it')
16.	Kəki e Lee Kisu Sənsæng kyesimyən com pakkwə cusipsiyo.	May I talk to Mr. Kisu Lee, please? ('If Mr. Kisu Kim is there, please change it.')

S

17.	Kəki nın əti (i)sici yo?	May I ask who is calling, please? ('Where is that place?')

James

18.	Mikuk Tæsakwan e Ceimsı imnita.	This is James at the American Embassy.

S

	kyesinın ci pokessımnita	I'll see if [he] is [in]
	thım i kyesinın ci pokessımnita	I'll see if [he] is free
19.	Camkan man kyesipsiyo. Cikim thım i kyesinın ci pokessımnita.	Wait just a moment, please. I'll see if he's free now.

James

20.	Komapsımnita.	Thank you.

22. 이 : 외환과의 최 선생(에게) 좀 부탁합니다.

통화
통화중
통화중 입니다
돌립니다
돌려 드리겠읍니다

23. 교환수 : 아, 지금 통화중인데요. 잠간 기다리세요.
곧, 돌려 드리겠읍니다. 예, 말씀 하십시오.

24. 이 : 여보세요. 최 준 선생 계십니까?

자리

25. 비서 : 지금 자리에 안 계시는데요. 점심에 나
가셨읍니다.

들어 옵니다

26. 이 : 몇 시에 들어 올지 아십니까?

돌아 옵니다
전합니다
전할 말씀

27. 비서 : 아마, 곧 돌아 올 것입니다. 전할 말씀이
있으시는지요?

28. 이 : 아니요, 괜찮습니다. 이따 다시 걸겠읍니다.

Dialogue C
(..on the telephone..)

Kyohwansu('Operator')

21. Hankuk ınhæng imnita.	Bank of Korea.

Lee

Wehwan Kwa	Foreign Currency Department
puthak	a favor to ask
puthak-hamnita	('I ask you for a favor')
22. Wehwan Kwa e Chwe Sənsæng (eke) com puthak-hamnita.	May I speak to Mr. Choe of the Foreign Currency Department?

Kyohwansu

thonghwa	('telephone talk')
thonghwa cung	('in the middle of telephone talk')
thonghwa cung imnita	line is busy
tollimnita	[I] rotate [it]; [I] switch [it]
tollyə tılikessımnita	I'll switch it for you
23. A, cikım thonghwa cung in te yo. Camkan kitalise yo. Kot tollyə tılikessımnita. Ne, malssım-hasipsiyo.	The line is busy now. Just a moment. I'll connect you right away. O.K., go ahead, please.

Lee

24. Yəpose yo. Chwe Cun Sənsæng kyesimnikka?	Hello, is Mr. Jhoon Choe there?

Pisə

cali	seat
25. Cikım cali e an kyesinın te yo. Cəmsim e na kasyəssımnita.	He is not in his office now. He went out for lunch.

Lee

tılə omnita	[he] comes in
26. Myəch-si e tılə ol ci asimnikka?	Do you know what time he will be back?

<u>Pisə</u>

tola omnita	[he] comes back
cənhamnita	[I] deliver
cənhal malssɪm	message to leave ('words to deliver')

27. Ama, kot tola ol kəs imnita. Cənhal malssɪm i issɪsinɪn ci yo? — He will probably be back soon. Would you like to leave a message for him?

<u>Lee</u>

28. Aniyo, kwænchanhsɪmnita. Itta tasi kəlkessɪmnita. — No, that's all right, thank you. I'll call later.

NOTES ON DIALOGUES

(Numbers correspond to the sentence numbers.)

2. Kəl- is a transitive verb which occurs after a certain object, and has various meanings depending on the object: cənhwa lıl kəl- 'to make a phone call' or 'to telephone'; os ıl kəl- 'to hang up clothes'; ssaum ıl kəl- 'to pick a quarrel' or 'to challenge (to someone)'; ton ıl kəl- 'to bet (money)' or 'to make a deposit'; sængmyəng ıl kəl- 'to risk life', etc.

5. Hok or hoksi 'by any chance', 'do [you] happen to...?' occurs as an adverb in question sentences or in conditional clauses. Poi- 'to be visible' or 'to be seen' is an intransitive verb, whereas po- 'to look at' is a transitive verb.

6. Camkan man ('only a short while') occurs as a time adverbial.

7. Tahæng imnita. ('[It] is a fortunate thing.') is a fixed expression which is used as the Korean equivalent of 'That's fortunate.'.

9. Myəch pən/myəppən/ means either 'what number?' or 'how many times?' in question sentences; 'several times' or '(on) several occasions' in other types of sentences.

13. Ne? which is pronounced with a sharp rising intonation means 'Beg your pardon!' or 'Pardon me!' when you didn't understand someone well; ne? with a prolonged mild rising intonation means 'Oh, is that right?' (Unit 18).

13. The inflected word khıke 'loudly', 'to be big' occurs as an adverbial before another inflected expression (See G. N. 3). Tılli- 'to be audible' or 'to be heard' is an intransitive verb, whereas tıt-~tıl- 'to listen to' or 'to hear' is a transitive verb.

22. Puthak is a noun which means 'a favor to ask'. (Sənsæng eke) puthak i issımnita. means 'I have a favor to ask of you.' Puthak-hamnita. is used to mean, among the more common English equivalents, 'Would you please do it?'; 'Please do it for me.'; 'Yes, please.'; 'Please take care of things.', etc. In telephoning, So-and-so eke com puthak-hamnita. is a fixed expression used something like 'May I speak to so-and-so?' or '(Mr.) so-and-so, please.'

28. Itta 'later' refers to 'the later time on the same day'.

Akka 'a little while ago' is its one-word antonym.

GRAMMAR NOTES

1. -n/ın/nın te 'while...', 'such is the case', 'in view of the fact that...', 'and then...', 'but...'

Remember that the post-noun te 'place' preceded by an inflected modifier word of an action verb occurred previously in the nominal positions (See Note 7 on Basic Dialogues, Unit 12). The selection of -n, -ın or -nın is the same as the present noun-modifier ending (Unit 5). Remember, however, -n/ın/nın te, -n/ın te and -l/ıl te should be distinguished. Examples:

(a)	il-hanın te	'the place where [I] work'
	məknın te	'the eating place'
(b)	kan te	'the place where [I] went'
	calan te	'the place where [I] grew up'
(c)	tıllıl te	'the place to stop by'
	sal te	'the place where [I] shall live'

Note that the construction -n/ın/nın te which may be followed by a pause may also occur before another inflected expression to signify some further explanation or remark in relation to or on the basis of the first action or description follows in the following inflected expression. The honorific and/or tense suffixes may occur in the -nın form of which inflected forms are the same in shapes for both action and description verbs: -(a,ə)ssnın te, for the past; -kessnın te, for the future. Observe the following examples:

Hankuk mal ıl pæunın te, sikan i manhi kəllimnita.	'When (or In) studying Korean it takes a lot of time.' / '[I]'m studying Korean and it takes a lot of time.'
Catongcha lıl sanın te, ton i philyohamnita.	'When buying a car [you] need money.'
I Sənsæng ıl chac(ı)nın te, chacıl su (ka) əpsımnita.	'[I]'m looking for Mr. Lee, but [I] cannot find him.'
Cə nın pæ ka kophın te, sənsæng ın pæ ka kophıci anhə yo?	'I am hungry; are you not?'

Ce sachon ın cocongsa in te, ton ıl manhi pələ yo. — 'My cousin is a pilot, and he makes ('earns') a lot of money?'

Cən e Ilpon mal ıl pæwəssnın te, cikım ın ta icəssımnita. — 'I studied Japanese before but I have forgotten [it] all now.'

Kı yəca ka hakkyo ttæ e phək yeppəssnın te, acik to kıləhci yo? — 'She was very pretty in her school days; she must be still pretty, isn't she?'

Næil nalssi ka cohkessnın te, əti e kal kka yo? — '(It seems) the weather will be nice tomorrow; shall we go someplace?'

-n/ın/nın te + yo may occur to end a sentence which, in this case, is a kind of informal polite statement sentence. The sentence final -n/ın/nın te yo occurs when the speaker shows slight surprise or hesitation.

Cham, cə pihængki ka ppalın te yo. — 'O, that airplane is really fast.'

Ceimsı Sənsæng i Hankuk mal ıl cal hanın te yo. — 'Mr. James speaks good Korean.'

Aniyo, cal molıkessnın te yo. — 'No, I don't know [it] well.'

2. Infinitive + {tu- / noh-}

As an independant verb, tu- or its synonym noh- means 'to put [something] (somewhere)' or 'to place [something] (somewhere)'.

However, tu- (or noh-) preceded by the infinitive of an action verb also occurs as an auxiliary verb. The verb phrase Infinitive + tu- which literally means something like 'does so-and-so and put [it] somehwere' is usually used to denote 'does so-and-so for future use or benefit' or 'does so-and-so in advance', or 'does so-and-so for the time being'. Compare the following pairs:

a. Han-Yəng sacən ıl sassımnita. — 'I bought a Korean-English dictionary.'

Han-Yəng sacən ıl sa tuəssımnita. — 'I have bought a Korean-English dictionary (for future use).'

b. Næil ın hal il i manhkessıni kka, onıl i il ıl ta kkıth-nækessımnita. — 'Since I'll have many things to do tomorrow, I will finish all this work today.'

Næil ın hal il i manhkessıni kka, onıl i il ıl ta kkıth-næ tukessımnita. — 'Since I'll have many things to do tomorrow, I will finish up all this work today (in advance).'

c. Sukce lıl hæ ya hamnita. — '[I] have to do homework.'

Sukce lıl hæ tuə ya hamnita. — '[I] have to do homework now {in advance. / (for some reason).}

d. Kim Cangkun e cənhwa pənho lɨl alə pwassɨmnikka? — 'Did you find out General Kim's telephone number?'

Kim Cangkun e cənhwa pənho lɨl alə pwa tuəssɨmnikka? — 'Have you found out General Kim's telephone number (for future use or in case)?'

3. -ke

The inflected form ending in -ke (or simply the -ke form) occurs before and modifies another inflected expression. Since the -ke form occurs as an adverbial, the ending -ke is called the Adverbializing Ending or simply the Adverbializer. The -ke form occurs in the following constructions:

(a) A description verb inflected in -ke occurs as a modifier before another inflected expression of an action verb.

Alɨmtapke calamnita.	'[It] is growing beautifully.'
Cohke mal-hæssə yo.	'[He] spoke well of [you].' / '[He] spoke nicely.'
Kɨləhke haci masipsiyo.	'Don't do it that way.'
Pissake sassɨmnita.	'I paid much for it.' ('I bought [it] to be expensive.')
Khɨke malssɨm hasipsiyo.	'Please speak loud.'

(b) An action verb inflected in -ke which may occur without a pause immediately before ha- is used with a causative meaning, of which English translations are {have / make / let} [someone] do...'. The personal nominal + {eke / ɨl/lɨl} may or may not precede the -ke ha- construction.

Kake hæssɨmnita.	'[I] had [him] go.'
Ai eke cake hasipsiyo.	'Please have the child go to bed.'
Cəngpu ka na eke wekukə lɨl pæuke hamnita.	'The government makes me study foreign languages.'

Note: As for the other contruction types where the -ke form occurs (e.g. -ke twe-) we will learn in further units.

4. -n/ın/nın ci

We learned that the construction, an interrogative + an inflected modifier word + the dependent noun ci, before an inflected expression occurs as a nominal expression (See Grammar Note 3, Unit 13).

The construction -n/ın/nın ci without being preceded by an interrogative may also occur as a nominal expression. If -n/ın/nın ci occurs as the object of the following inflected expression, the object particle ıl/lıl is usually omitted. The construction -n/ın/nın ci is used as the equivalent of the English nominal clauses which begin with 'if-', 'whether-' or 'that-'. Examples:

Kim Sənsæng i kyesinın ci pokessımnita.	'I'll see if Mr. Kim is in.'
Cip kaps i pissan ci alko siphsımnita.	'I want to know whether the rent is high.'
Sikan i manhi kəllinın ci alə posipsiyo.	'Please find out if it takes a lot of time.'
Miss Brown i Səul e sanın ci mollassımnita.	'I didn't know whether Miss Brown is living in Seoul.' / 'I didn't know that Miss Brown is living in Seoul.'

The honorific and/or tense suffixes may occur in the -n/ın/nın form in the above onstruction: -(a,ə)ssnın ci for the past, -kessnın (or its substitute -(ı)l ci for the future, respectively. Note that an inflected modifier word (e.g. -n/ın/nın) + ci + yo? may be used as a kind of informal polite question sentence final form. This form of a question sentence occurs only in a dialogue after a certain context has been established to denote the speaker's doubt or modesty. Examples:

(Hoksi) cənhal malssım i issısinın ci yo?	'Would you leave a message (by any chance)?' / 'May I take your message, sir?' / 'I wonder if you'd like to leave a message.'
Kəki nın nuku isin ci yo?	('As for there, who are you?') / 'May I ask whom I am speaking to?' / 'Who is speaking, please?'
Kıləm, Wəllam mal ın swiun ci yo?	'Well, is Vietnamese easy, then?'
Kılsse yo. Tangsin i Kimchi lıl cohahal ci yo?	'Well, I'm afraid if you'll like Kimchi.'
Hoksi sæ tæsa lıl mannasiəssnın ci yo?	'I wonder if you have met the new ambassador, sir.'

DRILLS

A. Substıtutıon Drıll

1.	Chæk i poici anhsımnita.	I cannot find the book ('The book is not seen.')
2.	Cənhwa pənho ka poici anhsımnita.	I cannot find the telephone number.
3.	(Næ) suchəp i poici anhsımnita.	I cannot find my address book.
*4.	(Næ) cikap i poici anhsımnita.	I cannot find my wallet.
5.	(Næ) kapang i poici anhsımnita.	I cannot find my briefcase.
6.	Ton i poici anhsımnita.	I cannot find money.
*7.	Ipku ka poici anhsımnita.	I cannot find the entrance.
*8.	Pata ka poici anhsımnita.	I cannot see the sea.
*9.	(Næ) cangkap i poici anhsımnita.	I cannot find my gloves.

B. Substitution Drill

1.	Cənhwa pənho lıl chacıl su (ka) əpsnın te yo.	I cannot find the telephone number.
2.	Næ suchəp ıl chacıl su (ka) əpsnın te yo.	I cannot find my address book.
*3.	Kı e cuso lıl chacıl su (ka) əpsnın te yo.	I cannot find his address.
*4.	Il cali lıl chacıl su (ka) əpsnın te yo.	I cannot find a job.
*5.	Cohın kihwe lıl chacıl su (ka) əpsnın te yo.	I cannot find a good chance.
*6.	Ton cikap ıl chacıl su (ka) əpsnın te yo.	I cannot find the (money) wallet.
*7.	Sikmo lıl chacıl su (ka) əpsnın te yo.	I cannot find a maid.
*8.	Chulku lıl chacıl su (ka) əpsnın te yo.	I cannot find the exit.
*9.	Ipku lıl chacıl su (ka) əpsnın te yo.	I cannot find the entrance.
*10.	Chulipku lıl chacıl su (ka) əpsnın te yo.	I cannot find the exit-entrance.

C. Substitution Drill

1.	Sənsæng e mal (soli) i/ka cal tıllimnita.	I [can] hear you well. ('Your speech (sound) is well heard.')
2.	Tangsin e mal (soli) i/ka cal tıllimnita.	I [can] hear you well.
3.	Kyosu e mal (soli) i/ka cal tıllimnita.	I [can] hear the professor well.
4.	Sangkwan e mal (soli) i/ka cal tıllimnita.	I [can] hear well what my boss says.
*5.	Latiyo soli ka cal tıllimnita.	I [can] hear the radio clearly.
*6.	Pihængki soli ka cal tıllimnita.	I [can] hear the airplane well.
*7.	Palam soli ka cal tıllimnita.	I hear the wind (well).
*8.	Kicha soli ka cal tıllimnita.	I hear the train (well).
*9.	Pal soli ka cal tıllimnita.	I hear the footsteps (well).
*10.	Mok soli ka cal tıllimnita.	I [can] hear [your] voice clearly.
*11.	Salam soli ka cal tıllimnita.	I hear the voices (well).

D. Substitution Drill

1.	Kim Sənsæng eke com pakkwə cusipsiyo.	May I speak to Mr. Kim? ('Exchange [it] to Mr. Kim.')
*2.	Kim Paksa eke com pakkwə cusipsiyo.	May I speak to Dr. (Ph.D.) Kim?
*3.	Kim Kyosu eke com pakkwə cusipsiyo.	May I speak to Professor Kim?
*4.	Kim Hakcang eke com pakkwə cusipsiyo.	May I speak to Dean Kim?
*5.	Kim Chongcang eke com pakkwə cusipsiyo.	May I speak to President (of university) Kim?
*6.	Kim Sacang eke com pakkwə cusipsiyo.	May I speak to President (of company) Kim?
*7.	Kim Cangkun eke com pakkwə cusipsiyo.	May I speak to General Kim?
*8.	Kim Phansa eke com pakkwə cusipsiyo.	May I speak to Judge Kim?
*9.	Kim Cangkwan eke com pakkwə cusipsiyo.	May I speak to Minister (in the government) Kim?
*10.	Kim Kyocang eke com pakkwə cusipsiyo.	May I speak to Principal Kim?
*11.	Kim Moksa eke com pakkwə cusipsiyo.	May I speak to Minister (of the church) Kim?

*12. <u>Kim Kwacang</u> eke com pakkwə cusipsiyo.	May I speak to Mr. ('Section Chief') Kim?
*13. <u>Kim Kukcang</u> eke com pakkwə cusipsiyo.	May I speak to Mr. ('Bureau Chief') Kim?
*14. <u>Kim (Kukhwe) ıywən</u> eke com pakkwə cusipsiyo.	May I speak to Congressman ('National Assembly Member') Kim?

E. Substitution Drill

1. Com tə khıke malssım hæ cusipsiyo.	Please speak a little louder.
*2. <u>Com tə chənchənhi</u> malssım hæ cusipsiyo.	Please speak a little more slowly.
*3. <u>Com tə ppalli</u> malssım hæ cusipsiyo.	Please speak a little faster.
*4. <u>Com tə cakke</u> malssım hæ cusipsiyo.	Please speak a little more softly.
*5. <u>Com tə coyonghi</u> malssım hæ cusipsiyo.	Please speak a little more quietly.
*6. <u>Com tə sokhi</u> malssım hæ cusipsiyo.	Please speak a little more quickly.
*7. <u>Com tə khın soli lo</u> malssım hæ cusipsiyo.	Please speak a little louder ('in a big voice').
8. <u>Tasi han pən</u> malssım hæ cusipsiyo.	Please say [it] once more ('once again').
*9. <u>Maım tælo</u> malssım hæ cusipsiyo.	{Please say as you like. Please say freely.

F. Substitution Drill

1. Kim Sənsæng i kyesinın ci pokessımnita.	I'll see if Mr. Kim is [in].
2. Kim Sənsæng i kyesinın ci <u>alə pokessımnita</u>.	I'll find out if Mr. Kim is [in].
3. Kim Sənsæng i kyesinın ci <u>mulə pokessımnita</u>.	I'll inquire if Mr. Kim is [in].
4. Kim Sənsæng i kyesinın ci <u>chacə pokessımnita</u>.	I'll try looking for Mr. Kim.
5. Kim Sənsæng i kyesinın ci <u>cənhwa-hakessımnita</u>.	I'll call [to see] if Mr. Kim is in.

6. Kim Sənsæng i kyesinın ci molıkessımnita.	I do not know if Mr. Kim is in.
7. Kim Sənsæng i kyesinın ci alko siphsımnita.	I'd like to know if Mr. Kim is in.
8. Kim Sənsæng i kyesinın ci allyə cusipsiyo.	Please let me know if Mr. Kim is in.

G. Substitution Drill

1. Kim Sənsæng i kyesinın ci alko siphsımnita.	I'd like to know if Mr. Kim is [in].
2. Pak Sənsæng i osinın ci alko siphsımnita.	I'd like to know if Mr. Park comes.
3. Pak Sənsæng i osinın ci molımnita.	I don't know if Mr. Park comes.
4. Sikan i manhi kəllinın ci molımnita.	I don't know if it takes a lot of time.
5. Sikan i manhi kəllinın ci mulə pokessımnita.	I'll ask if it takes a lot of time.
*6. Khıki ka kathın ci mulə pokessımnita.	I'll ask if the size is the same.
7. Khıki ka kathın ci alə pokessımnita.	I'll find out if the size is the same.
8. Kı pun i aphın ci alə pokessımnita.	I'll find out if he (honored) is sick.
9. Kı pun i aphın ci cənhwa-hæ pokessımnita.	I'll try calling to see if he is sick.

H. Substitution Drill

1. Kim Sənsæng i əti e sanın ci molımnita.	I don't know where Mr. Kim lives.
2. Cə puin i muəs ıl hanın ci molımnita.	I don't know what the lady does.
3. Tæthongyəng i myəch sal in ci molımnita.	I don't know how old the President is.
4. Kim Paksa ka nuku lıl chacnın ci molımnita.	I don't know whom Dr. Kim is looking for.
5. Sikmo ka muəs ıl wənhanın ci molımnita.	I don't know what the maid wants.
6. Sangkwan i ənce tola onın ci molımnita.	I don't know when [my] boss is coming back.

7. Sangkwan i ənce tola onın ci amnita.	I know when [my] boss is coming back.
8. Sangkwan i ənce tola onın ci alko siphsımnita.	I'd like to know when [my] boss is coming back.
*9. Sangkwan i ənce tola onın ci allyə cusipsiyo.	Please let [me] know when [your] boss is coming.

I. Substitution Drill

1. Chæk ıl ıyca e tuəssımnita.	I have put the book on the chair.
2. Ai lıl cip e tuəssımnita.	I have left the child at home.
3. Kapang ıl cha e tuəssımnita.	I have left the briefcase in the car.
4. Cikap ıl pang e tuəssımnita.	I have left my wallet in the room.
*5. Cha lıl chako e tuəssımnita.	I have left the car in the garage.
*6. Catongcha lıl cuchacang e tuəssımnita.	I have left the automobile in the parking lot.
*7. Cacənkə lıl untongcang e tuəssımnita.	I have left the bicycle in the playground.
*8. Cha lıl pakk e tuəssımnita.	I have left the car outside.
*9. Kong ıl an e tuəssımnita.	I left the ball inside.
*10. Kong ıl cəngwən e tuəssımnita.	I left the ball in the yard.
*11. Kılıs ıl puəkh e tuəssımnita.	I left the dish in the kitchen.

J. Grammar Drill (Use hoksi in the proper place.)

Tutor: Kim Sənsæng e cənhwa pənho lıl ase yo?	'Do you know Mr. Kim's telephone number?'
Student: Kim Sənsæng e cənhwa pənho lıl hoksi ase yo?	{'Do you know Mr. Kim's telephone number, by any chance? 'Do you happen to know Mr. Kim's telephone number?'

1. Tæthongyəng ıl mannassə yo?	Tæthongyəng ıl hoksi mannassə yo?
2. Cungkuk ımsik ıl məkə pon il i issə yo?	Cungkuk ımsik ıl hoksi məkə pon il i issə yo?
3. Sənsæng ın Panto Hwesa e kınmu-hase yo?	Sənsæng ın hoksi Panto Hwesa e kınmu-hase yo?
4. Cikım thım i kyese yo?	Cikım hoksi thım i kyese yo?

5. Kı pun i myəch-si e tola ol ci ase yo?	Kı pun i myəch-si e tola ol ci hoksi ase yo?
6. Ohu e sinæ e tıllıkessə yo?	Hoksi ohu e sinæ e tıllıkessə yo?
7. Kim Sənsæng e cuso lıl cəkə tuəssə yo?	Hoksi Kim Sənsæng e cuso lıl cəkə tuəssə yo?
8. Kimchi lıl capsusin cək i issə yo?	Hoksi kimchi lıl capsusin cək i issə yo?

K. Transformation Drill

Tutor: Kı e ilım ıl cəkəssımnita.	'I wrote his name.'
Student: Kı e ilım ıl cəkə tuəssımnita.	'I wrote his name down (for future use).'
1. Ssan kutu lıl sassə yo.	Ssan kutu lıl sa tuəssə yo.
2. Cən e Hankuk mal ıl pæwəssə yo.	Cən e Hankuk mal ıl pæwə tuəssə yo.
3. Inchən kanın kil ıl mulə pwassə yo.	Inchən kanin kil il mulə pwa tuəssə yo.
4. Yəl-han-si e cəmsim ıl məkəssə yo.	Yəl-han-si e cəmsim il məkə tuəssə yo.
5. Kim Sənsæng eke puthak-hæssə yo.	Kim Sənsæng eke puthak-hæ tuəssə yo.
6. Kim Sənsæng e cuso lıl aləssə yo.	Kim Sənsæng e cuso lıl alə tuəssə yo.
7. Ton ıl ınhæng e nəhəssə yo.	Ton ıl ınhæng e nəhə tuəssə yo.
8. Pam e phyənci lıl ssəssə yo.	Pam e phyənci lıl ssə tuəssə yo.
9. Il ıl ppalli kkıth-machiəssə yo.	Il ıl ppalli kkıth-machiə tuəssə yo.

L. Combination Drill (Make one sentence out of two in the pattern as in the example.)

Tutor: Cənhwa pənho lıl chacsımnita. Poici anhsımnita.	'I'm looking for the telephone number.' 'I cannot find it.'
Student: Cənhwa pənho lıl chacnin te, poici anhsımnita.	'I'm looking for the telephone number, but I cannot find it.'
1. Hankuk mal ıl pæumnita. Acik cal mal-haci mot hamnita.	Hankuk mal ıl pæunın te, acik cal mal-haci mot hamnita.
2. Palam i pumnita. Kıli chupci anhsımnita.	Palam i punın te, kıli chupci anhsımnita.
3. Cə yəca wa insa-hæssımnita. Ilım ıl molıkessımnita.	Cə yəca wa insa-hæssnın te, ilım ıl molıkessımnita.

4. Cəmsim ıl məkəssımnita. Tasi pæ ka kophımnita. — Cəmsim ıl məkəssnın te, tasi pæ ka kophımnita.
5. Catongcha lıl sako siphsımnita. Ton i əpsımnita. — Catongcha lıl sako siphın te, ton i əpsımnita.
6. Cə nın Səul pukın e samnita. Nal mata kicha lo il-halə omnita. — Cə nın Səul pukın e sanın te, nal mata kicha lo il-halə omnita.
7. Pak Sənsæng eke cənhwa lıl kəlləssımnita. Amu to patci anhəssımnita. — Pak Sənsæng eke cənhwa lıl kələssnın te, amu to patci anhəssımnita.
8. Cip esə hakkyo ka phək məmnita. I Sənsæng ın kələ sə tanimnita. — Cip esə hakkyo ka phək mən te, I Sənsæng ın kələ sə tanimnita.
9. Onil kkaci il ıl kkıth-næ ya hamnita. Sikan i pucok-hamnita. — Onıl kkaci il ıl kkıth-næ ya hanın te, sikan i pucok-hamnita.

M. Completion Exercise

Tutor: Cə nın Hankuk mal ıl pæunın te, — 'I am studying Korean but (<u>or</u> and)...

Student: Cə nın Hankuk mal ıl pæunın te, acik cal mal-haci mot hamnita. — 'I'm studying Korean but I can't speak it well yet.'

1. Catongcha lıl sako siphın te,
2. Cəmsim ıl məkəssnın te,
3. Hal il i manhın te,
4. Yəca chinku ka aphın te,
5. Hakkyo ka mən te,
6. Hankuk mal i phək əlyəun te,
7. Cip e cənhwa lıl kələssnın te,
8. Hyəng nim i Səul lo isa-hæssnın te,
9. Ton i com philyo-han te,
10. Palam i manhi punın te,

N. Grammar Drill (Use <u>itta</u> in the proper place and repeat after the teacher.)

Tutor: Tasi kəlkessımnita. — 'I'll call again.'

Student: Itta tasi kəlkessımnita. — 'I'll call again later.'

1. Tola osipsiyo. — Itta tola osipsiyo.

2. Chənchənhi ttənalyəko hamnita.	Itta chənchənhi ttənalyəko hamnita.
3. Tto pwepkessımnita.	Itta tto pwepkessımnita.
4. Tapang esə mannapsita.	Itta tapang esə mannapsita.
5. Kim Sənsæng i tıllıl kəs imnita.	Kim Sənsæng i itta tıllıl kəs imnita.
6. Kathi kal kka yo?	Itta kathi kal kka yo?
7. Khəphi han can sa cuse yo.	Itta khəphi han can sa cuse yo.
8. Tto wa to kwænchanhsımnikka?	Itta tto wa to kwænchanhsımnikka?
9. Sikan i issımyən, pwa ya hakessımnita.	(Itta) sikan i issımyən, (itta) pwa ya hakessımnita.

O. Grammar Drill (Use akka in the proper place and repeat after the teacher.)

Tutor: Cə nın cəmsim ıl məkəssımnita.	'I ate lunch.'
Student: Cə nın akka cəmsim ıl məkəssımnita.	'I ate lunch a little while ago.'
1. Kim Sənsæng ın ttənassımnita.	Kim Sənsæng ın əkka ttənassımnita.
2. Lætio esə kı mal ıl tıləssımnita.	Akka lætio esə kı mal ıl tıləssımnita.
3. I Paksa wa cənhwa lo mal-hæssımnita.	I Paksa wa cənhwa lo akka mal-hæssımnita.
4. Il ıl ta kkıth-machiəssımnita.	Il ıl akka ta kkıth-machiəssımnita.
5. Pi ka oki sicak-hæssımnita.	Pi ka akka oki sicak-hæssımnita.
6. Cə nın com swiəssımnita.	Cə nın akka com swiəssımnita.
7. Chinku ekesə cənhwa lıl patəssımnita.	Chinku ekesə akka cənhwa lıl patəssımnita.

EXERCISES

A. Read aloud the following telephone numbers:

1. 3-7506	8. 73-0193
2. 5-2673	9. 567-7065
3. 4-0407	10. 370-8731
4. 2-9716	11. 672-0409
5. 3-3654	12. 490-2089
6. 22-3402	13. 903-4356
7. 23-9781	14. 633-0295

B. Make a short statement in Korean for each of the following:

1. Dr. (Ph.D.) Kim
2. Professor Park
3. Dean Koh
4. President (of a university) Yoon
5. General Choe
6. Minister (of the Government) Lee
7. Judge Whang
8. Principal James
9. Reverand Yoo
10. President (of a company) Choe
11. Doctor Park
12. Mr. (chief of the department) Pae
13. Mr. (chief of the bureau) Seo
14. Senator/Sangwən ıywən/ Kennedy
15. Representative ('National Assembly Member') Kim
16. Mr. Kim's driver
17. a maid
18. your boss
19. a banker/ınhængka/
20. a politician/cəngchika/
21. a farmer/nongpu/
22. a laborer/notongca/
23. a businessman/saəpka/
24. a guest (or visitor)/sonnim/
25. the owner/cuin/

C. Telephone rings; answer it and say as follows:

1. 'Hello!'
2. 'I'm sorry but I can't hear you well.'
3. 'Please speak a little louder.'
4. 'One moment, please, the line is busy now.'
5. 'You have the wrong number but I'll connect you to his office in a minute.'
6. 'May I ask who is calling, please?'
7. 'Please wait just one second: he is on the line now.'
8. 'O.K.'

D. Call the Bank of Korea and conduct the following conversation:

	Secretary	You
1.	'Hello, Bank of Korea!'	'Hello, may I speak to Mr. Choe of the Foreign Currency Section?'
2.	'I'm sorry but he is not in the office now.'	'Do you happen to know where he has gone?'
3.	'Yes. He went out for lunch with a friend.'	'Do you know what time he'll be back?'
4.	'It's been nearly an hour since he left the office, so he'll be back soon. Do you want to leave a message?'	'No, that's all right. I have something to say to him directly /cikcəp/. I'll call again in about a half an hour.'
5.	'O.K., then, please do so.'	'Thank you.'

E. Make short dialogues so that the second partner uses the following expressions in his response:

1.	maım tælo	'as one pleases'
2.	tasi han pən	'once more'
3.	cohın kihwe	'a good chance'
4.	il cali	'a job'
5.	coyonghi	'quietly'
6.	com tə khıke	'a little more loudly'
7.	allyə cusipsiyo	'let [someone] know'
8.	khıki	'size'
9.	(ton) cikap	'wallet'
10.	pal soli	'foot-steps'
11.	itta	'later'
12.	akka	'a little while ago'
13.	chənchənhi	'slowly'
14.	camkan man	'just a moment'
15.	Puthak-hamnita.	'Yes, please.'

F. For each of the following pairs of words make short statements in Korean which include both words:

1. car: garage
2. automobile: parking lot
3. bicycle: playground
4. children: the outside
5. ball: the inside
6. dishes: kitchen
7. kids: yard (<u>or</u> garden)
8. address book: pocket/(ho)cumənI/
9. wallet: briefcase
10. Mr. Kim's address: his telephone number

G. Tell the class that:

1. you've jotted down Mr. Kim's address and telephone number.
2. you've deposited money in the bank.
3. you can hear the airplane well.
4. you've left the car on the street.
5. you don't know whom Dr. Kim is looking for.
6. you can answer any questions from the students.
7. you'll call the doctor a little while later.
8. you heard about the story just a little wile ago.

<u>End of Tape 11B</u>

Tape 12A

제 17 과 전화 (계속)

(대화 A)

(김 선생 부인은 부엌에 있다.)

엄마

1. 어린 딸: 엄마! 전화 왔어요.

받어라

너

네가

왔니

2. 어머니: 어디에서 왔니? 네가 받어라.

아빠

3. 어린 딸: 어느 분이 아빠를 찾어요.

4. 어머니: 그럼, 잠간만 기다려라. 곧 들어 가겠다.

(대화 B)

-조금 후에-

5. 미씨스 김: 여보세요.

댁

6 제임스: 여보세요. 김 기수 선생 댁입니까?

7. 미씨스 김: 예, 그렇습니다.

UNIT 17. Telephoning (Continued)

BASIC DIALOGUES FOR MEMORIZATION

Dialogue A

(..James tries to reach Mr. Kim..)
(Mrs. Kim is in the kitchen.)

Little Daughter

əmma	Mommy
1 əmma! Cənhwa wassə yo.	Telephone, Mommy!

Mother

patəla	receive [it]
nə	you (Plain Speech)
ne ka	you (Subject in Plain Speech)
wassni/wanni/	has [it] come?
2. əti esə wassni? Ne ka patəla.	Where is it? You get it.

Little Daughter

appa	Daddy
3. ənı pun i appa lıl chacə yo.	Somebody wants Daddy.

Mother

4. Kıləm, camkan man kitalyəla. Kot tılə kakessta.	Well, just a minute. I'm coming in right away.

Dialogue B

(..a little later..)

Mrs. Kim

5. Yəpose yo.	Hello.

James

tæk	home; residence
6. Yəpose yo. Kim Kisu Sənsæng tæk imnikka?	Is this Mr. Kisu Kim's residence?

Mrs. Kim

7. Ne, kıləhsımnita.	Yes, it is.

8. 제임스: 지금, 김 선생 댁에 계세요?

아이구

조금 전에

9. 미시즈 김: 아이구! 조금 전에 나 가셨는데요.
누구(이)시지요?

제임스(이)라고 합니다

10. 제임스: 김 선생의 친구입니다. (저는) 제임스(이)라고
합니다.

선생에 대해서, 선생에 관해서

이야기, 얘기

이야기 들었읍니다

11. 미시즈 김: 아, 그러세요? 선생에 대해서 이야기 많이
들었읍니다. 저는 미시즈 김입니다.

간다고 (말)합니다

12. 제임스: 그러세요? 전화로 실례합니다. 김 선생,
어디에 간다고 (말)했읍니까?

약속

만날 약속이 있읍니다

13. 미시즈 김: 친구와 만날 약속이 있다고 (말씀)하셨읍니다.
그리고, 다섯 시까지 집에 오겠다고 했어요.

14. 제임스: 그러면, 다시 걸겠읍니다.

James

8\. Cikım, Kim Sənsæng, tæk e kyese yo? — Is Mr. Kim at home now?

Mrs. Kim

aiku — Gee!; Oh!

cokım cən e — a little while ago

9\. Aiku! Cokım cən e na kasyəssnın te yo. Nuku (i)sici yo? — I'm sorry. He went out just a minute ago. Who is calling, please?

James

Ceimsı (i)lako hamnita — [they] say that [I]'m James

10\. Kim Sənsæng e chinku imnita. (Cə nın) Ceimsı (i)lako hamnita. — I'm Mr. James, a friend of Mr. Kim's.

Mrs. Kim

sənsæng e {tæhæ sə / kwanhæ sə} — about you; about teacher; concerning you

{yæki / iyaki} — story

iyaki tıləssımnita — I heard (the story)

11\. A, kıləse yo? Sənsæng e tæhæ sə iyaki manhi tıləssımnita. Cə nın Missisı Kim imnita. — Oh, yes? He has told me about you. ('I heard a lot about you.') I am Mrs. Kim.

James

kanta ko (mal-)hamnita — [they] say that [they] go

12\. Kıləse yo! Cənhwa lo sillye-hamnita. Kim Sənsæng, əti e kanta ko (mal-)hæssımnikka? — Is that so! Pardon me for calling. Did he say where he was going?

Mrs. Kim

yaksok — appointment, date

mannal yaksok i issımnita — [I] have an appointment to meet (someone)

13\. Chinku wa mannal yaksok i issta ko (malssım-)hasyəssımnita. Kıliko, tasəs-si kkaci cip e okessta ko hæssə yo. — He said that he has an appointment to meet with a friend. And he said that he'll come home by 5 o'clock.

전화하라고 (말)합니다

15. 미시스 김: 선생에게 전화하라고 말할까요?

말씀해 주십시요

16. 제임스: 그저, 제가 전화했다고 말씀해 주십시요.

17. 미시스 김: 예, 알겠읍니다. 그렇게 하겠읍니다.

18. 제임스: 그럼, 안녕히 계십시요.

19. 미시스 김: 고맙습니다. 안녕히 계세요.

James

14. Kıləmyən, tasi kəlkessımnita. — Well, I will call again.

Mrs. Kim

cənhwa-hala ko (mal-)hamnita — [he] tells [me] to call [him]

15. Sənsæng eke cənhwa-hala ko mal-hal kka yo? — Shall I tell [him] to call you?

James

malssım-hæ cusipsiyo — please tell [him]

16. Kıcə, ce ka cənhwa-hæssta ko malssım-hæ cusipsiyo. — Just tell him that I called.

Mrs. Kim

17. Ne, alkessımnita. Kıləhke hakessımnita. — Yes, I understand. I'll do so

James

18. Kıləm, annyənghi kyesipsiyo. — Goodbye, then.

Mrs. Kim

19. Komapsımnita. Annyənghi kyese yo. — Thank you. Goodbye.

NOTES ON DIALOGUES

(Numbers correspond to the sentence numbers.)

1.3. əmma 'Mommy' and appa 'Daddy' are the words frequently used by children. Girls use them much more than boys.

9. Aiku! 'Gee!' or 'Oh!' is a kind of exclamatory expression which indicates the speaker's surprise, delight, disappointment or helplessness, depending on the situation.

11. Iyaki ('story') and its contracted form yæki is used as a synonym of mal in all environments. Iyaki-ha- is equally interchangeable with mal-ha-.

12. Yaksok means either 'a promise' or 'an appointment (to meet someone)'. Its verb yaksok-ha- means 'to promise' or 'to make an appointment'.

GRAMMAR NOTES

Plain Speech: Formal and Informal

So far we have had the Polite Speech (Formal and Informal). As was mentioned in Units 2, 3, 4 the Polite Speech is the speech level spoken to the adults and/or the seniors in rank (e.g. age, school-grade, job, military, social status, etc.) in the hierarchy of the Korean social system. In general, a foreigner is expected to use the Polite Speech no matter who he speaks to, regardless of his age or status. At the same time he is spoken to in the Polite Speech. However, there is another commonly used speech level or style spoken to or among the children, which we shall call Plain Speech. Just like the Polite Speech, the Plain Speech has formal and informal styles, both of which are no different in level but are different only in the inflected forms of verbs at the end of the sentences. The two styles are usually mixed in one's speech. It is not easy to draw a strict line as to who uses the Plain Speech to whom, but it is very important to recognize the relationships of the two people by the speech levels they use each other. The following are the general rules governing how Plain Speech is used:

(a) The parents to their own children of any age.

(b) The older siblings in the family to the younger ones, or both another if there is little difference in age.

(c) The adults to the children of others who are under or around their teen age.

(d) Among the old and present classmates of all school ages (even in their adult life Plain Speech is often maintained).

(e) Among the friends of childhood or boyhood.

(f) The teachers to their students of pre-college ages.

(g) The senior graders of the same high school to their junior graders (in case of girls, even in college).

The reverse of the above rules is not possible.

(A). To form the Formal Plain Speech the final verbs in the sentences end in the following endings:

	Statement:	Question:	Imperative:	Propositative:
	-(nın/n)ta	-(ı)nyi? or -(ı)nya?	-(a, ə)la	-ca
1. Action Verb:				
a. Present	(1) -nınta/-nta	(2) -(ı)nyi?	(4) -(a,ə)la	-ca
b. Past	-(a,ə)ssta	-(a,ə)ssnyi?	-	-
c. Future	-kessta	-kessnyi?	-	-
2. Description Verb:				
a. Present	-ta	-nyi?	-	-
b. Past	-(a,ə)ssta	-(a,ə)ssnyi?	-	-
c. Future	-kessta	-kessnyi?	-	-
3. Copula:				
a. Present	ita	(3) (i)nyi?	-	-
b. Past	iəssta	iəssnyi?	-	-
c. Future	ikessta	ikessnyi?	-	-

Notes:

(1) -nınta is added to a stem ending in a consonant; -nta to a stem ending in a vowel. Exception: An action verb stem ending in either -ss- or -ps- takes -ta for a statement (in present tense), e.g. iss-→ issta/itta/, əps-→ əpsta/əptta/.

(2) -ɪnyi? is added to a stem ending in a consonant; -nyi? to a stem ending a vowel

(3) After a noun which ends in a vowel the copula stem i- is usually silent.

(4) The verb element to which -la is added is identical with an infinitive form. There are a few irregular forms for the imperative ending: 'go' o → wala or onəla, 'come' ka → kala or kakəla.

(B) The Informal Plain Speech has just one inflected form of a verb regardless of the sentence types, that is, all the four sentence types (statement, question, propositative, imperative) are in the Infinitive with different intonation patterns. When you drop off the particle yo from the Informal Polite Speech, the remaining part with the same intonation pattern is the Informal Plain Speech. Exception: the copula expression in Informal Plain Speech is (i)ya. Compare the following:

Informal Polite	Informal Plain	
Ka yo.	Ka.	'[I] go.'
Ka yo?	Ka?	'Do [you] go?'
Ka yo.	Ka. (in propositative intonation)	'Let's go.'
Ka yo.	Ka. (in imperative intonation)	'Go.'

2. Personal Nouns in the Polite and Plain Speeches

When the speech levels change, not only the final verb forms change but also the other words in the sentence such as personal nouns may require different forms (polite, less polite, humble, blunt, etc.) depending on what speech level the speaker uses. Study the following chart:

Speech Level:	Speaker:	Addressee:
Polite	cə 'I', ce ka 'I (as emphasis subject)' ce or cə e 'my', cə lɪl 'me', cə eke 'to me', uli or cəi or cəi tɪl 'we'	sənsæng or sənsæng nim or tangsin 'you', sənsæng tɪl or tangsin tɪl 'you (pl.), etc.
Plain	na 'I', næ ka 'I (as subject)', na lɪl	nə 'you', ne ka 'you (as subject)', nə lɪl 'you

	'me (as direct object)', næke (or na eke) 'to me', uli 'we'.	(as direct object)', ne or nə e 'your', nə eke 'to you', nəi or nəi tıl 'you (pl.)', nəi ka or nəi tıl i 'you (pl.) (as subject)', etc.

Note that ne 'yes' and aniyo 'no' in the plain speech are replaced by ıng or kılæ for ne; ani for aniyo.

3. Particles lako and ko

The particles lako and ko follow quotations and are called the Quotative Particles (or simply the quotatives). Since lako occurs after a direct quotation of the exact words of the original speaker - a word, a phrase, a sentence, an utterance, etc., it is called the Direct Quotative Particle. Examples:

(a) Original expression: Məli ka aphımnita. '[I] have a headache.'

Quoted: 'Məli ka aphımnita,' lako mal-hæssımnita. {'[He] said, '"I have a headache."' / '[He] said that he had a headache.'}

(b) Original expression: Kim Sənsæng (i) tæk e kyese yo? 'Is Mr. Kim at home?'

Quoted: 'Kim Sənsæng i tæk e kyese yo?' lako mal-hæssə yo. {'[He] asked if Mr. Kim is at home?' / '"Is Mr. Kim at home?", said [he].'}

(c) Original expression: Onıl ttənapsita. 'Let's leave today.'

Quoted: 'Onıl ttənapsita,' lako (kı ka) mal-hæssımnita. {'He suggested that we (he and I) lease today.' / '"Let's leave today," said he.'}

(d) Original expression: Annyənghi kasipsiyo. 'Good bye.'

Quoted: 'Annyənghi kasipsiyo,' lako kı yəca ka mal-hæssımnita. {'She said [to me] a good-bye.' / '"Good-bye," she said.'}

Ko follows a quotation which is said from the point of view of the speaker reporting the quotation. The tenses of the original is retained in the quotations but the forms of the verb are in indirect forms which we shall call the Indirect Quotations. Thus, ko is called the Indirect Quotative Particle. The Indirect Quotative verb forms are almost identical with the Formal Plain Speech verb forms with a few exceptions: in Indirect Quotations, the copula is (i)la: (la after a nominal ending in a vowel and ila after a nominal ending in a consonant); an imperative verb ending is -(ı)la: (ıla is added to a consonant verb stem and -la to a vowel stem); a question verb ending is always -(nı)nya instead of -(i)nyi. Observe the following chart:

	Indirect Quotation Ending	The Quotative Particle	Verbs which may be followed	Approximate Translations
1. Statement:				
a. Action Verb:				
Present	-nınta/nta			
Past	-(a,ə)ssta			
Future	-kessta			
b. Description Verb:				
Present	-ta	+ ko +	(mal-)ha-	'says that..'
Past	-(a,ə)ssta		sængkak-ha-	'thinks that..'
Future	-kessta		a(l)-	'understands that..'
c. Copula	(i)la			
2. Question:	-(nı)nya	+ ko +	(mal-)ha- mulə po-	'asks (if)..'
3. Imperative:	-(ı)la	+ ko +	(mal-)ha-	'tells [someone] to..'
4. Propositative:	-ca	+ ko +	(mal-)ha-	'suggests that..'

Examples:

1.

əti e kanta ko mal-hæssımnikka?	'Did [he] say where [he] is going?'
Yaksok i issta ko mal-hæssə yo.	'[He] said that [he] has an appointment.'
əməni ka tola kasyəssta ko mal-hamnita.	'[He] says that his mother died.'
Kim Sənsæng i Səul esə salkessta ko hæ yo.	'Mr. Kim says he'll live in Seoul.'
Chwe Ssi e atıl i phək ttokttokhata ko hamnita.	'[They] say that Mr. Choe's son is very bright.'
Kim Paksa nın puca (i)la ko hamnita.	'[They] say that Dr. Kim is (a) rich(man).'

2.

Hankıl ıl ilkıl su issnınya ko (Ceimsı eke) mulə pwassımnita.	'[I] asked (James) if he can read Hankıl.'
Taım kicha ka myəch-si e ttəna(nı)nya ko mulə posipsiyo.	'Ask [him] what time the next train leaves.'
Ilım i muəs inya ko kı salam i na eke mal-hæssə yo.	'That man asked me what my name is.'
Pak Sənsæng i tangsin eke Hankuk mal i əlyəpnya ko mal-hæssımnikka?	'Did Mr. Park ask you if Korean is difficult?'

3.

Sənsæng eke cənhwa-hala ko mal-hal kka yo?	'Shall I tell [him] to call you?'
(Ai eke) kongpu-hala ko hæssımnita.	'I told [my child] to study '
Nuka sənsæng eke wekukə lıl pæula ko mal-hæssə yo?	'Who told you to learn foreign languages?'
Sikmo eke cənyək (ıl) cunpi-hala ko mal-hæssımnita.	'I told the maid to prepare supper.'

4.

Cəmsim məkılə kaca ko chinku ka mal-hæssımnita.	'[My] friend suggested that we go (to) eat lunch.'
Com swica ko (kı eke) mal-hasipsiyo.	'Suggest (to him) that you (pl.) take a rest.'
Wæ kı yəca eke kyəlhon-haća ko mal-haci anhsımnikka?	'Why don't you propose to her? ('Why don't you propose that you [and she] get married?')'

DRILLS

A. Level Drill (based on Grammar Note 1)

Tutor: Cə nın hakkyo e kamnita.	'I'm going to school.' (Formal Polite)
Student: Na nın hakkyo e kanta.	'I'm going to school.' (Formal Plain)
1. Cə nın kimchi lıl cohahamnita.	Na nın kimchi lıl cohahanta.
2. Cə nın nal mata cənhwa lıl patsımnita.	Na nın nal mata cənhwa lıl patnınta.
3. Cə nın il cali lıl chacsımnita.	Na nın il cali lıl chacnınta.
4. Hankuk ımsik i mas i issımnita.	Hankuk ımsik i mas i issta.
5. Kyəul nalssi ka chupsımnita.	Kyəul nalssi ka chupta.
6. Pihængki ka ceil ppalımnita.	Pihængki ka ceil ppalıta.
7. Cəi ka pwassımnita.	Uli ka pwassta.
8. Cəi ka Kim Paksa lıl mannassımnita.	Uli ka Kim Paksa lıl mannassta.
9. Cə nın Yəngə lıl molımnita.	Na nın Yəngə lıl molınta.
10. Cikım pi ka oci anhsımnita.	Cikım pi ka oci anhnınta.
11. I Kyosu eke nın cənhal mal i əpsımnita.	I Kyosu eke nın cənhal mal i əpsta.
12. Acik pæ ka kophıci anhsımnita.	Acik pæ ka kophıci anhta.

B. Level Drill (based on Grammar Note 1)

Student 1: Hankuk mal i swipsımnikka?	'Is Korean easy?'
Student 2: Hankuk mal i swipnyi?	'Is Korean easy?'
1. Sənsæng ın Səul salam imnikka?	Nə nın Səul salam inya?
2. Tangsin in Yəngə lıl mal-hamnikka?	Nə nın Yəngə lıl mal-hanyi?
3. Pom e pi ka manhi omnikka?	Pom e pi ka manhi onyi?
4. Kulapha esə yəhæng-hæssımnikka?	Kulapha esə yəhæng-hæssnyi?
5. Pəlssə cəmsim ıl capsusyəssımnikka?	Pəlssə cəmsim ıl məkəssnyi?
6. Kim Sənsæng puin kwa cənhwa lo iyaki-hæssımnikka?	Kim Sənsæng puin kwa cənhwa lo iyaki-hæssnyi?
7. Pusan esə salə pon il i issımnikka?	Pusan esə salə pon il i issnyi?
8. Mikuk Tæsakwan e kınmu-hako siphsımnikka?	Mikuk Tæsakwan e kınmu-hako siphnyi?
9. əlma tongan tapang esə kitaliəssımnikka?	əlma tongan tapang esə kitaliəssnyi?
10. əce muəs halə sinæ e tılləssımnikka?	əce muəs halə sinæ e tılləssnyi?

C. Level Drill (based on Grammar Note 1)

Student 1: Hakkyo e kapsita.	'Let's go to school.'
Student 2: Hakkyo e kaca.	'Let's go to school.'
1. Com swipsita.	Com swica.
2. Cənyək (ıl) məkıpsita.	Cənyək ıl məkca.
3 Onıl pam e yənghwa polə kapsita.	Onıl pam e yənghwa polə kaca.
4. Hankuk mal lo iyaki-hapsita.	Hankuk mal lo iyaki haca.
5. Chənchənhi kələ kapsita.	Chənchənhi kələ kaca.
6. Onıl ın cip e issıpsita.	Onıl ın cip e issca.
7. Pul-koki lıl məkə popsita.	Pul-koki lıl məkə poca.
8. Kutu lıl saci mapsita.	Kutu lıl saci ma(l)ca.
9. Pak Sənsæng eke cənhwa-haci mapsita.	Pak Sənsæng eke cənhwa-haci ma(l)ca.
10. Kyosil esə tampæ lıl phiuci mapsita.	Kyosil esə tampæ lıl phiuci ma(l)ca.
11. Kılən kəs ıl yaksok-haci mapsita.	Kılən kəs ıl yaksok-haci ma(l)ca.
12. Hakkyo lıl kımantuci mapsita.	Hakkyo lıl kımantuci ma(l)ca.

D. Level Drill (based on Grammar Note 1)

Student 3: Hankuk mal lo mal-hasipsiyo.	'Speak (<u>or</u> say) in Korean.'
Student 4: Hankuk mal lo mal-hæla.	'Speak (<u>or</u> say) in Korean.'
1. Ohu e tto osipsiyo.	Ohu e tto {onəla. / wala.}
2. Cip e kasipsiyo.	Cip e {kakəla. / kala.}
3. əsə capsusipsiyo.	əsə məkəla.
4. Com tə khıke malssım-hasipsiyo.	Com tə khıke mal-hæla.
5. Yəki esə nælisipsiyo.	Yəki esə nælıəla.
6. Næil tasi cənhwa kəsipsiyo.	Næil tasi cənhwa kələla.
7. Ce cənhwa pənho lıl cəkə tusipsiyo.	Næ cənhwa pənho lıl cəkə tuəla.
8. I chæk ıl I Sənsæng eke cənhasipsiyo.	I chæk ıl I Sənsæng eke cənhæla.
9. Kı pun eke mal-haci masipsiyo.	Kı pun eke mal-haci maləla.
10. Kılən yaksok ın haci masipsiyo.	Kılən yaksok ın haci maləla.

E. Response Drill (based on Grammar Note 1)

Child:	Sənsæng ın Yəngə lıl mal-hasimnikka?	'Do you speak English, sir?'
Adult:	ıng, kılæ, (na nın) Yəngə lıl mal-hanta.	'Yes, I do.' ('That's right, I speak English.')
1.	Wekuk e ka pon il i issımnikka?	ıng, kılæ, wekuk e ka pon il i issta.
2.	Hankuk mal i pokcap-hamnikka?	ıng, kılæ, (Hankuk mal i) pokcap-hata.
3.	Sæ yangpok ıl sassımnikka?	ıng, kılæ, sæ yangpok ıl sassta.
4.	Sənsæng nim ın tampæ lıl phiumnikka?	ıng, kılæ, tampæ (lıl) phiunta.
5.	Ce apəci eke cənhal malssım i issımnikka?	ıng, kılæ, (nə e apəci eke) cənhal mal i issta.
6.	Onıl cənyək e tola osikessımnikka?	ıng, kılæ, onıl cənyək e tola okessta.
7.	Kı kəs i tahæng imnikka?	ıng, kılæ, kı kəs i tahæng ita.
8.	Ceimsı e tæhæ sə iyaki tıləssımnikka?	ıng, kılæ, (Ceimsı e tæhæ sə) iyaki tıləssta.
9.	Hankıl il mot ilksımnikka?	ıng, kılæ, (Hankıl il) mot ilknınta.
10.	Sənsæng ın ton i əpsımnikka?	ıng, kılæ, ton i əpsta.

F. Response Drill (based on Grammar Note 1)

Child:	(Uli) hakkyo e kal kka yo?	'Shall we go to school?'
Adult:	Kılæ, (hakkyo e) kaca.	'Sure, let's go.'
1.	Cəmsim ıl məkıl kka yo?	Kılæ, (cəmsim ıl) məkca.
2.	Cəncha pota ppəsı lıl thako kal kka yo?	Kılæ, (cəncha pota) ppəsı lıl thako kaca.
3.	Lætio nyussı lıl tılə pol kka yo?	Kılæ, (lætio nyussı lıl) tılə poca.
4.	Cəngkəcang aph esə nælil kka yo?	Kılæ, cəngkəcang aph esə nælica.
5.	Tasi sængkak-hæ pol kka yo?	Kılæ, tasi sængkak-hæ poca.
6.	Kicha lo Pusan e nælyə kal kka yo?	Kılæ, kicha lo (Pusan e) nælyə kaca.
7.	Ppəsı lo Nyuyok e olla kal kka yo?	Kılæ, ppəsı lo (Nyuyok e) olla kaca.
8.	Cənhwa pənho lıl pakkul kka yo?	Kılæ, (cənhwa pənho lıl) pakkuca.
9.	I sosik ıl halapəci eke cənhal kka yo?	Kılæ, (i sosik ıl halapəci eke) cənhaca.

G. Response Drill

Child: Cikɪm sicak-hæ to cohsɪmnikka?	'May I start now?'
Adult: Kɪlæ, əsə sicak-hæla.	'Go right ahead.'
1. Malssim com mulə pwa to cohsɪmnikka?	Kɪlæ, əsə mulə pwala.
2. Thipi lil pwa to cohsɪmnikka?	Kɪlæ, əsə pwala.
3. Sənsæng e mannyənphil ɪl ssə to cohsɪmnikka?	Kɪlæ, əsə ssəla.
4. Cə'mun ɪl yələ to cohsɪmnikka?	Kɪlæ, əsə yələla.
5. Mun ɪl tatə to cohsɪmnikka?	Kɪlæ, əsə tatəla.
6. Kyosil esə tampæ lil phiwə to cohsɪmnikka?	Kɪlæ, əsə phiwəla.
7. Sənsæng eke han kaci puthak-hæ to cohsɪmnikka?	Kɪlæ, əsə puthak-hæla.
8. I chæk ɪl ilkə to cohsɪmnikka?	Kɪlæ, əsə ilkəla.
9. Pak Yəngca wa kyəlhon-hæ to cohsɪmnikka?	Kɪlæ, əsə kyəlhon-hæla.

H. Response Drill

Adult: Hankuk mal il pæunyi?	'Are you learning Korean?'
Child: Ne, (Hankuk mal il) pæwə yo.	'Yes, I am (learning Korean,) (sir)
1. Hankuk mal ɪl anyi?	Ne, (Hankuk mal ɪl) alə yo.
2. Hakkyo ka {kakkapnyi? / kakkaunyi?}	Ne, (hakkyo ka) kakkawə yo.
3. Cikɪm pæ ka kophinyi?	Ne, pæ ka kopha yo.
4. Mom i phikon-hanyi?	Ne, (mom i) phikon-hæ yo.
5. Hakkyo ka kkɪth-nassnyi?	Ne, (hakkyo ka) kkɪth-nassə yo.
6. Nal mata Hankuk mal ɪl yənsɪp-hanyi?	Ne, nal mata (Hankuk mal ɪl) yənsɪp-hæ yo.
7. Kicha ka pəlssə ttənassnyi?	Ne, pəlssə ttənassə yo.
8. Ppəsɪ ka pəlssə tahassnyi?	Ne, pəlssə tahassə yo.
9. Onɪl cənyək e pi ka okessnyi?	Ne, (onɪl cənyək e) pi ka okessə yo.
10. Kim Sənsæng puin ɪn nai ka manhnyi?	Ne, (Kim Sənsæng puin ɪn) nai ka manhə yo.

I. Substitution Drill

1. I kəs ıl Yəngə lo muəs ila ko hamnikka?	How do you say this in English?
2. Cə kəs ıl Hankuk mal lo muəs ila ko hamnikka?	How do you say that in Korean?
3. Yaksok ıl Tokil mal lo muəs ila ko hamnikka?	How do you say appointment in German?
4. Cənhal mal ıl Səpana mal lo muəs ila ko hamnikka?	How do you say message in Spanish?
5. Puthak ıl Cungkuk mal lo muəs ila ko hamnikka?	How do you say a favor to ask in Chinese?
6. 'Yəpose yo.' lıl Ilpon mal lo muəs ila ko hamnikka?	How do you say 'Hello (there).' in Japanese?
7. 'Tahæng imnita.' lıl Mikuk mal lo muəs ila ko hamnikka?	How do you say 'That's fortunate.' in American language?
8. 'Camkan man kitalise yo.' lıl Pullansə mal lo muəs ila ko hamnikka?	How do you say 'Wait a minute.' in French?
9. 'Alkessımnita.' lıl Ssolyən mal muəs ila ko hamnikka?	How do you say 'I understand.' in Russian?

J. Substitution Drill

1. Sənsæng e tæhæ sə iyaki (manhi) tıləssimnita.	I heard (a lot) about you.
*2. Kı sosik e tæhæ sə iyaki tıləssımnita.	I heard about that news.
*3. Kı sinmun kisa e tæhæ sə iyaki tıləssımnita.	I heard about that newspaper article.
*4. Kı il cali e tæhæ sə iyaki tıləssımnita.	I heard about that job.
*5. Kı catongcha sako e tæhæ sə iyaki tıləssımnita.	I heard about that automobile accident.
*6. Kı sakən e tæhæ sə iyaki tıləssimnita.	I heard about that incident.
*7. Hankuk sænghwal e tæhæ sə iyaki tıləssımnita.	I heard about the Korean life.

8. Wekyokwan sænghwal e tæhæ sə iyaki tıləssımnita.	I heard about the life of foreign service.
*9. Hankuk nongpu e hæhæ sə iyaki tıləssımnita.	I heard about the Korean farmers.

K. Substitution Drill

1. Cə e ilım ın Ceimsı la ko hamnita.	My name is James. ('[They] say that my name is James.')
*2. I kənmul e ilım ın Kukce Ssenthə la ko hamnita.	The name of this building is said to be International Center.
*3. I kəli e ilım ın Congno la ko hamnita.	The name of this street is Congno.
*4. Hankuk Cəngpu e ilım ın Tæhan Minkuk ila ko hamnita.	The name of the Korean Government is Republic of Korea.
*5. Pullansə e səul ın Phali la ko hamnita.	The capital of France is Paris.
*6. Mikuk e suto nın Wəsingthon ila ko hamnita.	The capital city of the U.S. is Washington.
*7. I tosi e ilım ın Tæku la ko hamnita.	The name of this city is Taegu.
*8. Cə tæhakkyo e ilım in Yənse Tæhakkyo la ko hamnita.	The name of that university is Yonsei University.
*9. Cə yəca e ilım in Pak Yəngsuk ila ko hamnita.	That woman's name is Park Young-Sook.

L. Substitution Drill

1. Kim Sənsæng i əti e kanta ko (mal-)hæssımnikka?	{Did Mr. Kim say where he is going? Did [they] say where Mr. Kim is going?
2. Kim Sənsæng i muəs il kalıchinta ko hæssımnikka?	Did Mr. Kim say what he is teaching?
3. Kim Sənsæng i əti e santa ko hæssımnikka?	Did Mr. Kim say where he lives?
4. Kim Sənsæng i muəs ıl wənhanta ko hæssımnikka?	Did Mr. Kim say what he wants?
5. Kim Sənsæng i ənce onta ko hæssımnikka?	Did Mr. Kim say when he is coming?

6. Kim Sənsæng i myəch-si e tola onta ko hæssımnikka? — Did Mr. Kim say what time he is coming back?

7. Kim Sənsæng i nuku lıl chacnınta ko hæssımnikka? — Did Mr. Kim say whom he is looking for?

8. Kim Sənsæng i wæ Hankuk mal ıl pæunta ko hæssımnikka? — Did Mr. Kim say why he is studying Korean?

9. Kim Sənsæng i myəch sikan tongan il-hanta ko hæssımnikka? — Did Mr. Kim say how many hours he works?

M. Substitution Drill

1. Pak Sənsæng ın hakkyo e kanta ko (mal-)hæssımnita. — Mr. Park said that he is going to school.

2. Pak Sənsæng ın Hankuk salam ila ko (mal-)hæssımnita. — Mr. Park said that he is a Korean.

3. Pak Sənsæng ın Hankuk mal ıl kalıchinta ko (mal-)hæssımnita. — {Mr. Park said that he is teaching Korean. / [He] said that Mr. Park is teaching Korean.}

4. Pak Sənsæng ın Pul-koki lıl məkko siphta ko (mal-)hæssımnita. — Mr. Park said that he wants to eat Pul-koki.

5. Pak Sənsæng ın sənsæng il anta ko (mal-)hæssımnita. — Mr. Park said that he knows you.

6. Pak Sənsæng ın nal mata cənhwa lıl kənta ko (mal-)hæssımnita. — Mr. Park said that he makes phone-calls everyday.

7. Pak Sənsæng ın Yəngə lıl alə ya hanta ko (mal-)hæssımnita. — Mr. Park said that [he] has to know English.

8. Pak Sənsæng ın næil ttənalyə ko hanta ko (mal-)hæssımnita — Mr. Park said that he is going to leave tomorrow.

9. Pak Sənsæng ın sæ cha lıl sal kəs ila ko (mal-)hæssımnita. — Mr. Park said that he will buy a new car.

N. Substitution Drill

1. Hakkyo ka kakkapta ko Kim Sənsæng i mal-hæssə yo. — Mr. Kim said that the school is near.

2. Səul cip kaps i pissata ko Kim Sənsæng i mal-hæssə yo. — Mr. Kim said that the housing in Seoul is expensive.

3. Yəngə ka swipci anhta ko Kim Sənsæng i mal-hæssə yo. — Mr. Kim said that English is not easy.
4. Cəncha ka pəncap-hata ko Kim Sənsæng i mal-hæssə yo. — Mr. Kim said that streetcars are crowded.
5. Hansik i mas (i) issta ko Kim Sənsæng i mal-hæssə yo. — Mr. Kim said that Korean food is delicious.
6. Məli ka com aphıta ko Kim Sənsæng i mal-hæssə yo. — Mr. Kim said that he has a little headache.
7. Munce ka com pokcap-hata ko Kim Sənsæng i mal-hæssə yo. — Mr. Kim said that the problem is rather complicated.
8. Tasi cənhwa kəlkessta ko Kim Sənsæng i mal-hæssə yo. — Mr. Kim said that he will call again
9. Cikım thım i əpsta ko Kim Sənsæng i mal-hæssə yo. — Mr. Kim said that he is not free now.

O. Substitution Drill

1. Kı salam eke tasi cənhwa hala ko mal-hal kka yo? — Shall I tell him to call again?
2. Kı salam eke tasi ola ko mal-hal kka yo? — Shall I tell him to come again?
3. Kı salam eke kongpu-hala ko mal-hal kka yo? — Shall I tell him to study?
4. Kı salam eke tılə ola ko mal-hal kka yo? — Shall I tell him to come in?
5. Kı salam eke ohu e tıllıla ko mal-hal kka yo? — Shall I tell him to stop by in the afternoon?
6. Kı salam eke alə pola ko mal-hal kka yo? — Shall I tell him to find out?
7. Kı salam eke tola kala ko mal-hal kka yo? — Shall I tell him to go back?
8. Kı salam eke camkan man kyesila ko mal-hal kka yo? — Shall I tell him to wait a moment?
9. Kı salam eke yənsıp-hala ko mal-hal kka yo? — Shall I tell him to practise?
10. Kı salam eke kaci malla ko mal-hal kka yo? — Shall I tell him not to go?

P. Substitution Drill

1.	Kı salam eke kaci malla ko mal-hasipsiyo.	Please tell him not to go.
2.	Kı salam eke kaci malla ko mal-hæ cusipsiyo.	Please tell him not to go (for me).
3.	Kı salam eke kaci malla ko mal-haci masipsiyo.	Please don't tell him not to go.
4.	Kı salam eke kaci malla ko mal-hæssımnita.	I told him not to go.
5.	Kı salam eke kaci malla ko mal-hæssımnikka?	Did you tell him not to go?
6.	Kı salam eke kaci malla ko mal-hapsita.	Let's tell him not to go.
7.	Kı salam eke kaci malla ko mal-haci mapsita.	Let's not tell him not to go.
8.	Kı salam eke kaci malla ko mal-hakessə yo.	I'll tell him not to go.
9.	Kı salam eke kaci malla ko mal-haci anhkessə yo.	I'll not tell him not to go.
10.	Kı salam eke kaci malla ko mal-hanın kəs i cohkessə yo.	{You'd better tell him not to go. / It will be better to tell him not to go.
11.	Kı salam eke kaci malla ko mal-hæ to cohsımnita.	You may tell him not to go.

Q. Substitution Drill

1.	Kim Sənsæng i na eke Yəngə lıl pæuca ko mal-hamnita.	Mr. Kim suggests to me that he and I study English.
2.	Kim Sənsæng i na eke Hankuk mal lo mal-haca ko mal-hamnita.	Mr. Kim suggests to me that he and I speak in Korean.
3.	Kim Sənsæng i na eke Cungkuk ımsik ıl məkca ko mal-hamnita.	Mr. Kim suggests to me that he and I eat Chinese food.
4.	Kim Sənsæng i na eke sinæ lıl kukyəng-haca ko mal-hamnita.	Mr. Kim suggests to me that he and I go around the city.
5.	Kim Sənsæng i na eke cal sængkak-haca ko mal-hamnita.	Mr. Kim suggests to me that he and I give a second thought.

6. Kim Sənsæng i na eke il ɪl sicak-haca ko mal-hamnita. — Mr. Kim suggests to me that he and I start the work.

7. Kim Sənsæng i na eke hapsɪng ɪl thaca ko mal-hamnita. — Mr. Kim suggests to me that he and I take a jitney.

8. Kim Sənsæng i na eke yəca lɪl thæuca ko mal-hamnita. — Mr. Kim suggests to me that he and I give a ride to the girl.

9. Kim Sənsæng i na eke il ɪl kkɪth-machica ko mal-hamnita. — Mr. Kim suggests to me that he and I finish the work.

10. Kim Sənsæng i na eke yəki esə nælica ko mal-hamnita. — Mr. Kim suggests to me that he and I get off here.

R. Substitution Drill

1. Hankuk mal i əlyəpnya ko Ceimsɪ ka cə eke mulə pwassɪmnita. — James asked me if Korean is difficult.

2. Ilpon mal i swipnya ko Ceimsɪ ka cə eke mulə pwassɪmnita. — James asked me if Japanese is easy.

3. Kicha ka phyəlli-hanya ko Ceimsɪ ka cə eke mulə pwassɪmnita. — James asked me if the train is convenient.

4. Nuka Hankuk mal ɪl kalɪchi(nɪ)nya ko Ceimsɪ ka cə eke mulə pwassɪmnita. — James inquired me who teaches Korean.

5. əti esə sa(nɪ)nya ko Ceimsɪ ka cə eke mulə pwassɪmnita. — James asked me where I am living.

6. Myəch-si e hakkyo ka kkɪth-na(nɪ)nya ko Ceimsɪ ka cə eke mulə pwassɪmnita. — James asked me what time school is over.

7. Myəch sikan tongan kɪnmu-ha(nɪ)nya ko Ceimsɪ ka cə eke mulə pwassɪmnita. — James asked me how many hours [I] work.

8. əlma na mənya ko Ceimsɪ ka cə eke mulə pwassɪmnita. — James asked me how far [it] is.

9. Onɪl i myəchil inya ko Ceimsɪ ka cə eke mulə pwassɪmnita. — James asked me what date it is today.

S. Response Drill

Tutor: Kɪ i eke cənhwa-hala ko mal-hal kka yo?	'Shall I tell him to call [you]?'
Student 1: Ne, cənhwa-hala ko mal-hæ cusipsiyo.	'Yes, please tell him to call [me].'
Student 2: Aniyo, cənhwa-haci malla ko mal-hæ cusipsiyo.	'No, please tell him not to call [me].
1. Haksæng eke cip e kala ko mal-hal kka yo?	Ne, cip e kala ko mal-hæ cusipsiyo. Aniyo, cip e kaci malla ko mal-hæ cusipsiyo.
2. Ai eke ppəsɪ lɪl thako kala ko mal-hal kka yo?	Ne, ppəsɪ lɪl thako kala ko mal-hæ cusipsiyo. Aniyo, ppəsɪ lɪl thako kaci malla ko mal-hæ cusipsiyo.
3. Uncənsu eke mun aph esə nælið cula ko mal-hal kka yo?	Ne, mun aph esə nælið cula ko mal-hæ cusipsiyo. Aniyo, mun aph esə nælið cuci malla ko mal-hæ cusipsiyo.
4. Ceimsɪ eke cənhwa pənho lil cəkə tula ko mal-hal kka yo?	Ne, cənhwa pənho lil cəkə tula ko mal-hæ cusipsiyo. Aniyo, cənhwa pənho lil cəkə tuci malla ko mal-hæ cusipsiyo.
5. Pisə eke mun ɪl tatɪla ko mal-hal kka yo?	Ne, (mun ɪl) tatɪla ko mal-hæ cusipsiyo. Aniyo, (mun ɪl) tatci malla ko mal-hæ cusipsiyo.
6. I Sənsæng eke Kim Sənsæng e cuso lɪl alə pola ko mal-hal kka yo?	Ne, (Kim Sənsæng e cuso lɪl) alə pola ko mal-hæ cusipsiyo. Aniyo, (Kim Sənsæng e cuso lɪl) alə poci malla ko mal-hæ cusipsiyo.
7. Miss Chwe eke Hankuk mal ɪl kalɪchið cula ko mal-hal kka yo?	Ne, Hankuk mal ɪl kalɪchið cula ko mal-hæ cusipsiyo. Aniyo, Hankuk mal ɪl kalɪchið cuci malla ko mal-hæ cusipsiyo.

8. Pak Sənsæng eke khəphi han can sala ko mal-hal kka yo?
Ne, (khəphi han can) sala ko mal-hæ cusipsiyo.
Aniyo, (khəphi han can) saci malla ko mal-hæ cusipsiyo.

9. Kɪ yəca eke tangsin ɪl kitalila ko mal-hal kka yo?
Ne, (cə lɪl) kitalila ko mal-hæ cusipsiyo.
Aniyo, (cə lɪl) kitalici malla ko mal-hæ cusipsiyo.

T. Response Drill

Tutor: Ai eke cip e kala ko mal-hæssɪmnikka? — 'Did you tell the child to go home?'
Student 3: Ne, cip e kala ko mal-hæssɪmnita. — 'Yes, I did. ('I told [him] to go home.')'
Student 4: Aniyo, cip e kala ko mal-haci anhəssɪmnita. — 'No, I didn't. ('I didn't tell [him] to go home.')'

1. Haksæng tɪl eke cəmsim (ɪl) məkɪla ko mal-hæssɪmnikka?
Ne, cəmsil (ɪl) məkɪla ko mal-hæssɪmnita.
Aniyo, cəmsim (ɪl) məkɪla ko mal-haci anhəssɪmnita.

2. Puin eke phyənci (lɪl) puchila ko mal-hæssɪmnikka?
Ne, phyənci (lɪl) puchila ko mal-hæssɪmnita.
Aniyo, phyənci (lɪl) puchila ko mal-haci anhəssɪmnita.

3. Ai tɪl eke kil esə nolla ko mal-hæssɪmnikka?
Ne, kil esə nolla ko mal-hæssɪmnita.
Aniyo, kil esə nolla ko mal-haci anhəssɪmnita.

4. Chinku eke tapang esə kitalila ko mal-hæssɪmnikka?
Ne, tapang esə kitalila ko mal-hæssɪmnita.
Aniyo, tapang esə kitalila ko mal-haci anhəssɪmnita.

5. Uncənsu eke mun esə nælio cula ko mal-hæssɪmnikka?
Ne, mun esə nælio cula ko mal-hæssɪmnita.
Aniyo, mun esə nælio cula ko mal-haci anhəssɪmnita.

6. Kim Sənsæng eke chæk ɪl ponæla ko mal-hæssɪmnikka?
Ne, chæk ɪl ponæla ko mal-hæssɪmnita.
Aniyo, chæk ɪl ponæla ko mal-haci anhəssɪmnita.

7. Atɪl eke thipi lɪl pola ko mal-hæssɪmnikka?
Ne, thipi lɪl pola ko mal-hæssɪmnita.
Aniyo, thipi lɪl pola ko mal-haci anhəssɪmnita.

8. Kukmusəng i sənsæng eke Hankuk mal ɪl pæula ko mal-hæssɪmnikka?
Ne, Kukmusəng i na eke Hankuk mal ɪl pæula ko mal-hæssɪmnita.
Aniyo, Kukmusəng i Hankuk mal ɪl pæula ko mal-haci anhəssɪmnita.

9. ɪysa ka sənsæng eke khəphi lɪl masici malla ko mal-hæssɪmnikka?
Ne, ɪysa ka khəphi lɪl masici malla ko mal-hæssɪmnita.
Aniyo, ɪysa ka khəphi lɪl masici malla ko mal-haci anhəssɪmnita.

10. Kim Sənsæng i Səul esə cəncha lɪl thaci malla ko mal-hæssɪmnikka?
Ne, Kim Sənsæng i Səul esə cəncha lɪl thaci malla ko mal-hæssɪmnita.
Aniyo, Kim Sənsæng i Səul esə cəncha lɪl thaci malla ko mal-haci anhəssɪmnita.

U. Response Drill

Tutor: Pak Sənsæng i əti e kanta ko mal-hæssɪmnikka? /tapang/
'Did Mr. Park say where he was going? /tearoom/'

Student: Tapang e kanta kc mal-hæssə yo.
'He said (that) he was going to the tearoom.'

1. I Sənsæng i muəs ɪlo yəhæng-hanta ko mal-hæssɪmnikka? /catongcha/
Catongcha lo yəhæng-hanta ko mal-hæssə yo.

2. ənce kkaci kɪ il ɪl kkɪth-nænta ko mal-hæssɪmnikka? /taɪm cuil/
Taɪm cuil kkaci kkɪth-nænta ko mal-hæssə yo.

3. Kim Sənsæng ɪn atɪl i ənɪ tæhak e taninta ko mal-hæssɪmnikka? /Cungang Tæhak/
(Atɪl i) Cungang Tæhak e taninta ko mal-hæssə yo.

4. Sə Sənsæng i musɪn ɪmsik ɪl cohahanta ko mal-hæssɪmnikka? /yangsik/
Yangsik ɪl cohahanta ko mal-hæssə yo.

5. Ceimsı ka nuku wa kyəlhon-hanta ko mal-hæssımnikka? /Chwe Sənsæng e ttal/

Chwe Sənsæng e ttal kwa kyəlhon-hanta ko mal-hæssə yo.

6. Ceimsı Sənsæng i wæ Hankuk mal il pæunta ko mal-hæssımnikka? /Hankuk e kani kka/

Hankuk e kani kka, (Hankuk mal il) pæunta ko mal-hæssə yo.

7. Kı i ka əlma tongan Hankuk esə salkessta ko mal-hæssımnikka? /han sam sa nyən/

Han sam sa nyən (tongan) Hankuk esə salkessta ko mal-hæssə yo.

8. Pak Sənsæng ın muəs il masiko siphta ko mal-hæssımnikka? /mækcu/

Mækcu lil masiko siphta ko mal-hæssə yo.

9. Cəng Sənsæng i musın yoil e ttənakessta ko mal-hæssımnikka? /Hwayoil/

Hwayoil e ttənakessta ko mal-hæssə yo.

10. Chwe Sənsæng ın əlma e cha lıl sassta ko mal-hæssımnikka? /chən-ku-pæk Pul/

Chən-ku-pæk Pul e sassta ko mal-hæssə yo.

11. Hankuk mal sənsæng i Mikuk e onci myəch nyən tweəssta ko mal-hæssımnikka? /sam nyən pan/

(Mikuk e onci) sam nyən pan tweəssta ko mal-hæssə yo.

V. Transformation Drill

Tutor: (Kim Sənsæng i) i kəs i chæk ila ko mal-hæssə yo?

'Did Mr. Kim say that this is a book?'

Student: (Kim Sənsæng i) na eke i kəs i chæk inya ko mulə pwassə yo.

'Mr. Kim asked me if this is a book.'

1. (Kim Sənsæng i) Hankuk mal ıl anta ko mal-hæssə yo?

(Kim Sənsæng i) na eke Hankuk mal ıl a(nı)nya ko mulə pwassə yo.

2. (Kim Sənsæng i) Yəngə ka əlyəpta ko mal-hæssə yo?

(Kim Sənsæng i) na eke Yəngə ka əlyəpnya ko mulə pwassə yo.

3. (Kim Sənsæng i) Səul e cip kaps i pissata ko mal-hæssə yo?

(Kim Sənsæng i) na eke Səul e cip kaps i pissanya ko mulə pwassə yo.

4. (Kim Sənsæng i) Hansik i mas i issta ko mal-hæssə yo?
(Kim Sənsæng i) na eke Hansik i mas i iss(nı)nya ko mulə pwassə yo.

5. (Kim Sənsæng i) Miss Kim ın nai ka manhta ko mal-hæssə yo?
(Kim Sənsæng i) na eke Miss Kim ın nai ka manhnya ko mulə pwassə yo.

6. (Kim Sənsæng i) nai ka myəch sal ila ko mal-hæssə yo?
(Kim Sənsæng i) na eke nai ka myəch sal inya ko mulə pwassə yo.

7. (Kim Sənsæng i) yosæ muəs ıl hanta ko mal-hæssə yo?
(Kim Sənsæng i) na eke yosæ muəs ıl ha(nı)nya ko mulə pwassə yo.

8. (Kim Sənsæng i) əti e santa ko mal-hæssə yo?
(Kim Sənsæng i) na eke əti e sa(nı)nya ko mulə pwassə yo.

9. (Kim Sənsæng i) cikım myəch-si la ko mal-hæssə yo?
(Kim Sənsæng i) na eke cikım myəch-si nya ko mulə pwassə yo.

10. (Kim Sənsæng i) sikan i əlma na kəllinta ko mal-hæssə yo?
(Kim Sənsæng i) na eke sikan i əlma na kəlli(nı)nya ko mulə pwassə yo.

EXERCISES

(All the following exercises should be done in different speech levels: Formal and Informal Polite; Formal and Informal Plain.)

A. Tell the class that Mr. Park told you that:

1. he is sick.
2. he cannot come to work.
3. he will take a good rest.
4. he visited the doctor.
5. to call him anytime.
6. not to worry/kəkcəng-ha-ta/ about it.
7. not to ask him any questions.
8. to go to the movies with you.
9. not to speak in English while in the class.

B. Tell Pak Sənsæng that you think that:

1. they sell American newspapers and magazines at that bookstore.
2. the problem is rather complicated.
3. Mr. Yang will not buy a new car.
4. you've heard about the automobile accident.
5. Korea is called 'Tæhan Minkuk' in Korean.
6. anybody will be able to finish it easily.

C. Ask student A if he's heard:

1. that teaching Korean is easier than an European language.
2. that others also suggested eating Chinese food.
3. that James told the students to go home.
4. that all the students wanted to study Korean.
5. that the Government told James to teach English.

D. Tell Pak Sənsæng that:

1. you think that Jones speaks Korean very well.
2. Mr. Kim said that he will be back by 6:30.
3. you understood that Korean is difficult.

4. your Korean teacher told you to memorize/(ttala) we-ta/ the new words/tanə/.
5. Miss Brown asked you if you can teach her Korean.
6. Miss Choe suggested that you go together to the movies.
7. you heard that Mr. Chang's son is very bright.
8. you heard that Jones is a rich man.
9. James told you not to read that magazine.
10. your wife suggested that (she and) you not buy a foreign car.
11. 'I understand.' in Korean is expressed as 'I will know it.'
12. you heard about Korean customs.
13. the capital of France is called Paris.
14. you think riding taxis in Seoul is dangerous/wihəm-ha-ta/.
15. you think reading Korean newspapers is difficult.
16. you don't know if Korean is as easy as French.
17. you have an appointment to meet a friend at 3 p.m.
18. Jones asked you where you live.
19. your wife asked you what time the work ends.
20. the ambassador asked how difficult Korean was.

E. Mr. James has just telephoned and asked for Mr. Kim. Answer as follows:

1. 'Just a moment, please. I'll see if he is in.'
2. 'He isn't at his desk just now.'
3. 'Oh, gee, he went out just a minute ago.'
4. 'Who is calling, please?'
5. 'This is Miss Lee Suca (speaking). I'm Mr. Kim's secretary.'
6. 'He is in Mr. Park's office just now. It's extension/næsən/ 26.'
7. 'I mean Young-Soo Park.'
8. 'Would you like him to call you later?'
9. 'Yes, I understand, I will have him call you soon.'

F. Make the following telephone calls:

1. Call the Hanil Company and leave a message for Mr. Son that you are not coming today.
2. Call your home and tell the maid that you are going to the Kim's house for supper and will be home about 11:30.
3. Call a friend and ask her to go to the movies with you.
4. Call Mr. Kim's house and ask when Mr. Kim is returning to Seoul.
5. Call Mr. Han's house and ask Mr. Han to call Ambassador Wilson's office immediately.
6. Report that your telephone is out of order/kocang-na-ta/ and request that it be fixed/kochi-ta/.
7. Call your boss' house and tell his wife that he had some business in Inchon suddenly/kapcaki/ and that he said he'll call her from Inchon tonight around 9:00.
8. Call Mr. James' secretary and tell her Mr. James asked to call his office about his sickness.

End of Tape 12A

Tape 12B

제 18 과 일기에 대해서

(대화 A)

날씨
좋군요
1. A: 오늘은 날씨가 퍽 좋군요!

가을 날씨
이렇게
2. B: 예, 한국(의) 가을 날씨는 대개 이렇게 좋습니다.

이런 날씨
계속
계속합니까
3. A: 이런 날씨가 얼마 동안 계속합니까?

시월 말
하늘
하늘이 맑고
차차
(차차) 추워 집니다
4. B: 대개 시월 말까지는 하늘이 맑고 좋은 날씨가 계속합니다. 그러나, 십일월부터 차차 추워 집니다.

동북
미국 동북부

UNIT 18. Talking About Weather

BASIC DIALOGUES FOR MEMORIZATION

Dialogue A

A

nalssi	weather
cohkun yo	[it] is nice!
1. Onıl ın nalssi ka phək cohkun yo!	It's a nice day today!

B

kaıl nalssi	autumn weather
iləhke	this way; like this
2. Ne, Hankuk (e) kaıl nalssi nın tækæ iləhke cohsımnita.	Yes, Korea's autumn weather is usually nice like this.

A

ilən nalssi	this kind of weather
kyesok	continuation
kyesok-hamnikka	does [it] continue?; does [it] last?
3. Ilən nalssi ka əlma tongan kyesok-hamnikka?	How long does this kind of weather last?

B

Si-wəl mal	the end of October
hanıl	sky; heaven
hanıl i malkko	the sky is clear and..
chacha / cəmcəm	gradually
(chacha) chuwə cimnita	[it] gets colder, [it]'s getting colder
4. Tækæ Si-wəl mal kkaci nın hanıl i malkko, cohın nalssi ka kyesok-hamnita. Kıləna, Sip-il-wəl puthə chacha chuwə cimnita.	Until the end of October the sky is clear and nice weather countinues. But after November it gets gradually colder.

비슷합니다

비슷한 것 같습니다

5. A: 그럼, 한국의 기후가 미국 동북부와 비슷한 것 같습니다.

같다고 생각합니다

6. B: 예, 남한의 기후는 뉴욕 주와 대개 같다고 생각합니다.

봄 철

뉴욕처럼

7. A: 여기에도 봄 철에는 뉴욕처럼 비가 많이 오는가요?

늦은 봄

이른 여름

장마 철

장마 철이라고 부릅니다

8. B: 대개 늦은 봄과 이른 여름에 비가 많이 오지요. 그래서, 유월과 칠월을 장마 철이라고 부릅니다.

(대화 B)

-토요일 아침에-

밖에

9. A: 지금 밖에 날씨가 어떻습니까?

비가 올 것 같습니다

A

Tongpuk	Northeast ('eastnorth')
Mikuk Tongpukpu	the Northeastern part of the U.S
pisıthamnita	[it] is similar
pisıthan kəs kathsımnita	it seems that [it]'s similar; [it] looks like similar
5. Kıləm, Hankuk e kihu ka Mikuk Tongpukpu wa pisıthan kəs kathsımnita.	Well, Korea's weather seems to be similar to that of the Northeastern part of the United States.

B

kathta ko sængkak-hamnita	[I] think that [it]'s the same
6. Ne, Nam-Han e kihu nın Nyuyok Cu wa tækæ kathta ko sængkak-hamnita.	Yes, I think South Korea's weather is about the same as that of New York State.

A

pom chəl	spring season
Nyuyok chələm	like New York; just as New York
7. Yəki e to pom chəl e nın Nyuyok chələm pi ka manhi onın ka yo?	Does it rain here as much as it does in New York in the spring (season)?

B

nıcın pom	late spring
ilın yəlım	early summer
cangma chəl	rainy season
cangma chəl ila ko pulımnita	[we] call [it] the rainy season
8. Tækæ nıcın pom kwa ilın yəlım e pi ka manhi oci yo. Kılæ sə, Yu-wəl kwa Chil-wəl ıl cangma chəl ila ko pulımnita.	Yes, it usually rains a lot in late spring and early summer. So we call June and July the rainy season.

Dialogue B

(..on a Saturday morning..)

A

pakk (e)	outside
9. Cikım pakk (e) nalssi ka əttəhsımnikka?	What's the weather like outside now?

10. B: 아마, 비가 올 것 같습니다. 날이 흐리고, 바람이 좀 붑니다.

일기
일기 예보

11. A: 오늘 아침에 일기 예보를 들었읍니까?

래디오
개입니다
개인다고 (말)했읍니다
기상대
틀립니다

12. B: 예, 아침 래디오에서는 낮에 개인다고 말했지만 기상대도 가끔 틀리니까요.

큰 일
큰 일(이) 납니다

13. A: 비가 오면 큰 일 납니다.

계획
중대합니다, 중요합니다
중대한 계획, 중요한 계획

14. B: 왜요? 무슨 중대한 계획이라도 있읍니까?

등산
등산할 계획
등산할 계획입니다

15. A: 예, 오늘 오후에 등산할 계획이었읍니다.

B

pi ka ol kəs kathsımnita	it looks like rain
10. Ama, pi ka ol kəs kathsımnita. Nal i hıliko, palam i com pumnita.	It looks like it'll probably rain. It's cloudy and a little windy.

A

ilki	weather; climate
ilki yepo	weather forecast
11. Onıl achim e ilki yepo (lıl) tıləssımnikka?	Did you hear the weather forecast this morning?

B

lætio	radio
kæimnita	[it] clears up
kæinta ko (mal-)hæssımnita	[it] said that [it] clears up
kisangtæ	weather bureau; weather-man
thıllimnita/thılyimnita/	[it]'s wrong; [it] is not right
12. Ne, achim lætio esə nın nac e kæintako mal-hæssci man, kisangtæ to kakkım thıllini kka yo.	Yes, the radio this morning said it would clear up at noon, but the weather-man is occasionally wrong.

A

khın il	a big problem; a big trouble ('a big job')
khın il (i) namnita	('a big trouble comes up')
13. Pi ka omyən, khın il namnita.	It mustn't rain! ('If it rains, a big problem comes up.')

B

kyehwek	plan(ning); plans
cungtæ-hamnita / cungyo-hamnita	[it] is important
cungtæ-han / cungyo-han kyehwek	important plans
musın kyehwek ilato	any plans

예...
정말
바랍니다
개이기 바랍니다

16. B: 예..., 정말 오후에는 개이기 바랍니다.

14. Wæ yo? Musın cungtæ-han kyehwek ilato issımnikka? — Why? Do you have some important plans?

A

tıngsan — hiking

tıngsan-hal kyehwek — (a) plan to hike

tıngsan-hal kyehwek imnita — [I]'m planning to hike

15. Ne, onıl ohu e tıngsan-hal kyehwek iəssımnita. — Yes, I was planning to go hiking this afternoon.

B

ne...? — (oh, is that right?...)

cəngmal — certainly; truly; truth

palamnita — [I] desire; [I] hope

kæiki palamnita — [I] hope [it] cleras up

16. Ne...? Cəngmal ohu e nın kæiki palamnita. — Oh, you were? I hope it clears up in the afternoon.

NOTES ON DIALOGUES

(Numbers correspond to the sentence numbers.)

2. Iləhke 'this way' or 'like this', cələhke 'that way' or 'like that', kıləhke 'that way' or 'so' or 'in such a way', occur as adverbials which are inflected from the verb stems iləh- 'to be like this', cələh- 'to be like that' and kıləh- 'to be so'.

3. Ilən 'this kind of-', cələn 'that kind of-', kılən 'that kind of-', are the inflected present modifier words which are also based on the stem iləh- 'to be like this', cələh- 'to be like that', and kıləh- 'to be so', respectively. The stem final sound h is dropped when the ending -(ı)n is added.

4. Mal which occurs after certain time nominals is either a part of a word or a post-noun, meaning 'the end': wəlmal 'the end of the month', cumal 'weekend', nyənmal 'the end of the year', haknyən mal 'the end of the school year', Il-wəl mal 'the end of January', etc.

5. -Pu ('part') which occurs at the end of a word succeeding the names of directions (i.e. tong 'east, sə 'west', nam 'south', puk 'north') often designates geographical areas of the United States: Tongpu 'the Eastern part of U.S.', Səpu 'the Western part of U.S.', Nampu 'the South', Pukpu 'the North'. (See Drill B, Unit 15.)

8. X (i)la ko pulımnita. ('[We] call [it] X.') can be substituted by X (i)la ko hamnita. ('[We] say [it] is X.') (See Grammar Note 3, Unit 17.)

12. Thılli- 'to be wrong' has its antonymous verb mac- 'to be correct'. Mac- and olh- are synonymous.

GRAMMAR NOTES

1 -nınkun/kun yo

An inflected form ending in -nınkun/kun + yo may be used as a kind of emphatic or exclamatory sentence final form. This construction is usually accompanied by the intonation patterns the same as the one in -ci yo? (Unit 6) or the one in an exclamation sentence. -Nınkun is added to an action verb stem; -kun is added to the copula or a description verb stem, or to any verb stem plus the honorific and/or tense suffixes. However, to an action verb stem which ends in -ss, -kun is added. Observe the following examples:

(a)

Sənsæng ın Hankuk mal ıl cal hanınkun yo!	'You speak Korean very well!'
Cə mal i cham cal ttwinınkun yo!	'That horse runs sure fast!'
Ai tıl i cham manhi məknınkun yo!	'The kids sure eat a lot!'
Mikuk yəca tıl ın uncən ıl cal hanınkun yo!	'The American women certainly are good drivers, aren't they?' ('The American women do driving certainly well.')
A, næ ka kı kəs ıl mollasskun yo!	'Oh, gee, I didn't know that!'

(b)

Onıl nalssi ka phək cohkun yo!	'The weather is very nice today, isn't it?' / 'It's a nice day today!'
Kim Sənsæng ın cəngmal khi ka khıkun yo!	'Mr. Kim is really a tall man, isn't he?' / 'Mr. Kim really is tall.'
A, kıləhkun yo!	'Oh, that's right (I didn't know that).'
Aiku, phək aphıkesskun yo!	'Oh, no, [you] must hurt!'

Note: In the further Units, we will see that the construction -nınkun/kun + yo can be substituted by -nınku/ku + man + yo with the same meaning. The inflected word ending in -nınkun/kun is considered to be one-word contraction from the two-word phrase -nınku/ku + man.

2. Infinitive + ci-

As an independent verb ci- is an intransitive action verb, of which meanings vary depending on what is its subject or topic: Hæ ka cinta.

'The sun sets.', Kkoch i ciəssta. 'The flowers have withered.', (Namu) iph i cimnita. 'The leaves are falling.', etc. However, preceded by the infinitive of a description verb, ci- occurs as an auxiliary verb, which denotes gradual change of the description of the preceeding verb. The verb phrase Infinitive + ci- with or without an adverb cəmcəm (or chacha) 'gradually' is usually translated as either 'be getting -er' or 'become + adjective'. Examples:

Nalssi ka (chacha) chuwə cimnita.	'The weather is getting (gradually) colder.'
Hankuk mal i tə əlyəwə cimnita.	'Korean is getting more difficult.'
Yosæ mulkən kaps i phək pissa ciəssə yo.	'Things became quite expensive these days.'
Næil ilkɨ ka coha cil kka yo?	'Will the weather be nice tomorrow (do you think)?'

3. -n/ɪn/nɪn kəs kath-

The present inflected modifier word -n/ɪn/nɪn + kəs occurs without pause before the verb kath-, to denote the speaker's assumption for the probability of the action or description of the verb in the modifier word. The English translations for the construction -n/ɪn/nɪn kəs kath- are 'seems that...' or 'seems as if...' or 'looks like... ing', etc. Observe the following examples:

Pi ka onɪn kəs kathsɪmnita.	'It seems that it's raining (now).'
Kɪ ai ka tætanhi ttokttokhan kəs kathsɪmnita.	'That child seems to be very bright.'
Iyaki ka cæmi issnɪn kəs kathsɪmnikka?	'Does the story sound interesting?' ('Does it seem that the story is interesting?')
Cə khi (ka) khɪn salam i cangkun in kəs kathci yo?	'That tall man looks like a general, doesn't he?'
Il i kɪli swipci anhɪn kəs kathə yo.	'The work doesn't seem to be that easy
Tæsa ka ce ilɪm ɪl anɪn kəs kathci anhsɪmnita.	'The ambassador doesn't seem to know my name.'

Note that the tenses and/or speech levels of the whole construction are generated in the verb kath- (1), but the tenses for the speaker's assumption of the probability are made by replacing the present modifier word ending -nɪn with the past modifier word ending -n/ɪn form for the past and with the -(ɪ)l form for the future, respectively (2). Examples:

(1)

Pusan e yəkwan kaps i com pissan kəs kathəssımnita.	'It seemed that the hotels in Pusan were a little expensive.'
Kim Sənsæng e il i cæmi issnın kəs kathəssə yo.	'Mr. Kim's job sounded interesting.'
Uli Yəngə sənsæng ın ttal ıl calang-hanın kəs kathəssımnita.	'Our English teacher seemed to be proud of [his] daughter.'

(2a)

Kicha ka pəlssə ttənan kəs kathsımnita.	'It seems the train has already left.
Kaıl i kəi cinan kəs kathsımnita.	'It seems the autumn is almost over.' ('It seems that almost the autumn passed.')
Pak Sənsæng ın catongcha lıl pha(lı)n kəs kathsımnita.	'Mr. Park seems to have sold his car.

Note: In case of copula and description verbs, -(a,ə)sstən is added to the stem to show the past in the above construction. Example:

Kim Sənsæng puin ın cəlməssıl ttæ (e) yeppəsstən kəs kathsımnita.	'It seems Mrs. Kim was pretty when she was young.'

(2b)

Pi ka ol kəs kathsımnita.	'It looks like rain.' ('It seems that it will rain.')
Munce ka manhıl kəs kathə yo.	'It seems there're going to be a lot of problems.'
Nuka tæthongyəng i twel kəs kathsımnikka?	'Who do you think will be the President?' ('Who, does it seem, will become the President?')
Hankuk mal i Cungkuk mal pota tə əlyəul kəs kathsımnita.	'Korean looks more difficult than Chinese.'

4. Particle chələm

A nominal + the particle chələm (or its synonym kathi) 'like + the Nominal' occurs as an adverbial expression for the following inflected expression. Examples:

Kim Sənsæng chələm hasipsiyo.	'Please do [it] like Mr. Kim.'
Kkolphı chələm cohın untong i əpsımnita.	'There aren't any good sports like golf.'

I cip i sæ cip chələm kkækkıthamnita.	'This house is clean like a new house.'
Hankuk mal i Ilpon mal chələm əlyəpsımnikka?	'Is Korean difficult like Japanese?' 'Is Korean as difficult as Japanese?'

5. Particle lato/ilato

Lato occurs after a word ending in a consonant and ilato after a word ending in a vowel. The particle lato/ilato occurs after either inflected or uninflected words. Observe the following constructions where lato/ilato occurs: (Compare lato/ilato with na/ina, Grammar Note 4, Unit 10.).

(a) Interrogative expression + (i)lato = adverbial phrase 'any-'.

muəs ilato	'anything' or 'whatever [it] is'
musın yaksok ilato	'any appointment' or 'whatever appointment [it] may be'
nuku lato	'anybody' or 'whoever [it] may be'
ənce lato	'anytime' or 'whenever [it] may be'
əttəhke lato	'somehow' or 'whatever way [I] may take'

(b) After a nominal or an adverbial expression lato/ilato also occurs simply to emphasize the preceeding expression as the possible alternative of choice for the following inflected expression. Examples:

Onıl ın cip esə capci lato ilkessə yo.	'I'm going to read at home today, say, magazines.'
Na lato kılən il ın hal su issımnita.	'Even I can do such a job.'
Kıləm, tapang e lato kapsita.	'Well, let's go to, say, a tea-room, then.'
Yəngə lato kalıchiko siphci man,.....	'I would like to teach even English but.....'
Kalıchinın kəs i əlyəumyən, pæuki lato hal su isskessci yo?	'If teaching is hard, [he] can do, say, learning, can't [he]?'

Note that we will learn in further units about the constructions in which other inflected words + lato/ilato occur.

6. -(ı)l kyehwek i- 'be planning to...'

The construction the -(ı)l form + the noun kyehwek 'plan' + the copula i-, literally means '[it] is the plan to do...'. The usual translation, however, is 'be planning to do...'. The tense suffixes may occur in the copula i- for the whole construction. Examples:

Na nɪn næil tɪngsan-hal kyehwek imnita.	'I'm planning to go hiking tomorrow.'
Wəllæ Səul e kal kyehwek iəssci man, kyehwek ɪl pakkwəssə yo.	'Originally I was planning to go to Seoul, but I have changed plans.'
Miss Braun i kot kyəlhon-hal kyehwek in kəs kathsɪmnita.	'Miss Brown seems to be planning to get married soon.'
Kim Paksa nɪn appathɪ esə sal kyehwek ila ko mal-hæssɪmnita.	'Dr. Kim said that he was planning to live in an apartment.'

.DRILLS

A. Substitution Drill

1. Yu-wəl kwa Chil-wəl ɪl cangma chəl ila ko pulɪmnita. — [We] call June and July the rainy season.

*2. Səul ɪl Hankuk e suto la ko pulɪmnita. — Seoul is called the capital of Korea.

*3. Il hanɪn kos ɪl cikcang ila ko pulɪmnita. — The place where [you] work is called the place of work.

*4. Ton i manhɪn salam ɪl puca la ko pulɪmnita. — [We] call the person who has a lot of money a rich man.

*5. Kukhwe ɪywən tɪl ɪl cəngchika la ko pulɪmnita. — [We] call the members of the National Assembly politicians.

*6. Mikuk ɪl Hapcungkuk ila ko pulɪmnita. — America is called the United States.

*7. Pusan kathɪn tosi lɪl hangku la ko pulɪmnita. — A city like Pusan is called a harbor.

*8. Mulkən ɪl mantɪnɪn te lɪl kongcang ila ko pulɪmnita. — [We] call the place where goods are made a factory.

*9. Kongcang esə il-hanɪn salam ɪl cikkong ila ko pulɪmnita. — [We] call the people working at factories (factory) workers.

B. Substitution Drill

1. Nam-Han e kihu nɪn Mikuk Tongpu wa kathta ko sængkak-hamnita. — I think South Korea's weather is the same as that of the eastern U.S.

2. Nam-Han e kihu nɪn Mikuk Tongpu wa kathta ko sængkak-hamnikka? — Do you think South Korea's weather is the same as that of the eastern U.S.?

3. Cə yəca nɪn Mikuk salam ila ko sængkak-hamnikka? — Do you think that woman is an American?

4. Cə yəca nɪn Mikuk salam ila ko sængkak-haci anhsɪmnikka? — Don't you think that woman is an American?

5. Kakkɪm yənghwa ponɪn kəs i cohta ko sængkak-haci anhsɪmnikka? — Don't you think it is good to see the movies sometimes?

*6. Kakkɪm yənghwa ponɪn kəs i cohta ko mitsɪmnita. — I believe that it is good to see the movies sometimes.

7. Pak Sənsæng i Yəngə lɪl cal hanta ko mitsɪmnita. — I believe that Mr. Park speaks English well.

8. Pak Sənsæng i Yəngə lıl cal hanta ko tıləssımnita. — I heard that Mr. Park speaks English well.

9. Kim Ssi e apəci ka tola kasyəssta ko tıləssimnita. — I heard that Mr. Kim's father (had) passed away.

10. Kim Ssi e apəci ka tola kasyəssta ko (mal-)hæssımnita. — [They] (or Mr. Kim) said that Mr. Kim's (or his) father passed away.

11. Ceimsı nın tıngsan-hal kyehwek ila ko hæssımnita. — James told me (or said) that he was planning to go hiking.

12. Ceimsı nın tıngsan-hal kyehwek ila ko aləssımnita. — I understood (or knew) that James was planning to go hiking.

13. Sənsæng i Səul esə olæ tongan il-hæssta ko aləssımnita. — I understood that you worked in Seoul for a long time.

14. Sənsæng i Səul esə olæ tongan il-hæssta ko amnita. — I understand that you have worked in Seoul for a long time.

C. Response Drill

Tutor: Hankuk mal i əlyəwə yo? — 'Is Korean difficult?'

Student 1: Ne, (Hankuk mal i) əlyəpta ko sængkak-hamnita. — 'Yes, I think Korean is difficult.'

Student 2: Aniyo, (Hankuk mal i) əlyəpta ko sængkak-haci anhsımnita. — 'No, I don't think Korean is difficult.'

1. Kongpu-haki cæmi issə yo?

Ne, (kongpu-haki) cæmi issta ko sængkak-hamnita.

Aniyo, (kongpu-haki) cæmi issta ko sængkak-haci anhsımnita.

2. Cə yəca ka yeppə yo?

Ne, (cə yəca ka) yeppıta ko sængkak-hamnita.

Aniyo, (cə yəca ka) yeppıta ko sængkak-haci anhsımnita.

3. Kim Sənsæng i Pullansə mal ıl cal hæ yo?

Ne, (Kim Sənsæng i Pullansə mal ıl) cal hanta ko sængkak-hamnita.

Aniyo, (Kim Sənsæng i Pullansə mal ıl) cal hanta ko sængkak-haci anhsımnita.

4. Kicha ka phyəlli-hæ yo?

Ne, (kicha ka) phyəlli-hata ko sæ̈ngkak-hamnita.

Aniyo, (kicha ka) phyəlli-hata ko sæ̈ngkak-haci anhsımnita.

5. Hankuk san i alımtawə yo?

Ne, (Hankuk san i) alımtapta ko sæ̈ngkak-hamnita.

Aniyo, (Hankuk san i) alımtapta ko sæ̈ngkak-haci anhsımnita.

6. Nalssi ka phək chuwə cəssə yo?

Ne, (nalssi ka) phək chuwə cəssta ko sæ̈ngkak-hamnita.

Aniyo, (nalssi ka) phək chuwə cəssta ko sæ̈ngkak-haci anhsımnita.

7. Pakk e palam i tætanhi pulə yo?

Ne, (pakk e palam i) tætanhi punta ko sæ̈ngkak-hamnita.

Aniyo, (pakk e palam i) tætanhi punta ko sæ̈ngkak-haci anhsimnita.

8. Mikuk kwa Hankuk e kihu ka pisıthan kəs kathə yo?

Ne, (Mikuk kwa Hankuk e kihu ka) pisıthan kəs kathta ko sæ̈ngkak-hamnita.

Aniyo, (Mikuk kwa Hankuk e kihu ka) pisıthan kəs kathta ko sæ̈ngkak-haci anhsımnita.

9. I sikye ka thıllie yo?

Ne, (i sikye ka) thıllita ko sæ̈ngkak-hamnita.

Aniyo, (i sikye ka) thıllita ko sæ̈ngkak-haci anhsımnita.

10. Kı munce ka phək cungyo-hæ yo?

Ne, (kı munce ka) phək cungyo-hata ko sæ̈ngkak-hamnita.

Aniyo, (kı munce ka) phək cungyo-hata ko sæ̈ngkak-haci anhsımnita.

11. Cə ai ka ttokttokhan haksæ̈ng iye yo?

Ne, (cə ai ka) ttokttokhan haksæ̈ng ila ko sæ̈ngkak-hamnita.

Aniyo, (cə ai ka) ttokttokhan haksæ̈ng ila ko sæ̈ngkak-haci anhsımnita.

D. Response Drill

Tutor: Pak Sənsæng i Yəngə lıl cal hanta ko hæssə yo? — 'Did [they] say that Mr. Park speaks English well?'

Student: Ne, (Pak Sənsæng i Yəngə lıl) cal hanta ko tıləssə yo. — 'Yes, I heard [he] speaks English well.'

1. Consı Sənsæng i kot Səul e tola onta ko hæssə yo? — Ne, (Consı Sənsæng i) kot Səul e tola onta ko tıləssə yo.
2. Hankuk e yəlım nalssi ka Nyuyok pota tə mutəpta ko hæssə yo? ('Did [they] say that the summer weather in Korea is more muggy than in New York?') — Ne, (Hankuk e yəlım nalssi ka Nyuyok pota) tə mutəpta ko tıləssə yo.
3. Yang Sənsæng i cəngchika ka tweəssta ko hæssə yo? — Ne, (Yang Sənsæng i) cəngchika ka tweəssta ko tıləssə yo.
4. Pak Sənsæng puin i ınhæng e kınmu-hal kəs ila ko hæssə yo? — Ne, (Pak Sənsæng puin i) ınhæng e kınmu-hal kəs ila ko tıləssə yo.
5. Tæku e kyothong i phyəlli-hata ko hæssə yo? — Ne, (Tæku e kyothong i) phyəlli-hata ko tıləssə yo.
6. Hakkyo kal sikan i nıcəssta ko hæssə yo? — Ne, hakkyo kal sikan i nıcəssta ko tıləssə yo.

E. Response Drill

Tutor: Kakkım yənghwa lıl ponın kəs i cohta ko sængkak-hase yo? — 'Do you think it's nice to see the movies occasionally?'

Student: Ne, kakkım yənghwa lıl ponın kəs i cohta ko mitsımnita. — 'Yes, I believe it's nice to see movies occasionally.'

1. Cəng sənsæng i cikım Səul e kyesinta ko sængkak-hase yo? — Ne, Cəng Sənsæng i cikım Səul e kyesinta ko mitsımnita.
2. Hankuk mal ıl almyən, Hankuk esə il-haki phyənhata ko sængkak-hase yo? — Ne, Hankuk mal ıl almyən, Hankuk esə il-haki phyənhata ko mitsımnita.
3. Kı munce ka talıta ko sængkak-hase yo? — Ne, kı munce ka talıta ko mitsımnita.
4. Ilponə munpəp i Cungkukə pota pokcap-hata ko sængkak-hase yo? — Ne, Ilponə munpəp i Cungkukə pota pokcap-hata ko mitsımnita.

5. Sənsæng ın kuntæ kyənghəm i philyo-hata ko sængkak-hase yo? — Ne, kuntæ kyənghəm i philyo-hata ko mitsımnita.
6. Ceimsı Sənsæng ın Hankuk phungsok ıl cal ihæ-hanta ko sængkak-hase yo? — Ne, (Ceimsı Sənsæng ın) Hankuk phungsok ıl cal ihæ-hanta ko mitsımnita.
7. Pak Sənsæng (e) mal i thıllita ko sængkak-hase yo? — Ne, Pak Sənsæng (e) mal i thıllita ko mitsımnita.

F. Response Drill

Tutor: Cə pun ın wekyokwan imnikka? — 'Is that man in the foreign service?'
Student: Ne, (cə pun ın) wekyokwan ila ko aləssımnita. — 'Yes, I understood (<u>or</u> thought) that he is in the foreign service.'

1. Kim Sənsæng i Yəngə lıl kalıchimnikka? — Ne, (Kim Sənsæng i) Yəngə lıl kalıchinta ko aləssımnita.
2. Pak Yəngca ka kyəlhon-hæssımnikka? — Ne, (Pak Yəngca ka) kyəlhon-hæssta ko aləssımnita.
3. Cəng Sənsæng i tæsa ka tweəssımnikka? — Ne, (Cəng Sənsæng i) tæsa ka tweəssta ko aləssımnita.
4. Hankuk e kyəul kihu ka Mikuk Tongpu wa pisıthamnikka? — Ne, (Hankuk e kyəul kihu ka Mikuk Tongpu wa) pisıthata ko aləssımnita.
5. Hankuk sikol kil esə uncən-haki (ka) əlyəpsımnikka? — Ne, Hankuk sikol kil esə uncən-haki (ka) əlyəpta ko aləssımnita.
6. I Sənsæng e əməni nın nai ka manhsımnikka? — Ne, I Sənsæng e əməni nın nai ka manhta ko aləssımnita.

G. Response Drill (based on Grammar Note 1)

Tutor: Onıl nalssi ka phək cohci yo? — 'The weather is very nice today, isn't it?'
Student: Ne, (onıl nalssi ka) phək cohkun yo! — 'Yes, it certainly is!'

1. Cohın nalssi ka kyesok-haci yo? — Ne, cohın nalssi ka kyesok-hanınkun yo!
2. Il i pokcap-haci yo? — Ne, il i pokcap-hakun yo!
3. ımsik i mas i cohci yo? — Ne, ımsik i mas i cohkun yo!

4. Hanıl i tætanhi ma(l)kci yo? — Ne, hanıl i tætanhi ma(l)kkun yo!
5. Kim Sənsæng e atıl i phək ttokttokhaci yo? — Ne, (Kim Sənsæng e atıl i) phək ttokttokhakun yo!
6. Kot, pi ka ol kəs kathci yo? — Ne, kot, pi ka ol kəs kathkun yo!
7. Kı ai ka apəci wa pisıthaci yo? — Ne, (kı ai ka) apəci wa pisıthakun yo!
8. Onıl nalssi ka mutəpci yo? ('Today's weather is muggy, isn't it?') — Ne, (onıl nalssi ka) mutəpkun yo!
9. Kimchi ka cəngmal mæpci yo? — Ne, (kimchi ka) cəngmal mæpkun yo!

H. Grammar Drill (based on Grammar Note 2)

Tutor: Nalssi ka chupsımnita. — 'The weather is cold.'
Student: Nalssi ka cəmcəm chuwə cimnita. — 'The weather is getting colder.'

1. Hankuk mal i əlyəpsımnita. — Hankuk mal i cəmcəm əlyəwə cimnita.
2. Pang an i ttattıthamnita. — Pang an i cəmcəm ttattıthæ cimnita.
3. Cə nın nai ka manhsımnita. — Cə nın nai ka cəmcəm manhə cimnita.
4. Il e cæmi ka issımnita. — Cəmcəm il e cæmi ka issə cimnita.
5. Munce ka talımnita. — Munce ka cəmcəm talla cimnita.
6. Kyothong i phyəllihamnita. — Kyothong i cəmcəm phyəllihæ cimnita.
7. Kı ai nın khi ka khımnita. — Kı ai nın cəmcəm khi ka khə cimnita.
8. Namphyən kwa anæ e əlkul i pisıthamnita. — Namphyən kwa anæ e əlkul i cəmcəm pisıthæ cimnita.
9. Yosæ nın pihængki ka ppalımnita. — Yosæ nın pihængki ka cəmcəm ppalla cimnita.

I. Transformation Drill

Tutor: Pi ka omnita. — 'It's raining.'
Student: Pi ka onın kəs kathsımnita. — 'It seems to be raining (now).'

1. Il i acik kyesok-hamnita. — Il i acik kyesok-hanın kəs kathsımnita.
2. Pisə ka thaiphı lıl cal chimnita. — Pisə ka thaiphı lıl cal chinın kəs kathsımnita.
3. Acəssi ka kı sakən e tæhæ sə amnita. — Acəssi ka kı sakən e tæhæ sə anın kəs kathsımnita.

4. Miss Braun ın nai ka kıli manhci anhsımnita.	Miss Braun ın nai ka kıli manhci anhın kəs kathsımnita.
5. I Sənsæng i onıl ttənal kyehwek imnita.	I Sənsæng i onıl ttənal kyehwek in kəs kathsımnita.
6. Ceimsı nın yəngsa ka tweki wənhamnita.	Ceimsı nın yəngsa ka tweki wənhanın kəs kathsımnita.
7. Miss Chwe ka tangsin ıl salang-hamnita.	Miss Chwe ka tangsin ıl salang-hanın kəs kathsımnita.
8. Kı salam e acəssi ka puca imnita.	Kı salam e acəssi ka puca in kəs kathsımnita.
9. Cə haksæng i phək ttokttokhamnita.	Cə haksæng i phək ttokttokhan kəs kathsımnita.

J. Response Drill

Tutor: Onıl ilki ka əce wa pisıthamnikka?	'Is today's weather similar to that of yesterday?'
Student: Ne, (onıl ilki ka əce wa) pisıthan kəs kathsımnita.	'Yes, it looks the same.' ('It seems it is similar.')
1. Pakk e nalssi ka chupsımnikka?	Ne, chuun kəs kathsımnita.
2. Tæsa ka Hankuk mal ıl alə tıtsımnikka?	Ne, alə tıtnın kəs kathsımnita.
3. Hakkyo kal sikan i acik ilımnikka?	Ne, (acik) ilın kəs kathsımnita.
4. Hanıl i hılimnikka?	Ne, hılin kəs kathsımnita.
5. Samusil i com ətupsımnikka?	Ne, (com) ətuun kəs kathsımnita.
6. Kisangtæ e ilki yepo ka thıllimnikka?	Ne, thıllin kəs kathsımnita.
7. Kim Sənsæng e mal i macsımnikka?	Ne, macın kəs kathsımnita.
8. Wekyokwan sænghwal e wekukə ka cungyo-hamnikka?	Ne, cungyo-han kəs kathsımnita.
9. Mikuk tæsa ka tangsin e ilım ıl molımnikka?	Ne, molının kəs kathsımnita.

K. Response Drill

Tutor: Ohu e nun i ol kka yo?	'Will it snow in the afternoon?'
Student: Ne, (nun i) ol kəs kathsımnita.	'Yes, it looks like it.' ('It seems that it will snow.')
1. I os i pissal kka yo?	Ne, pissal kəs kathsımnita.
2. Hanıl i kæil kka yo?	Ne, kæil kəs kathsımnita.
3. Miss Braun i kot kyəlhon hal kka yo?	Ne, kot kyəlhon hal kəs kathsımnita.
4. Kı yəca ka kıləhke palal kka yo?	Ne, kıləhke palal kəs kathsımnita.
5. Kı chinku ka catongcha lıl tasi pakkul kka yo?	Ne, tasi pakkul kəs kathsımnita.
6. Puin i Hankuk ıl cohahal kka yo?	Ne, (anæ ka Hankuk ıl) cohahal kəs kathsımnita.
7. Næil nalssi ka mutəul kka yo?	Ne, mutəul kəs kathsımnita.
8. Ilki yepo ka thıllil kka yo?	Ne, thıllil kəs kathsımnita.
9. Kim Paksa mal i cəngmal il kka yo?	Ne, cəngmal il kəs kathsımnita.

L. Response Drill

Tutor: Hanıl i kæil kəs kathsımnita.	'It seems the sky will clear up.'
Student: Cəngmal, kæiki palamnita.	'I sure hope it does.' ('Truly, I hope it clears up.')
1. Ilki ka ttattıthal kəs kathsımnita.	Cəngmal, ttattıthaki palamnita.
2. Il i onıl ta kkıth-nal kəs kathsımnita.	Cəngmal, onıl ta kkıth-naki palamnita.
3. Ceimsı nın Hankuk mal kongpu lıl kımantuci anhıl kəs kathsımnita.	Cəngmal, kımantuci anhki palamnita.
4. Munce ka əpsıl kəs kathsımnita.	Cəngmal, (munce ka) əpski palamnita.
5. Mikuk e tola ka to, Hankuk mal kongpu ka kyesok-hal kəs kathsımnita.	Cəngmal, kyesok-haki palamnita.
6. Sənsæng kwa Wəsington esə tasi mannal kəs kathsımnita.	Cəngmal, tasi mannaki palamnita.
7. Kılən il-haki əlyəpci anhıl kəs kathsımnita.	Cəngmal, əlyəpci anhki palamnita.
8. Palam i pulci anhıl kəs kathsımnita.	Cəngmal, (palam i) pulci anhki palamnita.

9. Tæsakwan esə uli eke allyə cul kəs kathsɪmnita. — Cəngmal, allyə cuki palamnita.

10. Sinæ e kil i pəncap-hal kəs kathci anhsɪmnita. — Cəngmal, pəncap-haci anhki palamnita.

EXERCISES

A. Tell Pak Sənsæng that:

1. it's raining hard.
2. it's snowing outside.
3. it started to rain just a minute ago.
4. it has stopped snowing.
5. it is very windy and cloudy today.
6. it rained all morning/achim nænæ/.
7. it was snowy and cold yesterday at Panmunjom.
8. it was awfully muggy all summer in Washington.
9. it was hot but there was no humidity/sɪpki/.
10. it has begun to cloud up/kulɪm i kki-ta/.
11. it has begun to clear up.
12. the sky was clear and the temperature/onto/ was cool.
13. in winter, river always freeze/əl-ta/ but the sun shines most of the time.
14. the rainy season begins in the warm spring season and lasts until the end of July.
15. beginning early November the weather gets gradually colder.

B.

	James asks:	You:
1.	if you think the Korean winter is the same as that of New York State.	'Yes, I think so.'
2.	if it looks like rain.	'Yes, but I hope it won't rain.'
3.	if Koreans use chop-sticks like Japanese.	'Yes, they usually do.'
4.	whether it seems housing in Tokyo is less expensive than in the U.S.	'No, it seems to be about the same.'
5.	if you have any important plans.	'Yes, I have one, but not a specially important one.'

6. how long you're planning to to stay in Korea.	'Oh, maybe about two or three years.'
7. if you want to go hiking.	'Yes, only when the sky clears up.'
8. if you will go swimming /suyəng/ with him.	'Yes, if there is a good place to swim/suyəng-hal te/.'
9. if winter is good for hunting /sanyang-haki/.	'Yes, it is. But there are not many places to hunt/sanyang-hal kos/.'
10. if people go fishing/nakksi-cil (halə) ka-ta/ to the sea.	'Some people do, but you can also see people fishing/nakssi-cil hanın kəs/ by the river sides.'

C. Make a short dialogue so that one of the following expressions is included in the response:

1. iləhke	'this way'
2. cələhke	'that way'
3. kıləhke	'that way, in such a way'
4. ilən	'this kind of'
5. cələn	'that kind of'
6. kılən	'such kind of'
7. chacha or cəmcəm	'gradually'
8. onıl chələm	'like today'
9. Sənsæng e mal i macsımnita. (or macəssımnita).	'You are right.'
10. Næ ka thılliəssımnita.	'I am wrong.' ('I was not right.')
11. Næ ka cal mot hæssımnita.	'I was wrong.' ('I couldn't do well.')

End of Tape 12B

Korean-English Glossary

The following is all of the vocabulary introduced in this text, except words used for pronunciation drills in the Introductory Unit. There are three vertical columns: the left column is the Korean in transcription; the middle is the same in Hankıl; the right column is the meaning in English.

A verb is listed in the traditional Korean dictionary form ending in -ta with a hyphen after stem. Every verb or verb phrase is indicated as to transitive or intransitive by Vt & Vi respectively in the parenthesis immediately after the entry, and its Infinitive form is also entered right after Vt or Vi. A free noun or noun phrase is not indicated for its part-of-speech, but other entries are so indicated like verbs: (D) = Determinative, (DN) = Dependent Noun, (PN) = Post-Noun, (Ad) = Adverb, (P) = Particle, (C) = Counter, (Num Ch) = Numeral of Chinese Character origin, (Num K) = Numeral of Korean origin, (Int) = Interjection.

An Arabic number immediately following English meaning for each entry refers to the Unit in which it first occurs: the number alone refers to the Basic Dialogue or Dialogues of that unit; N, G or D preceded by a number refers to the Notes on Dialogues, Grammar Notes and Drills of the unit indicated by number respectively.

Examples:

9 means Unit 9, Basic Dialogue(s)
9-N means Unit 9, Notes on the Basic Dialogues
9-G means Unit 9, Grammar Notes
9-D means Unit 9, Drills

Entries are listed according to the alphabetical order of the Basic Syllable Chart in Introductory Unit: a, ə, o, u, ı, i, e, æ, y, w, k, kk, kh, n, t, tt, th, l, m, p, pp, ph, s, ss, c, cc, ch, h, ng.

<u>a</u>

a (Int)	아	Oh! 1
ai	아이	child 2-D
aiku! (Int)	아이구!	Gee!, Oh! 17
a(l)-ta (Vt: alə)	알다: 알어	knows 2-G
Amnikka?	압니까?	Do you know? 3
akka (Ad)	아까	a little while ago, a few minutes ago 16-N
atıl	아들	son 14
atınim	아드님	your son (honored) 14-N
alə tɨt-ta (Vt: alə tılə)	알어 듣다: 알어 들어	understands (by ears) 9
alə po-ta (Vt: alə pwa)	알어 보다: 알어 봐	finds out, recognizes 7-G
alə cu-ta (Vt: alə cuə)	알어 주다: 알어 줘	recognizes, gives credit 7-G
alımtap-ta (Vt: alımtawə)	아름답다: 아름다워	is beautiful 5-D
ama (Ad)	아마	perhaps, probably 11
amu (D)	아무	any
amu kəs (ina)	아무 것(이나)	anything, whatever 12
an (Ad)	안	not 3
An məmnita.	안 멉니다.	[It] is not far. 3
an	안	the inside 16-D
ani (Ad)	아니	no (plain speech) 17
aniyo (Ad)	아니요	no 1
Aniyo, kwænchanhsımnita.	아니요, 괜찮습니다.	(No), not at all. 1
anæ	아내	my wife 14

annyəng	안녕	peace, tranquility 1
Annyəng-hasımnikka?	안녕하십니까?	How are you? 1
annyənghi (Ad)	안녕히	peacefully 1
Annyənghi kasipsiyo.	안녕히 가십시요.	Good bye (to someone leaving).
Annyənghi kyesipsiyo.	안녕히 계십시요.	Good bye (to someone staying).
ancu	안주	relish [taken with liquor], sidedish 12
anc-ta (Vi: ancə)	앉다	sits 11-D
ancə iss-ta	앉어 있다	is seated 14-G
anh-ta (Vt: anhə)	않다: 않어	not 4
Pissaci anhsımnita.	비싸지 않습니다.	[It] is not expensive. 4
apənim	아버님	father (honored) 14-N
apəci	아버지	father 13-D
aphı-ta (Vi: aphə)	아프다: 아퍼	is sick, hurts 6
acəssi	아저씨	uncle 14-D
acik (Ad)	아직	(not) yet, still 6-N
acu (Ad)	아주	very, extremely 10
acuməni	아주머니	aunt 14-D
achim	아침	morning, breakfast 4-D
onıl achim	오늘 아침	this morning 4-D
Achim ıl məkəssımnita.	아침을 먹었읍니다.	I had my breakfast. 12-D
achim siksa	아침 식사	breakfast ('morning meal') 12-D
ahıle	아흐레	nine days, the 9th day of the month 6-D
ahın (Num K)	아흔	ninety 5
ahop (Num K)	아홉	nine 5

ə

əkkæ	어깨	shoulder 13
əti	어디	where, what place 2
əti e	어디에	where 2
əte (Ad)	어데	where 2
ətup-ta (Vi: ətuwə)	어둡다: 어두워	is dark 10-D
əttəh-ta (Vi: əttəhæ)	어떻다: 어떠해	how is? 4
əttən	어떤	what kind of 5
I kəs i əttəhsımnikka?	이것이 어떻습니까?	How is this? 4
əttəhke (Ad)	어떻게	how?, in what way? 1
əl-ta (Vi: ələ)	얼다: 얼어	freezes 18-D
əlım	어름	ice 12-D
əlım mul	어름 물	ice water 12-D
əli-ta (Vi: əlyə)	어리다 : 어려	is young, is childish 14
əlkul	얼굴	face 13
əlyəp-ta (Vi: əlyəwə)	어렵다: 어려워	is difficult 5-D
əlma	얼마	how much, what price 4
əlma imnikka?	얼마 입니까?	How much is it? 4
əlma na kəllimnikka?	얼마나 걸립니까?	How long does it take? 7
əlma tongan	얼마 동안	for how long, for some time 15-N
əməni	어머니	mother 13-G
əmənim	어머님	mother (honored) 14-N
əmma	엄마	mammy, mother 17
ənı (D)	어느	which, a certain 2
ənı kəs	어느 것	which one? 2
ənı hwesa esə	어느 회사에서	at some company 15

ənni	언니	older sister (of female) 14-D
ənce	언제	when 5-D
ənce tınci	언제든지	anytime 12
əps-ta (Vi: əpsə)	없다: 없어	does not exist, does not have 5
əsə	어서	quickly, please 4
əsə osipsiyo.	어서 오십시요.	Please come in. 4
əce	어제	yesterday 4
	오	
o (Num Ch)	오	five 4
o-ta (Vi: wa)	오다: 와	comes 2-G
olın (D)	오른	right 2
olın ccok	오른 쪽	the right (side) 2-N
olæ	오래	a long time
Olæ kan man imnita.	오래간만 입니다.	(I haven't seen you for a long time.), Long time no see. 8
olæ tongan	오래 동안	for a long time 8-N
olla o-ta (Vi: olla wa)	올라 오다: 올라 와	comes up 7-G
olla ka-ta (Vi: olla ka)	올라 가다: 올라 가	goes up 7-G
olh-ta (Vi: olha)	옳다: 옳아	is right 18-N
onıl	오늘	today 4
onto	온도	temperature 18-D
oppa	오빠	older brother (of female) 14-D
os	옷	clothes, dresses 4-D
ohu	오후	afternoon 4-D
onıl ohu	오늘 오후	this afternoon 4-D

u

uyu	우유	milk 12-D
uli	우리	we, our 14
uli kacok	우리 가족	our family 14
untong	운동	physical exercise, sport 9-D
untong-ha-ta (Vi: untong-hæ)	운동하다: 운동해	takes exercises, plays [balls] 9-D
untongcang	운동장	playground 16-D
uncənsu	운전수	driver 16-D
uphyənkuk	우편국	post office 3-D

ɪ

ɪywən	의원	congressman, member of the National Assembly 16-D
ɪl/lɪl (P)	을/를	
Sənsæng ɪn muəs ɪl hasimnikka?	선생은 무엇을 하십니까?	What do you do? 1
Yəngə lɪl mal-hamnita.	영어를 말합니다.	I speak English. 1-G
ɪlo/lo (P)	으로/로	to, as, by 2
Wen ccok ɪlo kasipsiyo.	왼쪽으로 가십시오.	Go to the left. 2
wekyokwan ɪlo	외교관으로	as a diplomat 7
pæ lo	배로	by ship 7
ɪmsik	음식	food 7-D
ɪmsikcəm	음식점	restaurant 10-D
ɪn/nɪn (P)	은/는	as far 1
Ce ilɪm ɪn Ceimsɪ imnita.	제 이름은 제임스입니다.	My name is James. 1
Cə nɪn haksæng imnita.	저는 학생입니다.	I'm a student. 1-G
Sənsæng ɪn muəs ɪl hasimnikka?	선생은 무엇을 하십니까?	What are YOU doing? 1-G
ɪnhæng	은행	bank 2-D

ɪysa	의사	medical doctor 8-D
ɪyca	의자	chair 2-D
ɪng (Ad)	응	yes (plain speech) 17

<u>i</u>

I	이	Lee (family name) 1-D
i (Num Ch)	이	two 4
i (D)	이	this 2
i	이	tooth 13
i/ka (P)	이/가	
tæsakwan i	대사관이	the embassy (as subject) 2
Tæsakwan i əti e issɪmnikka?	대사관이 어디에 있읍니까?	Where is the embassy? 2
i-ta (Copula: iye <u>or</u> iyə)	이다: 이예: 이여	
əlma iye yo?	얼마이예요?	How much is [it]? 5
iyaki	이야기	story 17 (see <u>yæki</u>)
iyaki-ha-ta (iyaki-hæ)	이야기하다: 이야기해	speaks, talks, tells
Sənsæng e tæhæ sə iyaki tɪləssɪmnita.	선생에 대해서 이야기 들었읍니다.	I heard about you. 17
il	일	work, job 6
il-ha-ta (il-hæ)	일하다: 일해	works 3-G
il cali	일 자리	job 16-D
il (DN)	일	experience, fact
Cungkuk ɪmsik ɪl məkə pon il i issɪmnikka?	중국 음식을 먹어 본 일이 있읍니까?	Have you ever eaten Chinese food? 13
il (Num Ch)	일	one 4
il (C)	일	day
il-il	일 일	the 1st day of the month 6
ilato (P)	이라도	18-G (see <u>lato</u>)

iləna-ta (Vi: iləna)	일어나다: 일어나	gets up 12-D
iləh-ta (Vi: ilæ or iləhæ)	이렇다: 이래: 이러해	is like this
ilən nalssi	이런 날씨	this kind of weather 18
ilɪ-ta (Vi: illə)	이르다: 일러	is early
ilɪn yəlɪm	이른 여름	early summer 18
ilɪm	이름	name 1
ilhɪn/ilɪn (Num K)	일흔/이른	seventy 5
ile	이레	seven days, the 7th day of the month 6-D
Ilyoil	일요일	Sunday 6-D
ilk-ta (Vt: ilkə)	읽다: 읽어	reads 1-D
ilkop (Num K)	일곱	seven 5
ilki	일기	weather 15 (see nalssi)
Ilpon	일본	Japan 1-G
Ilpon mal	일본 말	Japanese (language) 1-D
Ilpon salam	일본 사람	Japanese 1-G
Ilponə	일본어	Japanese (language) 8-D
ilsang (D)	일상	daily 4
ilsang yongphum	일상 용품	daily necessities, daily things 4
ilcciki (Ad)	일찌기	early 11-D
imnita (Copula)	입니다:	(see i-ta)
Kim Kisu imnita.	김 기수 입니다.	[I] am Kisu Kim.
insa-ha-ta (Vi: insa-hæ)	인사하다: 인사해	greets 9-D
insa-kwa	인사과	personnel section
insa-kwacang	인사 과장	personnel section chief, personnel officer 13-D

ina (P)	이나	10 (see na)
Into	인도	India 6-D
ip	입	mouth 13
ip-ta (Vt: ipə)	입다: 입어	puts on (clothes), dresses
ipə po-ta (ipə pwa)	입어 보다: 입어 봐	tries on (clothes) 7-G
ipku	입구	the entrance 16-D
itta (Ad)	이따	later (on the same day) 11
Itta mannapsita.	이따 만납시다.	See you later. 11
ithɪl	이틀	two days, the 2nd day of the month 6-D
Ithæli	이태리	Italy 6-D
Ithæliə	이태리어	Italian 8-D
ippal	이빨	tooth 13 (see i)
isa	이사	moving (house)
isa-ha-ta (isa-hæ)	이사하다: 이사해	moves (house, office, etc.) 1
iss-ta (Vt: issə)	있다: 있어	exists, is
Cal issɪmnita.	잘 있읍니다.	[I]'m fine. (lit. '[I] exists well.') 1
icɪm	이즘	these days 8 (see yocɨm)
ingkhɪ	잉크	ink 7-G
ihæ	이해	understanding
ihæ-ha-ta (ihæ-hæ)	이해하다: 이해해	understand, comprehends 18-D

e

e (P)	에	to
Səul yək e kamnita.	서울 역에 갑니다.	I'm going to the Seoul Station 3
e (P)	의	of, -'s 1
cə e ilɪm	저의 이름	my name 1-G

e (P)	에	at, on, in 2-G
eke (P)	에게	to (someone)
Kı chæk ıl na eke ilkə cusipsiyo.	그 책을 나에게 읽어 주십시오.	Please read me the book. 11-G
ekesə (P)	에게서	from (someone) 13
əməni ekesə	어머니에게서	from mother 13-G
esə (P)	에서	from, at, in 3
Yəki esə məmnikka?	여기에서 멉니까?	Is [it] far from here? 3
Kyosil esə konpu-hamnita.	교실에서 공부합니다.	[We] study in the classroom. 3-G

Y

ya (P)	야	only when, only if 11-G
Puchiə ya hamnita.	부쳐야 합니다.	[I] have to mail. 11
yakpang	약방	drugstore 10-D
yaksok	약속	appointment, date, promise 17
yaksok-ha-ta (yaksok-hæ)	약속하다: 약속해	promises, makes an appointment 17-N
yachæ	야채	vegitable 13
yangnyəm	양념	seasoning 13
yangmal	양말	sock(s), stocking(s) 4-D
yangpok	양복	suit(s) 4-D
yangsik	양식	western food 12-D
yangsikcəm	양식점	western restaurant 13
yək	역	railroad station 3
yəki	여기	here, this place 2-D
yəki e	여기에	here
Yəki e issımnita.	여기에 있읍니다.	[It]'s here. 2-D
Yəki issımnita.	여기 있읍니다.	Here you are! 5

yəkwan	여관	inn, hotel 2
yəksa	역사	history 9-D
yətəl - yətə(l)p (Num K)	여덟 - 여덟	eight 5
yətɪle	여드레	eight days, the 8th day of the month 6-D
yətɪn (Num K)	여든	eighty 5
yə-tongsæng	여동생	younger sister 16-D
yəl (Num K)	열	ten 5
yəl-ta (Vt: yələ)	열다: 열어	opens 11-D
yələ (D)	여러	several, many 4
yələ kaci	여러 가지	several kinds 4
yəlɪm	여름	summer 15
yəlhɪl	열흘	ten days, the 10th day of the month 6-D
yənphil	연필	pencil 2-D
yənsɪp	연습	practice 9
yənsɪp-ha-ta (Vt: yənsɪp-hæ)	연습 하다: 연습 해	practises 9-N
yənha-ta (Vi: yənhæ)	연하다: 연해	is tender (meat) 13-D
Yəpose yo!	여보세요!	Hello there!, Say! 3
Yəposipsiyo!	여보십시오!	Hello there! 3-N (see Yəpose yo.)
yəph	옆	the side 2
yəph e	옆에	beside, (near)by 2
Sichəng yəph e issɪmnita.	시청 옆에 있습니다.	[It]'s next to the City Hall. 2
yəsəs (Num K)	여섯	six 5

yessæ	엿새	six days, the 6th day of the month 6-D
yeca	여자	woman 1-D
yehæng	여행	travelling, trip 15
yehæng-ha-ta (yehæng-hæ)	여행하다: 여행해	makes a trip, travels 15
yeng	영	zero 16 (see kong)
Yenge	영어	English 1-G
Yengkuk	영국	England 1-G
Yengkuk salam	영국 사람	Englishman 1-G
yengsa	영사	consul 7-D
yengsakwan	영사관	consulate 7-D
Yeng-Han	영한	English-Korean, British-Korean 5
yenghwa	영화	movies 9
Yi	이	Lee (family name) 1-D
yo (Particle)	요	4-G
Chenman e yo.	천만에요.	Not at all. 2
yoil (PN)	요일	week-day
musın yoil	무슨 요일	what day of the week 6
yosæ	요새	these days 8
yocım	요즘	lately, these days 1
yongphum	용품	items 4
ilsang yongphum	일상 용품	daily necessities 4
yuk (Num Ch)	육	six 4
yukci	육지	the land (in contrast to sea) 15-D
yumyeng	유명	fame
yumyeng-han salam	유명한 사람	famous man 15-N

yepo	예보	forecast 18
yeppɪ-ta (Vi: yeppə)	예쁘다: 예뻐	is pretty 5-D
yesun (Num K)	예순	sixty 5

W

wa/kwa (P)	와/과	with, and 4
na wa kathi	나와 같이	with me 4
chæk kwa yənphil	책과 연필	book and pencil 4-G
waisyassi	와이샤쓰	dress shirt 4-D
wanhæng (cha)	완행(차)	local (train) 10-D
wihəm-ha-ta (Vi: wihəm-hæ)	위험하다	is dangerous, is in danger 17-D
wəl (C)	월	
Sam-wəl	삼월	March 6
wəllæ (Ad)	원래	originally, formerly 14
Wəlyoil	월요일	Monday 6-D
Wəllam	월남	Vietnam 6-D
wən (C)	원	Won (Korean monetary unit) 4
o-sip wən	오십 원	W50 4
wənha-ta (Vt: wənhæ)	원하다: 원해	wants 4
we-ta (Vt: weə or wewə)	외다: 외어: 외워	memorizes, learns by heart 17-D
we e	외에	besides, not only (see pakk e)
hyəng nim we e	형님외에	besides an older brother 14-N
wekyokwan	외교관	diplomat, foreign service personnel 3
wekuk	외국	foreign country
wekukə	외국어	foreign language 8-D
Wemupu	외무부	Ministry of Foreign Affairs (Korea) 3-1

wen (D)	왼	left 2
wen ccok ɨlo	왼쪽으로	to the left 2
wehwan	외환	foreign currency 16
wæ (Ad)	왜	why 6
Wæsik	왜식	Japanese food 12-D

<u>k</u>

ka (P)	가	2 (see <u>i</u>)
Hakkyo ka issɨmnita.	학교가 있습니다.	There is a school. ('A school exists.') 2-G
ka-ta (Vi: ka)	가다: 가	goes 1
Annyənghi kasipsiyo.	안녕히 가십시요.	Good bye (to someone leaving). 1
Wen ccok ɨlo kasipsiyo.	왼쪽으로 가십시요.	Go to the left. 2
kaɨl	가을	autumn 15
kakkap-ta (Vi: kakkawə)	가깝다: 가까워	is near 3
kakkai	가까이	a nearby place 11
kakkai (Ad)	가까이	nearby, at the nearby place 3-D
kakkɨm (Ad)	가끔	sometimes 9
kath-ta (Vi: kathə)	같다: 같어	is the same 5-D
kathi (Ad)	같이	together, with
Na wa kathi kapsita.	나와 같이 갑시다.	Lets go with me. 4
kathi (P)	같이	as, like
Nyuyok kathi	뉴욕같이	like New York 18-N
kalak	가락	spindle
son kalak	손가락	finger 13
pal kalak	발가락	toe 13
cəs kalak	젓가락	chopsticks 13
sut kalak	숟가락	(Korean) spoon 13
kalu	가루	powder 13

kalıchi-ta (Vt: kalıchiə)	가르치다: 가르쳐	teaches 1-D
kamsa	감사	gratitude
kamsa-ha-ta (Vi: kamsa-hæ)	감사하다: 감사해	is grateful 2
Kamsa-hamnita.	감사합니다.	Thank you. 2
kantan	간단	simplicity
kantan-ha-ta (Vi: kantan-hæ)	간단하다: 간단해	is simple 8-D
kancang	간장	(soy) sauce 13
kapang	가방	briefcase 13-D
kapyəp-ta (Vi: kapyəwə)	가볍다: 가벼워	is light (in weight) 10-D
kap(s)	값	price 4
cip kaps	집 값	rent, the price of a house 4-D
kapcaki (Ad)	갑자기	suddenly 17-D
kasım	가슴	chest 13-D
kacang (Ad)	가장	best, most
Kacang ppalımnita.	가장 빠릅니다.	[It]'s fastest. 10
kacok	가족	family, a family member 14
kaci (PN)	가지	sorts, kinds 4
Yələ kaci ka issimnita.	여러 가지가 있읍니다.	[We] have several kinds. 4
kaci-ta (Vt: kacə)	가지다: 가져	possesses
kacə o-ta	가져 오다	bring (something) 12
kacə ka-ta	가져 가다	takes (something) 12-N
kacə iss-ta	가져 있다	has, is possessing 14-G
kangsa	강사	instructor 8-D
tæhak kangsa	대학 강사	college instructor 8-D
kəi (Ad)	거의	almost, nearly 11
kəi ta	거의 다	almost (all) 11
kəki	거기	there, that place 3

kəki esə	거기에서	there, at that place, from there 3-G
kəkcəng	걱정	worry
kəkcəng-ha-ta (Vi&Vt)	걱정하다	worries 17-D
kəl-ta (Vt: kələ)	걸다: 걸어	hangs
cənhwa (lɪl) kəl-ta	전화를 걸다	makes a phone-call 16
kət-ta (Vi: kələ)	걷다: 걸어	walks 10
kələ ka-ta	걸어 가다	walks, goes on foot
Kələ kal kka yo?	걸어 갈까요?	Shall we walk? (in contrast to taking an automobile) 11
kələ sə	걸어서	on foot 10
kəli	거리	street 17-D
kəlli-ta (Vi: kəllyə)	걸리다: 걸려	takes (time) 7
(Sikan i) han sikan kəllimnita.	(시간이) 한 시간 걸립니다.	It takes an hour. 7-D
kəm-ta (Vi: kəmə)	검다: 검어	is dark 4-D
kənmul	건물	building 2
kənnə-ta (Vt: kənnə)	건너다: 건너	crosses
kənnən kil	건넌길	the street where you can cross 11-D
kil kənnə	길 건너	across the street 11-D
kəs (PN)	것	(thing) 2
cə kəs	저것	that (thing) (over there) 2
Cə kəs in muəs imnikka?	저것은 무엇입니까?	What is that? 2
ko (P)	고	
əti e kanta ko malhæssɪmnikka?	어디에 간다고 말 했읍니까?	Did [he] say where [he] is going? 17-G
koyangi	고양이	cat 5-G
koki	고기	meat 13
kot (Ad)	곧	soon, immediately 11
kotanha-ta (Vi: kotanhæ)	고단하다: 고단해	is tired, is fatigued 13

kotɨng (D)	고등	higher
kotɨng hakkyo	고등 학교	high school 10-D
kolmok	골목	corner (of the street) 11-D
komap-ta (Vi: komawə)	고맙다: 고마워	is grateful 1
Komapsɨmnita.	고맙습니다.	Thank you. 1
komthang	곰탕	(soup with rice and meet) 12
koppu	고뿌	cup 13
kophɨ-ta (Vi: kopha)	고프다: 고파	('is empty')
Pæ ka kophɨmnita.	배가 고픕니다.	I'm hungry. 12
kos (PN)	곳	place
kakkaun kos	가까운 곳	a nearby place 12
kocang	고장	**mechanical trouble**
kocang-na-ta (Vi: kocang-na)	고장나다	**is out of order 17-D**
kochi-ta (Vt: kochiə)	고치다	**fixes, repairs 17-D**
kochu	고추	red pepper 13
kochu kalu	고추 가루	(red pepper powder) 13
kohyang	고향	home town, native town 14
Kohyang i əti ise yo?	고향이 어디이세요?	Where do you come from?(H) 14
kong	공	zero 16
kong	공	ball 16-D
kongwən	공원	park 2-D
kongmuwən	공무원	civil servant 7-D
kongpo	공보	public information 2
kongpowən	공보원	information office 2
Mikuk Kongpowən	미국 공보원	USIS 2
kongpokwan	공보관	information officer 7-C
kongpu	공부	studying 1
kongpu-ha-ta (kongpu-hæ)	공부 하다: 공부 해	studies 1

kongcang	공장	factory 18-D
kongchæk	공책	notebook 4-D
ku (Num Ch)	구	nine 4
kuk	국	soup 13
kukyəng	구경	sightseeing, show 9
Kukmusəng	국무성	State Department (U.S.) 13-D
Kukpangpu	국방부	Ministry of National Defence (Korea) 13-D
Kukpangsəng	국방성	the Defense Department (U.S.) 13-D
kukcang	국장	bureau chief 16-D
kukce	국제	international 9
Kukce Kıkcang	국제 극장	International Theatre 9
Kukhwe	국회	National Assembly, Congress, Parliament 13-D
kutu	구두	shoe(s) 4-D
Kulapha	구라파	Europe 6-D
kulim	구름	cloud
kulim i kki-ta	구름이 끼다	clouds up 18-D
kunin	군인	soldier, military man 7-D
kuntæ	군대	military 7
kı (D)	그	that, the 2-G
kı kəs	그것	that (thing), it 2
Kı kəs ın yəkwan imnita.	그것은 여관입니다.	It's an inn. 2
kıkcang	극장	theatre 3-D

kıləh-ta (Vi: kılæ or kıləhæ)	그렇다: 그래: 그러해	is so, is such 1
Kiləhsımnita.	그렇습니다.	It's so., That's right. 1
Kıləhsımnikka?	그렇습니까?	Is that so?, Is that right? 1
kıləm (Ad)	그럼	then, if so 4 (see kılyəmyən)
kıləna (Ad)	그러나	but, however 5
kilən kəs	그런 것	such a thing 8
kilənte	그런데	by the way 8
kıləha-ta (Vi: kıləhæ)	그러하다: 그러해	is so, does so 4 (see kıləh-ta)
kiləhke (Ad)	그렇게	so, in such a way 9
kıləmyən (Ad)	그러면	if so, then 5 (see kıləm)
kıləhci man	그렇지만	however, neverthless 9
kılæsə	그래서	therefore, so 9
kılıs	그릇	container, dish 13
kıli (Ad)	그리	(not) so, like that 4
Kıli pissaci anhsımnita.	그리 비싸지 않습니다.	[It]'s not so expensive. 4
kılıko (Ad)	그리고	and 5
kılim	그림	picture, painting 4-D
kılphi	글피	two days after tomorrow 6-D
kılsse (Ad)	글쎄	well, maybe 4
Kılsse yo.	글쎄요.	Well. 4
kımantu-ta (Vi: kimantwə)	그만두다: 그만둬	stops (doing), quits 11-D
Kımyoil	금요일	Friday 6-D
kımnyən	금년	this year 6-D
kınmu	근무	(paid) service

kinmu-ha-ta (Vi: kınmu-hæ)	근무하다: 근무해	works, is employed 8
kiphæng(cha)	급행(차)	express (train) 10-D
kıcə (Ad)	그저	just 1
Kıcə kiləhsımnita.	그저 그렇습니다.	Just so so. 1
kıcəkke	그저께	the day before yesterday 4-D
kitali-ta (Vt: kitaliə)	기다리다: 기다려	waits (for) 9
Kitalinin kəs i cohkessımnita.	기다리는 것이 좋겠습니다.	[You]'d better wait. ('That you wait will be good.') 11
kil	길	street, road 2-D
ki(l)-ta (Vi: kilə)	길다: 길어	is long, is lengthy 10-D
Kim	김	(a family name) 1
Kim Kisu	김 기수	(a full name) 1
Kimchi	김치	(pickled vegetable) 13-D
kipun	기분	feeling 13
kisa	기사	article, column 17-D
kisangtæ	기상대	weather bureau, weatherman 18
kisuksa	기숙사	dormitory 13-D
kica	기자	reporter 8-D
sinmun kica	신문 기자	journalist 8-D
kicha	기차	train 7-G
kihu	기후	climate, weather 15
kihwe	기회	chance, opportunity 16-D
kæ (C)	개	
Yənphil han kæ cuse yo.	연필 한 개 주세요.	Please give a pencil. 5-G

kæ	개	dog 5-G
kæi-ta (Vi: kæiə)	개이다: 개여	(weather) clears up 18
kwa (PN)	과	department, section
Wehwan Kwa	외환과	the Foreign Currency Department 16
kwanha-ta (Vi: kwanhæ)	관하다: 관해	is concerned
kwanhæ sə	관해서	concerning, about 17 (see tæhæ sə)
sənsæng e kwanhæ sə	선생에 관해서	about you 17
kwacang	과장	department chief 16-D
kwi	귀	ear 13
kwa (P)	과	with, and 4 (see wa)
kwail	과일	fruit 13
kwasil	과실	fruil 13
kwən (C)	권	volume of
Yəngə chæk tu kwən	영어 책 두 권	two English books 5-G
kwænchanh-ta (Vi: kwænchanhə)	괜찮다: 괜찮어	is OK, is alright 1
(Aniyo), kwænchanhsimnita.	아니요, 괜찮습니다.	Not al all., That's OK., It's not bad. 1
kyəul	겨울	winter 15
kyəlan	겨란	egg 13 (see talkyal)
kyəngchal	경찰	police
kyəngchalkwan	경찰관	policeman 8-D
kyəngchalsə	경찰서	police station 10-D
kyəlhon	결혼	marriage
kyəlhon-ha-ta (Vi: kyəlhon-hæ)	결혼하다: 결혼해	gets married, has a wedding 14

kyənghəm	경험	experience 18-D
kyesi-ta (Vi: kyesiə)	계시다: 계셔	is, exists, stays (honored) 1 (see <u>iss-ta</u>)
Annyənghi kyesipsiyo.	안녕히 계십시오.	Good bye (to someone staying).
kyesok	계속	continuation
kyesok-ha-ta (Vi: kyesok-hæ)	계속 하다: 계속 해	continues, lasts 18
kyehwek	계획	plans 18
Tıngsan-hal kyehwek imnita.	등산 할 계획입니다.	[I]'m planning to hike. 18
kyothong	교통	traffic, transportation 10-D
Kyothong i pəncaphamnita.	교통이 번잡합니다.	The traffic is jammed. 10-D
kyosu	교수	professor 8-D
kyosil	교실	classroom 2-D
kyocang	교장	principal (of school) 16-D
kyohwansu	교환수	telephone operator 16
kyohwe	교회	church 10-D

<u>kk</u>

kka (DN)	까	
Kal kka yo?	갈까요?	Shall we go? 5
ssani kka	싸니까	because [it]'s cheap 12
kkamah-ta (Vi: kkamæ)	까맣다: 까매	is black 4-N
kkaman sæk	까만색	black color 4-D
kkaci (P)	까지	as far as, to, until, by 7
Mikuk kkaci	미국 까지	as far as America 7
næil kkaci	내일까지	by tomorrow 7-G
kkok (Ad)	꼭	exactly, without fail, by all means 15
kkolphı	골프	golf 18-G

kkɪth	끝	the end, the ending
kkɪth-machi-ta (Vt: kkɪth-machiə)	끝마치다: 끝마쳐	finishes, completes 14-D
kkɪth-na-ta (Vi: kkith-na)	끝나다: 끝나	ends, is over 6-D
kkɪth-næ-ta (Vt: kkith-næ)	끝내다: 끝내	finishes, completes 8-D
kkækkɪtha-ta (Vi: kkækkɪthæ)	깨끗하다: 깨끗해	is clean 18-G

<u>kh</u>

khal	칼	knife 5-D
kho	코	nose 13
khokhakhola	코카콜라	coca cola 12-D
khokhoa	코코아	cocoa 12-D
khong	콩	beans 12
khɪ-ta (Vi: khə)	크다: 커	is big 5
khɪn chæk	큰 책	a big book 5
khɪ-ta (Vi: khə)	크다: 커	grows up, 15-D
khɪki	크기	size 16-D
khɪke (Ad)	크게	loudly 16
khi	키	height (of person) 18
khi ka khɪ-ta	키가 크다	is tall 18-D

<u>n</u>

na	나	I 1 (see <u>cə</u>)
na e	나의	my 1 (see <u>cə e</u>)
na-ta (Vi: na)	나다: 나	comes out
Hæ ka nanta.	해가 난다.	Sun shines. 18-D
Khɪn il nassɪmnita.	큰 일 났읍니다.	('[I] have a big problem.') 18

na/ina (P)	나/이나	
ppəsɪ na cəncha	뻐스나 전차	bus or streetcar 10
muəs ina	무엇이나	anything 12
nai	나이	age 14
Nai ka manhsɪmnita.	나이가 많습니다.	[He] is old. 14
Nai ka cəksɪmnita.	나이가 적습니다.	[He] is young. 14
na o-ta (Vt-Vi: na wa)	나 오다: 나 와	comes out, graduates 7-G
ənce hakkyo lɪl na wassɪmnikka?	언제 학교를 나 왔읍니까?	When did you finish school? 1
na ka-ta (Vi: na ka)	나 가다: 나 가	goes out 9
nakksi-cil	낚시질	fishing
nakksi-cil-ha-ta	낚시질 하다	does fishing 18-D
nal	날	day 6-D
nala	나라	country, nation 10-D
nalssi	날씨	weather 15 (see ilki)
Nam-Mi	남미	South America 6-D
Nampu	남부	the Southern part, the South (U.S.) 15-D
namphən	남편	hustand 14-D
Nam-Han	남한	South Korea 6-D
namtongsæng	남동생	younger brother 16-D
nappɪta (Vi: nappə)	나쁘다: 나빠	is bad 4-N
nac	낮	daytime, noontime
nac e	낮에	in the daytime 6-D
nac-ta (Vi: nacə)	낮다: 낮아	is low 10-D
nah-ta (Vi: naha)	낳다: 낳아	is born, gives a birth 15

nahıl	나흘	four days, the 4th day of the month 6-D
nə	너	you (plain speech) 17-G
nəi	너희	you (plural in plain speech) 17-G
nək (Num K)	넉	(see <u>ne(s)</u>)
nək tal pan	넉 달 반	four months and a half 8-D
nəlp-ta (Vi: nəlpə)	넓다: 넓어	is wide 5-D
nəmu (Ad)	너무	too
Nəmu nıcsımnita.	너무 늦습니다.	[It]'s too late. 11
nəngnəkha-ta (Vi: nəngnəkhæ)	넉넉하다: 넉넉해	is enough 13
nəh-ta (Vt: nəhə)	넣다: 넣어	puts in, deposits 16-G (see <u>noh-ta</u>)
nola(h)-ta (Vi: nolæ)	노랗다: 노래	is yellow 4
nolan sæk	노란 색	yellow color 4
nolla-ta (Vi: nolla)	놀라다: 놀라	is surprised 13-G
noph-ta (Vi· nopha)	높다: 높아	is high 10-D
noh-ta (Vt: noha)	놓다: 놓아	places, puts 16-G (see <u>tu-ta</u>)
Cəkə nohassımnita.	적어 놓았읍니다.	I jot it down (for future use). 16-G
nongpu	농부	farmer 17-D
nongcang	농장	farm 15-D
nui	누이	sister (for male siblings)
nui tongsæng	누이 동생	younger sister 14
nuku	누구	who, what person 3
nuka	누가	who (subject) 3-N
nuku lıl	누구를	whom 3-N

nuləh-ta (Vi: nulæ)	누렇다: 누래	is yellowish 4-D
nun	눈	eyes 13
nun	눈	snow
Nun i omnita.	눈이 옵니다.	It snows. 15
nunim	누님	older sister (of male) 14-D
nɪl (Ad)	늘	all the time, always 9
nɪli-ta (Vi: nɪlyə)	느리다: 느려	is slow 10-D
nɪ(l)k-ta (Vi: nɪlkə)	늙다: 늙어	is old, is aged 14-N
nɪn (P)	는	as for 1 (see ɪn)
nɪc-ta (Vi: nɪcə)	늦다: 늦어	is late 11
nɪcke/nɪkke/ (Ad)	늦게	late 10-D
nim	님	sweet-heart, lover 14-N
nim (PN)	님	
pumo nim	부모님	parents (honored) 14-N
ne (Ad)	네	yes 1
Ne?	네?	Beg your pardon!, Pardon me. 16-N
Ne.. .	네....?	Is that right? 18
ne ka	네가	you (subject in plain speech) 17-G
nekthai	넥타이	neck-tie 4-D
ne(s) (Num K)	넷	four 5
ne kəli	네 거리	crossroad 11-D

næ ka	내가	I (subejct) 1 (see <u>ce ka</u>)
næil	내일	tomorrow 4-D
næli-ta (Vi: næliə)	내리다: 내려	gets off, descends 7-N
næliə cu-ta (Vt: næliə cuə)	내려 주다: 내려 주어	drops [someone] off
Næliə cusipsiyo.	내려 주십시오.	Please drop [me] off. 11
næliə o-ta (Vi: næliə wa)	내려 오다: 내려 와	comes down 7-G
næliə ka-ta (Vi: næliə ka)	내려 가다: 내려 가	goes down 7-G
nænæ (Ad)	내내	all the way
achim nænæ	아침 내내	all morning 18-D
næ-nyən	내 년	next year 6-D
næphıkhin	내프킨	napkins 13-D
næsən	내선	(telephone-line) extension 17-D
nængmyən	냉면	(cold noodle) 12

<u>t</u>

ta	다	all 9
taım	다음	next, next time 5
taim cip	다음 집	the next door 5
tat-ta (Vt: tatə)	닫다: 닫어	closes 11-D
ta(l)-ta (Vi: talə)	달다: 달어	is sweet, is sugary 13

tal	달	month, moon 6
talɨ-ta (Vi: talla)	다르다: 달라	is different 5
talɨn kəs	다른 것	different one, other one 5
tali	다리	leg 13
tali	다리	bridge 10-D
ta(l)k	닭	chicken
ta(l)k koki	닭 고기	chicken 13
talkyal	달걀	egg 13 (see <u>kyəlan</u>)
tampæ	담배	cigarettes, tobacco 4-D
tanə	단어	word 17-D
tani-ta (Vi: taniə)	다니다: 다녀	attends (school)
Hakkyo e tanimnita.	학교에 다닙니다.	[I]'m attending school. 8
tapang	다방	tearoom 3-D
tasəs (Num K)	다섯	five 5
tasi (Ad)	다시	again 3
Tasi (hanpən) malssɨm hasipsiyo.	다시 한번 말씀 하십시요.	Please say it again. 3
tassæ	닷새	five days, the 5th day of the month 6-D
tah-ta (Vi: taha)	닿다: 닿아	arrives 6-N
tahæng	다행	fortunate thing
tahæng-ha-ta (Vi: tahæng-hæ)	다행하다: 다행해	is fortunate 16
A, tahæng imnita.	아, 다행입니다.	Oh, that's fortunate. 16
tə (Ad)	더	more 5
Tə ssamnita.	더 쌉니다.	[It]'s cheaper. 5
tə ssan kəs	더 싼 것	cheaper one 5

təkpun	덕분	favor, mercy 1
təkpun e	덕분 에	(at your favor) 1
Təkpun e cal cinamnita.	덕분 에 잘 지납니다.	I'm doing fine, thank you. 1
təl (Ad)	덜	less
təl əlyəwn mal	덜 어려운 말	(a) less difficult language 5-G
təp-ta (Vi: təwə)	덥다: 더워	is hot 13
to (P)	도	also, too 1, ven though 10
puin to	부인도	your wife also 1
na to	나도	me too 4
issə to	있어도	even though there is 10
toyaci	도야지	pig
toyaci koki	도야지 고기	pork 13 (see tweci)
Tokil	독일	Germany 1-D
Tokilə	독일어	German (language) 8-D
tol-ta (Vi: tola)	돌다: 돌아	turns, make a turn 11-D
tola o-ta (Vi: tola wa)	돌아 오다: 돌아 와	comes back 7-G
tola ka-ta (Vi: tola ka)	돌아 가다: 돌아 가	goes back 7 passes away 11-G
tola po-ta (Vt: tola pwa)	돌아 보다: 돌아 봐	looks back 12-G
tollita (Vi: tolliə)	돌리다: 돌려	rotates, switches, turns around 16
ton	돈	money 7-G
top-ta (Vt: towa)	돕다: 도와	helps
towa cu-ta (Vt: towa cuə)	도와 주다: 도와 주어	gives help, gives a helping hand 7-G
tosəkwan	도서관	library 10-D
tosi	도시	city, urban community 10-D

tohweci	도회지	metropolitan area, city 15-I
tongan (PN)	동안	for, during, while
Yətə(l)p sikan tongan il-hamnita.	여덟 시간 동안 일합니다.	[I] work for eight hours. 6
Kulapha e issnın tongan	구라파에 있는 동안	while [I] was in Europe 15
tongyo	동료	collegue, co-worker 13-D
Tongpu	동부	the East (U.S.), the eastern part 15-D
tongmul	동물	animal
tongmulwən	동물원	zoo ('animal house') 10-D
tongsæng	동생	a younger sibling 14
tu(l) (Num K)	둘	two 5
tu-ta (Vt: tuə)	두다: 두어	places, puts
tuə iss-ta	두어 있다	is being placed 14-C
Cəkə tuəssımnita.	적어 두었읍니다.	[I] wrote it down (for future use). 16-G
tıl (PN)	들	
kı kəs tıl	그것들	they, those (things) 10
ta tıl	다들	all, everybody 14
tı(l)-ta (Vt: tılə)	들다: 들어	eats or drinks (food), lifts
əsə tısipsiyo.	어서 드십시요.	Please help yourself. 13
tıt-ta (Vt: tılə)	듣다: 들어	listens to, hears 9
tılə o-ta (Vi: tılə wa).	들어 오다: 들어 와	comes in 7-G
tılə ka-ta (Vi: tılə ka)	들어 가다: 들어 가	goes in 7-G
tılə ka po-ta (Vi: tılə ka pwa)	들어 가 보다: 들어 가 봐	enters and sees, goes in to see 12-G
tıllı-ta (Vt: tıllə)	들르다: 들러	stops by, drops in 4
tılli-ta (Vi: tıllyə)	들리다: 들려	is heard, is audible 16

tɪnci/itɪnci (P)	든지: 이든지	(see itinci)
muəs itɪnci	무엇이든지	anything 12-G
Yəngə tɪnci Tokilə	영어든지 독일어	either English or German 12-G
tɪng (PN)	등	and so on, etc. 12
tɪng	등	back
Ting i aphimnita.	등이 아픕니다.	I have a backache. 13
tɪngsan	등산	hiking
tingsan-ha-ta (Vi: tɪngsan-hæ)	등산하다: 등산해	hikes 18
te (PN)	데	place 10-D
kakkaun te	가까운 데	nearby place 12
tæ (C)	대	
catongcha tu tæ	자동차 두 대	two automobiles 6-G
tæk	댁	your home, home (honored) 4
tækæ (Ad)	대개	usually, generally 6
tætanhi (Ad)	대단히	very 2
tæthongyəng	대통령	the President 8-D
tælo (P)	대로	
maɪm tælo	마음대로	as one pleases, as you like 16-D
kɪ tælo	그대로	as it is
Tæman	대만	Formosa, Taiwan 6-D
tæmun	대문	gate 11-D
tæsa	대사	ambassador 7-G
tæsakwən	대사관	embassy 2
tæhak	대학	college 8-D
tæhakwən	대학원	graduate school 15-G
tæhakwən kongpu	대학원 공부	graduate studies 15-G

tæhakkyo	대학교	university 10-D
tæha-ta (Vt: tæhæ)	대하다: 대해	faces, confronts with
kihu e tæhæ sə	기후 에 대해서	concerning (or about) the weather 15
Tæhan Minkuk	대한 민국	the Republic of Korea 17-D
twe-ta (Vi: tweə)	되다: 되어	becomes, has been
Sam nyən tweəssimnita.	삼년 되었읍니다.	It's been 3 years. 8
Sənsæng i tweəssimnita.	선생이 되었읍니다.	[He] has become a teacher. 8-
tweci	돼지	pig
tweci koki	돼지 고기	pork ('pig meat') 13
twi	뒤	back, rear 2-D
twi e	뒤에	behind, in back of
Cip twi e issımnita.	집 뒤에 있읍니다.	[It]'s behind the house. 2-D
ttattıtha-ta (Vi: ttattıthæ)	tt 따뜻하다: 따뜻해	is warm 15
ttal	딸	daughter 14
(ttala) we-ta	따라 외다	memorizes, learns by heart 17-D (see we-ta)
ttanim	따님	your daughter (honored) 14-N
ttəna-ta (Vt: ttəna)	떠나다: 떠나	leaves 6
Ttənalyəko hamnita.	떠나려고 합니다.	[I]'s going to leave. 7
tto (Ad)	또	again 1
Tto pwepkessımnita.	또 뵙겠읍니다.	So long., See you again. 1
Tto talın kəs i philyo-hamnikka?	또 다른 것이 필요 합니까?	Do you need anything else? 5
ttokttokha-ta (Vi: ttokttokhæ)	똑똑하다: 똑똑해	is intelligent, is bright 17-
ttokpalo (Ad)	똑바로	straight, straight ahead 3
ttıkəp-ta (Vi: ttıkəwə)	뜨겁다: 뜨거워	is hot (solid, liquid) 13

ttæ (PN)	때	time, occasion, when
ki ttæ (e)	그 때(에)	(at) that time 7
ttæ ttæ lo	때때로	occasionally 9-D
hakkyo e kal ttæ (e)	학교에 갈때(에)	when [I] go to school 14-G
ttwi-ta (Vi: ttwiə)	뛰다: 뛰어	runs 18-G
Tækæ ttwiə kamnita.	대개 뛰어 갑니다.	[I] usually run. ('I usually run and go.') 14-G

th

tha-ta (Vt: tha)	타다: 타	rides, gets on 7
thako ka-ta	타고 가다	takes (bus, taxi, etc.) 10
thaiphı	타이프	typing
thaiphı congı	타이프 종이	typing paper 5
thək	턱	chin, jaw 13-D
Thoyoil	토요일	Saturday 6-D
thongyəkkwan	통역관	interpreter 8-D
thonghwa	통화	telephone conversation
Thonghwa cung imnita.	통화 중 입니다.	The line is busy. 16
thım	틈	free time, spare time 9
thılli-ta (Vi: thılliə)	틀리다: 틀려	is wrong 18
thipi	티비	television 14-G
thæu-ta (Vt: thæwə)	태우 다: 태워	gives a ride (to someone), loads 7-N
thæwə cu-ta (Vt: thæwə cuə)	태워 주 다: 태워 주 어	gives [someone] a ride 11-N
Thækuk	태국	Tailand 6-D
thækssi	택시	taxi 7-D

l

lako (P)	라고	
'Məli ka aphimnita.' lako mal-hæssɪmnita.	머리가 아픕니다 라고 말 했읍니다.	[He] said, "I have a headache." 18-G
lato/ilato (P)	라도/이라도	18-G
muəs ilato	무엇이라도	whatever [it] is 18-G
na lato	나라도	even I 18-G
lætio	래디오	radio 9-D
lo (P)	로	to, as, by 2 (see ɪlo)
Hakkyo lo kamnita.	학교로 갑니다.	[I] go to school. 2-G
wekyokwan ilo	외교관으로	as a diplomat 7
pæ lo	배로	by boat 7
lɪl (P)	를	1 (see ɪl)

m

maɪm	마음	mind, heart 13-D
maɪm tælo	마음대로	as one pleases 16-D
moksa	목사	minister (of church) 16-D
mat (D)	맏	first
mat atɪl	맏 아들	the first son 14-G
mata (P)	마다	every, each
nal mata	날마다	everyday 8
mal	말	language, utterance, speech, word 1
Hankuk mal	한국 말	Korean (language) 1
mal-ha-ta (Vi-Vt: mal-hæ)	말하다: 말해	speaks 1-D
Sacən mal imnikka?	사전 말입니까?	Do you mean a dictionary? 4
mal	말	horse 5-G
ma(l)-ta (Vt: malə)	말다: 말어	not do 11-G
Thaci mapsita.	타지 맙시다.	Let's not ride. 11

Kaci masipsiyo.	가지 마십시오.	Don't go. 11-G
malı-ta (Vi: mallə)	마르다: 말러	dries
Mok i malımnita.	목이 마릅니다.	I'm thirsty. ('Throat is dry.'). 12
mali (C)	마리	head of
mal ne mali	말 네 마리	four heads of horses, four horses 5-G
malk-ta (Vi: malkə)	맑다: 맑어	is clear (water, air, etc.) 18
man (Num Ch)	만	ten-thousands 4
man (P)	만	only, just
Mianhaci man	미안하지만	I'm sorry but... 9
Mækcu tu pyəng man kacə osipsiyo.	맥주 두 병만 가져 오십시오.	Please bring me just two bottles of beer. 12
manna-ta (Vt: manna)	만나다: 만나	meets 3
mannyənphil	만년필	fountain-pen 4-D
manh-ta (Vi: manhə)	많다: 많어	is plenty, are many 9
manhi (Ad)	많이	a lot, much 8-D
mas	맛	taste 13
mas i iss-ta (or coh-ta)	맛이있다 (or 좋다)	is delicious 13
mas i əps-ta	맛이 없다	is tasteless 13
masi-ta (Vt: masyə)	마시다: 마셔	drinks 10
mac-ta (Vi: macə)	맞다: 맞어	is correct, fits 18-N
mahın (Num K)	마흔	forty 5
mangnæ	막내	the last child 14-N
mangnæ atıl	막내 아들	the last son 14-N
mək-ta (Vt: məkə)	먹다: 먹어	eats 2-G
məkə po-ta (Vt: məkə pwa)	먹어 보다: 먹어 봐	tries (food) 7-G

mə(l)-ta (Vi: mələ)	멀다: 멀어	is far 3
Yəki esə məmnikka?	여기에서 멉니까?	Is [it] far from here? 3
məli	머리	head, hair 13
məli ka coh-ta	머리가 좋다	has brain 13-D
məlli (Ad)	멀리	far away 11-N
məmul-ta (Vi: məmulə)	머물다: 머물어	stays 6-D
məmchu-ta (Vt-Vi: məmchwə)	멈추다: 멈추워	stops (car, taxi, etc.) 11-D
məncə (Ad)	먼저	first of all, above all 10
mok	목	neck, throat 12
Mok i malɪmnita.	목이 마릅니다.	I'm thirsty. 12
Mok i aphɪmnita.	목이 아픕니다.	I have a sore throat. 13
Mokyoil	목요일	Thursday 6
molɪ-ta (Vt: malla)	모르다: 몰라	doesn't know 3
mole	모레	the day after tomorrow 4-D
mom	몸	body 6
Mom i aphɪmnikka?	몸이 아픕니까?	Are you sick? 6
mot (Ad)	못	cannot
Ilkci mot hamnita.	읽지 못 합니다.	[I] cannot read. 8
Mot kamnita.	못 갑니다.	[I] cannot go. 8-G
motu	모두	all, in all, altogether 14
moca	모자	hat, cap 4-D
mocala-ta (Vi: mocala)	모자라다: 모자라	is not enough 13
muəs	무엇	what (thing) 1
muəs ɪl	무엇을	what (as direct object) 1
mukəp-ta (Vi: mukəwə)	무겁다: 무거워	is heavy 10-D

muke	무게	weight 10-D
mul	물	water 12-D
mut-ta (Vt: mulə)	묻다: 물어	inquires
mulə po-ta (Vt: mulə pwa)	물어보다: 물어봐	inquires 2
mulkən	물건	goods 9-D
mun	문	door, window 11
aph mun	앞문	the front door 11
munpəp	문법	grammar 10-D
munce	문제	problem 10-D
musɪn (D)	무슨	what kind of 4
musɪn sæk	무슨 색	what color, what kind of color 4
munpangku	문방구	stationaries
munpangkucəm	문방구점	stationary shop 5
Mianhamnita.	미안합니다.	I'm sorry. 1
Mianhaci man	미안하지만	I'm sorry but... 9
Mikuk	미국	America, the United States 1
Mikuk salam	미국 사람	an American 1
Mikuk mal	미국 말	the American language 1-D
mit-ta (Vt: mitə)	믿다: 믿어	trusts, believes 18-D
menyu	메뉴	menu 12
mæil (Ad)	매일	everyday 9-D
mækcu	맥주	beer 12
mæp-ta (Vi: mæwə)	맵다: 매워	is (spicy) hot 13
mæcuil	매주일	every week 9-D

myənuli	며누리	daughter-in-law ('son's wife') 14-D
myəch/myət/ (D)	몇	how many, what
ɪyca ka myəch kæ issɪmnikka?	의자가 몇 개 있읍니까?	How many chairs are there? 5
myəch-si	몇 시	what time 6
myəchil	며칠	what day, some days, how many days
Onil i myəchil ici yo?	오늘이 며칠이지요?	What's today's date? 6
myəngnyəng	명령	(excutive) order 13-D

P

Pak	박	Park (family name) 1-D
pakmulkwan	박물관	museum 10-D
paksa	박사	doctor (of philosophy) 16-D
pakk	밖	the outside 14-N
pakk e	밖 에	outside, to the outside 16-D
Hankuk mal pakk e molɪmnita.	한국 말 밖 에 모릅니다.	I know only Korean. ('Outside of Korean, I don't know.') 16-G
pakku-ta (Vt: pakkwə)	바꾸다: 바꿔	exchanges, changes
Kim Sənsæng eke com pakkwə cusipsiyo.	김 선생에게 좀 바꿔 주십시요.	May I talk to Mr. Kim (on the phone)? 16
pata	바다	sea 16-D
pat-ta (Vt: patə)	받다: 받어	receives, gets 6
pal	발	foot 13
pal kalak	발가락	toe 13
pala-ta (Vt: palæ)	바라다: 바래	hopes, wishes 8-G

pala po-ta (Vt: pala pwa)	바라 보다: 바라 봐	looks over (from the distance) 12-G
palam	바람	wind
Palam i pu(lı)mnita.	바람이 붑니다.	It is windy. 15
palo (Ad)	바로	just, right 2
palo aph e	바로 앞에	right ahead 2
Palo aph e issımnita.	바로 앞에 있읍니다.	[It]'s right up ahead. 2
palk-ta (Vi: palkə)	밝다: 밝어	is light 10-D
pam	밤	night 4-D
pan	반	half 6-D
panto	반도	peninsula
Panto Hwesa	반도 회사	Bando Company 8
pap	밥	rice (cooked), meal 12
pappıta (Vi: pappə)	바쁘다: 바뻐	is busy 9
pang	방	room 4-D
pangsong	방송	broadcasting
pangsongkuk	방송국	broadcasting station, radio station 11-D
panghak	방학	school vacation 6-D
pəl (C)	벌	
yangpok tu pəl	양복 두 벌	two suits 5-G
pəlssə (Ad)	벌써	already 6
pən (PN)	번	time, number
i pən	이번	this time 7
han pən	한 번	once 7
myəch pən	몇 번	what number, how many times 16
pəncap-ha-ta (Vi: pəncap-hæ)	번잡하다: 번잡해	is crowded 10

pənho	번호	number 16
cənhwa pənho	전화 번호	telephone number 16
po-ta (Vt: pwa)	보다: 봐	looks at, sees 4
poi-ta (Vi: poyə)	보이다: 보여	is seen, is visible 16
poyə cu-ta (Vt: poyə cuə)	보여 주다: 보여 주어	shows 5
pokcap	복잡	complexity
pokcap-ha-ta (Vi: pokcap-hæ)	복잡하다: 복잡해	is complicated 8-D
pota (P)	보다	than
Hankuk mal i Tokil mal pota tə əlyəpsımnita.	한국 말이 독일 말보다 더 어렵습니다.	Korean is more difficult than German. 8
pothong	보통	ordinary, ordinairly
pothong samu	보통 사무	ordinary office work 8
pom	봄	spring (season) 15
ponæ-ta (Vt: ponæ)	보내다: 보내	sends 11-D
ponkuk	본국	home country 15-D
pontho	본토	mainland 15-D
pongkıp	봉급	pay, salary 13-D
puəkh	부엌	kitchen 16-D
puin	부인	lady, your wife, Mrs.____. 1
pukın (PN)	부근	vicinity 10
i pukın	이 부근	this vicinity, around here 10
puk-pu	북부	the Northern part 15-D
Puk-Han	북한	North-Korea 6-D
putıləp-ta (Vi: putıləwə)	부드럽다: 부드러워	is tender, is soft 13-D

puthak	부탁	request of a favor, a favor
Chwe Sənsæng (eke) com puthak-hamnita.	최 선생(에게) 좀 부탁합니다.	May I speak to Mr. Choe, please? 16
Chinku ekesə puthak ɪl patəssɪmnita.	친구 에게서 부탁을 받었읍니다.	My friend asked me of a favor. ('I received a request of favor from a friend.') 18-D
puthə (P)	부터	from
cikɪm puthə	지금 부터	from now on 8-D
pul	불	fire, light
pul-koki	불고기	Korean style barbecue ('fire meat') 13
pu(l)-ta (Vi: pulə)	불다: 불어	blows
Palam i pu(lɪ)mnita.	바람이 붑니다.	It's windy. ('Wind blows.') 15
pulɪ-ta (Vt: pullə)	부르다: 불러	calls 18
nolæ lɪl pulɪ-ta	노래를 부르다	sings a song 18-N
pu(l)k-ta (Vi: pulkə)	붉다: 붉어	is reddish 4-D
Pullansə	불란서	France 1
Pullansə mal	불란서 말	French (language) 8-D
Pullansə salam	불란서 사람	Frenchman 1-D
Pullansəə	불란서어	French 8-D
pulphyən	불편	inconvenience, discomfort
pulphyən-ha-ta (Vi: pulphyən-hæ)	불편하다: 불편해	is inconvenient, is uncomfortable 10-D
pumo	부모	parents 14
pun (PN)	분	person (honored) 3
kɪ pun	그분	he ('that person') 3
sənsæng se pun	선생 세 분	three teachers 5-G
pun (C)	분	minute 6
puncuha-ta (Vi: puncuhæ)	분주하다: 부조해	is busy, is hectic 8
Pusan	부산	Pusan 1-G

puca	부자	a rich man 17-G
pucok	부족	insufficiency, lack
pucok-ha-ta (Vi: pucok-hæ)	부족하다: 부족해	is not enough, is insufficient 13
puchi-ta (Vt: puchiə)	부치다: 부쳐	mails, ships 11
pi	비	rain
Pi ka omnita.	비가 옵니다.	It rains. ('Rain comes.') 8-G
pilli-ta (Vt: pillyə)	빌리다: 빌려	borrows
pillyə cu-ta (Vt: pillyə cuə)	빌려주다: 빌려 주어	loans, lends 7-G
pisə	비서	secretary 7-G
pisıtha-ta (Vi: pisıthæ)	비슷하다: 비슷해	is similar 15
pissa-ta (Vi: pissa)	비싸다: 비싸	is expensive 4
pihængki	비행기	airplane 7
pihængcang	비행장	airport 7-D
pæ	배	ship 7
pæ	배	stomach
Pæ ka kophımnita.	배가 고픕니다.	I'm hungry. 12
pæ (PN)	배	times
i (or tu) pæ	이 (두) 배	two times 7-G
pæu-ta (Vt: pæwə)	배우다: 배워	learns 1-D
pæk (Num Ch)	백	hundred 4
pækhwacəm	백화점	department store 2
pyəllo (Ad)	별로	(not) particularly
Pyəllo manhi məkci anhəssımnita.	별로 많이 먹지 않었읍니다.	I didn't eat so much. 13

pyənhosa	변호사	lawyer 8-D
pyəng	병	sickness, disease 15-G
pyəng i na-ta	병이 나다	gets sick 15-G
pyəng	병	bottle
pyəng (C)	병	bottle of 12
pyəngwən	병원	hospital 10-D
pwep-ta (Vi: pwewə)	뵙다: 뵈워	('meets')
Chəɪm pwepsɪmnita.	처음 뵙습니다.	(I'm glad to meet you.) ('I see you for the first time.') 1
Tto pwepkessɪmnita.	또 뵙겠읍니다.	See you again., So long. 1

<u>pp</u>

ppata	빠다	butter 13-D
ppalɪta (Vi: ppallə)	빠르다: 빨러	is fast 10
ppalli (Ad)	빨리	quickly, fast 16-D
ppang	빵	bread 13-D
ppəsɪ	뻐스	bus 7-G
ppilu	삐루	beer 13
ppyam	뺨	cheek 13

<u>ph</u>

phal (Num Ch)	팔	eight 4
phal	팔	arm 13
pha(l)-ta (Vt: phalə)	팔다: 팔어	sells 4
phala(h)-ta (Vi: phalæ)	파랗다: 파래	is blue 4-N
phalan sæk	파란 색	blue color 4-D

phansa	판사	judge 16-D
phək (Ad)	퍽	quite, very 9
phulɪ-ta (Vi: phulɪlə)	푸르다: 푸르러	is bluish 4-D
phungsok	풍속	custom 15-G
phiu-ta (Vt: phiwə)	피우다: 피워	smokes
Kim ɪn tampæ lɪl phiuko siphə hæ yo.	김은 담배를 피우고 싶어 해요.	Kim wants to smoke. 9-D
phikon	피곤	fatigue
phikon-ha-ta (Vi: phikon-hæ)	피곤하다: 피곤해	is tired 13
philo	피로	fatigue
philo-ha-ta (Vi: philo-hæ)	피로하다: 피로해	is fatigued 13
philyo	필요	need, necessity
philyo-ha-ta (Vi: philyo-hæ)	필요하다: 필요해	is necessary, is needed 5
phen	펜	pen 5
phyən (PN)	편	side, way
ənɪ phyən	어느 편	which way 10
phyənci	편지	letter, mail 9-D
phyənha-ta (Vi: phyənhæ)	편하다: 편해	is comfortable 10-D
phyo	표	ticket 14-G

<u>S</u>

sa (Num Ch)	사	four 4
sa-ta (Vt: sa)	사다: 사	buys 4
Sassə yo?	샀어요?	Did [you] buy? 4
saəp	사업	business, enterprise
saəpka	사업가	business-man 16-D
saita	사이다	(a kind of soft drink) 12
sawi	사위	son-in-law ('daughter's husband') 14-D
sakən	사건	incident, trouble 17-D
sako	사고	accident 17-D
sa(l)-ta (Vi: salə)	살다: 살어	lives 9-G
sal (C)	살	year old 5-G
han sal	한 살	one year old 14
salam	사람	person, man 1
salam (C)	사람	
haksæng tu salam	학생 두 사람	two students 5-G
salang	사랑	love 9-G
salang-ha-ta (Vt: salang-hæ)	사랑하다: 사랑해	loves 9-G
sam (Num Ch)	삼	three 4
samu	사무	office work 6-D
samuwən	사무원	clerk, office worker 7-D

samusil	사무실	office 3-D
san	산	mountain 10-D
sanyang	사냥	hunting
sanyang ka-ta	사냥가다	goes hunting 18-D
sanpo	산보	a walk, a stroll
sanpo-ha-ta (Vi: sanpo-hæ)	산보하다: 산보해	takes a walk, strolls 9-D
sacang	사장	president of company 8-D
sacən	사전	dictionary 5
sachon	사촌	cousin 14-D
sahɨl	사흘	three days, the 3rd of the month 6
sangyəng	상영	showing of movies
sangyəng-ha-ta (Vt: sangyəng-hæ)	상영하다: 상영해	shows movies 9
Sangwən	상원	Senate (U.S.)
Sangwən ɨywən	상원 의원	Senator 16-D
sangkwan	상관	supervisor, boss 13-D
sangcəm	상점	store, shop 2-D
sə (P)	서	so, and so
kilæ sə	그래서	so, therefore 9
Səul	서울	Seoul (Capital of Korea) 1-G
səul	서울	capital 17-D

sək (Num K)	석	8-D (see <u>se(s)</u>)
sək tal	석 달	three months 8-D
səlhın (Num K)	설흔	thirty 5
səlthang	설탕	sugar 13
səm	섬	island 15-D
sənmul	선물	present, gift 13-G
sənsənha-ta (Vt: sənsənhæ)	선선하다: 선선해	is cool (air) 15
sənsæng	선생	teacher, you, Mr. 1-N
Səpu	서부	the West (U.S.), the western part 15-D
sə-ta (Vi: sə)	서다: 서	stands up, stops (walking, vehicles) 11-D
sə iss-ta	서 있다	is standing 14-G
so	소	cattle, cow 5-G
so koki	소고기	beef 13
sokım	소금	salt 13
sohki (Ad)	속히	quickly 16-D
soli	소리	noise, sound, voice
mal soli	말 소리	voice 16-D
salam soli	사람 소리	voices 16-D
pal soli	발 소리	foot steps 16-D
son	손	hand 13
son kalak	손 가락	finger 13

sonnim	손님	customer, quest 13-D
sonnyə	손녀	granddaughter 14-D
sonca	손자	grandson 1/ -D
sopangsə	소방서	fire station 11-D
sosik	소식	news, whereabout 15-G
sohakkyo	소학교	elementary school 10-D
su (DN)	수	
(Mal) hal su issımnita.	(말) 할 수 있읍니다.	[I] can speak. 8
Hal su əpsımnita.	할 수 없읍니다.	[I] cannot do., I'm unable to do. 8-N
suəp	수업	class (work) 6-D
ənce suəp i kkıth-namnikka?	언제 수업이 끝납니까?	When does the class end? 6-D
suyəng	수영	swimming 18-D
suyəng ka-ta	수영 가다	goes swimming 18-D
Suyoil	수요일	Wednesday 6-D
sukən	수건	towel 4
son sukən	손수건	handkerchief 4-D
sukce	숙제	homework 16-G
suto	수도	capital city 17-D
sut kalak	숟가락	(Korean) spoon 13
sul	술	liquor, wine 12-D
suchəp	수첩	address book 16

sɨmu (Num K)	스무	twenty 5
sɨmu nal	스무 날	twenty days 6-D
sɨmul (Num K)	스물	twenty 5
sɨpki	습기	humidity 18-D
sɨngkɨp	승급	promotion 13-D
si (D)	시	(husband's side)
si pumo	시부모	husband's parents 14-D
si apəci	시아버지	husband's father 14-D
si əməni	시어머니	husband's mother 14-D
si tongsæng	시동생	husband's younger siblings 14-D
si nui	시누이	husband's sister 14-D
si cip	시집	husband's family 14-D
si-ta (Vi: siə)	시다: 시어	is sour 13
siwe	시외	suburb, out skirt of city 10-D
sikan	시간	time, hour 6
myəch sikan	몇 시간	how many hours 6
Sikan i issɨmnikka?	시간이 있읍니까?	Do you have time. 6-N
sikol	시골	country, rural area 15-D
sikye	시계	watch, clock 2-D
siktang	식당	restaurant, dining hall 3-D
siksa	식사	meal 12-D
achim siksa	아침 식사	breakfast 12-D
sikmo	식모	maid 16-D
Sikhako	시카고	Chicago 15
sillye	실례	rudeness 1
Sillye-hamnita.	실례합니다.	Excuse me (on leaving <u>or</u> on interrupting) 1

Sillye-hakessɪmnita.	실례하겠읍니다.	Excuse me (for what I'm going to do). 1
Sillye-hæssɪmnita.	실례했읍니다.	Excuse me (for what I did). 1
silhəha-ta (Vt: silhəhæ)	싫어하다: 싫어해	dislikes 4-N
sinæ	시내	downtown 4
sinmun	신문	newspaper 4-D
sinmunsa	신문사	newspaper publisher 11-D
sip (Num Ch)	십	ten 4
siph-ta (Vt: siphə)	싶다: 싶어	
Poko siphsɪmnita.	보고 싶습니다.	I want to see. 9
sicak	시작	beginning
sicak-ha-ta (Vi-Vt: sicak-hæ)	시작하다: 시작해	begins 3-G
sicang	시장	market-place 3-D
sicang po-ta	시장 보다	goes food shopping 9-D
sichəng	시청	city hall 2
sihəm	시험	test, examination
sihəm (il) po-ta	시험(을) 보다	takes an examination 15-G
singkəp-ta (Vi: singkəwə)	싱겁다: 싱거워	is not salty, is bland 13
se(s) (Num K)	셋	three 5
seu-ta (Vt: sewə)	세우다: 세워	parks, stops, erects 11-D
sæ (D)	새	new 14-D
sæk	색	color 4
sængil	생일	birthday 13-G
sængkak	생각	idea, thought 9
sængkak-ha-ta (Vt-Vi: sængkak-hæ)	생각하다: 생각해	thinks 15

sængmyəng	생명	life 16-N
sængsən	생선	fish 13
sænghwal	생활	life, livelihood 15-D
syassı	샤쓰	shirts 4-D
swi-ta (Vi: swiə)	쉬다: 쉬어	rests, takes a rest 6
swin (Num K)	쉰	fifty 5
swip-ta (Vi: swiwə)	쉽다: 쉬워	is easy 5-D

<u>ss</u>

ssa-ta (Vi: ssa)	싸다: 싸	is cheap 4
ssau-ta (Vi: ssawə)	싸우다: 싸워	fights, quarells 14-G
Ssolyən	쏘련	Soviet Union 6-D
Ssolyənə	쏘련어	Russian 8-D
ssi-ta (Vt: ssə)	쓰다: 써	writes, uses 8-D
ssı-ta (Vi: ssə)	쓰다: 써	is bitter (in taste) 13
ssik (P)	씩	each 14
hana ssik	하나씩	one at a time, one each 14

<u>c</u>

Ca! (Int)	자!	Here!, Well! 5
ca-ta (Vi-Vt: ca)	자다: 자	sleeps 11-G
cak-ta (Vi: cakə)	작다: 작어	is small 5
cakin kəs	작은것	a small one 5
Cakke malssım-hasipsiyo.	작게 말씀 하십시요.	Please speak softly. 16-D
caknyən	작년	last year 6-D
catongcha	자동차	automobile 7-G

cal (Ad)	잘	well 1
cala-ta (Vi: cala)	자라다: 자라	grows up 14-D
calang	자랑	boasting
calang-ha-ta (Vt: calang-hæ)	자랑하다: 자랑해	is proud of (something) 18-G
cali	자리	seat 11-D
il cali	이 자리	job 16-D
cam	잠	sleep
Cam i omnita.	잠이 옵니다.	I'm sleepy. ('Sleep comes.') 13
(Cam ɨl) camnita.	잠을 잡니다.	[I]'m sleeping. 13
camkan (Ad)	잠간	for a moment 2
Camkan man kitalise yo.	잠간만 기다리세요.	Just a minute. 16
can (C)	잔	cup of
khəphi han can	커피 한 잔	a cup of coffee 5-G
capsusi-ta (Vt: capsusyə)	잡수시다: 잡수셔	eats (honored) 12 (see mək-t
capci	잡지	magazine 4-D
cacənkə	자전거	bicycle 16-D
cacu (Ad)	자주	frequently, often 9-D
əlma na cacu	얼마나 자주	how often 9-D
cang (C)	장	sheet of, piece of 5
swin cang	쉰 장	50 sheets 5
cang	장	(soy) sauce 13 (see kancang)
cangin	장인	father-in-law ('wife's father' 14-D
cangkun	장군	general (of armed forces) 16-
cangkap	장갑	gloves 16-D

cangkwan	장관	minister (of government) 16-D
cangma (chəl)	장마(철)	rainy season 18
cangmo	장모	mother-in-law ('wife's mother) 14-D
cə	저	I (polite) 1
cə e or ce	저의, 제	my 1
cə (D)	저	that 2
cə kənmul	저 건물	that building (over there) 2
cə(h)i	저희	we (polite) 17-G
cək (DN)	적	
Məkə pon cək i issɨmnikka?	먹어 본 적이 있읍니까?	Have you ever eaten? 13
cək-ta (Vi: cəkə)	적다: 적어	is little 5-N
cək-ta (Vt: cəkə)	적다: 적어	writes down, jots down
Cəkə tuəssɨmnita.	적어 두었읍니다.	[I] wrote it down (for later use). 16
cəki	저기	there, that place 2
cəki e	저기에	over there, at that place 2
cələh-ta (Vi: cəlæ)	저렇다: 저래	is like that
cələn kəs	저런 것	that kind of thing 18-D
cələhke (Ad)	저렇게	that way, like that 18-N
cə(l)m-ta (Vi: cəlmə)	젊다: 젊어	is young, is youthful 14-N
cəmsim	점심	lunch 12
cəmcəm (Ad)	점점	gradually 18
cən	전	before
yətəl-si o pun cən	여덟 시 오 분 전	five minutes to eight 6
cən e	전에	previously 7
Səul e oki cən e	서울에 오기 전에	before coming to Seoul, before [I] came to Seoul 15

cənyək	저녁	evening 4-D
onil cənyək	오늘 저녁	this evening 4-D
cənyək (siksa)	저녁 식사	supper 12-D
cənpo	전보	telegram, cable 13-D
cəncha	전차	streetcar 7-G
cənha-ta (Vt: cənhæ)	전하다: 전해	delivers 16
cənhal mal(ssɪm)	전할 말(씀)	message (to leave) 16
cənhwa	전화	telephone 13-D
cənhwa-ha-ta (cənhwa-hæ)	전화하다: 전화해	telephones 16
cənhwa (lɪl) kəl-ta	전화를 걸다	makes a telephone call 16
cənhwa pənho chæk	전화 번호 책	telephone book 16
cəs kalak	젓가락	chopsticks 13
Cəng	정	Chung (family name) 1-D
cəngwən	정원	the yard, garden 16-D
cəngkəcang	정거장	station, railroad station 3
cəngpu	정부	government 8-D
cəngmal (Ad)	정말	certainly 18
cəngmal	정말	truth 18
Cəngmal imnikka?	정말입니까?	Are you sure?, Is it true? 1[illegible]
cəngchika	정치가	politician 18-D
cæphanso	재판소	(law) court 10-D
coyonghi (Ad)	조용히	quietly 16-D
cokim (Ad)	조금	a little 8 (see com)
cokha	조카	nephew 14-D
cokha ttal	조카딸	niece 14-D

coləp	졸업	graduation
coləp-ha-ta (coləp-hæ)	졸업하다: 졸업해	graduates (from) 14
com (Ad)	좀	a little 2
cop-ta (Vi: copa)	좁다: 좁아	is narrow 5-D
cocongsa	조종사	pilot 16-G
coh-ta (Vi: coha)	좋다: 좋아	is good, is nice 4
cohaha-ta (Vt: cohahæ)	좋아하다: 좋아해	prefers, likes 4
congi	종이	paper 5
Cu	주	State (U.S.) 15
cu-ta (Vt: cuə)	주다: 주어	gives 4
Cusipsiyo.	주십시요.	Please give [me]. 4
Ka cusipsiyo.	가 주십시요.	Please go (for me). 11
cuil	주일	week 6
cuin	주인	master, owner, my husband
uli cuin	우리 주인	my husband ('our master') 14-D
cuk-ta (Vi: cukə)	죽다: 죽어	dies 11-G
culo (Ad)	주로	mainly, mostly 8
cumal	주말	weekend 12-D
cumun	주문	order (of goods, food, etc) 1 13-D
cunpi	준비	preparation 15-G
cunpi-ha-ta (cunpi-hæ)	준비하다: 준비해	prepares for 17-G
cuso	주소	(one's) address 16-D
cuchacang	주차장	parking lot 16-D

cung (PN)	중	among, during 10
ki (kəs til) cung esə	그(것들) 중 에서	among them 10
cungang	중앙	center, central 11
cungyoha-ta (Vi: cungyohæ)	중요하다: 중요해	is important 18
Cungkuk	중국	China 1-G
Cungkuk mal	중국 말	Chinese (language) 1-G
Cungkuk salam	중국 사람	Chinese (man)
Cungkukə	중국어	Chinese (language) 8-D
cungtæha-ta (Vi: cungtæhæ)	중대하다: 중대해	is important 18
cunghakkyo	중학교	junior high school ('middle school') 10-D
ci (DN)	지	
əti e issnin ci asimnikka?	어디에 있는지 아십니까?	Do you know where [it] is? 13
Kukmusəng e tilə on ci,	국무성에 들어 온지	since I joined the State Department, 15
ci-ta	지다	
chuwə ci-ta (chuwə cə)	추워 지다: 추워 저	gets colder 18
cikap	지갑	wallet 16-D
cikəp	직업	occupation, profession 18-D
cikim	지금	now, present 5
cikcang	직장	place of work 18-D
cikkong	직공	factory worker, technician 18-
cilki-ta (Vi: cilkiə)	질기다: 질기어	is tough 13
cilmun	질문	question(iars) 13-D

cina-ta (Vi: cina)	지나다: 지나	passes by, gets along
Yocɪm əttəhe cinasimnikka?	요즘 어떻게 지나십니까?	How are you getting along these days? 1
cinan	지난	last, past
cinan sahil	지난 사흘	last three days 6
cito	지도	map 2-D
cip	집	house, home 2-D
ce ka	제가	I (polite subject) 17-G
ceil (Ad)	제일	most, best, No. 1 10-N
Ceil phyəllihamnita.	제일 편리합니다.	[It]'s most convenient. 10
cæmi	재미	fun, interest 1
Sənsæng in cæmi əttəhsimnikka?	선생은 재미 어떻습니까?	And how are YOU doing? 1
Cæmi (ka) issɪmnita.	재미(가) 있읍니다.	[It]'s interesting. 8
Ceimsɪ	제임스	James 1
	cc	
cca-ta (Vt: cca)	짜다: 짜	is salty 13
ccali (PN)	짜리	worth, value 5
o-sip Wən ccali	오십 원 짜리	50 Wən worth, W50 bill 5
ccalp-ta (Vi: ccalpə)	짧다: 짧어	is short (in length) 10-D
ccok (PN)	쪽	side, direction 2
wen ccok	왼쪽	the left (side) 2
i ccok	이쪽	this way 2-D
Sichəng ccok ɪlo	시청쪽으로	in the direction of the City Hall 2-D
ccɪm (PN)	쯤	around, about
tasəs si ccɪm	다섯 시 쯤	around 5 o'clock 6
ccæ (PN)	째	
tu pən ccæ	두 번째	the second time 7

ccæm	잼	jam 13-D

<u>ch</u>

cha	차	car 4-N
cha	차	tea 12-D
hongcha	홍차	black tea 10-G
cha-ta (Vi: cha)	차다: 차	is cold
chan mul	찬물	cold water 12-D
chako	차고	garage 16-D
cham (Ad)	참	really, very 9
Cham (Int)	참	By the way, Oh! 9-N
chac-ta (Vt: chacə)	찾다: 찾어	looks for, seeks 3
əti lɪl chac(s)ɪmnikka?	어디를 찾습니까?	What (place) are you looking for? 3
chacha (Ad)	차차	gradually 18
chang (mun)	창(문)	window 11-D
chə	처	my wife 14-D
chəɪm	처음	first, the first time 1
chəim ɪlo	처음으로	for the first time 7-N
chəl	철	season 18
chələm (P)	처럼	
Nyuyok chələm	뉴욕처럼	like (<u>or</u> just as) New York 18
chən (Num Ch)	천	thousand 4
chənam	처남	brother-in-law ('wife's brother') 14-D
chənyə	처녀	maiden, single woman, spinster 14-D

chənchənhi (Ad)	천천히	slowly 11-D
chənman	천만	ten-million 1
chənman e	천만에	of ten-million
Chənman e malssɨm imnita.	천만에 말씀입니다.	You're welcome. 1
chət (D)	첫	first 7 (see chəɨm)
chət ccæ	첫째	first, the first 7
chət pən ccæ	첫 번째	the first, the first time 7
chəce	처제	wife's younger sister 14-D
chəhyəng	처형	wife's older sister 14-D
chiəta po-ta (Vt: chiəta pwa)	쳐다 보다: 쳐다 봐	looks up to, beholds 12-G
cho	초	vinegar 13
chon	촌	village, rural area 15-D
chongcang	총장	president (of university) 16-D
chotæ	초대	invitation 13-D
chongkak	총각	bachelor, unmarried man 14-G
chulipku	출입구	exit-entrance 16-D
chulku	출구	exit 16-D
chum	춤	dancing
chum (ɨl) chu-ta (chum (ɨl) chwə)	춤을 추다: 춤을 춰	dances 9-D
chup-ta (Vi: chwə)	춥다: 추워	is cold 18
chungpun	충분	sufficiency
chungpun-ha-ta (chungpun-hæ)	충분하다: 충분해	is sufficient, is enough 13
chil (Num Ch)	칠	seven 4

chinku	친구	friend 3
chinchək	친척	relatives 14-D
chæk	책	book 1-G
chækpang	책방	book store 4
chæksang	책상	table, desk 2-D
Chwe	최	Choe (family name) 1-D
	<u>h</u>	
ha-ta (Vt: hæ <u>or</u> hayə)	하다: 해: 하여	does 1
Muəs (il) hasimnikka?	무엇을 하십니까?	What do you do (sir)? 1
haya(h)-ta (Vi: hayæ)	하얗다: 하애	is white 4-N
hayan sæk	하얀 색	white color 4-D
hako (P)	하고	with, and 9
na hako	나하고	with me 9
chæk hako yənphil	책하고 연필	book and pencil 9-G
hakki	학기	semester 10-D
hakkyo	학교	school 2
haknyən	학년	grade (school year), grader
haksæng	학생	student 1
hakca	학자	scholar 8-D
hakcang	학장	dean (of college) 16-D
halapəci	할아버지	grandfather 13-G
halu	하루	one day, the 1st day of the month 6
halməni	할머니	grandmother 14-D

han (D)	한	approximately 8
han sam nyən	한 삼 년	about 3 years 8
han(a) (Num K)	하나	one 4
hanil	하늘	heaven, sky 18
Hansik	한식	Korean food 12
Hankuk	한국	Korea 1
Hankuk mal	한국 말	Korean (language) 1
Hankuk salam	한국 사람	(a) Korean 1-G
Hankukə	한국어	Korean 8-D
hanthe (P)	한테	to 11-G (see eke)
hapsing	합승	jitney 7-G
Hapcungkuk	합중국	United States 18-D
hangsang (Ad)	항상	all the time 9-N
hangku	항구	harbor 18-D
hangsi (Ad)	항시	always 9-N
həli	허리	waist 13-D
hok (Ad)	혹	by any chance 16
hoksi (Ad)	혹시	by any chance 16
hothel	호텔	hotel 2-D
honca	혼자	single, alone 14
Hocu	호주	Australia 6-D
hongcha	홍차	(black) tea 10-G
hu	후	the later time
hu e	후 에	later, after a while 7

tæhak ɪl coləp-han hu e	대학을 졸업한 후 에	after graduation from the college 15
hullyungha-ta (Vi: hullyunghæ)	훌륭 하다: 훌륭 해	is excellent, is outstanding 13
huchu	후추	black pepper 13
huchu kalu	후추 가루	black pepper (power) 13
hɪli-ta (Vi: hɪliə)	흐리다: 흐리어	is cloudy 18
hɪlkiə po-ta (Vt: hɪlkiə pwa)	흘겨 보다: 흘겨 봐	steers 12-G
hi-ta (Vi: hiə)	희다: 희어	is whitish 4-D
hæ	해	year, sun 6-D
musɪn hæ	무슨 해	what year 6-D
hæwe	해외	overseas, abroad 15-D
hyənkɪm	현금	cash 7-G
hyonkɪm ɪlo	현금으로	in cash 7-D
hyuka	휴가	vacation 6
Hyuka lɪl patəssɪmnita.	휴가를 받었읍니다.	[I] took a vacation. 6
hyəng	형	older brother
nyəng nim	형님	older brother (honored) 14
hyəngcə	형제	siblings, brothers and sisters 14
Hwayoil	화요일	Tuesday 6-D
Hwalan	화란	Holland 6-D
hwesa	회사	company, firm 8

Index to the Grammar Notes

References are to Unit and Grammar Note: for example, 3.1. refers to Unit 3, Grammar Note 1. The alphabetical order of the Index follows that of Korean-English Glossary. The letters which are not used in the Glossary are inserted as follows: D after T; F and Q after P; V after H.